reader's digest

Low fat no fat cookbook

Low Fat No Fat Cookbook was edited and designed by
The Reader's Digest Association Limited, London

The typeface used in this book is Gill Sans
Printed in Barcelona, Spain
ISBN 0 276 42393 3

reader's digest

Low fat no fat

cookbook

PUBLISHED BY THE
READER'S DIGEST ASSOCIATION LIMITED
LONDON • NEW YORK • SYDNEY
CAPE TOWN • MONTREAL

contributors

COOKERY ADVISER
Jenni Muir

NUTRITIONAL ADVISER
Amanda Ursell

WRITERS
Pat Alburey
Mridula Baljekar
Clare Brigstocke
Roz Denny
Christine France
Sybil Kapoor
Jo Middleditch
Jenni Muir
Louise Pickford
Oded Schwartz
Wendy Veale
Lorna Wing

RECIPE TESTERS
Terry Farris
Angela Kingsbury

PHOTOGRAPHERS
Gus Filgate
William Lingwood
Craig Robertson
Simon Smith
Philip Webb
Philip Wilkins

HOME ECONOMISTS
Alison Austin
Maxine Clark
Jacqueline Clarke
Lucy Knox
Sarah Lowman
Kathy Man
Sally Mansfield
Jane Oddie
Louise Pickford
Sunil Vijayakar
Fran Ward

STYLISTS
Clare Louise Hunt
Penny Markham
Helen Payne
Helen Trent

EDITOR
Brenda Houghton

ART EDITOR
Joanna Walker

SENIOR DESIGNER
Jane McKenna

ASSISTANT EDITORS
Alison Candlin, Celia Coyne,
Kim Davies, Beverley LeBlanc,
Marion Moisy,
Rachel Warren Chadd

SUB-EDITORS
Chloë Garrow, Jane Hutchings

EDITORIAL ASSISTANTS
Louise Catcheside
Abigail MacIntyre

PROOFREADERS
Roy Butcher, Barry Gage

reader's digest
general books

EDITORIAL DIRECTOR
Cortina Butler

ART DIRECTOR
Nick Clark

EXECUTIVE EDITOR
Julian Browne

MANAGING EDITOR
Paul Middleton

DEPUTY MANAGING EDITOR
Alastair Holmes

EDITORIAL GROUP HEADS
Ruth Binney, Noel Buchanan

PICTURE RESEARCH EDITOR
Martin Smith

STYLE EDITOR
Ron Pankhurst

contents

INTRODUCTION

SPECIAL FEATURES

THE RECIPES

introduction

This book is first and foremost about enjoying food, and is packed with recipes to tempt your appetite and please your taste buds. It is also about following a healthy lifestyle, and here we explain how you and your family can achieve a balanced diet and eat great meals, all at the same time.

HOT CAJUN POTATO WEDGES (PAGE 240)

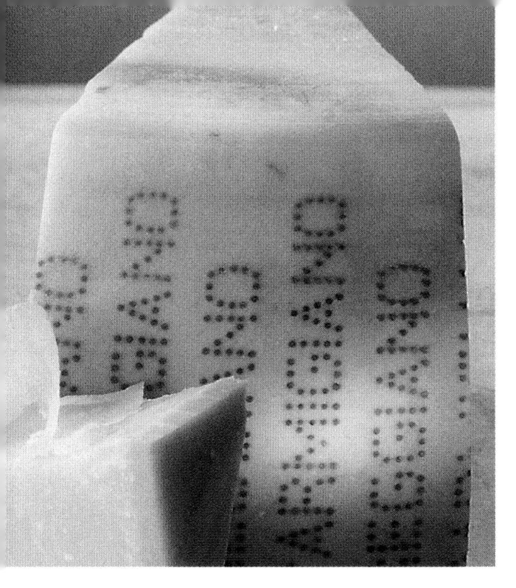

at – the ood news nd the bad

o many theories surround he issue of fat in the diet hat most of us feel onfused. To help you to nake sensible choices, here re answers to some of the ey questions about fat.

What is fat and what does it do?

Fat is one of the main nutrients in food and is the most concentrated source of calories, those units of energy which fuel our bodies every day of our lives. One helping of fat yields more than twice as much energy as the same sized helping of carbohydrate or protein.

Between them, the different types of fat and oil supply our bodies with the vitamins A, D, E and K and enable the body to absorb them. Fat also makes food succulent: adding butter to bread or soured cream to baked potatoes makes them seem more palatable.

The basic building blocks of fat are called fatty acids, and there are two main types – saturated and unsaturated. Fats that are solid at room temperature, such as butter and the fat you see on meat, generally contain a lot of saturated fatty acids. Fats that are liquid at room temperature, such as most vegetable oils, usually have a high level of unsaturated fatty acids.

Is one sort of fat worse than another?

In recent years unprecedented attention has been paid to fats and their role in our health. As so often happens, certain foods are cast in the role of villain while others play the hero. In the case of fat, saturated fats have been deemed 'bad' and unsaturated fats have assumed the 'good' image – a reputation that is largely deserved.

Unsaturated fats come in two forms: monounsaturated and polyunsaturated, according to how much hydrogen they contain. All fatty acids are made up of carbon, hydrogen and oxygen in different proportions. Saturated fats have a full complement of hydrogen, monounsaturates have a little less and polyunsaturated fats have least.

All fats are actually a mixture of saturated, monounsaturated and polyunsaturated fatty acids. Whichever one is present in the highest proportion dictates how the fat or oil is known. So, for example, butter is high in saturated fatty acids and is categorised as a saturated fat; olive oil is richest in monounsaturated fatty acids and is called a monounsaturated fat; and sunflower oil is rich in polyunsaturated fatty acids and is known as a polyunsaturated fat.

Research indicates that a high consumption of saturated fat can lead to a raised level of cholesterol in the blood, and this contributes to the growth of fatty deposits on the walls of the arteries. These can block the flow of blood, causing heart failure and stroke.

Unsaturated fats, such as olive oil, do not appear to raise cholesterol levels and may even help to keep them low. So, in this sense, they are better for you than saturated fats.

The key to a healthy diet is to eat a wide variety of foods, to maintain the proportion of the calories you get from fat at around 35 per cent or less of your total calorie intake, and to keep saturated fats to the minimum. This low-fat diet is best combined with regular exercise for overall well-being.

Are there any fats that I should eat?

There are two unsaturated fatty acids, linoleic and alpha-linolenic acids, otherwise known as omega-6 and omega-3, which play a vital role in building and maintaining healthy nerve tissue. As these acids cannot be made by our bodies they must be obtained from our diet, so they are known as essential fatty acids (EFAs).

SMOKED SALMON BAGEL WITH QUARK (P

EFAs are crucial for the correct development of an infant's brain in the womb and after birth. They are needed to maintain the structure of every cell in our bodies and to keep skin smooth and watertight. They help to damp down the inflammatory processes in rheumatoid arthritis and psoriasis, and the risk of coronary heart disease is reduced because of the role that EFAs play in reducing the stickiness of blood.

EFAs are also necessary for the production of hormone-like substances called prostaglandins. These control second-by-second reactions throughout our bodies, including the dilation of blood vessels, the level of blood pressure and blood-clotting mechanisms.

In other words, EFAs are as necessary to our well-being as any vitamin. The amount we need is small but crucial: about 1 per cent of our calories should come from omega-6 and 0.2 per cent from omega-3. Omega-6 is found in sunflower, safflower and corn oil, and in almonds and walnuts. Omega-3 is found in fish oils and in soya bean and rapeseed oil.

What is special about fish oil?

Fish oils are important because they contain omega-3. The benefits became clear when it emerged that there was something in fish that was protecting from heart disease people who eat very large amounts of it, such as the Inuit of the Arctic.

Research showed that the essential fatty acid omega-3 was found throughout the oily flesh of fish such as herring, mackerel, salmon, sardines and tuna, and it is now recommended that these should become regular ingredients in a healthy diet. Try the great oily fish recipes in this book, such as the quick and easy Smoked Salmon Bagel with Quark (page 45).

Is margarine better for me than butter?

Margarine was invented as a substitute for butter. By law in Britain, margarine must be fortified with vitamins A and D, and polyunsaturated versions are also an important source of vitamin E and essential fatty acids.

The best margarines are made with olive or sunflower oil; cheaper versions contain palm oil, beef tallow and lard. However, whether hard or soft, margarines contain just as much fat as butter, around 80 per cent of the whole.

Butter is a natural product, with none of the emulsifiers, colouring agents or preservatives that are used in the manufacture of margarine. While it is higher in saturated fats than margarine, if you only use it occasionally and sparingly, there is no reason to drop butter from your diet completely.

On some labels I see trans fats listed: what are these?

In the manufacture of margarine from vegetable oil, some of the soft unsaturated fatty acids in the oil are converted into hard saturated ones. During this process, some unsaturated fatty acids with an unusual shape are formed. The body reacts to these 'trans' fats as if they were saturated fats, and they have been linked to heart disease.

Trans fatty acids make up 5-7 per cent of the fat in margarines labelled 'high in polyunsaturates' (with hard margarine containing more than soft) and 40 per cent of the fat in white cooking fats. They also occur naturally in butter, but in this instance do not pose a health risk.

It has been suggested that trans fatty acids are not the cause of the problem but are simply the sign of a diet that contains too many processed foods and too few protective ones, such as fruit and vegetables.

The cautionary advice is to study labels to keep consumption of trans fats to a minimum. They are found in lard and cheap hard margarine, and in convenience and processed foods which contain them, such as some biscuits.

Can I use as much olive oil as I like?

No. The health benefits of the Mediterranean diet continue to attract attention and olive oil has gained the reputation of being a golden elixir, but its virtue needs to be kept in perspective. It is one of the healthiest vegetable oils available, because it is high

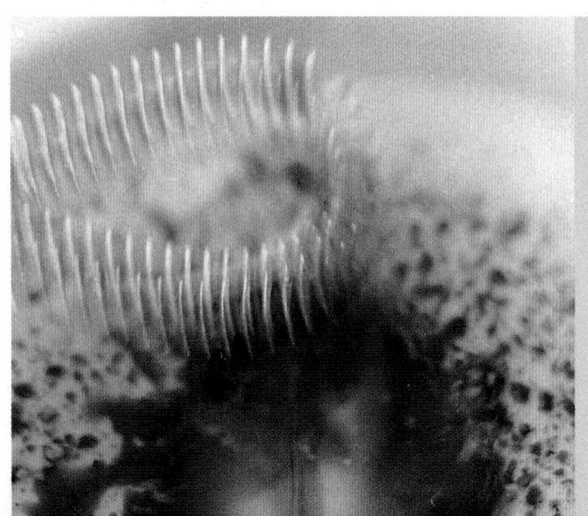

Do not use oily dressings on your salad: try fruit juice or freshly squeezed lemon and herbs instead.

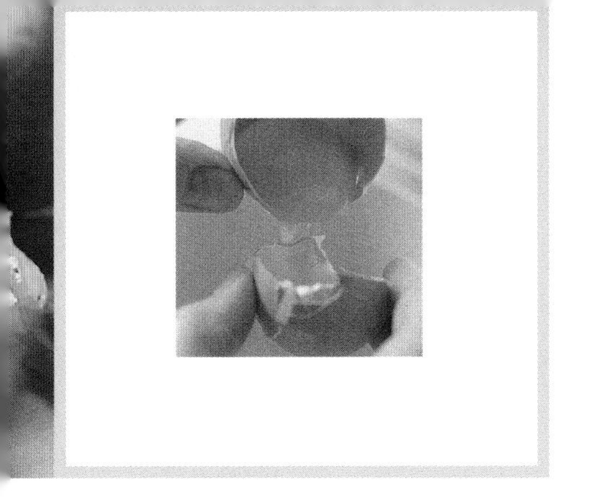

in monounsaturated fatty acids, which seem to help to lower blood cholesterol.

However, it is a mistake to think that because a saturated fat like butter is more likely to increase cholesterol to harmful levels than an unsaturated fat such as olive oil, you can consume as much of the latter as you like.

Olive oil and butter are equally high in calories and fat: 1 teaspoon of butter provides 37 calories and 4 g of fat while 1 teaspoon of olive oil supplies 45 calories and 5 g of fat.

Being too generous with olive oil will make you put on weight just as surely as eating too much butter, and excess weight is linked to many diseases, from diabetes and joint problems to heart disease. So use olive oil by all means, but use it sparingly.

Are all vegetable oils unsaturated?

No. The exceptions are coconut and palm oil. Unusually for a vegetable oil, coconut oil contains more saturated fats than unsaturated: 91 per cent (palm oil is 47 per cent fat). Coconut oil is widely used in West Indian cuisine for its delicious flavour, but it should be used in moderation on a low-fat diet, and avoided if you are trying to reduce cholesterol levels.

Vegetable oils without the word 'polyunsaturated' included on the label often contain a large amount of palm oil, and are high in saturated fat.

Should I avoid foods that are rich in cholesterol?

It used to be thought that because foods such as eggs and shellfish contain cholesterol, eating them must raise blood cholesterol levels. However, it has been discovered that the amount of cholesterol we eat has little effect on the cholesterol levels in our blood. It is saturated fats which raise blood cholesterol and which should be restricted. So foods rich in saturated fats, for example fatty cuts of meat, should be eaten in moderation, but having four or five eggs a week as part of a balanced diet will do you no harm.

How can I be sure of spotting all the fat in food?

Fats are present in a huge variety of foods. There are the obvious ones that you can see and which taste fatty, like butter and margarine, and those that are harder to detect because they occur in processed foods.

Fats and oils are concealed in many processed foods, like cakes and crisps. Equally, labels that describe foods as 'less fat', 'reduced fat', 'lower', 'light' or 'lite' are confusing and do not always mean very much.

A food labelled 'less fat' or 'reduced fat' must contain at least 25 per cent less fat than the standard version. If a standard sausage contains 32 g of fat per 100 g (3½ oz), then a 'reduced fat' sausage will have no more than 24 g, but that is still quite a lot of fat.

'Low fat', however, is a legally defined term. Under British food-labelling guidelines drawn up in 1996, products labelled 'low fat', with the exception of spreads, must contain less than 5 g of fat per 100 g, or per serving if a normal serving weighs 100 g or more. So while a small pot of ordinary Greek yoghurt contains 11 g of fat, a 'low-fat' yoghurt has only 2 g.

Fat spreads, however, can be labelled 'low-fat' even though they do not meet this 5 g guideline and reduced-fat spreads have 42-62 g of fat per 100 g. This is less than butter, which has 80 g of fat per 100 g, but they remain high-fat foods and should be used with care.

The answer is to scrutinise the small print on packaging to check the actual quantity of fat that the food contains. And, since most manufacturers now provide a breakdown of nutrients which includes the unsaturated and saturated fat content, look for products with a low saturated fat content.

Aren't most reduced-fat foods rather tasteless?

Certainly not, as proved by the recipes in this book. You will discover how the rich tastes of butter, oil and cream can be replaced by equally mouth-watering low-fat or no-fat alternatives, such as good stocks, wine, soy sauce, flavoured vinegars and fruit juices.

Experiment to find out which low-fat products you enjoy, as they vary in quality and taste. There are some good options available, such as low-fat yoghurts and reduced-fat cheeses, which are useful to the low-fat cook.

However, changing directly from whole milk to skimmed can be too big a leap. It is better to use semi-skimmed and progress from there. If you try whole milk a few weeks later, you may find it tastes cloying.

Changing to a low-fat diet can be gradual, but once you are used to the clear flavourings of fresh herbs and subtle spicing you will be amazed how over-rich and unappetising fat-laden meals will seem.

the main sources of fat in our diet ▶

the **main sources** of **fat** in our **diet**

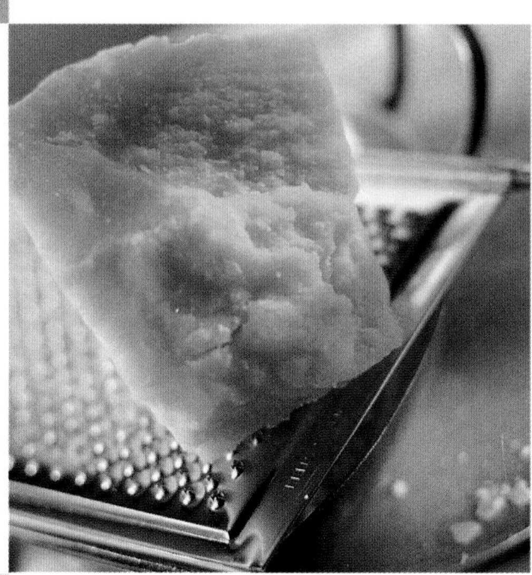

Knowing which foods are high in fat is step one in controlling your fat intake. These guidelines will help you to steer clear of the worst culprits and to choose the healthiest ingredients to cook with every time.

Butter

Butter is made by churning rich cream, so it is not surprising that it is one of the most concentrated sources of fat in the diet: there is a massive 80 g of fat in 100 g (3½ oz) of butter, and 740 calories. Most of this is saturated fat which, if eaten to excess, can contribute to raised blood cholesterol. It does, however, provide vitamins A and D. Half-fat butter has had water whipped into it to achieve the same volume with only half the amount of butter.

Margarine

Margarine was invented in 1869 as a cheap substitute for butter and by law in Britain it must be fortified with vitamins A and D. Polyunsaturated versions are also an important source of essential fatty acids and vitamin E. Hard or soft, most have the same amount of fat and just as many calories as butter.

Low-fat spreads

It is possible to buy spreads that have been designed to look and taste like margarine but have a lower fat content. A '70 per cent fat spread' contains 635 calories and 70 g of fat per 100 g (3½ oz); a 'low-fat spread' contains 390 calories and 41 g of fat or less; and a 'very low-fat spread' has 273 calories and 25 g of fat. What this means is that even the lowest-fat spreads are made up of a quarter of fat and should not be eaten to excess.

Much of the fat in these reduced-fat spreads has been replaced by water, with emulsifiers used to bind it in. This water evaporates when the spread is heated, which is why the very low-fat spreads, which contain most water, are labelled 'unsuitable for cooking'.

As a general rule, if you want to avoid the saturated fat of butter or lard in your cooking, it is better to use small amounts of olive or sunflower oil.

Milk

The amount of fat contained in milk varies according to where it comes from: 600 ml (1 pint) of sheep's milk contains 35 g of fat, cow's milk has 23 g and goat's milk 20 g. What was once known as 'soya milk' but is now termed 'soya drink' has 11 g.

Since the mid 1980s there has been a big switch from purchases of whole milk to semi-skimmed or skimmed, and it makes good sense. Where a pint of ordinary milk has 23 g of fat, semi-skimmed contains 9 g and skimmed 1 g. If you add up all the milk you use during the day, in drinks, on cereals and in cooking, then changing over from whole milk to skimmed can make a significant difference to your fat intake.

Cream

All cream is high in fat, as the table below shows. Synthetic creams are made from buttermilk or skimmed milk and vegetable oil rather than whole milk, but this is to prolong their shelf life, not to lower the fat content, which is often as high as in real cream. On a low-fat diet it is best to check the labels.

Reduced-fat creams, homogenised to give them a creamy texture, are a better option. Where single cream, for instance, has 19 g of fat per 100 g, half-fat single cream has 13 g. Reduced-fat creams keep well because of the lower fat content, and although there is some loss of flavour, they are useful in cooked dishes. Half-fat crème fraîche, with 15 g of fat per 100 g, tastes and behaves in cooking much like the full-fat version and in small quantities adds a welcome voluptuousness to soups and sauces.

TYPE	FAT PER 100 g	CALORIES PER 100 g
Single cream	19 g	198
Soured cream	20 g	205
Crème fraîche	30 g	320
Whipping cream	39 g	373
Double cream	48 g	449
Clotted cream	63 g	586

STRAWBERRY YOGHURT ICE (PAGE 275)

Yoghurt

The fat content of yoghurt depends on the type of milk it is made from and whether it has been enriched. Read the labels carefully.

Greek yoghurt usually has cream added, which raises the fat content of an individual 150 g (5½ oz) pot to 11 g. Plain yoghurts manufactured from whole milk but without added cream have about 5 g of fat in a pot of that size, while low-fat versions have 2 g.

Very low-fat yoghurts, made from skimmed milk, contain almost no fat at all and their texture may be runny. Yet they are still useful ingredients to include in marinades, salad dressings and sauces.

Do not spread butter on your freshly baked teabread – a little fruit conserve is all the extra you need on Banana Bread (page 295).

CHARGRILLED PORK WITH LITTLE BAKED APPLES (PAGE 186)

Cheese

In general, hard cheeses contain the most fat and soft cheeses least. Cheddar and Double Gloucester, for example, have 34 g of fat per 100 g (3½ oz) while cottage cheese has only 4 g. Soft, full-fat cream cheese is the exception, as it is made from cream rather than milk and is 47 per cent fat.

If you are looking for a low-fat cheese, you can choose a soft cheese such as quark, which has the merest trace of fat, creamy ricotta with 11 g of fat per 100 g or a soft goat's milk cheese with 16 g.

However, choosing low-fat varieties is not the only option. You may find that you get more satisfaction and still cut down on fat by eating a smaller portion of a cheese with a more powerful flavour, such as a Port Salut or Saint Paulin with 23 g of fat per 100 g, Camembert with 24 g, Brie with 27 g or a great hard cheese such as Stilton with 35 g. And you need only a little grated Parmesan to brighten up a host of pastas, pizzas and gratins.

Reduced-fat cheeses have about half the fat of their full-fat cousins. Reduced-fat Cheddars average 16 g of fat in each 100 g of cheese and although they lack the great flavour of the full-fat version, they are useful for cooking.

Fromage frais is a soft cheese whose fat content depends on the type of milk used. Plain fromage frais made from whole milk contains only 7 g of fat per 100 g and makes a delicious spread. Low-fat fromage frais, made from skimmed milk, has only a trace of fat, and although there is some reduction in taste and texture, it adds a welcome creamy note to sauces and stews.

Meat

Meat and processed meat products, such as pies, pâtés, sausages and sausage rolls, currently contribute around 22 per cent of fat to the average adult diet in the UK. On a low-fat diet, most processed meat products are best avoided.

Not all the fat in meat is the saturated kind: around half the fat in lean beef, lamb and pork is unsaturated. New approaches in farming have lowered the fat content of meat dramatically. Through selective breeding, in which the leanest animals become the parents of the next generation, and with changes to animal feeds, the amount of fat surrounding meat and between its fibres has been very much reduced. When combined with modern butchery, which removes most of the visible fat, the reduction that has been achieved is remarkable, as the table below shows.

GRAMS OF FAT PER 100 g OF RAW MEAT

	Beef	Lamb	Pork
1950s	25 g	31 g	30 g
1990s	8 g	5 g	4 g

Poultry and game

Chicken is still one of our most popular sources of protein and, like turkey, both light and dark meat are low in fat, as the table on the right shows.

However, it is best to remove the skin of poultry before you eat it as 100 g of roast chicken breast with the skin on has 14 g of fat, which drops to just 5 g for a skinless breast.

Furred and feathered game, such as rabbit, venison, pheasant and partridge, once considered luxury items, are now widely available. Game is naturally lean, and the strong flavours of these meats mean that they do not need to be boosted with high-fat sauces.

GRAMS OF FAT PER 100 g (ROAST MEAT WITHOUT SKIN)	
Turkey	2g
Chicken	5g
Rabbit	6g
Venison	6g
Partridge	7g
Pheasant	9g
Duck	10g

Fish

White fish such as plaice and cod store virtually all their body oils in their livers (hence cod liver oil), so a 100 g (3½ oz) portion of cod or haddock provides less than 1g of fat; the same sized portion of halibut and plaice only 2 g.

Fish such as herring, mackerel, salmon, sardines, trout and tuna contain oil throughout their flesh. So a 100g portion of trout or tuna provides 5 g of fat, salmon has 11 g, herring 13 g and mackerel 16 g.

This is no reason to shun them, however, because this fat is good for us. Fish oil is rich in vitamins A and D and essential fatty acids (see page 10) and we should aim to eat plenty.

Shellfish

A wide range of shellfish is available in Britain, including crabs, crayfish and lobsters, mussels, oysters and scallops, prawns and shrimps.

All shellfish are low in fat. Raw scallops, shrimps, oysters and prawns all have 1 g per 100 g (3½ oz); lobster, mussels and squid 2 g; and even the highest in fat, crab, has only 5 g.

Shellfish are also rich in minerals and protein, and with their fresh flavours and different textures, they make a delicious nutritional contribution to low-fat cooking.

Nuts

Nearly all nuts, including almonds, brazils, cashews, hazelnuts, peanuts, pine nuts, pistachios and walnuts, are rich in fat, having from 49 g to 69 g of fat per 100 g (3½ oz). A 50 g bag of roasted peanuts, for instance, contains the equivalent of nearly 2 tablespoons of oil.

Switching to dry-roasted nuts is no solution: they contain almost as much fat as standard roasted nuts. The exception is chestnuts, which have just 3 g of fat per 100 g and are the low-fat cook's best nutty friend.

However, most of the oil in nuts is unsaturated and provides essential fatty acids and vitamin E. Nuts also provide important minerals such as selenium. As long as they are only eaten in small quantities, they can make a useful contribution to the diet.

Seeds

Like most nuts, seeds are a rich source of oils, and a single tablespoon of sunflower seeds scattered over your salad will add 7 g of fat to it.

Although seeds provide useful amounts of essential fatty acids and vitamin E, they should be used in moderation. Make the most of their strong flavours and add teaspoons rather than tablespoons of plain or toasted seeds to your salads and pilafs, bread and cakes.

POACHED CHICKEN WITH SPRING VEGETABLES (PAGE 137)

fat and the family

The amount of fat we need to eat for a healthy diet fluctuates during our lives. The recommended intake for a child is not the same as an adult's. Here are the latest guidelines suggesting how much fat it is wise to eat at different ages.

Judging the right amount

Fat intake fluctuates widely around the world and tends to be much higher in the West than in developing countries. Currently in the UK, the average adult obtains around 42 per cent of his or her total calories from fats, mostly from those found in meat, meat products, table fats and baked foods such as biscuits, pastries and cakes.

We do not need all this fat – indeed, it can be harmful to our health. The Department of Health recommends that our consumption of fat should fall to around 35 per cent of our total calorie consumption, which would be 700 calories out of a daily allowance of 2000.

However, some organisations, such as the World Cancer Research Fund, recommend a fat intake of 30 per cent or less, because they believe this reduces the risk of cancer.

Our daily diet

Most of us need to reduce our current daily fat consumption to 99 g a day or less for men, and to 77 g a day or less for women, assuming a typical daily calorie count of 2550 and 2000 calories respectively.

If you wish to lower your consumption to 30 per cent, then an average man should consume only 85 g of fat in his daily diet, and an average woman 67 g.

When selecting recipes from this book, consider how the amount of fat you are eating adds up over the course of the day. If, for instance, you fancy bacon and egg for breakfast rather than fresh fruit, you should compensate for the higher fat level at breakfast by choosing a lower-fat lunch or dinner. Consult the Menu Planner on pages 306-311 for helpful suggestions on putting balanced meals together. These are the healthy eating recommendations from the Department of Health:

- Eat five servings of fruit and vegetables (excluding potatoes) for their fibre, carbohydrate, minerals and vitamins.
- Eat lots of carbohydrate, including potatoes, cereals, pasta, rice, oats, noodles, sweetcorn, millet and cornmeal.
- Eat moderate amounts of protein from beans and pulses, dairy products, meat, poultry, fish, eggs and nuts, choosing lower-fat versions wherever you can.
- Eat sparingly of fatty foods such as butter, margarine and other fat spreads, oils, dressings and crisps.
- Processed foods rich in sugar, such as chocolates, sweets and sugary snacks, should also be eaten sparingly because they add few nutrients to the diet and can contribute to tooth decay.

Babies and toddlers from birth to four years old

Infants need the energy provided by whole milk and should never be given skimmed or semi-skimmed milks and dairy products. When they are no longer taking breast milk or formula milks that are fortified with all the nutrients they require, it is vital that they get these nutrients from their food.

A well-balanced and varied diet is important for growth and development. Essential fatty acids (EFAs), contained in oily fish such as salmon and tuna, and in vegetable oils such as sunflower and olive oil, are important because they are needed for the development of the brain and other vital organs, which are growing at a very fast rate at this age. But do not try to boost children's intake by giving them nuts or seeds, even though they do contain EFAs, as they could cause choking.

Fish is an important part of a healthy diet – all it needs to boost its flavour is a squeeze of lemon.

Children from five to twelve years old

Only when children are over the age of five can they progress to reduced-fat dairy products. It is better to give them semi-skimmed milk, because it will still provide them with vitamins A and D, than to switch to skimmed, which lacks them. Aim to keep up children's intake of EFAs, which research shows are necessary for healthy eyes and ears.

Teenagers

All teenagers need fats in their diets to supply sufficient energy to support their rapid physical development during adolescence. But be sure they are not overloading on the saturated fats in fast foods, crisps, biscuits and chocolate. They also need vitamin D, in particular, to enhance calcium absorption to support their growing bones.

So offer them the oily fish that contain both EFAs and vitamin D, such as salmon and fresh tuna. Fish canned in brine are not such a good source of EFAs because most of the fish oil is removed before canning; canned fish in oil retains the EFAs.

Men

Up to the age of 50, men are more at risk from heart disease than women of a similar age, and need to keep their arteries clear. They will benefit from one or two meals a week containing fish rich in EFAs. If they are watching their waistlines, they also need to keep an eye on their total fat intake, eating lean meat, cutting down on processed meals, pies and sausages and switching to reduced-fat dairy products.

Men should also include some nuts and seeds in their diet, as these provide the antioxidant vitamin E, which again is good for helping to protect the heart.

Women

Natural fats, such as evening primrose oil, may help to smooth out the hormonal ups and downs that women face after puberty, and will provide the skin with the nourishment it needs to keep in good condition.

The vitamin D that oily fish provides also helps in the battle to preserve a good calcium balance in the body, by ensuring absorption of the maximum amount of calcium from the diet. This is important to help to fight the loss of bone mass and osteoporosis, which can lead to fractures and broken limbs. Women are particularly prone to this after the menopause, so building up this healthy bone mass should start in the twenties and thirties.

For weight watchers, keeping overall fat intake down will play a big role both in losing excess pounds and maintaining the correct body weight once it is achieved. And over the age of 50, women are just as much at risk of heart disease as men and need to keep their arteries clear in the same way.

Elderly peole

As people get older, inflammatory problems such as rheumatoid arthritis often develop. Research has revealed that the essential fatty acids contained in fish oil may help to relieve the symptoms, so there is an added incentive to keep enjoying mackerel, salmon and tuna dishes.

Vegetarians

Becoming a vegetarian does not automatically ensure that you are eating a low-fat or healthy diet. Although vegetarians avoid the saturated fat found in meat, going overboard on cheese, nuts and seeds to compensate can really push the fat up. Vegetarians also need to be aware of the importance of balancing foods. If you are not getting any protein from meat, poultry or fish, you must make sure you get the moderate amounts the body needs from foods such as tofu and pulses.

Step-by-step to a lower-fat eating plan

The first step in reducing your fat intake is to cut back on all the visible fats. That means having less butter or margarine on your bread, using less oil in cooking and salad dressings, cutting off all the fat from around chops and steaks, and discarding the skin of poultry.

However, it is important to think about invisible fat too. Did you know, for example, that an inviting pot of pale pink taramasalata has 53 g of fat hidden in every 100 g (3½ oz)? Or that an average, 200 g (7 oz) serving of steak and kidney pie has 42 g, an ordinary beefburger and large fries 40 g, and a small 100 g bar of milk chocolate 30 g?

If you are serious about cutting down on fat, you have to read patiently the labels of all the processed food you buy.

BULGUR WHEAT PILAF WITH NUTS AND SEEDS (PAGE 219)

other ingredients in the balance ▶

other **ingredients** in the **balance**

Reducing the amount of fat you eat is not the only way to improve your diet. Aim to eat a wide variety of fresh, non-processed food every day and your diet will not only be low in fat, but you will also get all the nutrients your body needs to stay vigorous and healthy.

Choose carbohydrates for satisfaction

For a healthy diet, we need to structure each meal around a base of starchy carbohydrates because they supply us with a low-fat form of energy as well as B vitamins and some calcium, iron and fibre. These carbohydrate foods help to fill us up, too, so we do not pine for succulent, high-fat dishes.

All types of cereal food contain fibre, but wholegrain products, such as wholemeal bread and pasta and brown rice, provide most.

A healthy diet should include plenty of bread, breakfast cereals, bulgur wheat, cornmeal, maize, millet, noodles, oats, pasta, potatoes, pulses and rice. However, you must avoid frying these foods, spreading lots of fat on your bread, and heaping rich sauces onto pasta or rice dishes.

Ease up on protein foods

Protein is part of the structure of every cell in our bodies and, as the cells are constantly dying, they need continual replacement. Most of us know that protein is important for building and maintaining our bodies so we tend to eat much more than we need. This can be harmful because

DAILY PROTEIN NEEDS

0-3 years	12.5 g increasing to 15 g
4-6 years	20 g
7-10 years	28 g
11-14 years (boys)	42 g
11-14 years (girls)	41 g
15-18 years (boys)	55 g
15-18 years (girls)	45 g
Men over 18	55 g
Women over 18	45 g

any surplus is broken down to release energy, which is stored in our bodies as fat. As the table (below left) shows, adult men need only 55 g (2 oz) of protein a day and women need just 45 g (1½ oz).

Good sources of protein include milk and hard cheeses, in which about 20-30 per cent of the weight is protein; meat and fish with about 20 per cent; and beans, peas and lentils with 5 per cent. Most other vegetables and fruit have less than 5 per cent. Choose lean or reduced-fat sources of protein, so that you do not eat too much fat alongside your protein.

Don't stint on fruit and vegetables

Fruit and vegetables are highly nutritious but add comparatively few calories to the diet. They are packed with vitamins such as A, C and E, a host of minerals such as calcium, iron, magnesium and potassium, and other active compounds which help to protect against cancer and heart disease.

With the exception of avocado pears, which are high in unsaturated fat, fruit and vegetables are also virtually fat-free. The Department of Health recommends that we eat 400 g (14 oz) of fruit and vegetables a day. The motto is: 'Fresh, frozen, cooked, raw, it doesn't matter, just eat more'.

Eat plenty of fibre

Eating plenty of foods rich in fibre, such as wholemeal bread, wholegrain cereals, fruit and vegetables, can help to protect your health. Insoluble fibre, found mainly in wholegrain cereals and nuts, helps to prevent constipation and, by speeding the passage of food through the intestine, can help to reduce the risk of colonic and bowel cancer. Soluble fibre, found principally in pulses and oats such as porridge oats, has been shown to help to reduce blood cholesterol.

At least 18 g of fibre a day is recommended, which is easily achieved. For instance, one slice of wholemeal bread provides 2 g of fibre and fits comfortably into the daily diet.

Go easy on salt

There are two schools of thought on sodium and blood pressure. There are those who say that a high intake definitely raises blood pressure and we should cut back as much as possible, and there are those who say that only some people are susceptible to a high intake. Since there is no easy way of telling whether you are susceptible or not, it is best to favour caution: use as little salt as possible in your cooking and do not add any at the table.

Watch out for 'hidden' salt in ingredients such as soy sauce, anchovies and smoked fish, and in processed food, where the levels can be high. Stock cubes, for example, are generally very salty, so it is better to make your own stock to add a really rich, deep flavour to your food (see the great stock recipes on page 64).

Other ways to compensate for less salt in food include using top-quality ingredients with lots of natural flavour, generously sprinkling food with fresh herbs and using salty cheeses, such as feta and blue cheeses. Cutting back on salt may make food seem bland at first, but your taste buds will soon adapt.

Enjoy alcohol in small doses

Most doctors accept that alcohol is fine in moderation, but that it is safer to drink a little four or five days a week than to 'save up' units for a weekend binge. Current guidelines are up to four units a day for men; three units for women. A unit is equivalent to half a pint of beer, lager or cider, a pub measure of spirits or wine, or a small glass of fortified wine.

Alcohol also adds lots of empty calories: a typical 287 ml (10 fl oz) bottle of lager has 83 calories, a 125 ml (4 fl oz) glass of wine, 85 calories. Alcohol contributes few if any nutrients and, because it makes you feel full, may stop you eating more nutritious foods. The antioxidants in red wine have been said to be good for the heart, but you should still drink it only in moderation.

SPAGHETTI WITH SCALLOPS AND ROASTED PEPPERS (PAGE 209)

low-fat cooking techniques

Good low-fat cooking is no different from ordinary cooking: you just add fat more judiciously. Use the low-fat methods explained here to adapt your favourite recipes to healthy eating. As this guide shows, even frying is not completely off limits.

Braising

Braising involves cooking meat and vegetables slowly in a flavoursome liquid in a covered casserole in the oven. It is particularly good for bringing juicy tenderness to tougher, lean meats such as game, and to fibrous vegetables such as celery, leeks and onions. You do not need to add oil or butter to the braising liquid: the flavour should come from ingredients such as good stock, wine and fresh herbs, as in Daube of Beef and Vegetables Provençale (page 169).

Casseroling

This is similar to braising, but the meat is cut into small pieces. Traditionally these are sealed or browned in fat before the liquid and other ingredients are added: see Beef Stew with Parsley Dumplings (page 166). Provided the low-fat frying techniques detailed below are followed, there is no need to omit this step.

Casseroles usually taste better the day after they are made. Chilling the dish overnight has the added advantage that any fat will rise to the surface and solidify, so it can be lifted off before the casserole is reheated, to make an even healthier dish.

Frying

- Shallow-frying: there is no need for you to throw away the frying pan. The keys to successful low-fat frying are: invest in a good quality heavy-based nonstick frying pan and/or wok, and always measure the oil, butter or margarine, if using, carefully. Fat expands as it heats, so add it to a hot pan and you will probably find you need less than you thought. It helps to use a brush or piece of kitchen paper to spread the very thinnest film of fat or oil over the pan.

Stir-frying is so quick and easy that you can have a healthy meal on the table faster than the time it takes to heat up a ready-made frozen meal.

- Dry-frying: this is an excellent method for cooking meat and oily fish without the addition of fat. A nonstick frying pan is useful but not essential: the most important thing is for the pan to have a heavy base. It should be heated until very hot before the fish or meat is added and, once in the pan, they should not be moved or turned over until a light crust has formed.
- Sautéeing and stir-frying can be turned into no-fat cooking techniques by replacing the usual butter or oil with liquids such as good quality stock, soy sauce and lemon juice, as in the Onion, Feta Cheese and Marjoram Pizzas (page 252). These methods are particularly good for cooking vegetables quickly.

  To prevent sticking, a nonstick pan is helpful, or a well-seasoned wok, but what is most important is to keep the food moving around the pan so that it has no time to catch and burn.

Grilling

Successful low-fat grilling demands a rack which allows the fat in the food to drip down into the base of the pan. Laying the food on foil or using a baking sheet under the grill, although it may be necessary with delicate foods like some fish which would break up on a rack, traps the fat around the food and so is best avoided.

- Grilling is an excellent choice for fattier meats such as bacon, as well as tender pieces of meat and poultry, and juicy vegetables such as courgettes and peppers. It is also a very good way of cooking highly absorbent aubergines with little or no oil.

  This is a quick cooking technique best done with intense heat. For extra flavour and tenderness, food can be marinated before it is grilled.
- Chargrilling or griddling is similar to grilling except that it is done on the hob, with the heat coming from below rather than above. A ridged, iron griddle or grill pan allows the fat to drip away from the food.

  Make sure the griddle or grill pan is really hot before adding the food, and very lightly oil the griddle or the food before cooking to stop it sticking. This should not be necessary if the food has been marinated.
- Barbecuing has all the low-fat advantages of grilling, and the burning wood or charcoal also imparts a delicious smoky flavour to the food. This method is suitable for fish, poultry, meat and vegetables such as aubergines, courgettes, onions, peppers, potatoes and sweet potatoes. Using fat-free and low-fat marinades to flavour foods before they are cooked can turn a barbecue into an aromatic feast.

Microwaving

The microwave oven's main selling point has always been its speed, but another advantage for the low-fat cook is that microwaved dishes often require little or no cooking fat. For example, you can soften onions in the bare minimum of fat before adding them to other dishes. Microwaving is a particularly successful method for cooking delicate fish and vegetables. To expand your repertoire, invest in a good microwave cookbook and experiment using less fat.

En papillote

This French term refers to foods that are wrapped in greaseproof paper or foil and baked in the oven. This method is best for seafood, poultry, vegetables and fruits, and it is usually most convenient to wrap servings individually. Rather than fat, flavouring ingredients such as a dash of wine or vermouth, citrus juices, herbs and spices are included in the parcels. A couple of tablespoons of liquid is generally required for each parcel to help to steam the food and keep it moist.

SMOKED HADDOCK WITH POACHED EGG (PAGE 42)

Poaching

Not merely a healthy method of cooking eggs, poaching can also be used as the basis of an entire low-fat meal, provided the cooking liquid is flavoured with herbs and spices, and a dash of an acidic agent such as citrus juice, vinegar, vermouth or wine. It is excellent for fish and other seafood and poultry – as in Chilled Chicken with a Herb and Tomato Sauce (page 136). Even large joints such as hams and legs of lamb benefit from being poached because it keeps the meat tender and extraordinarily juicy (see Ham Simmered in Cider, page 187).

For best results, make sure the liquid does not come to boiling point, or even a lively simmer, as this can toughen the food and leech out the flavour. When poaching, the liquid should only shiver; at most it can simmer very gently.

BAKED HALIBUT WITH STEAMED PAK CHOI (PAGE 117)

Roasting

Depending on the fat content of the food being prepared, roasting can be a no-fat cooking method. Whole birds and joints of red meat do not usually require the addition of extra fat to the roasting pan, and using a trivet in the base of the pan allows any fat in the meat to drip away from the food during cooking. Roasting can also be a good means of preparing large, firm pieces of white fish such as cod, monkfish and sea bass.

All kinds of vegetables can be roasted too: brush them very lightly with oil before placing them in the oven. Mixing the oil with a little balsamic or sherry vinegar, or with syrup or soy sauce, not only helps to make a very small amount of oil go further, but also adds extra flavour, as the recipe for Sweet Roasted Squash with Shallots (page 231), which uses maple syrup or honey, shows.

Steaming

Cooking food in the hot vapours rising from boiling water, rather than in the water itself, helps to preserve nutrients, maintains the colour and texture of food and is almost as quick as boiling. Steaming can be used for fish and seafood, poultry and vegetables.

You can use a purpose-made steamer, a bamboo steaming basket placed over a saucepan or wok, or a metal colander or collapsible metal steamer resting in a saucepan. The most important thing is to keep the lid on so that the steam does not escape.

Always use top quality fresh ingredients when you are steaming: the flavour of the food is not going to be masked by butter or oil so it is essential that they taste good in their own right.

Invest in these useful items for easier low-fat cooking.

Brushes: useful for oiling foods lightly and to help to spread a thin layer of oil around the base of the cooking pan.

Food processor or blender: either of these make easy work of puréeing fruit and vegetables to make creamy sauces and soups, and to make dried-fruit purée, so useful for replacing some fat in baking recipes. You can also use a food processor to mince meat and poultry, after you have carefully trimmed off all the fat.

Measuring spoons and scales: many foods do not require strict measuring but any food containing fat, such as butter, margarine and oils, creams and yoghurts, should be measured carefully. Cultivating the habit of measuring, not guessing, is really helpful in controlling fat intake.

Nonstick frying pan and/or wok: even for the low-fat cook, careful frying is a useful, quick cooking method. A nonstick pan or wok allows you to do it without fat, or with the bare minimum. Invest in the best you can afford, one with a heavy base.

Ridged, iron grill pan: any fat collects in the hollows between the ridges so the food does not sit in fat, nor does the fat end up on your plate. In addition, the ridges give an attractive lined appearance to foods cooked in such a pan.

Steamer: enables you to cook food without fat or immersion in water, keeping it fresh and full of flavour. You can improvise a steamer by using a metal colander placed over a saucepan, but for regular use, a stainless steel steamer is a good investment as it can cook larger quantities, or even a whole meal.

Zester: a quick way to remove the zest from citrus fruit and add zing to savoury and sweet dishes without fat.

easy ways to cut the fat in your diet

Use your imagination to think of different ways of cooking without using fat. Whether it's a fruit juice dressing for salad, or a fat-free topping for baked potatoes, try these suggestions to stimulate your culinary creativity.

- Choose extra-lean cuts of meat and trim off all visible fat.
- If using ingredients such as anchovies, olives or sun-dried tomatoes preserved in oil, drain them well then mop off any remaining oil with kitchen paper.
- Do not garnish soup with high-fat cream, fried croutons or bacon. Choose finishing touches that look appetising without adding fat, such as sprigs of fresh herbs or a few pretty salad leaves. Or emphasise one of the ingredients, using shreds of carrot with carrot or vegetable soup, or prawns with a fish soup.
- You can often substitute two egg whites for one whole egg in baking. The whites, which have no fat, can also be whisked to make very light sponges such as Angel Food Cake (page 296).
- To make 'creamy' soups, add potatoes or white beans to the soup while it is simmering, then purée before serving.
- Go easy on garnishes: they can add a surprising amount of fat. For instance, a single tablespoon of pine nuts contains 10 g of fat; flaked almonds 9 g; croutons 6 g; ordinary crème fraîche 5 g and crispy bacon bites 3 g.
- Instead of using a roux made with butter, thicken sauces with cornflour or arrowroot mixed to a paste with skimmed milk, low-fat yoghurt, stock or water as in Chicken with Asparagus in a White Wine Sauce (page 130).
- Accompany grilled fish, poultry and meat with salsas made from fresh fruit and vegetables instead of creamy sauces or high-fat gravy.
- Instead of greasing baking trays, use baking paper to line them and prevent food from sticking.
- Purée fresh fruit to make dessert sauces that are as luscious as cream.
- Mash potatoes with some cooked celeriac or parsnip for extra flavour and they will not need butter or cream. Or infuse a crushed clove of garlic in some hot skimmed milk while they are cooking (you can do it in a cup in the microwave) then beat it in to help make a tasty mash.
- Split your jacket potato open and squeeze lots of lemon juice and black pepper over for a strong, fat-free flavour.
- Spread marmalade or jam straight onto your toast – you will soon find you do not miss the butter. Do not add butter when having snacks on toast like baked beans, scrambled egg or grilled tomatoes; just let the flavour of the topping come through. Spread sandwiches with a little low-fat mayonnaise.
- If you want a cheese topping, a little grated Parmesan goes a long way when mixed with breadcrumbs and/or herbs.
- Cut the fat in some cake and pudding recipes, such as Apricot Oat Flapjacks (page 296), by replacing up to half the amount of butter, margarine or vegetable oil with a dried-fruit purée. Look for ready-made prune purée, or prune spread as it may be labelled, in health food shops. Alternatively, make your own by puréeing ready-to-eat stoned prunes in a food processor with a little hot water to give a smooth texture.

  Just try the Squidgy Chocolate Cake (page 299) to appreciate the wonderful texture and flavour that prunes add. Dried apricot, apple, banana and date purées are other excellent fat substitutes because they, too, add the moisture and flavour that would otherwise be supplied by fat.

how to use this book

Before you rush to try out the hundreds of delicious recipes on the following pages, please take time to read these guidelines. They explain how the recipes are set out and are designed to help you to get the very best out of this cookbook.

GRILLED CHICKEN, BROCCOLI AND PASTA GRATIN (PAGE 139)

Using the recipes

- Ingredients are given in both metric and imperial measures, but these are not exact equivalents so use either all-metric or all-imperial measures when cooking.
- All spoon measures are for a level spoonful. For accuracy, it is best to use cooks' measuring spoons: the 5 ml spoon equals 1 level teaspoon and the 15 ml spoon equals 1 level tablespoon.
- All eggs are large unless otherwise indicated.
- Most recipes specify black pepper and for the best flavour this should be freshly ground. Likewise, Parmesan cheese should be freshly grated.
- Use fresh herbs rather than dried if you can as they add wonderful tastes and fragrances to low-fat food. If you cannot find the herb specified in the recipe, you may find another that complements the dish, so enjoy experimenting. If you cannot get fresh herbs at all, then substitute 1-1½ teaspoons of the dried herb for 1 tablespoon of fresh.
- For best results, use high quality ingredients. Recipes assume that the fruit and vegetables you select are fresh and ripe and that meat and fish is fresh, carefully reared or handled and has plenty of flavour.

Using the nutritional analyses

The figures given with each recipe do not include optional accompaniments, such as bread with soup.

With main course dishes, the analysis includes vegetables or accompaniments only if they are part of the dish, such as in Grilled Chicken, Broccoli and Pasta Gratin (page 139). If the recipe is for fish or meat on its own or with a sauce, allow for the nutrients – especially fat – that will be provided by any accompaniment.

In poultry recipes, figures are calculated assuming the meat has been skinned. In recipes using beef, lamb and pork, the assumption is that the leanest cuts have been chosen and all visible fat trimmed off.

Vegetables are generally specified by weight and not number – for example, 60 g (2¼ oz) onions, rather than 1 small onion – for precise calculations.

Eggs

Salmonella bacteria, which can cause fatal food poisoning in the most extreme cases, affect poultry flocks in the United Kingdom, and the risk is highest with soft-boiled, lightly cooked or raw eggs. These, and any dishes containing them, should be avoided by elderly or infirm people, pregnant women, and children. For safety, cook eggs to 71°C (160°F), the temperature at which the yolk sets hard and the salmonella bacteria are destroyed.

eakfasts and snacks

Breakfast fruit cocktail

Nutrients per serving

- Calories 163
- Carbohydrate 39 g
- Protein 3 g
- Fat 1 g (no saturated fat)

Take one grapefruit, one papaya, one orange and one banana, add a handful of strawberries and you have the most mouth-watering alarm call imaginable.

PREPARATION TIME: 10 minutes, plus overnight chilling
SERVES 2

1 small orange
2 teaspoons orange flower water or rosewater, optional
1 large pink grapefruit
1 papaya
1 large banana
100 g (3½ oz) strawberries
To garnish: 2 sprigs of fresh mint

1 Grate the zest from the orange and squeeze out the juice, then mix them together in a large bowl. Stir in the flower water, if using.
2 Add each fruit to the bowl as you prepare it. Cut the top and bottom off the grapefruit, then stand it on a flat end and slice off the skin. Slice the grapefruit into rounds, then cut each round into two halves.
3 Halve the papaya, scoop out and discard the seeds and membrane, then peel and slice the flesh. Peel the banana and slice it on the diagonal. Hull the strawberries and slice any large ones.
4 Stir the fruit together, coating them well with the orange juice and zest. Cover and chill overnight in the refrigerator.
5 In the morning, spoon the fruit into two bowls. Scatter some mint leaves over them and serve.

Ruby grapefruit and grape refresher

Sparkling grape juice and fresh grapefruit segments make a vibrant and flavourful pick-you-up to start the day. Enjoy it pure, or with creamy yoghurt.

PREPARATION TIME: 10 minutes, plus 30 minutes, or overnight, chilling
SERVES 2

1 ruby grapefruit
125 g (4½ oz) seedless black grapes
4 tablespoons sparkling red grape juice
To serve: low-fat natural yoghurt, optional

1. Using a sharp knife, cut all the peel and white pith from the grapefruit, holding it over a bowl to catch the juice. Cut down the side of each segment in turn, as close to the membrane as you can, and ease it out. Squeeze any remaining juice from the membrane, then discard it.
2. Cut the grapes in half if they are large, otherwise leave them whole. Add them to the grapefruit segments and juice. Chill for at least 30 minutes, or overnight if that is easier.
3. Spoon the sparkling grape juice over the grapefruit just before serving. Serve the fruit on its own, or top with yoghurt.

Variations: if you cannot find sparkling grape juice, use still grape juice and add it to the fruit before chilling. Orange segments can also be added, or used as a substitute for the grapefruit.

Nutrients per serving

- Calories 115
- Carbohydrate 28 g
- Protein 2 g
- No fat

RUBY GRAPEFRUIT

Apricot oat warmer

Nutrients per serving

- Calories 340
- Carbohydrate 66 g
- Protein 13 g
- Fat 4 g (including saturated fat 1 g)

Here's a cosy start to a winter's day. This spicy cinnamon porridge, with its cargo of rich apricots, is sweetened with golden syrup. Best of all, it takes only minutes to prepare.

PREPARATION TIME: 2 minutes
COOKING TIME: 5 minutes
SERVES 1

40 g (1½ oz) instant porridge oats
200 ml (7 fl oz) skimmed milk
4 ready-to-eat dried apricots
2 teaspoons golden syrup
A pinch of ground cinnamon

1. Simmer the porridge oats and milk together in a small saucepan for 4-5 minutes until the mixture is slightly thickened and smooth, stirring frequently. If necessary, add a little water to get the texture you prefer.
2. Meanwhile, chop the apricots.
3. Stir the syrup and ground cinnamon into the porridge. Pour the porridge into a bowl, sprinkle the chopped apricots on top and serve.

Variation: replace the apricots with a small chopped banana. You can also sprinkle four chopped hazelnuts over the porridge for extra crunch, but this will add 3 g of fat.

Whipped berry porridge

Nutrients per serving

- Calories 143
- Carbohydrate 33 g
- Protein 4 g
- Fat 1 g (no saturated fat)

Fluffy crimson semolina is swollen with juicy fruit to bring a refreshing lightness to this warming comforter.

PREPARATION TIME: 5 minutes, plus 5 minutes cooling
COOKING TIME: 25 minutes
SERVES 2

125 g (4½ oz) berries, such as raspberries and blackberries, defrosted if frozen
1 tablespoon caster sugar
Salt
50 g (1¾ oz) semolina
To serve: 2 tablespoons natural or lemon-flavoured low-fat yoghurt, optional

1. Pick over the berries, reserving a few as a garnish, and purée the rest with 500 ml (18 fl oz) of water, using a hand-held mixer. Strain the mixture through a fine nylon sieve into a small saucepan.
2. Add the sugar and a pinch of salt to the pan and place it over a medium heat. Bring the purée to a rolling boil then gently whisk in the semolina, taking care the mixture does not boil over. Then reduce the heat as far as possible and leave the mixture to simmer for about 20 minutes, stirring frequently, until it thickens.
3. Pour the porridge into two bowls and leave them to cool for 5 minutes. Serve garnished with the reserved fruit and yoghurt, if using.

Dried fruit compote

Nutrients per serving

- Calories 302
- Carbohydrate 72 g
- Protein 5 g
- Fat 2 g (no saturated fat)

In this cool compote a spoonful of unusual dried fruits helps to make a stunning high-fibre breakfast.

PREPARATION TIME: 5 minutes, plus overnight chilling
COOKING TIME: 4-5 minutes
SERVES 4

Grated zest of 1 orange
300 ml (10 fl oz) freshly squeezed orange juice
1-2 tablespoons clear honey, optional
1 stick cinnamon
6 cloves
300 g (10½ oz) mixed dried fruit
1 tablespoon unusual dried fruit, such as blueberries, cherries or mango
Juice of 1 lemon
½ lemon
To serve: 4 tablespoons muesli

1. Place the orange zest, juice, the honey, if using, cinnamon, cloves and 200 ml (7 fl oz) of water in a small saucepan and bring to the boil.
2. Meanwhile, place all the dried fruit in a heatproof bowl and pour the lemon juice over it. Divide the half-lemon in two lengthways, then slice it across into very thin crescents. Add these to the dried fruit then pour the boiling orange juice over the top. Allow to cool, then refrigerate overnight to allow the flavours to mature.
3. To serve, spoon the compote into individual bowls and sprinkle with muesli.

Canadian pancake feast

Nutrients per serving

- Calories 517
- Carbohydrate 87 g
- Protein 24 g
- Fat 10 g (including saturated fat 3 g)

Treat yourself to a brunch of low-fat buckwheat pancakes drizzled with Canadian maple syrup and piled high with grilled gammon and pineapple.

PREPARATION TIME: 5 minutes, plus 20 minutes standing

COOKING TIME: 25 minutes

SERVES 2

2 slices fresh pineapple, about 1 cm (½ in) thick
2 unsmoked gammon steaks, about 75 g (2¾ oz) each
4 tablespoons maple syrup

For the batter:

75 g (2¾ oz) self-raising white flour
25 g (1 oz) buckwheat flour
A pinch of bicarbonate of soda
Salt
1 egg
150 ml (5 fl oz) skimmed milk

1 To make the batter, sift both the flours into a bowl and stir in the bicarbonate of soda and a pinch of salt. Make a well in the centre, break in the egg and stir in a little of the flour, then gradually whisk in the milk to give a smooth batter. Alternatively, place all the batter ingredients in a food processor and blend until smooth. Set aside for 20 minutes to allow the starch grains to swell.
2 When the batter is ready, heat a nonstick frying pan or griddle until very hot (lightly grease the pan with vegetable oil if necessary, blotting off the excess with kitchen paper). Stir the batter, then pour a small ladleful into the pan and cook it for about 3 minutes, until the top has bubbled and is no longer wet. Turn it over and cook for 2-3 minutes on the other side. Keep the first pancake warm and cook three more the same way.
3 Heat the grill to high then cook the pineapple and the gammon steaks for 8 minutes, turning them over halfway through cooking.
4 To serve, stack two pancakes on each plate and top with the grilled gammon, then the pineapple. Pour some maple syrup over the top and serve.

Variation: if you cannot find buckwheat flour, use plain wholemeal flour instead.

Bacon, egg and tomatoes with mustard pancakes

Tuck into a leaner version of the British breakfast, served on filling mustard pancakes.

PREPARATION TIME: 15 minutes, plus 20 minutes standing
COOKING TIME: 25 minutes
SERVES 4

4 rindless rashers of lean bacon
4 tomatoes, halved
Salt and black pepper
½ teaspoon dried mixed herbs
4 eggs
For the pancakes:
90 g (3¼ oz) plain white flour
1 teaspoon baking powder
1 egg, separated
2 teaspoons wholegrain mustard
175 ml (6 fl oz) buttermilk, or 175 g (6 oz) low-fat natural yoghurt
1 teaspoon sunflower oil

1. Set the bacon and tomatoes on the rack of the grill pan. Sprinkle the tomatoes with pepper and herbs then set aside.
2. To make the pancakes, sift the flour, baking powder and a pinch of salt into a mixing bowl and make a well in the centre. Add the egg yolk, mustard and buttermilk or yoghurt, then whisk to a smooth, thick batter. Set aside for 20 minutes to rest.
3. Whisk the egg white until it forms soft peaks. Fold a little into the batter to loosen it, then fold in the rest.
4. Heat a large nonstick frying pan over a medium heat and wipe the surface with kitchen paper dipped in the oil. Set the paper aside to oil the pan for each pancake. Drop 2 tablespoons of batter into the pan and cook the pancakes for 1-2 minutes, until they are golden brown underneath and bubbles start to form on top. Then turn them over and cook the other side for 1 minute, or until golden.
5. Transfer the pancakes to a plate lined with kitchen paper and keep them warm. Make six more pancakes the same way, oiling the frying pan again if necessary. In the meantime, heat the grill to high.
6. Grill the bacon and tomatoes until the tomatoes are just softened and the bacon is golden and slightly crisp, turning the rashers over as they begin to brown.
7. Meanwhile, poach the eggs in an egg poacher for about 3 minutes until the whites are set and the yolks still runny. Or fill a frying pan one-third full of water, add 2 teaspoons of vinegar and bring to a simmer. Break each egg into a teacup, swirl a small whirlpool in the water with a spoon, slide the eggs in and poach them for about 3 minutes.
8. Arrange the eggs, bacon, tomatoes and pancakes on warmed plates, season and serve.

Nutrients per serving

- Calories 277
- Carbohydrate 24 g
- Protein 20 g
- Fat 12 g (including saturated fat 3 g)

Light and fruity French toast

This luscious eggy bread, made without any yolks, is topped with a sweet fruity spread.

PREPARATION TIME: 5 minutes
COOKING TIME: 6 minutes
SERVES 2

3 tablespoons skimmed milk
2 egg whites
Salt and black pepper
4 slices day-old crusty white bread
1-2 teaspoons butter
4 tablespoons ready-made apple and pear spread
To serve: 1 tablespoon demerara sugar and a pinch of cinnamon, optional

1. Whisk together the milk and egg whites in a shallow dish and season lightly. Dip both sides of the bread into the liquid.
2. In a large frying pan, melt a little of the butter over a medium heat until it froths. Add two slices of bread and fry for 2-3 minutes until the bottoms are firm and golden brown.
3. Remove the toast, melt more butter if needed, then cook the other side for 2-3 minutes until golden brown. Repeat with the remaining two slices.
4. Coat with the apple and pear spread, sprinkle with a little sugar and cinnamon if you like, and serve.

Variation: use raisin loaf instead of white bread, sprinkle with caster sugar and a pinch of cinnamon and top with a sliced banana.

Nutrients per serving

- Calories 305
- Carbohydrate 56 g
- Protein 10 g
- Fat 6 g (including saturated fat 3 g)

Egg white omelette with asparagus

The delicate flavour of asparagus replaces the taste of egg yolk in this feather-light, low-cholesterol omelette.

PREPARATION TIME: 10 minutes
COOKING TIME: 16 minutes
SERVES 1

100 g (3½ oz) asparagus, trimmed, or asparagus tips
Salt and black pepper
4 egg whites
½ teaspoon sunflower oil

1. Put a steamer on to boil then steam the asparagus for 8 minutes, or until tender, and drain. Season to taste while still warm.
2. Whisk the egg whites until frothy but not forming peaks: the mixture should be pourable. Do not add salt as it will break down the froth.
3. Heat the oil in a small nonstick omelette pan or frying pan, swirling it around until it covers the bottom in a thin film. Pour in the omelette mixture and cook over a low to medium heat for 2-3 minutes, until the bottom is firm.
4. Slide the omelette onto a plate. Lay the asparagus in the pan, then carefully invert the omelette on top. Cook for another 2-3 minutes, until the bottom has just set and the asparagus is golden brown, then serve.

Variation: if asparagus is out of season, use chopped spinach or broccoli instead.

Nutrients per serving

- Calories 89
- Carbohydrate 2 g
- Protein 14 g
- Fat 3 g (no saturated fat)

Spicy scrambled eggs on toast

Scrambled eggs become a tasty treat when cooked with fresh herbs, spices and a splash of lime juice.

PREPARATION TIME: 15 minutes
COOKING TIME: 8-10 minutes
SERVES 4

4 thick slices wholemeal bread
1 tablespoon butter
1 green chilli, deseeded and diced
2 teaspoons curry paste
1 clove garlic, crushed
1 teaspoon grated ginger
4 spring onions, chopped
85 g (3 oz) tomatoes, peeled and diced
6 eggs
1 tablespoon chopped fresh coriander
1 teaspoon lime juice
Salt and black pepper
4 tablespoons low-fat natural yoghurt, optional

1 Toast the bread and keep it warm.
2 Melt the butter in a nonstick frying pan and add the chilli, curry paste, garlic, ginger and spring onions, reserving a few for a garnish. Fry them over a low heat for 5 minutes, until softened but not browned. Stir in the tomatoes and cook for a further 1 minute.
3 Beat the eggs with the coriander, lime juice and salt and pepper to taste. Add the eggs to the pan and stir gently over a low heat until just set.
4 Lay the toast on plates, top with the curried eggs, sprinkle with the reserved spring onions and add some yoghurt if you wish.

Nutrients per serving

- Calories 272
- Carbohydrate 17 g
- Protein 17 g
- Fat 16 g (including saturated fat 5 g)

Fresh ideas for healthy packed lunches

A lunch box can hold a miniature, but satisfying, low-fat feast if you are watching your fat intake. Variety and flavour are vital not only to make the meal appealing but also to ensure that your diet has a full range of nutrients, and the ideal packed lunch has a variety of small items.

Think of your lunch in courses: start with soup or a vegetable juice cocktail and follow it with something more substantial, such as these freezer-friendly recipes. Maintain your vegetable intake with a salad, or some crudités and a no-fat salsa dip, and finish with fresh or dried fruit or a slice of nutritious cake for a healthy alternative to high-fat snacks.

Make a friend of your freezer

Creating enticing lunch boxes is easy using a freezer. Choose recipes that can be frozen in single servings, like Hi-veg Muffins, Curried Tuna Slices and Sweet Pumpkin and Apricot Cakes (right). Freeze two or three different items and, in the morning, choose the one you fancy and it will defrost by lunch time.

- To freeze lunch box items, wrap individual portions in greaseproof paper, then place them in a freezer bag and label it. They can be frozen for up to three months.

Latin-American chicken parcels

Tortillas enclose a filling with all the flavour of traditional guacamole, but far less fat.

PREPARATION TIME: 20 minutes
COOKING TIME: 15 minutes
MAKES 4

2 skinned and boned chicken breasts, about 125g (4½ oz) each
Salt and black pepper
150g (5½ oz) frozen peas
1 small green chilli, deseeded and chopped
1 clove garlic, crushed
3 tablespoons low-fat Greek yoghurt
2-3 tablespoons chopped fresh coriander
Juice of 1 lime
150g (5½ oz) canned kidney beans, drained and rinsed
100g (3½ oz) tomatoes, deseeded and chopped
2 spring onions, chopped
4 soft wheat flour tortillas

1. Put a kettle of water on to boil and heat the grill to high. Grill the chicken breasts for 6-8 minutes, turning them over halfway through, until the juices run clear when they are pierced with a knife. Set them aside to cool then cut into cubes.
2. Meanwhile, simmer the peas in salted water for 5 minutes, or until tender. Drain and rinse.
3. Place the peas in a food processor, add the chilli, garlic and yoghurt, and some of the coriander and lime juice, then purée. Adjust the flavour with more coriander and lime juice and add salt and pepper to taste.
4. Stir the beans, tomatoes and spring onions into the purée. Spread it over each tortilla, top with chicken and roll it up. Wrap each parcel tightly in kitchen foil.

Nutrients per parcel

- Calories 316
- Carbohydrate 45g
- Protein 30g
- Fat 3g (including saturated fat 1g)

LATIN-AMERICAN CHICKEN PARCELS
CURRIED TUNA SLICES
HI-VEG MUFFINS

Hi-veg muffins

These flavour-packed, savoury muffins will banish hunger.

PREPARATION TIME: 30 minutes
COOKING TIME: 30-40 minutes
MAKES 16

100g (3½ oz) squash or sweet potatoes, peeled and chopped
100g (3½ oz) courgettes, grated
250g (9oz) onions, grated
100g (3½ oz) red pepper, finely diced
100g (3½ oz) spinach, shredded, or broccoli, finely chopped
100g (3½ oz) canned sweetcorn, drained
75ml (2½ fl oz) vegetable oil, plus extra for greasing
225g (8oz) reduced-fat Cheddar cheese
Salt and black pepper
225g (8oz) self-raising white flour, sifted
4 eggs

1. Steam the squash or sweet potatoes for 10-15 minutes until tender. Mash and set aside. Meanwhile, heat the oven to 180°C (350°F, gas mark 4) and lightly grease 16 muffin tins.

2 Place the courgettes, onions, red pepper, spinach or broccoli and sweetcorn in a mixing bowl with the oil, grate the cheese in and season to taste. Fold the flour in, then the mashed squash or sweet potatoes.
3 Whisk the eggs until frothy, then fold them into the vegetable mixture and spoon it into the muffin tins. Bake the muffins for 20-25 minutes until slightly risen and browned.
4 Let the muffins cool thoroughly before removing them from the tins.

Nutrients per muffin

- Calories 165
- Carbohydrate 14 g
- Protein 8 g
- Fat 9 g (including saturated fat 2 g)

Curried tuna slices

Tuna and rice topped with cheese makes a hearty snack.

PREPARATION TIME: 30 minutes
COOKING TIME: 1 hour
MAKES 12 slices

50 g (1¾ oz) onions, grated
225 g (8 oz) long-grain white rice
1 whole egg plus 2 egg whites
4 tablespoons chopped fresh parsley
Salt and pepper
400 g (14 oz) canned tuna in brine, drained and flaked
40 g (1½ oz) butter
2 tablespoons plain white flour
2 tablespoons curry powder
350 ml (12 fl oz) skimmed milk
125 g (4 oz) low-fat yoghurt
2 teaspoons lemon juice
50 g (1¾ oz) reduced-fat Cheddar cheese, finely grated

1 Line a 18 x 28 cm (7 x 11 in) ovenproof dish with baking paper. Boil the onions and rice in salted water for 12 minutes, or until the rice is tender.
2 Drain the rice and onions, then place in a mixing bowl. Lightly beat the whole egg and add it to the rice, with 2 tablespoons of the parsley, and season to taste. Press the mixture into the base and up the sides of the dish.
3 Spread the tuna over the rice base, then set the dish aside.
4 Melt the butter in a saucepan, stir in the flour and curry powder and cook for 1 minute. Take off the heat and gradually add the milk, stirring. Add the yoghurt and bring to the boil, then simmer for 10-15 minutes until thick.
5 Meanwhile, heat the oven to 180°C (350°F, gas mark 4). Off the heat, add the lemon juice and remaining parsley to the sauce. Allow to cool slightly, then stir in the egg whites and season. Pour the sauce over the tuna, sprinkle the cheese on top and bake for 25-30 minutes until golden.
6 When it is cool, remove from the tin and cut into 12 slices.

Nutrients per slice

- Calories 174
- Carbohydrate 20 g
- Protein 14 g
- Fat 4 g (including saturated fat 3 g)

Sweet pumpkin and apricot cakes

Apricot purée replaces fat in these sweet, moist cakes.

PREPARATION TIME: 30 minutes, plus 30 minutes soaking and 20 minutes cooling
COOKING TIME: 45-55 minutes
MAKES 24 squares

85 g (3 oz) ready-to-eat dried apricots
500 g (1 lb 2 oz) pumpkin
450 g (1 lb) plain white flour
2 teaspoons baking powder
1 teaspoon bicarbonate of soda
2 teaspoons ground cinnamon
½ teaspoon salt
450 g (1 lb) caster sugar
4 eggs, lightly beaten
125 ml (4 fl oz) vegetable oil, plus extra for greasing

1 Cover the apricots with boiling water and leave them to plump up for at least 30 minutes. Drain them and reserve 4-5 tablespoons of the liquid.
2 Peel, deseed and chop the pumpkin. Steam it for 15-20 minutes until very tender. Drain it thoroughly and mash to make 450 ml (16 fl oz) of purée then set aside for 20 minutes to cool.
3 Purée the apricots in a food processor or with a hand-held mixer until very smooth, adding the reserved water if necessary to make 125 ml (4 fl oz) of purée.
4 Heat the oven to 180°C (350°F, gas mark 4) and grease two 23 cm (9 in) square cake tins.
5 Place the flour, baking powder, bicarbonate of soda, cinnamon, salt and sugar in a large mixing bowl and make a well in the centre. Add the eggs, oil, apricot and pumpkin purées and mix until they are just combined.
6 Pour the mixture into the cake tins, smooth the tops and bake for 30-35 minutes, rotating the tins half-way through, until the cakes have risen and a skewer comes out clean.
7 Cut each cake into 12. Leave to cool in the tins on wire racks for at least 20 minutes, then turn them out onto the racks to cool completely.

Nutrients per square

- Calories 209
- Carbohydrate 36 g
- Protein 3 g
- Fat 7 g (including saturated fat 1 g)

SWEET PUMPKIN AND APRICOT CAKES

Low-fat tip

For a lower-fat dish, brush the mushrooms and tomatoes with Worcestershire sauce, then grill them.

Turkey patties with tomatoes and mushrooms

Spiced minced turkey makes a lean and flavoursome substitute for traditional breakfast sausages. Add tomatoes and mushrooms for a great brunch.

PREPARATION TIME: 10 minutes
COOKING TIME: 15 minutes
SERVES 4

3 tablespoons olive oil
1 large green chilli, deseeded and finely chopped
2 large cloves garlic, crushed
A large pinch of ground cumin
500 g (1 lb 2 oz) minced turkey
Salt and black pepper

To serve:

4 large field mushrooms
2 large tomatoes, halved
8 slices French bread
4 large fresh basil leaves
Relish or mustard, optional

1 Heat 1 tablespoon of the oil in a small saucepan, then cook the chilli and garlic for 1-2 minutes until softened. Add the cumin and cook for a further few seconds, then leave to cool.
2 Stir the chilli and garlic mixture into the minced turkey and add salt and pepper to taste. Divide the mixture into four and shape each portion into a flat patty.
3 Heat a nonstick frying pan and brush it lightly with 1 tablespoon of oil. Fry the patties for 3-4 minutes on each side, then remove and keep them warm.
4 Add the mushrooms and tomatoes to the pan, adding more oil if necessary. Fry them for 3-4 minutes, turning once.
5 Meanwhile, toast the bread then brush the slices lightly with oil. Slice the basil and sprinkle it over the tomatoes. Serve everything together, with some relish or mustard to go with the turkey patties if you like.

Nutrients per serving

- Calories 306
- Carbohydrate 25 g
- Protein 33 g
- Fat 9 g (including saturated fat 2 g)

Sweetcorn griddlecakes with yoghurt sauce

A delicious Sunday breakfast treat, these griddlecakes are also good as a light lunch or served with roast chicken.

PREPARATION TIME: 5 minutes, plus 20 minutes standing
COOKING TIME: 20 minutes
MAKES 12

75 g (2¾ oz) cornmeal
75 g (2¾ oz) strong white flour
2 teaspoons baking powder
Salt and black pepper
1 tablespoon vegetable oil, plus extra for greasing
150 ml (5 fl oz) skimmed milk or water
1 cob fresh sweetcorn, or 125 g (4½ oz) canned sweetcorn, or frozen sweetcorn, defrosted
2 tablespoons chopped fresh coriander
2 egg whites
For the sauce:
150 g (5½ oz) low-fat Greek yoghurt
Grated zest of 1 lemon
1 tablespoon lemon juice
2 tablespoons chopped fresh coriander

1. Combine the cornmeal, flour, baking powder and some black pepper in a large bowl. Add the oil and the milk or water, and stir until the batter has a thick, dropping consistency.
2. If using fresh sweetcorn, cut the tip off and stand the cob upright on a chopping board. Hold it firmly by the stem and, using a sharp knife, slice off the kernels, following the hard cob as your guide. Add the sweetcorn kernels and chopped coriander to the batter, mix well, cover and allow to rest for 20 minutes.
3. Whisk the egg whites and a pinch of salt into soft peaks. Add a little beaten white to the batter to loosen it, then fold in the rest.
4. Heat a griddle or large frying pan and spread a thin coating of oil over it with a piece of kitchen paper. Keep the paper to hand and use it to grease the pan for the next batch.
5. Dip a large tablespoon in water and use it to drop spoonfuls of the batter onto the hot griddle or pan. Cook for 2-3 minutes until browned, then turn them over and cook for a further 3-4 minutes. Keep the first batch warm and repeat until all the batter has been used, greasing the griddle or pan after each batch.
6. In a bowl, mix together all the sauce ingredients and serve it with the griddlecakes.

Nutrients per cake, with sauce

- Calories 79
- Carbohydrate 12 g
- Protein 3 g
- Fat 2 g (including saturated fat 1 g)

Smoked haddock with **poached egg**

Nutrients per serving

- Calories 183
- Carbohydrate 3 g
- Protein 27 g
- Fat 7 g (including saturated fat 2 g)

Start your day with this light version of the traditional combination of salty, smoked fish and a smooth rich egg.

PREPARATION TIME: 5 minutes
COOKING TIME: 12 minutes
SERVES 4

2 small fillets undyed smoked haddock, about 175 g (6 oz) each
275 ml (9½ fl oz) skimmed milk
4 eggs
2 teaspoons vinegar, optional
Black pepper

1 Rinse the haddock, pat it dry with kitchen paper and cut each fillet in half to make four pieces. Place the fillets, skin side down, in a single layer in a frying pan and add enough milk to cover (do not add salt as the fish is salty enough). Bring to the boil, cover, reduce the heat and simmer for 5-7 minutes until the flesh flakes easily.
2 Meanwhile, poach the eggs in an egg poacher for 3 minutes, or until the whites are set but the yolks are still runny. Alternatively, fill a large frying pan one-third full of water, add 2 teaspoons of vinegar to help to hold the egg whites firm and bring it to simmering point. Break the eggs into a cup one at a time, use a spoon to swirl a small whirlpool in the simmering water and slide them into the pan. Cook for 4 minutes, or until they are lightly set.
3 Lift out the cooked fish fillets with a slotted spoon, drain them on kitchen paper, then transfer to serving plates, skin side still down. Lay a poached egg on each fillet, sprinkle with black pepper and serve.

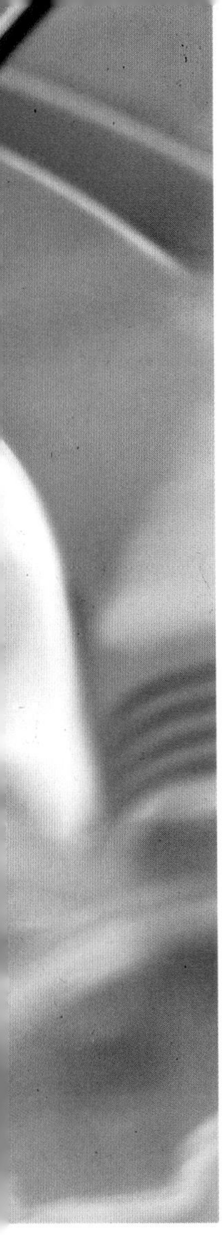

Quick smoked salmon pâté

Smoked salmon trimmings blended with fresh herbs and white beans make a delicious pâté that needs no cooking.

PREPARATION TIME: 5 minutes, plus 30 minutes-1 hour chilling
SERVES 4

200 g (7 oz) canned cannellini beans, drained
2 tablespoons chopped fresh herbs, such as chervil, dill and parsley
Juice of ½ lemon
200 g (7 oz) smoked salmon trimmings
Salt and black pepper
To serve: brown toast, crackers or crudités

1 Blend the beans, herbs, lemon juice and salmon in a food processor or with a hand-held mixer until it is really smooth. Add salt and black pepper to taste, then transfer the pâté to a serving dish and chill for 30 minutes-1 hour. Serve it with brown toast, crackers or crudités. The pâté is best eaten very fresh.

Nutrients per serving

- Calories 127
- Carbohydrate 9 g
- Protein 13 g
- Fat 3 g (no saturated fat)

Low-fat tip

Using soft white beans instead of the usual cream cheese makes the pâté low in fat but very filling.

Baked mixed mushrooms with **ciabatta**

Nutrients per serving, when serving 4
- Calories 254
- Carbohydrate 34 g
- Protein 9 g
- Fat 9 g (including saturated fat 2 g)

A mix of olive oil, garlic and rosemary releases a wonderful Mediterranean aroma while the mushrooms are cooking.

PREPARATION TIME: 15 minutes
COOKING TIME: 20-25 minutes
SERVES 4 as a snack, or 8 as a starter

3 cloves garlic, crushed
2 teaspoons lemon juice
2 tablespoons olive oil
2 teaspoons balsamic vinegar
Salt and black pepper
675 g (1 lb 8 oz) mixed button, chestnut and open mushrooms
300 g (10½ oz) tomatoes
2-4 sprigs of rosemary
1 teaspoon chopped fresh parsley or sage
1 ciabatta loaf

1 Heat the oven to 200°C (400°F, gas mark 6). Whisk together the garlic, lemon juice, olive oil, vinegar and seasoning in a large bowl.
2 Clean and slice the mushrooms; peel, deseed and dice the tomatoes. Add both to the bowl of dressing. Chop the rosemary, reserving some for a garnish, then add it to the mushroom mixture with the parsley or sage and stir.
3 Tip the mushroom mixture into a roasting tin. Cover with foil, make slits in the top to release a little of the steam during cooking and bake for 20-25 minutes until the mushrooms are tender.
4 When they are nearly done, heat the bread in the oven. Cut it in half lengthways and cut each half into four equal pieces, or eight if serving as a starter.
5 Place two pieces of bread on each serving plate, cut side up, top with the mushroom mixture and serve immediately, garnished with the reserved rosemary.

Irish grilled steak sandwich with onion salad

Nutrients per serving

- Calories 338
- Carbohydrate 38 g
- Protein 28 g
- Fat 10 g (including saturated fat 3 g)

For a really satisfying snack, try this classic from the Irish races: juicy grilled lean steak in a warm, crusty baguette.

PREPARATION TIME: 10 minutes, plus 1 hour soaking, optional
COOKING TIME: 4-6 minutes
SERVES 2

60 g (2¼ oz) onion, finely sliced
1 small baguette or 2 long crusty rolls
A little low-fat spread, optional
1 large lettuce leaf, torn
1 large tomato, sliced
2 thin steaks of beef, about 100 g (3½ oz) each
A little vegetable oil, to brush
Salt and black pepper
To serve: horseradish or mustard

1. If you have time, soak the onion slices in cold water for 1 hour: it helps to cut their pungency.
2. Drain the onions and pat them dry. Warm the baguette or rolls very gently. Split them in half and spread lightly with the low-fat spread, if using, then fill with the lettuce and tomato.
3. Heat the grill, or a ridged, iron grill pan, until it is piping hot. Trim any fat off the steaks, brush them with just a little oil and grill or fry them for 2-3 minutes on each side until cooked to your liking.
4. Place the steaks in the sandwiches, brush them with mustard or horseradish and top with the onion slices. Season to taste.
5. Press the sandwiches firmly to seal, cut on the diagonal and eat them immediately, wrapped in paper napkins.

Smoked salmon bagel with quark

Nutrients per serving

- Calories 336
- Carbohydrate 48 g
- Protein 29 g
- Fat 4 g (including saturated fat 1 g)

Finely sliced healthy smoked salmon makes an ideal partner to serve with virtually fat-free quark.

PREPARATION TIME: 7 minutes
SERVES 1

50 g (1¾ oz) quark
1 teaspoon lemon juice
1 bagel
50 g (1¾ oz) smoked salmon, finely sliced
Black pepper
To garnish: a few sprigs of dill, chopped

1. Mix together the quark and lemon juice.
2. Warm the bagel briefly, slice it in half and spread the bottom piece with the quark mixture. Sprinkle it with the slices of salmon then add black pepper to taste and a little dill. Cover with the top half and eat while the bagel is still warm.

Low-fat tip

Quark, a very light soft cheese, makes a fresh alternative to the rich cream cheese usually served in bagels.

Garlic, tomato and anchovy toasts

Nutrients per serving
- Calories 144
- Carbohydrate 23 g
- Protein 5 g
- Fat 4 g (including saturated fat 1 g)

Enjoy the wonderful taste of toasted bruschetta topped with a sharp, lemony paste and sweet grilled tomato.

PREPARATION TIME: 5 minutes, plus 10 minutes soaking
COOKING TIME: 2-3 minutes
SERVES 4

3 anchovy fillets
2 tablespoons skimmed milk
1 clove garlic, crushed
1 teaspoon lemon juice
4 slices bread, cut from a large crusty loaf
600 g (1 lb 5 oz) tomatoes
1 tablespoon olive oil
Black pepper
To garnish: fresh basil leaves

1. Place the anchovies in a small dish, add the milk and leave to soak for 10 minutes to remove excess saltiness and draw out some of the oil.
2. Drain, rinse and pat the anchovies dry with kitchen paper. Place them in a food processor with the garlic and lemon juice and pulse to make a paste. Alternatively, mash them with a fork, or with a pestle and mortar.
3. Heat the grill to high. Toast the bread on both sides, then spread a quarter of the paste over one side of each slice: it is very strong, so you only need a little.
4. Slice the tomatoes, discard the ends and arrange the slices on top of the anchovy paste. Drizzle with oil, sprinkle with black pepper and return to the grill for 1-2 minutes until the tomatoes are softened. Serve scattered with basil leaves.

ANCHOVIES

soups

Chilled melon soup

Nutrients per serving
- Calories 143
- Carbohydrate 25g
- Protein 6g
- Fat 2g (including saturated fat 1g)

This unusual, velvety soup is actually Parma ham with melon in a new guise.

PREPARATION TIME: 20 minutes, plus at least 4 hours chilling and 30 minutes standing
SERVES 4

1.5kg (3lb 5oz) honeydew melon
2 tablespoons medium (oloroso) sherry
1 tablespoon balsamic vinegar
1 teaspoon chopped fresh mint leaves
To garnish: 3 slices Parma ham, trimmed of some of its fat

1 Cut the melon into quarters, then peel and deseed it and cut it into large chunks. Place them in a food processor with 100ml (3½fl oz) of cold water, the sherry, vinegar and mint and process until smooth and velvety.
2 Transfer the soup to a bowl, cover and refrigerate for at least 4 hours, and preferably longer, for the flavours to develop. Half an hour before serving, allow the soup to come back to room temperature.
3 Finely slice the Parma ham into strips. Serve the soup in individual bowls, garnished with the ham.
Variation: you can leave out the Parma ham garnish to make a no-fat soup.

Chilled leek, pear and potato soup

Nutrients per serving
- Calories 104
- Carbohydrate 17g
- Protein 4g
- Fat 2g (no saturated fat)

This cold golden soup with its hint of sweetness is delicious on a summer's day.

PREPARATION TIME: 20 minutes, plus at least 30 minutes chilling
COOKING TIME: 25 minutes
SERVES 4

2 teaspoons olive oil
225g (8oz) leeks, finely sliced
125g (4½oz) potatoes, diced
2 dessert pears, peeled, cored and diced
10-12 strands saffron
900ml (1 pint 12fl oz) vegetable stock
Salt and black pepper
To garnish: a few snipped fresh chives
To serve: 4 tablespoons low-fat natural yoghurt

1 Heat the oil in a saucepan. Add the leeks and potatoes and cook for 5-6 minutes, stirring frequently, until slightly softened.
2 Add the pears, saffron and stock. Slowly bring to the boil, then reduce the heat, cover and simmer for 15 minutes, or until the vegetables are tender.
3 Blend or liquidise the soup until very smooth. Season to taste.
4 Cool the soup, then cover and chill for at least 30 minutes, or until required. When serving, swirl 1 tablespoon of yoghurt into each bowl and garnish with black pepper and a sprinkling of chives.
Variation: serve the soup warm, adding 1 tablespoon of mild curry powder, stirred in at the end of Step 1.

Chilled spinach and yoghurt soup

Nutrients per serving
- Calories 84
- Carbohydrate 10g
- Protein 8g
- Fat 1g (saturated fat 1g)

Dried mint gives an authentic Middle Eastern flavour to this refreshing soup.

PREPARATION TIME: 15 minutes
SERVES 4

250g (9oz) frozen leaf spinach, defrosted
1 clove garlic, finely crushed
500g (1lb 2oz) low-fat natural yoghurt
Salt and black pepper
3 teaspoons dried mint
To garnish: fresh mint leaves and grated nutmeg, optional

1 Add some ice cubes to 300ml (10fl oz) of cold water and chill it in the refrigerator. Squeeze the water from the spinach, then chop the spinach finely and place in a large bowl.
2 Mix in the garlic and yoghurt, season and stir in the dried mint. If the spinach was not chopped finely enough, briefly process the mixture in a food processor or with a hand-held mixer.
3 Add the iced water gradually, stirring continuously, until you achieve the desired soup consistency. Check the seasoning, cover and chill until ready to serve.
4 Decorate with fresh mint leaves, and a little grated nutmeg if you like, and serve.

Lemony lentil soup

Nutrients per serving

- Calories 261
- Carbohydrate 40g
- Protein 18g
- Fat 5g (including saturated fat 1g)

This sturdy, soothing winter soup has a delicious citrus overtone combined with the warm flavours of roasted spices.

PREPARATION TIME: 5 minutes
COOKING TIME: 35 minutes
SERVES 4

1 tablespoon olive oil
3 cloves garlic, coarsely chopped
250g (9oz) onions, coarsely chopped
250g (9oz) red lentils, rinsed and drained
1.2 litres (2 pints) chicken or vegetable stock
1 teaspoon ground coriander
½ teaspoon ground cumin
Juice of 1 lemon
4 wafer-thin slices of lemon
Salt and black pepper

1 Heat the oil in a heavy-based saucepan. Add the garlic and onions and cook them over a medium heat for 6-7 minutes until they turn a rich brown colour, stirring frequently to prevent them sticking.
2 Add the lentils and cook for a further 1-2 minutes. Then add the stock, raise the heat and bring the soup to the boil. Reduce the heat, cover and simmer for 15-20 minutes until the lentils are almost soft.
3 Place a nonstick frying pan over a high heat, add the coriander and cumin and dry-fry them for 1-2 minutes until the aroma rises, then add them to the soup.
4 Raise the heat under the soup, add the lemon juice and lemon slices and season to taste, then let it simmer for 5 minutes. Sprinkle the soup with a little black pepper and serve.

Goan seafood soup

Nutrients per serving

- Calories 149
- Carbohydrate 10g
- Protein 16g
- Fat 4g (including saturated fat 2g)

A lightly spiced prawn soup from the west coast of India makes an exciting start to any meal. Add the fresh oysters for a special occasion.

PREPARATION TIME: 30 minutes
COOKING TIME: 30 minutes
SERVES 4

8 fresh oysters, optional
15g (½oz) butter
125g (4½oz) onions, finely chopped
2 cloves garlic, crushed
1 green chilli, deseeded and chopped
125g (4½oz) potatoes, peeled and diced
2 teaspoons ground coriander
200g (7oz) cooked, peeled prawns
75g (2¾oz) low-fat fromage frais
150ml (5fl oz) skimmed milk
3 tablespoons dry white wine
For the stock:
250ml (9fl oz) fish stock
125g (4½oz) carrots, sliced
2 cloves garlic, crushed
3 tablespoons roughly chopped fresh coriander
1 teaspoon cumin seeds
1 teaspoon coarsely chopped ginger
1 teaspoon black peppercorns
To garnish: 1 tablespoon roughly chopped fresh coriander leaves

1. Put all the ingredients for the stock into a large saucepan and add 900ml (1 pint 12fl oz) of water. Bring it to the boil over a high heat, then reduce the heat, cover and simmer for 15 minutes. Strain 750ml (1 pint 7fl oz) of the stock into a measuring jug, adding more water if necessary.
2. If you are adding the oysters, scrub the shells well with a vegetable brush then rinse them several times. Open the oysters over a bowl to catch the juices, then ease away the flesh from the half shell with a knife and add them to the juices in the bowl.
3. Melt the butter in a heavy-based saucepan over a medium heat and sauté the onions, garlic and chilli for 2-3 minutes.
4. Add the potatoes and coriander and continue to cook for 2 minutes. Add the reserved stock and bring to the boil, then cover and simmer for 5-7 minutes until the potatoes are tender. Remove from the heat.
5. Add half the prawns, then purée the soup in a food processor or with a hand-held mixer. Return the soup to the saucepan, add the remaining prawns, fromage frais and milk and heat slowly until the soup is just beginning to bubble, taking care not to let it boil.
6. Stir in the wine, and the oysters and all their juices, if using. Simmer for 1-2 minutes, then garnish the soup with the coriander leaves and serve.

Fennel, pea and mint soup

Nutrients per serving, when serving 4

- Calories 127
- Carbohydrate 18 g
- Protein 10 g
- Fat 3 g (no saturated fat)

An intensely coloured soup with great flavours that sing through clearly.

PREPARATION TIME: 5 minutes
COOKING TIME: 25 minutes
SERVES 4-6

600 g (1 lb 5 oz) fennel, chopped
500 g (1 lb 2 oz) fresh or frozen peas
900 ml (1 pint 12 fl oz) vegetable stock
3 tablespoons chopped fresh mint
Salt and black pepper
To garnish: a few small lettuce leaves, such as oak-leaf lettuce, and a few sprigs of fresh herbs, such as chervil and mint

1. Place the fennel, peas and stock in a large saucepan and bring to the boil, then reduce the heat, cover and simmer for 20 minutes, or until the fennel is tender.
2. Add the chopped mint and simmer for a further 1 minute.
3. Reserve a cupful of the vegetables and purée the remaining mixture in a food processor or with a hand-held mixer. Scrape the purée back into the pan.
4. Return the reserved vegetables to the soup and reheat. Season to taste with salt and pepper then serve, garnished with the lettuce leaves and herbs.

Carrot and butter bean soup

Nutrients per serving, when serving 4

- Calories 185
- Carbohydrate 31g
- Protein 8g
- Fat 4g (including saturated fat 2g)

The flavours of fresh and ground coriander give this filling soup extra bite.

PREPARATION TIME: 10 minutes
COOKING TIME: 30 minutes
SERVES 4-6

15g (½ oz) butter
150g (5½ oz) onions, finely chopped
450g (1 lb) carrots, finely chopped
100g (3½ oz) leeks, chopped
300g (10½ oz) potatoes, chopped
1 teaspoon ground coriander
1 clove garlic, crushed
225g (8oz) canned butter beans, rinsed and drained
300ml (10fl oz) skimmed milk
2 tablespoons chopped fresh coriander
Salt and black pepper
To garnish: sprigs of fresh coriander

1. Melt the butter in a large saucepan, add the onions, cover and cook over a low to medium heat for 5-8 minutes until softened.
2. Stir in the carrots, leeks, potatoes, ground coriander and garlic, cover and cook for a further 5 minutes.
3. Add the butter beans and 900ml (1 pint 12fl oz) of water and bring to the boil. Then reduce the heat and simmer, covered, for 20 minutes, or until the vegetables are tender.
4. Remove the soup from the heat and purée it with a hand-held mixer or in a food processor. Stir in the milk and chopped coriander and season to taste. Gently reheat the soup to warm through the added milk then serve it, garnished with sprigs of coriander.

Oriental vegetable soup

A selection of finely sliced vegetables is briefly cooked in a flavoursome chicken stock.

PREPARATION TIME: 10 minutes
COOKING TIME: 10 minutes
SERVES 4

100 g (3½ oz) baby pak choi (Chinese cabbage)
85 g (3 oz) carrots
4 spring onions
50 g (1¾ oz) shiitake mushrooms
60 g (2¼ oz) tofu
4 thin slices ginger
1 clove garlic
600 ml (1 pint) chicken stock
1 tablespoon soy sauce, or to taste
Black pepper

1. Finely shred the pak choi and set it aside in a bowl. Cut the carrots in half lengthways, slice them at an angle into thin half moons and add them to the pak choi. Cut the spring onions into thin, angled slices; finely slice the mushrooms; chop the tofu. Add them all to the bowl.
2. Cut the ginger slices and garlic into thin matchsticks and place them in a saucepan with the stock. Bring to the boil, then reduce the heat and simmer for 3 minutes.
3. When you are almost ready to serve, bring the stock back to the boil, add the vegetables and tofu and season to taste with soy sauce and pepper. Reduce the heat and simmer for 2 minutes, then serve.

Variations: for a vegetarian dish, use vegetable stock instead of chicken. Enoki mushrooms can be used instead of shiitake, and peeled, deseeded cucumber can replace the carrots.

Nutrients per serving

- Calories 31
- Carbohydrate 2 g
- Protein 3 g
- Fat 1 g (no saturated fat)

Spring vegetable soup with lemon

This refreshing soup mixes unusual sour and sweet flavours. Serve it hot or chilled, with a glass of ice-cold vodka.

PREPARATION TIME: 15 minutes
COOKING TIME: 20-25 minutes
SERVES 4

125 g (4½ oz) potatoes, cut into cubes
150 g (5½ oz) onions, chopped
2 stalks lemongrass, tough outer leaves removed, finely chopped
1.2 litres (2 pints) chicken or vegetable stock
50 g (1¾ oz) sorrel, finely shredded
50 g (1¾ oz) spinach, finely shredded
50 g (1¾ oz) spring onions, finely sliced
1 fresh red chilli, deseeded and finely chopped
2 cloves garlic, finely sliced
1-2 tablespoons sugar or clear honey
Salt
3-4 tablespoons lemon juice

1. Place the potatoes, onions, chopped lemongrass and stock in a large heavy-based saucepan and bring it to the boil. Reduce the heat, cover and simmer for 15-20 minutes until the potatoes are just cooked.
2. Stir in the sorrel, spinach, spring onions, chilli, garlic, sugar or honey and a pinch of salt. Bring the soup to the boil and cook for 1 minute.
3. Remove the soup from the heat and add lemon juice to taste. Serve it hot or chilled, as you prefer.

Variation: if sorrel is not in season, use another strong-flavoured leaf such as rocket or watercress.

Nutrients per serving

- Calories 59
- Carbohydrate 10 g
- Protein 4 g
- Fat 1 g (no saturated fat)

Spiced pumpkin and bacon soup

Aromatic cumin enlivens a hearty cold-weather soup of colourful pumpkin and bacon.

PREPARATION TIME: 15 minutes
COOKING TIME: 40 minutes
SERVES 4

I tablespoon olive oil
200 g (7 oz) onions, sliced
1.3 kg (3 lb) pumpkin, peeled, deseeded and cut into chunks
125 g (4½ oz) extra-trimmed smoked back bacon, diced
I tablespoon ground cumin
750 ml (1 pint 7 fl oz) vegetable stock
Salt and black pepper
To garnish: sprigs of fresh coriander
To serve: crusty bread rolls, optional

1 Heat the oil in a saucepan and add the onions. Stir to coat them with oil, then cover and cook them over a low heat for 5-10 minutes until they start to soften, stirring occasionally.
2 Add the pumpkin, bacon and cumin to the pan. Stir, then cover and simmer for 10 minutes, stirring occasionally.
3 Add the stock, raise the heat and bring to the boil. Lower the heat and simmer, uncovered, for 20 minutes, or until the pumpkin is tender.
4 Purée the soup with a hand-held mixer or in a food processor. Season to taste, garnish with coriander and black pepper and serve, accompanied by a crusty bread roll, if you like.

Variation: if you cannot get fresh pumpkin, use 425 g (15 oz) canned, unsweetened pumpkin, usually found on supermarkets' canned fruit shelves.

Nutrients per serving

- Calories 90
- Carbohydrate 29 g
- Protein 13 g
- Fat 7 g (including saturated fat 1 g)

Borshch with **coriander** and **cumin**

Beetroot is delicious teamed with other vegetables, as in this version of the Russian classic.

PREPARATION TIME: 15 minutes
COOKING TIME: 40 minutes
SERVES 6

500 g (1 lb 2 oz) raw beetroot, chopped
1 stick celery, chopped
50 g (1¾ oz) button mushrooms, sliced
150 g (5½ oz) onions, chopped
1 small red or yellow pepper, deseeded and chopped
175 g (6 oz) potatoes, chopped
2 tablespoons olive or sunflower oil
2 teaspoons ground coriander
1 teaspoon cumin seeds
1.2 litres (2 pints) vegetable stock
A pinch of dried thyme
Salt and black pepper
To garnish: 150 g (5½ oz) low-fat natural yoghurt and chopped fresh chives

1 Put the beetroot, celery, mushrooms, onions, pepper and potatoes into a large saucepan and stir in the oil. Cook over a high heat, stirring, until the vegetables start to sizzle. Cover the pan, reduce the heat to low and simmer for 10 minutes without lifting the lid.
2 Stir in the coriander and cumin and cook for a further 1-2 minutes. Add the stock and thyme, bring to the boil, then lower the heat and simmer for 20 minutes, stirring occasionally.
3 Season with salt and pepper to taste. Pour the soup into bowls and garnish each serving with yoghurt and a sprinkling of chives.

Variation: to make a smooth soup, purée all the ingredients at the end of Step 2 in a food processor or by using a hand-held mixer.

Nutrients per serving

- Calories 115
- Carbohydrate 16 g
- Protein 4 g
- Fat 5 g (including saturated fat 1 g)

Broccoli and cauliflower cheese soup

Nutrients per serving

- Calories 156
- Carbohydrate 15 g
- Protein 15 g
- Fat 5 g (including saturated fat 2 g)

A favourite family dish is transformed into a tasty, speckled soup, perfect for a light lunch or supper.

PREPARATION TIME: 10 minutes
COOKING TIME: 25 minutes
SERVES 4

250 g (9 oz) broccoli, broken into florets
250 g (9 oz) cauliflower, broken into florets
1 shallot, or 50 g (1¾ oz) onions, chopped
600 ml (1 pint) vegetable stock
300 ml (10 fl oz) skimmed milk
40 g (1½ oz) tiny pasta shapes for soup
75 g (2¾ oz) half-fat mature Cheddar cheese, grated
1 tablespoon chopped fresh chives
Salt and black pepper
To garnish: a pinch of grated nutmeg

1. Put the broccoli, cauliflower, shallot, or onions, and stock into a large saucepan. Bring to the boil, cover, then reduce the heat and simmer for 10 minutes, or until the florets are tender. Purée in a food processor or with a hand-held mixer.
2. Return the soup to the pan and add the milk and pasta. Gently bring it to a steady simmer, then cover and cook for a further 10 minutes, or until the pasta is tender.
3. Stir in the cheese and chives, reserving some chives for a garnish, and simmer for a few more minutes, stirring occasionally, until the cheese has melted and the soup has thickened slightly. Do not boil it or the cheese will become stringy.
4. Season to taste, garnish with the reserved chives and a sprinkling of nutmeg, and serve.

Variation: use all broccoli or all cauliflower, if you prefer.

Tip: this soup also freezes well.

Tomato and bread soup

Nutrients per serving

- Calories 126
- Carbohydrate 18 g
- Protein 3 g
- Fat 5 g (including saturated fat 1 g)

This variation on the traditional Italian peasant soup made with day-old bread gains a wonderful flavour from garlic, herbs and balsamic vinegar.

PREPARATION TIME: 15 minutes, plus 10 minutes soaking time
COOKING TIME: 25 minutes
SERVES 6

2 tablespoons olive oil
150 g (5½ oz) onions, chopped
1 red chilli, deseeded and chopped
2 cloves garlic, crushed
1 tablespoon chopped fresh thyme
1 kg (2 lb 4 oz) tomatoes, cut into quarters
600 ml (1 pint) vegetable stock
A pinch of sugar
125 g (4½ oz) day-old white bread, cubed
2 tablespoons balsamic vinegar
2 tablespoons chopped fresh basil leaves
Salt and black pepper
To garnish: fresh basil leaves

1. Heat 1 tablespoon of the oil in a saucepan and fry the onions, chilli, garlic and thyme on a low heat for 5 minutes, or until they have softened and are lightly golden.
2. Add the tomatoes, stock and sugar to the onions and bring them to the boil. Cover, reduce the heat and simmer for 20 minutes.
3. Meanwhile, put the bread cubes into a small bowl, add the vinegar, the remaining oil and 4 tablespoons of cold water and leave them to soak for 10 minutes.
4. Purée the tomato mixture, bread and basil together with a hand-held mixer or in a food processor until very smooth.
5. Return the soup to the pan, season to taste and reheat it gently. Pour the soup into bowls, garnish with a few leaves of basil and serve.

Crabmeat, mussel and prawn soup

Light and healthy seafood, gently simmered in wine and flavoured with herbs, gives a wonderful suggestion of long afternoons at the seaside.

PREPARATION TIME: 30 minutes
COOKING TIME: 20 minutes
SERVES 4 for a light lunch or supper, or 6 as a starter

Nutrients per serving, when serving 4

- Calories 310
- Carbohydrate 13 g
- Protein 36 g
- Fat 10 g (including saturated fat 2 g)

1 kg (2 lb 4 oz) live mussels
1 clove garlic, unpeeled
1 sprig of fresh parsley
1 shallot, roughly chopped
1 small sprig of fresh thyme
150 ml (5 fl oz) dry white wine
300 ml (10 fl oz) skimmed milk
30 g (1¼ oz) 70 per cent fat spread
30 g (1¼ oz) plain white flour
450 ml (16 fl oz) fish stock
1 small lemon
150 g (5½ oz) fresh white crabmeat, or canned crabmeat, drained
200 g (7 oz) peeled cooked prawns, defrosted if frozen
Black pepper
2-3 tablespoons finely chopped fresh dill
60 g (2¼ oz) virtually fat-free fromage frais
To garnish: sprigs of fresh dill and thin strips of lemon zest

1. Scrub and debeard the mussels and rinse them thoroughly. Discard any open mussels that do not close when tapped, and any with broken shells. Then put them into a large saucepan with the garlic, parsley, shallot, thyme and wine, and cover with a tight-fitting lid. Place over a very high heat and cook for 6-8 minutes until the mussels have opened, shaking the pan frequently. Do not overcook the mussels or they will become tough.
2. Meanwhile, place a large colander over a mixing bowl and line it with kitchen paper.
3. Pour the cooked mussels into the prepared colander and leave them to drain and cool slightly. Then remove the mussels from their shells, discarding any that have not opened, and put them into a small bowl. Pour the mussel liquid into a measuring jug and make it up to 600 ml (1 pint) with the milk.
4. Melt the spread in a large saucepan, stir in the flour, then gradually stir in the milky mussel liquid. Add the fish stock and bring to the boil, stirring continuously, then reduce the heat and allow to simmer for 5 minutes.
5. Meanwhile, pare the zest from the lemon into thin strips or finely grate it, and squeeze out the juice. Reserve half the zest for a garnish.
6. Flake the crabmeat and add it to the soup with the lemon juice and zest, the mussels and the prawns. Season with pepper (because the mussel liquid will be naturally salty, you should not need to add salt), then heat it through gently for 3-4 minutes. Do not boil or the seafood will toughen.
7. Stir the dill and fromage frais into the soup and ladle it into bowls. Garnish it with sprigs of dill and strips of lemon zest and serve the soup on its own as a starter, or with crusty bread and a salad for a light meal.

MUSSELS

Hot Moroccan bean soup

This filling soup is given extra heat with harissa, the fiery chilli paste from North Africa.

PREPARATION TIME: 10 minutes
COOKING TIME: 45 minutes
SERVES 4 as a main meal, or 6 as a starter

200 g (7 oz) canned cannellini beans
400 g (14 oz) canned chickpeas
150 g (5½ oz) onions, chopped
150 g (5½ oz) tomatoes, peeled and chopped
2 tablespoons lemon juice
1 teaspoon ground cumin
1 teaspoon turmeric
50 g (1¾ oz) rice noodles
2 tablespoons chopped fresh coriander
1-2 teaspoons harissa paste
Salt and black pepper
To garnish: sprigs of fresh coriander

1. Rinse and drain the beans and chickpeas and place them in a large saucepan with the onions, tomatoes, lemon juice, cumin and turmeric. Add 1.7 litres (3 pints) of water. Bring to the boil, then reduce the heat, cover and simmer for 30 minutes.
2. Stir the rice noodles into the soup and simmer for a further 5 minutes. Then stir in the chopped coriander and the harissa and add salt and pepper to taste.
3. Ladle the soup into warmed bowls, garnish with sprigs of coriander and serve.

Variation: you can substitute haricot beans for cannellini beans, if you like.

Tip: harissa paste is available from most major supermarkets and can be added to dishes or served separately as a condiment. If you cannot find it, use Tabasco sauce to taste instead.

Nutrients per serving, when serving 4

- Calories 434
- Carbohydrate 83 g
- Protein 16 g
- Fat 5 g (saturated fat 1 g)

The finest stocks

Homemade stocks add superb taste and body to low-fat cooking so that you won't yearn for butter or cream. Risottos, casseroles, braised vegetables and exquisite Oriental soups are among the many dishes enhanced by a good stock.

Stock cubes may be tempting when you are in a hurry, but they lack the depth of flavour of fresh stock. Instead, you can combine convenience and quality by freezing homemade stock in small cartons to use as needed.

Try the following stocks in the recipes in this book. If you chill them after making, any trace of fat will set on top and can then be lifted off and discarded.

Fresh stock cubes from the freezer

Tiny portions of well-flavoured frozen stock are particularly useful to add directly to dishes. Strain some fresh stock into a saucepan and boil until reduced by at least half. Leave it to cool, then pour it into ice-cube trays and freeze. Transfer the frozen stock cubes to a freezer bag and freeze until required.

Chicken stock

This deliciously light stock is the ideal flavour booster for delicate soups and sauces.

PREPARATION TIME: 20 minutes
COOKING TIME: 3 hours 30 minutes
MAKES 2 litres (3 pints 10 fl oz)

225 g (8 oz) onions
1 chicken, about 2 kg (4 lb 8 oz), jointed, or 3 raw chicken carcasses, chopped
200 g (7 oz) carrots, chopped
3 sticks celery, chopped
2 cloves garlic
225 g (8 oz) tomatoes, cut into quarters
1 small bay leaf
3 sprigs of fresh parsley
1 sprig of fresh thyme
500 ml (18 fl oz) dry white wine
4 black peppercorns

1. Cut off the onion roots and outer skins, leaving the inner brown skins on to colour the stock. Chop the onions then set them aside.
2. If you are using a whole chicken, cut off the breasts for another recipe. Cut off the parson's nose and pull away the fat inside the cavity. Put the chicken into a large non-corrosive stockpot, flameproof casserole or heavy-based saucepan. Add the onions, carrots, celery, garlic, tomatoes, bay leaf, parsley, thyme, wine and 3.5 litres (6 pints) of cold water and bring to the boil, frequently skimming the grey froth and fat from the surface.
3. As soon as the liquid boils, reduce the heat, add the peppercorns, partially cover and leave to simmer for 3 hours, skimming occasionally.
4. Line a colander or large sieve with a piece of damp muslin. Discard the bones and strain the stock, leaving any cloudy sediment at the bottom of the pan. Leave to cool then skim off any fat. The stock will keep in the refrigerator for up to three days, if boiled and cooled each day; or divide the stock between three or four suitable containers and freeze for up to three months.

Meat stock

Roasting bones extracts their robust flavour for casseroles and soups, and melts the fat so that it can be poured off.

PREPARATION TIME: 10 minutes
COOKING TIME: 4 hours
MAKES 1.5 litres (2 pints 15 fl oz)

4 lamb leg bones, chopped
500 g (1 lb 2 oz) onions
250 g (9 oz) carrots, chopped
450 g (1 lb) celeriac, chopped
1 whole head garlic, unpeeled and cut in half
200 g (7 oz) leeks, chopped
75 g (2¾ oz) mushrooms, cut in half
250 g (9 oz) tomatoes, cut in half
3 sprigs of fresh parsley
2 sprigs of fresh thyme
750 ml (1 pint 7 fl oz) dry red wine
4 black peppercorns

1. Heat the oven to its highest setting. Put the bones in a large roasting tin and roast them for 10 minutes, or until they begin to colour and release their fat.

MEAT STOCK, USED IN COUNTRY LAMB AND VEGETABLE COBBLER, PAGE 175

CHICKEN STOCK, USED IN PAELLA, PAGE 220

2 Meanwhile, cut off the onion roots and outer papery skins, leaving on the inner brown skins to colour the stock. Then chop the onions and set them aside.
3 Skim off the fat from the roasting tin. Add the carrots, celeriac, garlic, leeks, mushrooms and onions to the bones, and return the tin to the oven for 25 minutes, or until the vegetables begin to turn golden brown. Stir occasionally so that they colour evenly, but be careful not to let them burn or the stock will taste bitter.
4 Transfer the bones and vegetables to a large non-corrosive stockpot, flameproof casserole or heavy-based saucepan, discarding any fat. Add the tomatoes, parsley, thyme, wine and 4.2 litres (7 pints 7 fl oz) of cold water and bring to the boil, frequently skimming the froth and fat from the surface.
5 As soon as the liquid boils, reduce the heat, add the peppercorns, partially cover and leave to simmer for 3 hours, skimming occasionally.
6 Strain the stock and skim to remove fat as for Chicken Stock in Step 4. Use the stock at once, or allow it to cool then chill or freeze it until required. It will keep in the refrigerator for up to four days, if boiled and cooled each day; freeze for up to three months.

Variation: you can also use game or pork bones, but for a clear flavour, restrict them to one animal or bird.

FISH STOCK, USED IN GOAN SEAFOOD SOUP, PAGE 53

VEGETABLE STOCK, USED IN POTATOES BOULANGÈRE, PAGE 241

Fish stock

The best fish stock is made from the gelatine-rich bones of brill, Dover sole or turbot.

PREPARATION TIME: 15 minutes
COOKING TIME: 40 minutes
MAKES 2 litres (3 pints 10 fl oz)

2 kg (4 lb 8 oz) white fish bones and trimmings
175 g (6 oz) carrots, chopped
3 sticks celery, chopped
600 g (1 lb 5 oz) leeks, white parts only, chopped
1 bay leaf
3 large sprigs of fresh parsley
500 ml (18 fl oz) dry white wine
5 black peppercorns

1 Rinse any blood off the bones, chop them and place them in a large non-corrosive stockpot, flameproof casserole or heavy-based saucepan. If the trimmings include heads, snip out and discard the gills, then rinse. Remove and discard any black skin, because it will colour the stock. Add the trimmings to the pot.
2 Add the carrots, celery, leeks, bay leaf, parsley, wine and 2 litres (3 pints 10 fl oz) of cold water and bring to the boil, frequently skimming the grey froth from the surface.
3 As soon as the liquid boils, reduce the heat, add the peppercorns, partially cover and leave to simmer for 30 minutes, skimming occasionally.
4 Strain and skim as for Chicken Stock in Step 4. For a clear stock, leave the strained stock to sit for 1 hour, then strain it again. The stock will keep in the refrigerator for up to two days; freeze for up to two months.

Vegetable stock

Use this stock for vegetarian dishes such as risottos, soups and casseroles.

PREPARATION TIME: 20 minutes
COOKING TIME: 2 hours 20 minutes
MAKES 2 litres (3 pints 10 fl oz)

425 g (15 oz) carrots, chopped
700 g (1 lb 9 oz) celeriac, chopped
2 sticks celery, chopped
1 whole head garlic, unpeeled and cut in half
400 g (14 oz) leeks, white parts only, chopped
75 g (2¾ oz) mushrooms, cut in half
300 g (10½ oz) onions, chopped
175 g (6 oz) tomatoes, cut into quarters
1 bay leaf
3 sprigs of fresh parsley
1 sprig of fresh thyme
1.5 litres (2 pints 15 fl oz) dry white wine
4 black peppercorns

1 Put the carrots, celeriac, celery, garlic, leeks, mushrooms, onions, tomatoes, bay leaf, parsley, thyme, wine and 2.5 litres (4 pints 10 fl oz) of cold water into a large non-corrosive stockpot, flameproof casserole or heavy-based saucepan. Bring to the boil, skimming any grey froth from the surface as necessary.
2 As soon as the liquid boils, reduce the heat, add the peppercorns, partially cover and simmer for 2 hours, or until reduced by half, skimming the surface as necessary.
3 Strain as for Chicken Stock in Step 4. The stock will keep for up to four days in the refrigerator; freeze for up to three months.

Pigeon soup

A rich and gamy soup makes an impressive starter, or can be served with crusty rolls for a memorable light lunch.

PREPARATION TIME: 15 minutes

COOKING TIME: 1 hour 15 minutes - 1 hour 30 minutes

SERVES 4

1 teaspoon unsalted butter
2 young pigeons, about 225 g (8 oz) each, rinsed and dried
2 large cloves garlic, crushed
2 small sticks celery, finely chopped
200 g (7 oz) leeks, thickly sliced
175 g (6 oz) potatoes, diced
½ teaspoon cayenne pepper
Salt
½ teaspoon cumin seeds
150 ml (5 fl oz) skimmed milk
75 g (2¾ oz) low-fat fromage frais
To garnish: 1 tablespoon finely chopped fresh parsley or coriander

1. Melt the butter in a large heavy-based saucepan over a medium heat, then fry the whole pigeons for about 5 minutes, or until they have browned all over. Remove them and keep to one side.
2. Pour off most of the fat, leaving about 2 teaspoons in the pan, then add the garlic and fry for 30 seconds. Add the celery, leeks and potatoes and cook for 2-3 minutes, stirring frequently. Put a kettle of water on to boil.
3. Add the cayenne pepper and some salt to the vegetables, then add the pigeons, breast side down. Pour in 600 ml (1 pint) of boiling water, return to the boil and reduce the heat to low. Cover and simmer for 1 hour-1 hour 15 minutes until the pigeons are cooked through.
4. Meanwhile, heat a small heavy-based frying pan over a medium heat, add the cumin seeds, then turn off the heat and stir the seeds for 30 seconds-1 minute until they release their aroma. Crush them finely with a pestle and mortar or the back of a wooden spoon.
5. Remove the pigeons with a slotted spoon and purée the broth. When the pigeons are cool enough to handle, pull off and discard the skins. Cut off the meat using a small knife, then chop it into small pieces.
6. Put the meat and the puréed broth into a saucepan over a medium heat. Add the crushed cumin and milk and stir until the soup begins to bubble. Reduce the heat, stir in the fromage frais and cook for a further 1-2 minutes, then adjust the seasoning if necessary. Garnish with parsley or coriander and serve.

Variation: quail can be used instead of pigeon: just reduce the cooking time to 45-50 minutes.
Tip: young pigeons are available from some supermarkets and from fish and game shops.

Nutrients per serving

- Calories 120
- Carbohydrate 10 g
- Protein 10 g
- Fat 5 g (including saturated fat 1 g)

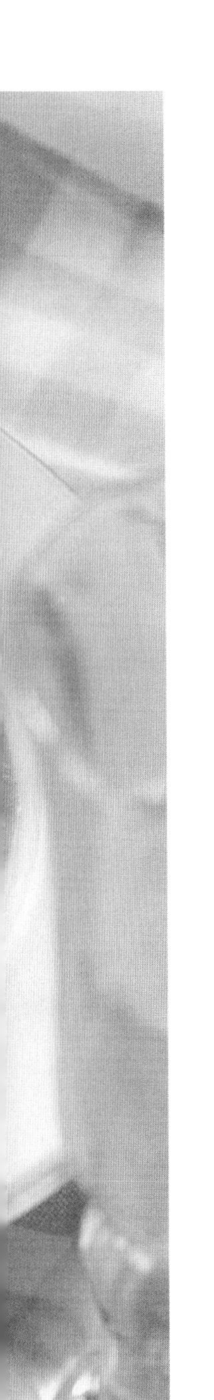

Oriental soup with **spicy meatballs**

Far Eastern cuisine abounds with light, flavoursome soups, such as this fragrant broth with spicy turkey meatballs.

PREPARATION TIME: 15 minutes
COOKING TIME: 10-15 minutes
SERVES 4

For the meatballs:
250 g (9 oz) minced turkey
1 small egg white
1 large clove garlic, crushed
1 teaspoon finely grated ginger, or ginger purée
2 spring onions, finely chopped
1 tablespoon dark soy sauce
Black pepper

For the soup:
1.2 litres (2 pints) light chicken stock, or Japanese dashi
1 tablespoon dark soy sauce
2 tablespoons dry vermouth, or dry sherry
200 g (7 oz) savoy cabbage

To garnish: 1 small fresh red chilli, deseeded and cut into very thin strips, optional

1. First make the meatballs: mix the turkey with the egg white, garlic, ginger, onions and soy sauce and add pepper to taste. If you prefer your meatballs very smooth, combine the mixture in a food processor.
2. Dip your hands in cold water and divide and shape the mixture into 20 evenly sized small balls. Set the meatballs aside.
3. To make the soup, put the stock, or dashi, soy sauce and vermouth, or sherry, into a saucepan and bring to the boil. Drop in the meatballs one by one, so they do not stick together. Return the soup to the boil then let it simmer for 8 minutes.
4. Core and finely shred the cabbage, add it to the soup and simmer for a further 2-3 minutes until it is just wilted.
5. Ladle the soup into warm bowls, and garnish with a few strips of red chilli, if you like.

Nutrients per serving

- Calories 103
- Carbohydrate 3 g
- Protein 19 g
- Fat 1 g (no saturated fat)

Chicken, leek and sweetcorn chowder

Nutrients per serving

- Calories 183
- Carbohydrate 16 g
- Protein 25 g
- Fat 3 g (no saturated fat)

Sweetcorn is added to the traditional pairing of chicken and leek, to make a hearty, chunky soup for all the family to enjoy.

PREPARATION TIME: 15 minutes, plus 5 minutes cooling

COOKING TIME: 35 minutes

SERVES 4

350 g (12 oz) chicken breasts
1 bay leaf
6 black peppercorns
350 g (12 oz) sweetcorn, canned, or defrosted if frozen
250 g (9 oz) leeks, thinly sliced
Salt and black pepper
To serve: crusty wholemeal bread, optional

1 Remove the skin and any fat from the chicken breasts and place them in a large saucepan. Add 800 ml (1 pint 9 fl oz) of water, the bay leaf and the peppercorns. Bring to the boil and skim off any foam that comes to the top, then cover the pan and let the chicken simmer for 20 minutes, or until the meat comes off the bones easily. Leave it to cool for 5 minutes.
2 Lift the chicken from the liquid and slice the meat, or shred it with two forks, and set it aside. Strain the liquid and measure 150 ml (5 fl oz) into a bowl or jug. Add half the sweetcorn and purée it in a food processor or with a hand-held mixer. Return the purée to the pan, whisk in the remaining liquid and bring it to the boil.
3 Add the leeks to the pan, then cover and simmer for 6-8 minutes until they are tender.
4 Add the cooked chicken to the chowder with the remaining sweetcorn and simmer for 2-3 minutes to heat both through. Taste and adjust the seasoning then serve hot, with crusty wholemeal bread, if you like.

Variation: for a quicker version, substitute ready-cooked, skinned chicken breasts and use chicken stock instead of water, to enhance the flavour.

BAY LEAVES

Turkey and **coconut soup** with **lemongrass**

Nutrients per serving

- Calories 133
- Carbohydrate 4 g
- Protein 17 g
- Fat 5 g (including saturated fat 4 g)

An excellent way of using up the Christmas turkey is to make a delicious stock as the base for this unusual soup.

PREPARATION TIME: 20 minutes
COOKING TIME: 45-50 minutes
SERVES 4

125 g (4½ oz) cooked turkey breast, skinned
25 g (1 oz) coconut milk powder
1 fresh red chilli, deseeded and chopped
Salt
1 tablespoon cornflour
1 tablespoon finely chopped fresh coriander
For the stock:
Carcass of a 3 kg (6 lb 8 oz) turkey
2 teaspoons coriander seeds
100 g (3½ oz) carrots, chopped
1 stick celery, chopped
5 cm (2 in) cinnamon stick, broken
4 cloves
1 teaspoon cumin seeds
4 large cloves garlic, unpeeled and lightly crushed
5 cm (2 in) cube ginger, unpeeled and sliced
2 stalks lemongrass, bruised
225 g (8 oz) onions, unpeeled and quartered
To garnish: 4 small fresh red chillies, optional

1. First make the stock. Cut the turkey carcass into manageable pieces and crush the coriander seeds with a pestle and mortar. Place them in a large saucepan, add 1.2 litres (2 pints) of water and all the other ingredients. Bring it to the boil, reduce the heat to low, cover the pan and simmer for 35-40 minutes.
2. Meanwhile, finely chop the turkey breast.
3. Remove and discard the largest pieces of turkey carcass from the stock then strain the stock through a large sieve into a measuring jug. There should be 750 ml (1 pint 7 fl oz); if not, add water to make up the amount.
4. Put the coconut milk powder in a large saucepan and pour the measured stock onto it. Place the pan over a medium heat and whisk the stock and milk powder to eliminate any lumps.
5. When the coconut mixture begins to bubble, reduce the heat to low and add the turkey and chilli, and salt to taste.
6. Blend the cornflour with 1-2 tablespoons of cold water, add it to the soup and stir for 2-3 minutes until the soup thickens.
7. Add the fresh coriander, stir briefly, remove the soup from the heat and serve, garnished with a chilli in each bowl, if you wish.

Variation: you could also make the stock with the carcasses of two large chickens.

starters and salads

Mixed mezes

For a charming start to a meal, try this trio of spicy vegetable purées drawn from around the Mediterranean. Serve at room temperature with bread sticks, grilled pitta breads or crudités.

Aubergine dip

Roasting the aubergine gives this *moutabal*, as it is known in the Lebanon, or *baba ganoush*, as it is known in Egypt, its mellow flavour.

PREPARATION TIME: 15 minutes, plus 10 minutes cooling
COOKING TIME: 15 minutes
SERVES 4-6

500 g (1 lb 2 oz) aubergine
1 tablespoon chopped fresh coriander
1-2 cloves garlic, crushed
1 tablespoon lemon juice
4-6 tablespoons half-fat Greek yoghurt
Salt and black pepper

1. Heat the oven to 200°C (400°F, gas mark 6). Roast the aubergine for 15 minutes, or until the skin is blistered and charred, turning it over halfway through.
2. Place the aubergine in a bowl, seal with cling film and leave to cool for 10 minutes. Peel off the skin, then place the flesh in a sieve and press it lightly to squeeze out any excess liquid. Transfer the flesh to a mixing bowl.
3. Mash the aubergine thoroughly with a fork or potato masher, stir in the coriander, garlic, lemon juice and yoghurt and blend well. Season to taste and add a little more crushed garlic if desired.

Nutrients per serving, when serving 4

- Calories 31
- Carbohydrate 3 g
- Protein 2 g
- Fat 1 g (saturated fat 1 g)

Moroccan carrot dip

Hot, sweet spices bring a taste of North African sun to this dip.

PREPARATION TIME: 10 minutes
COOKING TIME: 25 minutes
SERVES 4-6

500 g (1 lb 2 oz) carrots, thickly sliced
1 teaspoon ground cinnamon
1 teaspoon ground cumin
2 cloves garlic, crushed
½ teaspoon ground ginger
1 tablespoon clear honey
1 tablespoon olive oil
1 teaspoon paprika
3 tablespoons vinegar or lemon juice
Salt and black pepper

1. Place the carrots in a large saucepan, cover with water, bring to the boil and simmer for 20-25 minutes until they are very soft. Rinse under cold running water, then drain thoroughly.
2. Put them in a bowl and mash with a potato masher. Stir in the cinnamon, cumin, garlic, ginger, honey, oil, paprika and vinegar or lemon juice. Blend well and season to taste.

Nutrients per serving, when serving 4

- Calories 79
- Carbohydrate 12 g
- Protein 1 g
- Fat 3 g (including saturated fat 1 g)

Fava

Moroccan carrot dip

Fava

This traditional Greek split pea dip is rich and filling.

PREPARATION TIME: 10 minutes, plus 10 minutes cooling

COOKING TIME: 45 minutes

SERVES 4-6

225 g (8 oz) yellow split peas
75 g (2¾ oz) onions, chopped
1 small clove garlic, crushed
Juice of ½ lemon, or to taste
1 teaspoon olive oil
Salt and black pepper
To garnish: paprika

1. Pick over and rinse the split peas, then place them in a large saucepan with the onions and enough water to cover. Bring to the boil, then reduce the heat and simmer for 30-45 minutes until the split peas are thick and mushy (the exact time will depend on the age of the peas). If there is still some water remaining, drain it off before transferring the peas to a bowl.
2. Beat in the garlic, lemon juice and oil until thick and well blended. Leave to cool, then add salt and pepper to taste and garnish with paprika.

Nutrients per serving, when serving 4

- Calories 200
- Carbohydrate 34 g
- Protein 13 g
- Fat 2 g (no saturated fat)

Aubergine dip

Refreshing tomato and watercress spread

A pretty starter, bursting with flavour.

PREPARATION TIME: 20 minutes, plus 1 hour setting

SERVES 4

400 g (14 oz) canned chopped tomatoes
75 g (2¾ oz) cucumber, roughly chopped
1 red pepper, roughly chopped
1 spring onion, roughly chopped
2 tablespoons sherry vinegar
75 g (2¾ oz) watercress leaves, finely chopped
Salt and black pepper
2 sachets powdered gelatine
Olive oil for greasing
To garnish: a few sprigs of watercress
To serve: brown bread, such as pumpernickel

1. Purée the tomatoes, cucumber, pepper, spring onion and vinegar in a food processor or with a hand-held mixer. Transfer to a large bowl.
2. Stir in the watercress (do not purée it or it will become sloppy). Season to taste.
3. Place 3 tablespoons of water in a teacup, sprinkle the gelatine over the surface and leave it for 5 minutes until it becomes spongy. Then stand the cup in a pan of simmering water until the gelatine is runny and clear. Pour it into the tomato mixture in a steady stream, stirring to combine it thoroughly.
4. Grease four 200 ml (7 fl oz) ramekins. Spoon in the mixture and chill for 1 hour, or until set.
5. Turn out the moulds by dipping the bases in hot water then inverting them over a plate. Garnish with watercress and serve with brown bread.

Nutrients per serving

- Calories 135
- Carbohydrate 21 g
- Protein 9 g
- Fat 2 g (no saturated fat)

Low-fat tip

Ridged, iron grill pans are especially good for cooking aubergine, which otherwise soaks up oil like a sponge.

Turkish aubergine with tomato and yoghurt sauce

Nutrients per serving

- Calories 89
- Carbohydrate 6 g
- Protein 3 g
- Fat 6 g (including saturated fat 1 g)

Flavoursome spoonfuls of yoghurt, tomato and toasted cumin seeds make a tasty partner for slices of smoky aubergine grilled with very little fat.

PREPARATION TIME: 10 minutes
COOKING TIME: 15 minutes, plus cooling
SERVES 4

600 g (1 lb 5 oz) aubergines
2 tablespoons olive oil
2 teaspoons cumin seeds
100 g (3½ oz) canned chopped tomatoes
100 g (3½ oz) low-fat natural yoghurt
Salt and black pepper
To garnish: fresh coriander leaves

1. Heat a ridged, iron grill pan over a medium-high heat. Cut the aubergines widthways into 12 thick slices, discarding the ends. Lightly brush both sides of each slice with oil and cook for 3-4 minutes on each side until the flesh is soft when pierced. Alternatively, you can cook the aubergine slices under a hot grill.
2. Set the cooked aubergine slices aside to cool: they taste best at room temperature.
3. Meanwhile, heat a small frying pan over a high heat. Dry-fry the cumin seeds for a few seconds, or until they turn dark brown. Remove them from the pan immediately and set aside. When they are cool, grind them to a powder in a spice mill or with a pestle and mortar.
4. Put the tomatoes in a saucepan and cook over a medium heat for 3-4 minutes, stirring occasionally, until they are reduced to a thick sauce, then set this aside to cool.
5. When the tomato sauce has cooled, add the ground spice and yoghurt, mix together and season to taste. If you have time, chill the sauce a little.
6. To serve, lay three slices of the chargrilled aubergine on each of four plates and add a spoonful of the tomato and yoghurt sauce along the side of each. Garnish with a few fresh coriander leaves and serve.

Wild mushrooms and blueberries on rice noodles

Nutrients per serving

- Calories 177
- Carbohydrate 30 g
- Protein 4 g
- Fat 4 g (including saturated fat 1 g)

This stylish first course offers a rich and unusual contrast of tender mushrooms and refreshingly tart juicy fruit, tossed on a bed of mild rice noodles.

PREPARATION TIME: 20 minutes, including soaking
COOKING TIME: 30 minutes
SERVES 6

10 g (¼ oz) dried porcini mushrooms
150 g (5½ oz) baby chestnut mushrooms
150 g (5½ oz) oyster mushrooms
150 g (5½ oz) shiitake mushrooms
2 tablespoons olive oil
4 large cloves garlic, finely sliced
1 tablespoon finely sliced ginger
6 spring onions, sliced diagonally
350 ml (12 fl oz) chicken or vegetable stock
2 tablespoons soy sauce
200 g (7 oz) thin rice noodles
100 g (3½ oz) blueberries, defrosted if frozen

1 Rinse any grit off the porcini mushrooms, then leave them to soak in hot water for 20 minutes. Drain them, reserving the soaking liquid. Rinse, then dry them on kitchen paper and slice thinly.
2 Meanwhile, slice the baby chestnut and oyster mushrooms; remove and discard the stalks from the shiitakes then slice them. Set them all aside.
3 Heat the oil in a wok or a heavy-based frying pan. Add the garlic, ginger and spring onions and stir-fry for 4-5 minutes until the garlic is nicely browned. Add all the mushrooms and continue stir-frying for 2-3 minutes.
4 Make the reserved mushroom liquor up to 400 ml (14 fl oz) with the stock and add it, with the soy sauce, to the mushrooms. Bring the mixture to the boil, then reduce the heat and simmer, uncovered, for 20 minutes, stirring occasionally.
5 Meanwhile, put a kettle of water on to boil. Put the rice noodles in a large heatproof bowl, cover them with the boiling water and leave them to soak for the time indicated on the packet.
6 Add the blueberries to the mushrooms, increase the heat and boil for 2-3 minutes until the liquid has thickened slightly and the blueberries are heated through.
7 Drain the noodles, add them to the mushroom mixture in the wok or frying pan and toss together. Spoon into six serving bowls and serve while still hot.

Variation: blackberries, cranberries or raspberries can be used instead of blueberries.
Tip: you can find the easy-to-cook thin rice noodles in most supermarkets or in Oriental grocers.

Roasted asparagus with **caramelised shallot dressing**

Nutrients per serving
- Calories 61
- Carbohydrate 3 g
- Protein 3 g
- Fat 4 g (including saturated fat 1 g)

Make the most of the short asparagus season in early summer. Roasting the asparagus is a healthier alternative to drenching them in butter.

PREPARATION TIME: 10 minutes, plus 2-3 hours cooling, optional
COOKING TIME: 20 minutes
SERVES 4

500 g (1 lb 2 oz) asparagus, trimmed
4 teaspoons olive oil
6 large cloves garlic
4 shallots
3 tablespoons balsamic vinegar
Salt and black pepper
1 tablespoon chopped fresh thyme, sage and rosemary mixed, or all thyme

1 Heat the oven to 230°C (450°F, gas mark 8).
2 Place the asparagus in an ovenproof dish, drizzle with 2 teaspoons of the oil and use your fingers to rub it in so that all the spears are well coated. Roast the asparagus for 15-20 minutes, depending on the thickness of the spears, until they have softened and browned slightly.
3 Meanwhile, peel and quarter the garlic and shallots. Heat the rest of the oil in a wok or heavy-based pan, add the garlic and shallots and stir-fry over a high heat for 5-7 minutes until they are golden brown.
4 Add 4 tablespoons of water, reduce the heat, cover and simmer for 10-15 minutes until softened. Then increase the heat and boil hard until most of the water has evaporated.
5 Add the vinegar and bring to the boil, then pour the dressing over the hot asparagus. Season with salt and pepper to taste, and sprinkle with the herbs. Serve immediately, or set aside for a few hours to allow the flavours to mature, then serve at room temperature.

Variation: for a smoky flavour, cook the asparagus on the barbecue. Brush the spears with 2 teaspoons of the oil and place them on the rack above hot coals. Using tongs, turn them at least once and cook until they have softened and browned slightly.

Brandied chestnut and mushroom terrine

Nutrients per serving, when serving 8

- Calories 234
- Carbohydrate 38 g
- Protein 6 g
- Fat 4 g (including saturated fat 1 g)

This luxurious dish can also be served as a meatless main course.

PREPARATION TIME: 20 minutes
COOKING TIME: 55 minutes
SERVES 8-10

1 tablespoon olive oil, plus extra for greasing
2-4 cloves garlic, crushed
175 g (6 oz) mushrooms, sliced
175 g (6 oz) red onions, thinly sliced
6 tablespoons brandy
8 vacuum packed or canned unsweetened, whole chestnuts
1 egg, beaten
125 g (4½ oz) wholemeal breadcrumbs
400 g (14 oz) canned unsweetened chestnut purée
Grated zest of ½ orange plus juice of 1 orange
1 tablespoon each chopped fresh parsley and thyme
Salt and black pepper
To garnish: chopped fresh coriander or basil
To serve: mixed salad leaves

1. Heat the oven to 180°C (350°F, gas mark 4). Lightly grease a 900 g (2 lb) loaf tin.
2. Heat the oil in a large saucepan over a medium heat and gently fry the garlic, mushrooms and onions for 7-8 minutes until they are tender and lightly browned, stirring frequently.
3. Add the brandy to the pan and allow it to simmer for 1-2 minutes until reduced, then remove the pan from the heat and leave the mixture to cool for about 3 minutes.
4. Break the chestnuts into pieces and stir them into the mushroom mixture with the egg, breadcrumbs, chestnut purée, orange zest and juice, parsley, thyme and salt and pepper to taste, using a wooden spoon to break up the chestnut purée.
5. When the mixture is thoroughly combined, spoon it into the loaf tin, smooth over the top and bake it for 45 minutes, or until the top is browned.
6. Leave the terrine to cool in the tin, then turn it out onto a plate and cut it into neat slices. Sprinkle a little chopped coriander or basil over the top and serve it with mixed salad leaves.

Low-fat tip

Chestnuts not only have a great flavour, they have just a fraction of the fat of most other nuts.

Stuffed chicken breasts with red onion marmalade

The sweetness of a fruit stuffing and the onion marmalade is balanced by bitter salad leaves. For easy entertaining, this dish can be made up to a day ahead.

PREPARATION TIME: 30 minutes

COOKING TIME: 1 hour, plus 3-4 hours, or overnight, chilling

SERVES 4

1 dessert apple, peeled and coarsely grated
75 g (2¾ oz) ready-to-eat stoned prunes, chopped
2 skinned and boned chicken breasts, about 175 g (6 oz) each
A pinch of ground mace
Salt and black pepper

For the marmalade:
1 teaspoon olive oil
250 g (9 oz) red onions, thinly sliced
150 ml (5 fl oz) chicken stock
2 tablespoons balsamic vinegar

To serve: a salad of mixed, slightly bitter leaves, such as red chard, red mustard or rocket

1 To make the onion marmalade, heat the oil in a saucepan, add the onions and cook over a medium heat for 2-3 minutes until they start to soften. Add the stock and vinegar, reduce the heat to low, partially cover the pan and simmer for 30-45 minutes, stirring frequently, until the onions are very soft and the stock is reduced to a thick syrup. Remove the pan from the heat and allow the marmalade to cool, then cover and refrigerate until needed.
2 Meanwhile, mix the apple and prunes together in a small bowl and set aside.
3 Place each chicken breast between two large sheets of cling film, then use a meat mallet or a rolling pin to beat each one out to a thin rectangular shape, about 15 x 20 cm (6 x 8 in). Place them on a board with the inner side uppermost. Remove and discard the white sinews and trim each breast into a neat rectangle, reserving the trimmings.
4 Put a kettle on to boil. Finely chop the chicken trimmings and mix them into the apple and prune mixture. Season the stuffing and the chicken breasts well with mace and salt and pepper to taste.
5 Lay a spoonful of the stuffing along the shorter side of each chicken breast, then roll them up.
6 Take a large sheet of cling film and place a chicken breast at one end. Then roll up the breast so that it is enclosed in several layers of film. Tightly twist the ends of the film and gently roll the chicken breast back and forth several times to form a neat, sausage-shaped roll, twisting the ends tightly each time you roll. Tie the ends with string to seal securely. Repeat with the other breast.
7 Put the chicken breasts side by side into a small saucepan and cover with boiling water. Return to the boil, reduce the heat to low, cover the pan and poach the chicken for 10-15 minutes until a skewer inserted into the centre of each roll feels hot on the back of your hand.
8 Transfer the chicken rolls to a plate and allow to cool (do not remove the cling film). Then chill for 3-4 hours, or overnight, to allow the flavours to develop.
9 To serve, unwrap the chicken breasts and slice them thinly. Divide the salad leaves between four serving plates, top with a spoonful of onion marmalade and arrange the chicken slices alongside.

RED ONIONS

Nutrients per serving

- Calories 190
- Carbohydrate 17 g
- Protein 26 g
- Fat 2 g (no saturated fat)

Steamed prawn won tons

Easy to assemble, these tasty won tons make an ideal first course of an Oriental meal.

PREPARATION TIME: 30 minutes
COOKING TIME: 5 minutes
SERVES 4

200 g (7 oz) raw, headless tiger prawns
½ tablespoon finely chopped bamboo shoots
1 clove garlic, crushed
½ teaspoon finely chopped ginger
1 tablespoon mirin, or dry sherry
1 tablespoon soy sauce
3 spring onions, finely chopped
24 won ton wrappers
A little oil for greasing, optional
To serve: ready-made chilli sauce and soy sauce

1. Peel the prawns, then run a sharp knife along the length of each back and pull away the dark digestive thread. Rinse the prawns and pat them dry with kitchen paper. Finely chop the prawns, either with a sharp knife or in a food processor.
2. Mix the prawns with the bamboo shoots, garlic, ginger, mirin or sherry, soy sauce and spring onions.
3. Spread out six won ton wrappers at a time on a dry surface. Place 1 teaspoon of the filling in the middle of each and lightly brush two adjacent edges of the first won ton with water. Fold it into a triangle, pressing the edges together firmly. Then press the two bottom corners together to seal. Repeat with the remaining wrappers.
4. If using a metal rather than a bamboo steamer, lightly grease it with a little oil. Arrange the won tons in a single layer on the steamer and steam for 5 minutes. If they will not fit in one layer, steam the won tons in batches.
5. Serve them warm with chilli sauce and soy sauce served separately, for dipping.

Tip: mirin and packets of won ton wrappers are available from Chinese supermarkets. If the won ton wrappers are frozen and defrosted, use them at once because they dry out very quickly.

Nutrients per serving

- Calories 79
- Carbohydrate 7 g
- Protein 10 g
- Fat 1 g (no saturated fat)

Grilled spiced trout fillets

These tangy fillets sharpen the appetite for the main course.

PREPARATION TIME: 15 minutes, plus 30 minutes marinating

COOKING TIME: 5 minutes

SERVES 4

4 trout fillets, 125 g (4½ oz) each

For the marinade:

1 teaspoon tamarind concentrate or compressed pulp

½-1 teaspoon cayenne pepper

1 tablespoon chopped fresh coriander

½ teaspoon ground coriander

½ teaspoon ground cumin

2 teaspoons garlic purée, or crushed garlic

Salt

A little oil for greasing

To garnish: fresh coriander; 1 lemon

To serve: salad leaves and tomatoes

1. Put the fillets side by side in a single layer, skin side down, in a shallow non-corrosive dish.
2. To make the marinade, blend the tamarind with 2 tablespoons of hot water in a bowl. If it does not dissolve, stand the bowl over a pan of simmering water and stir until it does. Allow it to cool.
3. Add the cayenne pepper, chopped and ground coriander, cumin, garlic and salt to taste to the tamarind water, then pour it over the fish. Using the back of a spoon, spread the marinade so that it covers the fillets evenly and completely. Leave them to marinate for 30 minutes.
4. Heat the grill to high. Line the grill pan with foil, then brush it with a little oil. Place the fish on the foil and grill for 5 minutes, or until the flesh flakes easily.
5. Remove the fillets from the grill and garnish with a few sprigs of fresh coriander and the lemon, cut into wedges, and serve with mixed salad leaves and tomatoes.

Tip: Tamarind, a sour tropical fruit, is sold in concentrated form in bottles and in compressed blocks of pulp in supermarkets and Asian food shops. If you do not have any tamarind, stir the spices into 1 tablespoon of lemon juice mixed with 1 tablespoon of water.

Nutrients per serving

- Calories 188
- Carbohydrate 1 g
- Protein 27 g
- Fat 8 g (including saturated fat 1 g)

Indian patties

Nutrients per serving

- Calories 158
- Carbohydrate 24 g
- Protein 7 g
- Fat 5 g (including saturated fat 1 g)

These spinach patties are usually deep-fried, but here they are grilled to give plenty of flavour with much less oil.

PREPARATION TIME: 25 minutes, plus 2-3 hours soaking
COOKING TIME: 25 minutes
SERVES 8

225 g (8 oz) split yellow lentils (channa dhal)
5 cm (2 in) cinnamon stick, broken into several pieces
4 cloves
2 teaspoons coriander seeds
2 teaspoons cumin seeds
½ teaspoon black peppercorns
2 teaspoons garlic purée, or crushed garlic
2 teaspoons ginger purée, or grated ginger
225 g (8 oz) fresh spinach
2 tablespoons roughly chopped fresh coriander
8-10 fresh mint leaves, or ½ teaspoon dried mint
1-2 green chillies, deseeded
1 egg
Salt
50 g (1¾ oz) onion, roughly chopped
1 tablespoon sunflower oil
To garnish: sprigs of fresh mint
To serve: 8 small pitta breads, grilled

1. Rinse the lentils, cover them with plenty of cold water and leave to soak for 2-3 hours.
2. Heat a small, heavy-based frying pan over a medium heat. Add the cinnamon, cloves, coriander and cumin seeds and peppercorns, then dry-fry them for 1 minute, or until they release their aromas. Transfer them to a plate to prevent further cooking and leave to cool.
3. Drain the lentils and put them into a pan with the garlic, ginger and spinach. Cook over a medium heat, stirring, for 1-2 minutes until the spinach begins to release its juice. Reduce the heat, cover and simmer for 10-12 minutes, stirring occasionally, until the liquid has been absorbed – take the lid off towards the end, if necessary, to allow it to evaporate.
4. Meanwhile, grind the roasted spices finely in a spice mill or with a pestle and mortar, then transfer them to a food processor. Add the lentil and spinach mixture, fresh coriander, mint, chilli, egg, and salt to taste and process. When the mixture is well blended, add the onion and pulse for a few seconds to chop the onion finely rather than puréeing it.
5. Heat the grill to high and divide the mixture into 16 equal balls. Shape them into round, flat patties about 5 cm (2 in) in diameter.
6. Line the grill pan with foil and brush lightly with some of the oil. Place the patties on top, brush them with half of the remaining oil and grill for 4 minutes. Turn them over, brush with the rest of the oil and grill for a further 3-4 minutes until brown and crisp. Serve two patties on a grilled pitta bread, garnished with a sprig of mint.

Variations: yellow split peas can be used instead of the lentils. The patties also taste good served with a spoonful of raita (page 192).

Seared pigeon breasts and **blueberries**

Nutrients per serving

- Calories 269
- Carbohydrate 4 g
- Protein 27 g
- Fat 16 g (including saturated fat 1 g)

Rich, gamy pigeon breasts and hot, juicy blueberries are set on a bed of mixed leaves, given their own fruity dressing.

PREPARATION TIME: 10 minutes
COOKING TIME: 3 minutes, plus 5 minutes resting
SERVES 4

1½ tablespoons olive oil
8 pigeon breasts, skinned
175 g (6 oz) blueberries, defrosted if frozen
150 g (5½ oz) mixed salad leaves
2 tablespoons chopped fresh herbs, such as basil, chives and parsley
For the dressing:
1½ tablespoons extra virgin olive oil
1 tablespoon raspberry or other fruit vinegar
1 teaspoon lemon juice
1 teaspoon wholegrain mustard
Salt and black pepper

1. Heat the oil in a frying pan, add the pigeon breasts and fry for 1 minute on each side, then remove them from the pan and leave to rest for 5 minutes. Reserve the meat juices in the pan.
2. To make the dressing, beat together all the ingredients in a small bowl, then set aside.
3. Return the frying pan to the heat, add the blueberries and cook gently for 30 seconds. Strain any pan juices through a fine nylon sieve into the dressing and adjust the seasoning if necessary. Reserve the blueberries.
4. Place the salad leaves and herbs in a bowl and spoon 2 tablespoons of the dressing over them. Toss the salad to coat it lightly, then arrange on four serving plates.
5. Slice the breasts in half lengthways and lay four slices on each salad. Using a slotted spoon, lift the blueberries out of the sieve and lay them around the edges. Drizzle the remaining dressing over the salads.

Variation: if pigeon is unavailable, you can use four duck breasts, skinned and cut in half crossways.

Great winter salads

It is tempting to reach for comforting hot dishes when the weather is cold. But winter vegetables served raw or lightly cooked make surprisingly good and nourishing additions to the salad bowl.

Root vegetables and brassicas, at their peak during the coldest months, can replace summer's softer salad leaves as a crisp contrast to hearty stews and roasts. Even the much-maligned Brussels sprout gets a new lease of life in Fruity Brussels Sprouts, offering a low-fat solution to the problem of what to serve with leftover Christmas turkey.

Fragrant Oriental ingredients complement the fresh flavours of the other salads, and both the versatile Ratatouille Chinese-style and the Green Vegetable Salad can be enjoyed hot or cold.

Low-fat herb dressing

In a food processor, mix 175 g (6 oz) virtually no-fat fromage frais, 1 teaspoon tarragon vinegar, 1 spring onion, ½ tablespoon chopped chives and 2 tablespoons parsley, basil or coriander leaves until green and blended. Season to taste. It will keep in the refrigerator for three days but start to thicken: stir in 1 tablespoon of low-fat yoghurt to thin it.

Fruity Brussels sprouts

Sprouts give a pale, frilly look to this crisp raw salad.

PREPARATION TIME: 25 minutes
SERVES 4

225 g (8 oz) Brussels sprouts
1 dessert apple
125 g (4½ oz) carrot, grated
3 celery sticks, chopped
2 tablespoons chopped fresh coriander
125 g (4½ oz) natural dates, stoned and chopped

For the dressing:
1 tablespoon half-fat crème fraîche
2 tablespoons reduced-calorie mayonnaise
2 teaspoons olive oil
Grated zest and juice of 1 orange
2 teaspoons white wine vinegar
Salt and black pepper

1. To make the dressing, whisk together the crème fraîche, mayonnaise, oil, orange zest and juice and vinegar, then season to taste and set aside.
2. Trim off and discard the bases and outer leaves of the sprouts, then shred them finely and put them into a large bowl. Cut the apple into quarters without peeling it, remove the core then chop into small chunks and add to the bowl with the carrot and celery.
3. Stir in enough dressing to coat the salad, saving any left over to serve on the side. Scatter the coriander and dates over the salad and serve.

Nutrients per serving

- Calories 125
- Carbohydrate 18 g
- Protein 3 g
- Fat 5 g (including saturated fat 1 g)

RATATOUILLE CHINESE-STYLE

Ratatouille Chinese-style

This vegetable salad is given a piquant flavour with Oriental black bean and hoisin sauces.

PREPARATION TIME: 25 minutes, plus 20 minutes marinating
COOKING TIME: 8 minutes
SERVES 2 as a main course, 4 as a side dish

125 g (4½ oz) courgettes
125 g (4½ oz) aubergine
125 g (4½ oz) small chestnut, oyster or shiitake mushrooms
125 g (4½ oz) tomatoes, peeled, deseeded and cut into small dice
125 g (4½ oz) canned water chestnuts, drained and sliced

For the dressing:
1 tablespoon black bean sauce
1 tablespoon hoisin sauce
2 tablespoons dry sherry
A few drops of Tabasco sauce
1 teaspoon red or white wine vinegar

1. Put a kettle on to boil. To make the dressing, put all the ingredients into a bowl, mix together and set aside.
2. Heat the grill to high. Cut the courgettes in half lengthways and then into 2 cm (¾ in) chunks. Blanch them in boiling water for 2 minutes,

FRUITY BRUSSELS SPROUTS

CABBAGE AND CARROT SALAD WITH SPICED YOGHURT DRESSING

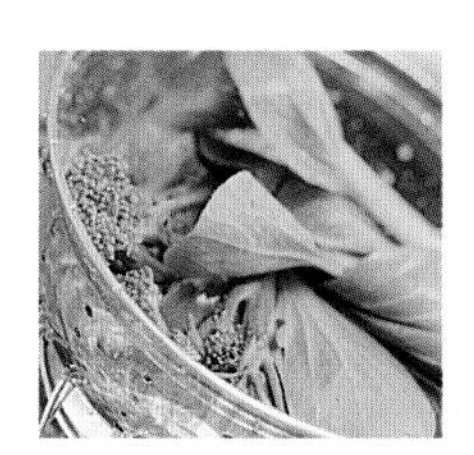

GREEN VEGETABLE SALAD WITH GARLIC AND GINGER

then drain and refresh them under running cold water. Dry them on kitchen paper.

3. Cut the aubergine into 1 cm (½ in) slices. Cook the slices on a baking tray under the grill for 3 minutes on each side, or until they are tender. Leave them to cool, then cut them into quarters.
4. Grill the mushrooms for 5 minutes, turning occasionally, then set them aside to cool.
5. Put the vegetables into a serving dish and add the tomatoes and water chestnuts. Pour the dressing over them, mix well and set aside to marinate for 20 minutes for the flavours to blend (do not refrigerate).
6. As a salad, serve the ratatouille at room temperature. As a side dish, tip the dressed salad into a hot, nonstick wok or frying pan and stir-fry over a high heat for 5-8 minutes, until steaming hot. Serve with stir-fried meat, fish or poultry dishes, or with rice as a vegetarian meal.

Nutrients per serving, when serving 2

- Calories 113
- Carbohydrate 19 g
- Protein 4 g
- Fat 1 g (no saturated fat)

Cabbage and carrot salad with spiced yoghurt dressing

Two winter favourites are given a spicy, minted dressing to bring out all their flavours.

PREPARATION TIME: 15 minutes
SERVES 4

125 g (4½ oz) white cabbage, finely shredded
125 g (4½ oz) carrots, grated
For the dressing:
125 g (4½ oz) low-fat natural yoghurt
1 tablespoon finely chopped red onion
1 green chilli, deseeded and finely chopped, optional
2 tablespoons finely chopped fresh coriander
1 teaspoon bottled mint sauce, or 1 teaspoon each chopped fresh mint and white wine vinegar
A pinch of salt
½ teaspoon sugar
To garnish: ½ teaspoon ground cumin and ½ teaspoon paprika

1. Place the cabbage and carrots in a large bowl.
2. To make the dressing, mix all the ingredients together and beat them with a fork until well blended.
3. Stir the dressing into the cabbage and carrots, sprinkle with cumin and paprika and serve.

Nutrients per serving

- Calories 38
- Carbohydrate 7 g
- Protein 2 g
- No fat

Green vegetable salad with garlic and ginger

Crisp, healthy and delicately flavoured, these lightly steamed vegetables can be enjoyed hot or cold.

PREPARATION TIME: 20 minutes, plus chilling time if serving cold
COOKING TIME: 3-4 minutes
SERVES 4

150 g (5½ oz) broccoli
150 g (5½ oz) small pak choi, or other Chinese leaves
50 g (1¾ oz) spring onions
100 g (3½ oz) sugar snaps or mangetout, topped and tailed
1 small clove garlic, crushed
1 teaspoon finely grated ginger
1 teaspoon soft dark brown sugar
1 tablespoon Thai fish sauce

1. Fill a steamer with water to just below the basket. Bring the water to the boil.
2. Cut the broccoli into small florets, trimming the stalks to about 1 cm (½ in). Peel the remaining stalk and cut it into 1 cm (½ in) diagonal slices. Split the pak choi lengthways. Trim the spring onions and cut them into thin diagonal slices.
3. Put all the vegetables into a bowl, add the garlic and ginger and toss well. Transfer them to the steamer basket, cover and steam for 3-4 minutes until the vegetables are tender but still slightly crunchy.
4. Add the sugar to the fish sauce, stirring until it dissolves. Arrange the vegetables in a serving dish, pour the dressing over them and serve hot. Alternatively, leave them to cool, then chill until about 10 minutes before serving.

Nutrients per serving

- Calories 32
- Carbohydrate 4 g
- Protein 3 g
- No fat

Green beans and celeriac in a stir-fry dressing

Lightly steamed vegetables in a sweet and sour sauce make a pretty starter or party dish.

PREPARATION TIME: 15 minutes, plus 1-2 hours standing

COOKING TIME: 10-15 minutes

SERVES 4

250 g (9 oz) celeriac, cut into matchsticks
300 g (10½ oz) green beans

For the dressing:

1 tablespoon groundnut or olive oil
1 teaspoon sesame oil
1-2 fresh red chillies, deseeded and finely sliced
4 cloves garlic, coarsely chopped
1 tablespoon grated ginger
1-2 tablespoons clear honey
2 tablespoons soy sauce
5 tablespoons cider, or wine, vinegar

To garnish: sprigs of fresh coriander

1 Steam the celeriac for 1 minute, add the beans and steam for another 4 minutes, or until they are tender but still crisp. Then transfer them to a heatproof bowl.
2 To make the dressing, heat the oils in a wok or a heavy-based frying pan, add the chilli, garlic and ginger and stir-fry over a high heat until they start to brown – do not let them burn. Add the honey, soy sauce and vinegar and boil for 1-2 minutes until thickened.
3 Stir the dressing into the vegetables and leave to stand for 1-2 hours. Serve at room temperature, garnished with sprigs of coriander.

Variation: broccoli, carrots or parsnips can replace the beans and celeriac.

Nutrients per serving

- Calories 83
- Carbohydrate 9 g
- Protein 2 g
- Fat 4 g (including saturated fat 1 g)

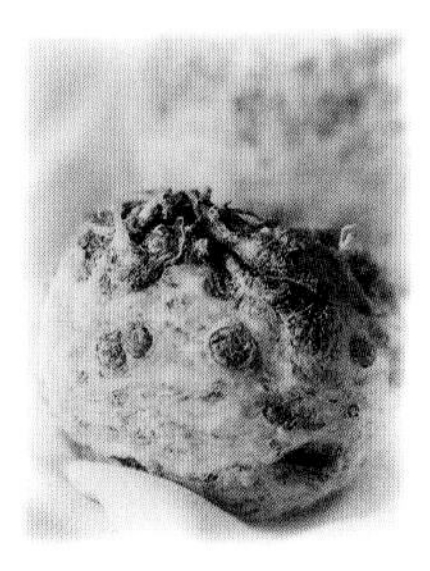

CELERIAC

Spinach and apple salad

A herb dressing and grilled croutons make great partners for crisp young spinach leaves.

PREPARATION TIME: 15 minutes
COOKING TIME: 6-8 minutes
SERVES 4

2 cloves garlic, unpeeled
2 slices wholemeal bread, crusts removed
100 g (3½ oz) young spinach leaves
2 crisp, red-skinned dessert apples, cored and sliced
For the dressing:
6 tablespoons chopped mixed fresh chives, mint and parsley
90 ml (3 fl oz) apple juice
1 teaspoon mild mustard
2 tablespoons cider vinegar
Salt and black pepper
To garnish: a few fresh chives

1. Heat the grill to high. To make the dressing, place all the ingredients in a food processor and blend until smooth, or use a hand-held mixer. Season to taste.
2. Place the garlic cloves under the hot grill for 4-5 minutes until the skins are blackened, turning once. Let them cool enough to handle, then squeeze out the flesh and mash it.
3. Spread one side of the bread slices with the garlic paste, then cut the slices into dice. Arrange them in one layer on a baking sheet and toast under the hot grill for 1-2 minutes, turning from time to time, until the croutons are golden brown.
4. Toss the spinach and apple together in a serving bowl, then scatter the garlic croutons on top. To serve, drizzle the dressing over and garnish with fresh chives.

Nutrients per serving

- Calories 69
- Carbohydrate 14 g
- Protein 2 g
- Fat 1 g (no saturated fat)

Quinoa salad with **dried fruit**

High in protein and low in fat, quinoa grains absorb flavours to make a substantial salad.

PREPARATION TIME: 15 minutes
COOKING TIME: 20 minutes
SERVES 4

180 g (6½ oz) quinoa grains
Salt and black pepper
2 tablespoons pine nuts
1 stick celery, finely diced
50 g (1¾ oz) red onion, finely diced
½ yellow pepper, deseeded and finely diced
12 dried cranberries, snipped into pieces
50 g (1¾ oz) currants
For the dressing:
½-1 teaspoon ground coriander
½-1 teaspoon ground cumin
1 tablespoon lemon juice
½ teaspoon paprika
1 tablespoon chopped fresh parsley
To garnish: fresh flat-leaved parsley

1. Put a kettle on to boil. Put the quinoa in a large sieve and rinse it thoroughly several times in cold running water to remove its bitter flavour.
2. Put the quinoa in a saucepan with 500 ml (18 fl oz) of boiling water and a pinch of salt and return to the boil. Cover, reduce the heat and simmer for 15 minutes, or until the grains are tender but not mushy. Strain over a large bowl to catch the cooking liquid, then set both aside.
3. Toast the pine nuts in a dry frying pan for 1-2 minutes until they are golden brown. Transfer the quinoa to a large bowl and stir in the celery, onion, pepper, cranberries, currants, and pine nuts.
4. To make the dressing, mix together the coriander, cumin, lemon juice, paprika and parsley. Add up to 4 tablespoons of the quinoa cooking liquid until you have the desired sharpness. Season to taste, then stir it into the salad. Garnish with parsley and serve.

Nutrients per serving

- Calories 241
- Carbohydrate 37 g
- Protein 8 g
- Fat 8 g (including saturated fat 1 g)

QUINOA

Low-fat tip

Rubbing oil into the potatoes and baking them on a tray instead of in a dish of oil produces crisp roast potatoes with almost no fat.

Roasted potato salad with cumin and yoghurt dressing

This hot potato salad is served with a lightly spiced, cool dressing.

PREPARATION TIME: 15 minutes
COOKING TIME: 50-55 minutes
SERVES 4

I tablespoon olive oil
Salt and black pepper
5 small baking potatoes, scrubbed
125 g (4½ oz) mixed salad leaves
For the dressing:
½ teaspoon ground cumin
Juice of ½ lemon
100 g (3½ oz) half-fat Greek yoghurt

1 Heat the oven to 200°C (400°F, gas mark 6). In a bowl, stir together the oil and ½ teaspoon salt, then use your hands to turn and coat the potatoes in the mixture. Place the potatoes on a baking tray and roast for 50-55 minutes until soft when squeezed and crisp on the outside.
2 Meanwhile, to make the dressing, place the cumin in a small ovenproof dish, such as a ramekin, and toast it in the hot oven for no more than 2 minutes while the potatoes are roasting. Do not let it burn. Remove from the oven and leave it to cool.
3 In a small bowl, stir together the cooled cumin, lemon juice and yoghurt and add salt and pepper to taste. Cover and chill, or set aside at a cool room temperature.
4 Arrange the salad leaves on four serving plates. When the potatoes are done, remove them from the oven and, using an oven mitt for protection, quarter them lengthways into wedges.
5 Put five potato wedges on each plate. Drizzle the warm potatoes with the dressing and serve.

Nutrients per serving

- Calories 189
- Carbohydrate 32 g
- Protein 5 g
- Fat 5 g (including saturated fat 2 g)

Marinated leeks

Enjoy this simple salad with its herb and mustard dressing as a light first course or as an accompaniment to cold meat.

PREPARATION TIME: 20 minutes, plus 30 minutes marinating
COOKING TIME: 10 minutes
SERVES 4

8 slim young leeks
Salt and black pepper
For the marinade:
2 tablespoons extra virgin olive oil
2 teaspoons white wine vinegar
1 tablespoon wholegrain mustard
2 tablespoons finely chopped fresh chives
2 tablespoons finely chopped fresh parsley
1 teaspoon finely chopped fresh tarragon
To garnish: 4 sprigs of fresh tarragon
To serve: wholemeal bread slices, optional

1. Bring a wide pan of salted water to the boil. Cut the leeks lengthways or, for a dinner party presentation, cut a cross from the top of each leek through the leaves to halfway down the white part of the stem. Rinse the cut leeks in lots of cold water to remove any grit.
2. Drop half the leeks into the boiling water and boil them for 4-5 minutes until they are tender. Remove with a slotted spoon and cool them under cold water. Drain and pat them dry then arrange them in a shallow dish. Repeat with the remaining leeks.
3. Meanwhile, to make the marinade, whisk together the oil, vinegar, mustard and herbs and season to taste. Spoon the mixture over the leeks then use your hands to turn them so that they are well coated. Cover and leave to marinate at room temperature for 30 minutes, turning occasionally.
4. Divide the leeks between four plates, fan out the leaves if cut crossways, and garnish with tarragon.

Variation: if you only have large leeks, cut them into chunks.

Tip: you can make this a day ahead and chill it. Return it to room temperature before serving.

Nutrients per serving

- Calories 81
- Carbohydrate 3 g
- Protein 2 g
- Fat 6 g (including saturated fat 1 g)

Chinese-style hot noodle salad with **vegetables**

Fragrant ginger and lemongrass flavour this hearty vegetable and noodle salad.

PREPARATION TIME: 30 minutes

COOKING TIME: 10 minutes

SERVES 4

100 g (3½ oz) thin egg noodles
2 teaspoons sunflower oil
1 fresh red chilli, deseeded and finely chopped
2-3 cloves garlic, chopped
2 tablespoons finely grated ginger
1 tablespoon lemongrass, very finely chopped
200 g (7 oz) carrots, cut into matchsticks
1 red pepper, diced
1 yellow pepper, diced
150 g (5½ oz) baby sweetcorn, cut in half lengthways
100 g (3½ oz) sugarsnap peas
250 g (9 oz) Chinese leaves, finely shredded
6 spring onions, finely sliced
4 tablespoons soy sauce
1 teaspoon sesame oil
3 tablespoons fresh coriander leaves
25 g (1 oz) salted peanuts, finely chopped

1. Put a kettle on to boil. Cook the noodles in boiling water according to the instructions on the packet, then drain them well.
2. Heat the sunflower oil in a hot wok or large frying pan and stir-fry the chilli, garlic, ginger, lemongrass, carrots, peppers, sweetcorn and sugarsnap peas for 4-5 minutes.
3. Add the Chinese leaves, spring onions, drained noodles, soy sauce and sesame oil. Toss everything together over a medium heat for a further minute until they are thoroughly combined and hot.
4. Finally, add the coriander and peanuts, toss together once more and serve.

Nutrients per serving

- Calories 236
- Carbohydrate 36 g
- Protein 9 g
- Fat 9 g (including saturated fat 2 g)

Chunky watermelon and **cucumber salad**

A specially light and refreshing salad – the perfect dish for steamy summer days.

PREPARATION TIME: 15 minutes
SERVES 4

700 g (1 lb 9 oz) watermelon
½ cucumber
40 g (1½ oz) stoned black olives in brine, drained
For the dressing:
25 g (1 oz) feta cheese, rinsed and dried
3 tablespoons low-fat natural yoghurt
1 tablespoon chopped fresh dill
Salt and black pepper
To garnish: sprigs of fresh dill
To serve: crusty wholemeal bread, optional

1 Cut the flesh away from the hard rind of the watermelon. Then cut it into bite-size chunks and pick out the seeds, reserving any juice.
2 Halve the cucumber lengthways and scoop out the seeds with a teaspoon. Cut the flesh into 2 cm (¾ in) chunks.
3 In a large bowl, toss together the watermelon, cucumber and olives.
4 To make the dressing, crumble the feta cheese into a small bowl, add the watermelon juice and yoghurt and mash them together. Stir in the dill and season to taste.
5 Divide the salad between four plates, sprinkle it with pepper and garnish with dill. Place a spoonful of the dressing alongside and serve with wholemeal bread, if you like.
Variation: when watermelon is out of season, cantaloupe or charentais melons make good substitutes.

Nutrients per serving

- Calories 102
- Carbohydrate 16 g
- Protein 4 g
- Fat 3 g (including saturated fat 1 g)

Pear, chicory and **Roquefort salad**

A pale and pretty salad with a great balance of flavours.

PREPARATION TIME: 15 minutes
COOKING TIME: 2 minutes
SERVES 4

25 g (1 oz) walnut halves
2 pears
3 heads chicory, or 1 large head radicchio
80 g (3 oz) Roquefort cheese
For the dressing:
1 teaspoon clear honey
1 teaspoon Dijon mustard
2 tablespoons white wine vinegar or cider vinegar

1 In a heavy-based frying pan, dry-fry the walnuts for 1-2 minutes until they brown slightly. Be careful not to over-brown them or they will taste bitter. Tip the toasted nuts into a small dish and set aside to cool.
2 Core and dice the pears and place them in a salad bowl. Discard the outer leaves of the chicory or radicchio, then toss the remaining leaves in the salad bowl with the pears. Roughly chop the toasted walnuts and set them aside.
3 To make the dressing, combine the honey, mustard and vinegar in a small bowl, then pour it over the pears and leaves and toss to coat.
4 Use your fingers to crumble the cheese over the salad, then sprinkle it with the chopped walnuts and serve.

Nutrients per serving

- Calories 165
- Carbohydrate 11 g
- Protein 6 g
- Fat 12 g (including saturated fat 5 g)

Watercress, kiwi, mushroom and tomato salad

Serve this flavour-packed salad as a vibrant first course or as an accompaniment to meat.

PREPARATION TIME: 20 minutes
SERVES 4

125 g (4½ oz) watercress sprigs
2 kiwi fruit, peeled and thinly sliced
125 g (4½ oz) button or chestnut mushrooms, thinly sliced
250 g (9 oz) tomatoes, sliced
For the dressing:
1 teaspoon red wine vinegar
Salt and black pepper
4 teaspoons olive oil

1. Arrange a bed of watercress in a bowl, then scatter the kiwi fruit, mushrooms and tomatoes on top.
2. To make the dressing, pour the vinegar into a small bowl, season to taste and whisk thoroughly to dissolve the salt. Add the oil and whisk again.
3. Just before serving, pour the dressing over the salad, taking care not to disturb the arrangement.

Variation: add a few pale purple chive or lavender flowers when they are in season, for extra colour.

Nutrients per serving

- Calories 64
- Carbohydrate 5 g
- Protein 2 g
- Fat 4 g (including saturated fat 1 g)

KIWI FRUIT

Smoked chicken Caesar salad

This version of a classic salad features smoked chicken rather than oily anchovies.

PREPARATION TIME: 15 minutes
COOKING TIME: 8-11 minutes
SERVES 4

125 g (4½ oz) day-old bread, cubed
300 g (10½ oz) cos lettuce, torn into bite-size pieces
200 g (7 oz) skinned and boned smoked chicken breast, cubed
25 g (1 oz) Parmesan cheese, grated
For the dressing:
1 medium egg
1 clove garlic, crushed
2 teaspoons Dijon mustard
1 tablespoon extra virgin olive oil
A few drops Tabasco sauce, optional
½ teaspoon Worcestershire sauce
4 tablespoons low-fat natural yoghurt
Salt and black pepper

1. Put a kettle on to boil. Heat the oven to 200°C (400°F, gas mark 6).
2. Place the bread cubes on a baking sheet and bake for 5-8 minutes until they are crisp and golden. Transfer them to a large bowl and leave to cool.
3. To make the dressing, boil the egg for 3 minutes, then immediately plunge it into cold water.
4. Shell the egg and place it in a food processor with the garlic, mustard, oil, Tabasco, if using, Worcestershire sauce and yoghurt. Blend until smooth, then season to taste.
5. Add the lettuce and chicken to the croutons. Add the dressing and cheese. Toss well to coat and serve.

Variation: if smoked chicken is unavailable, use barbecued chicken.

Nutrients per serving

- Calories 237
- Carbohydrate 20 g
- Protein 22 g
- Fat 8 g (including saturated fat 3 g)

SMOKED CHICKEN CAESAR SALAD

Sizzling turkey and orange salad

The whole family will enjoy this juicy salad with hot turkey. Serve it on its own, or with a jacket potato for a main course.

PREPARATION TIME: 15 minutes, plus 15 minutes marinating
COOKING TIME: 15-25 minutes
SERVES 4

500 g (1 lb 2 oz) skinned and boned turkey
1 tablespoon sunflower oil
4 spring onions, sliced
Salt and black pepper
A bunch of watercress, thick stalks removed
For the marinade:
2 large oranges
2 teaspoons honey
2 teaspoons wholegrain mustard
1 shallot, finely chopped

SIZZLING TURKEY AND ORANGE SALAD

1 To make the marinade, cut the peel and white pith from one orange, then cut out the segments over a large bowl to collect any juice. Cut the segments in half and set them aside. Squeeze the juice from the second orange into the bowl. Stir in the honey, mustard and shallot.
2 Cut the turkey into thin strips. Add them to the marinade, coating them well, then cover and leave in a cool place for 15 minutes.
3 Heat the oil in a large nonstick wok or frying pan and, working in batches, stir-fry the marinated turkey strips for 5-6 minutes until they are golden brown. Add the spring onions to the last batch and cook for a further 2 minutes. When the last batch has cooked, return all the turkey to the pan. Season lightly, pour in any remaining marinade and bring to the boil.
4 Divide the watercress between four plates and scatter some of the reserved orange segments on top. Spoon the turkey over, top with the remaining orange and serve.

Variation: for a hot dish, add the watercress and orange segments to the wok with the marinade. To make a creamy sauce, stir in 4 tablespoons of low-fat fromage frais off the heat.

Nutrients per serving

- Calories 214
- Carbohydrate 12 g
- Protein 33 g
- Fat 4g (including saturated fat 1 g)

Mixed shellfish and **pasta salad**

Nutrients per serving

- Calories 256
- Carbohydrate 43 g
- Protein 14 g
- Fat 1 g (no saturated fat)

A cool pasta salad tasting of the sea makes a luxurious starter or a lovely dish to take on a grand picnic.

PREPARATION TIME: 20 minutes, plus 3-4 hours standing
COOKING TIME: 15 minutes
SERVES 4

500 g (1 lb 2 oz) live mussels
75 ml (2½ fl oz) white wine
Juice of 1-2 lemons
Salt and black pepper
250 g (9 oz) pasta shapes, such as fusilli (spirals) or farfalle (butterflies)
50 g (1¾ oz) peeled, cooked prawns, defrosted if frozen
2 cloves garlic, finely chopped
50 g (1¾ oz) fresh flat-leaved parsley, finely chopped
4 spring onions, chopped

1 Clean the mussels under running water, pulling out all the beards. Discard any with damaged shells or open ones that do not close when tapped. Place them in a pan with the wine, cover and bring to the boil. Cook over a high heat for 2-3 minutes until they have opened. Take the pan off the heat and leave the mussels to cool.
2 Strain the cooking liquid through a fine sieve into a small bowl and discard any mussels that have not opened. Whisk the lemon juice into the strained mussel liquor to make a dressing. Add salt and pepper to taste and set it aside.
3 Bring a large pan of water to the boil, add the pasta and a pinch of salt and cook according to the instructions on the packet. Strain and place in a large bowl with a little of the mussel dressing stirred through to prevent it from drying out.
4 Cut the prawns in half if they are large. Add the mussels, prawns, garlic, parsley and spring onions to the pasta and mix them thoroughly.
5 Pour the rest of the mussel dressing over the salad and mix well. Cover and chill for a few hours for the flavours to develop, then adjust the seasoning to taste. Bring the salad to room temperature before serving.

Variation: the mussels are essential to this recipe, but you can substitute scallops and/or squid for the prawns.

Bulgur wheat and fish salad in a lemon dressing

A gutsy fish salad using orange roughy, a New Zealand import with a hint of shellfish flavour.

PREPARATION TIME: 20 minutes, plus 45 minutes soaking and 1-2 hours chilling

COOKING TIME: 15 minutes

SERVES 4-6

200 g (7 oz) bulgur (cracked) wheat
300 g (10½ oz) orange roughy fillets
½ lemon, thinly sliced
2 sprigs fresh parsley
5 black peppercorns
150 g (5½ oz) cucumber, diced
100 g (3½ oz) spring onions, thinly sliced
250 g (9 oz) cherry tomatoes, halved
3 tablespoons chopped fresh coriander, optional
3 tablespoons chopped fresh mint
3 tablespoons chopped fresh parsley

For the dressing:
Grated zest of ½ lemon
2 tablespoons lemon juice
2 tablespoons red wine vinegar
2 tablespoons olive oil
1 teaspoon Dijon mustard
1 clove garlic, crushed
Salt and black pepper

To garnish: a few sprigs of fresh mint

1 Put a kettle on to boil. Place the bulgur wheat in a large heatproof bowl, cover it with 600 ml (1 pint) of boiling water and leave it to stand for 45 minutes, or until it is tender and has absorbed all or most of the water.
2 Meanwhile, place the fish fillets in a large lidded frying pan, add the lemon slices, parsley sprigs and peppercorns and enough cold water to cover. Bring it to the boil, then reduce the heat and simmer, covered, for 5 minutes, or until the fish is opaque and flakes easily.
3 Remove the fish from the liquid and leave it to cool, then break it gently into large flakes.
4 Drain off any excess water from the bulgur wheat and squeeze it dry. Put it into a large salad bowl and add the cucumber, spring onions, tomatoes and chopped herbs. Gently mix in the fish without breaking it up.
5 To make the dressing, whisk all the ingredients together. Pour the dressing over the salad and mix gently without breaking up the fish.
6 Cover the bowl and chill in the refrigerator for 1-2 hours to allow the flavours to develop. Check the seasoning before serving and garnish with extra sprigs of mint.

Variation: you can substitute any firm white fish for the orange roughy, or use canned tuna in water, drained and flaked.

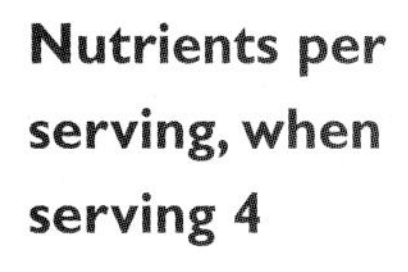

Nutrients per serving, when serving 4

- Calories 347
- Carbohydrate 42 g
- Protein 17 g
- Fat 12 g (including saturated fat 1 g)

fish and shellfish

Scallops with tomato and orange sauce

A simple, fresh sauce makes a vibrant accompaniment to sweet, chunky scallops.

PREPARATION TIME: 25 minutes
COOKING TIME: 10 minutes
SERVES 2

10-14 scallops, about 250 g (9 oz) altogether
For the sauce:
225 g (8 oz) tomatoes
50 ml (2 fl oz) fish stock
Juice of 1 orange
2 tablespoons dry white wine
1 teaspoon white wine vinegar
½ teaspoon caster sugar
Black pepper
1 tablespoon olive oil
Olive oil for greasing
To garnish: a few fresh basil leaves

1 To make the sauce, cover the tomatoes with boiling water and leave for 1-2 minutes. Then peel, deseed and chop them.
2 Place them in a food processor with the stock, orange juice, wine, vinegar, sugar and pepper to taste, and blend until smooth. Alternatively, beat them by hand in a mixing bowl.
3 Transfer the mixture to a saucepan, bring it to the boil and cook rapidly for 5 minutes, or until reduced by half to a thick coating consistency. Whisk in the oil to make a glossy sauce, and keep it warm.
4 Cut away and discard the tough white muscle on each scallop and the coral, if attached. Lightly grease a ridged, iron grill pan or a nonstick frying pan with oil, and place it on a high heat.
5 When the oil is hot, add the scallops and sear them for 2 minutes, then turn and cook them for a further 30 seconds. Remove them from the pan and let them rest for 1 minute.
6 Pour the sauce onto two plates and divide the scallops between them. Garnish with basil leaves and serve.
Serving suggestion: Braised Fennel (page 234) and Peppers Stuffed with Minted Rice (page 222).

Nutrients per serving

- Calories 257
- Carbohydrate 11 g
- Protein 30 g
- Fat 9 g (including saturated fat 2 g)

Steamed mussels with fennel and vermouth

The distinctive fragrances and flavours of fennel and vermouth blend perfectly with succulent mussels.

PREPARATION TIME: 20 minutes
COOKING TIME: 15 minutes
SERVES 4

2 kg (4 lb 8 oz) live mussels
1 large head fennel
25 g (1 oz) butter
150 g (5½ oz) onions, chopped
1 clove garlic, chopped
175 ml (6 fl oz) dry vermouth
1 tablespoon chopped fresh parsley
Black pepper

1 Scrub the mussels, removing any beards still attached to the shells, and wash them well. Discard any that are damaged, or opened ones that do not close when tapped.
2 Dice the fennel and finely chop the fronds, then set the fronds aside. Melt the butter in a large nonstick saucepan, add the diced fennel, onions and garlic, cover and cook gently for 10 minutes, or until tender.
3 Stir in the vermouth, parsley, fennel fronds and black pepper and bring to the boil. Add the mussels, cover and cook for 4-5 minutes, shaking the pan occasionally, until the shells have opened. Discard any mussels that remain closed.
4 Transfer the mussels to four bowls, pour over the pan juices and serve.
Serving suggestion: serve with lots of crusty French bread to mop up all the juice.

Nutrients per serving

- Calories 243
- Carbohydrate 10 g
- Protein 24 g
- Fat 9 g (including saturated fat 4 g)

Grilled prawns with **apple** and **fennel dressing**

The tenderness of juicy prawns is set off by a sharp dressing.

PREPARATION TIME: 30 minutes

COOKING TIME: 4 minutes

SERVES 4

600 g (1 lb 5 oz) headless raw tiger prawns
1 tablespoon olive oil
Salt and black pepper
For the dressing:
1 teaspoon fennel seeds
2 tablespoons lemon juice
2 tablespoons apple juice
50 g (1¾ oz) fennel, finely sliced
1 clove garlic, crushed
1 tablespoon extra virgin olive oil
To garnish: a few fresh chives

1 Peel the prawns, leaving the tail shells on. Run a sharp knife along the length of each back and pull away the dark digestive thread. Rinse the prawns and pat them dry with kitchen paper.
2 Heat a small nonstick frying pan over a medium heat and dry-fry the fennel seeds for 1-2 minutes, then grind them coarsely in a spice mill or with a pestle and mortar. Whisk them together with 1 tablespoon of the lemon juice and the other ingredients for the dressing, adding more lemon juice to taste.
3 Heat the grill to medium-high. Toss the prawns in the oil and season to taste, then grill them for 2 minutes on each side, or until they turn pink and opaque.
4 Divide the prawns between four plates, pour over the dressing, garnish with chives and serve warm or at room temperature.

Variation: you could barbecue the prawns on skewers instead of grilling them, if you like, or cook them on a ridged, iron grill pan.

Serving suggestion: boiled rice or steamed potatoes.

Nutrients per serving

- Calories 149
- Carbohydrate 1 g
- Protein 22 g
- Fat 6 g (including saturated fat 1 g)

Crab and prawn parcels with sweet and sour sauce

Crisp filo parcels open to reveal a creamy seafood filling that contrasts wonderfully with a ginger and pineapple sauce.

PREPARATION TIME: 40 minutes
COOKING TIME: 25-30 minutes
SERVES 4

150 g (5½ oz) cooked, peeled prawns, defrosted if frozen
2 tablespoons chopped fresh chives
100 g (3½ oz) fresh crabmeat, or canned crabmeat, drained
3 tablespoons half-fat crème fraîche
Black pepper
8 sheets fresh filo pastry, each about 18 x 31 cm (7 x 12½ in)
1 tablespoon olive oil

For the sauce:
25 g (1 oz) stem ginger preserved in syrup, drained and cut into fine shreds
1 tablespoon syrup from the ginger
2 small canned pineapple rings, drained and finely chopped
20 g (¾ oz) soft dark brown sugar
A pinch of cayenne pepper
1 tablespoon seasoned rice vinegar, or white wine, or cider vinegar
1½ teaspoons arrowroot

To garnish: a few watercress leaves and fresh chives

1 Heat the oven to 220°C (425°F, gas mark 7). Roughly chop the prawns and put them into a mixing bowl. Stir in the chives, crabmeat and crème fraîche. Season well with pepper.
2 Brush one sheet of filo lightly with a little of the oil. Lay a second sheet on top and brush it lightly with oil, then cut them in half lengthways to make two long strips, two layers thick.
3 Divide the crab mixture into eight equal portions. Place one portion at the bottom right-hand end of one of the double-layered strips of filo pastry, then fold the top right-hand corner over the filling to make a triangle. Continue folding the parcel over at right angles, all the way along the length of the strip, enclosing the filling with many layers of pastry.
4 Make seven more parcels the same way, using two strips of pastry and one portion of filling for each parcel. Place the parcels on a baking tray, brush them with the remaining oil and bake in the centre of the oven for 20-25 minutes until the pastry is crisp and golden brown.
5 Meanwhile, prepare the sauce. Put all the ingredients except the arrowroot into a saucepan with 150 ml (5 fl oz) of water and stir over a medium heat until the mixture comes to the boil, then reduce the heat to low and simmer it for 5 minutes.
6 Blend the arrowroot with 2 teaspoons of cold water, stir it into the sauce and return the sauce to the boil, stirring continuously, until it thickens and becomes clear. Reduce the heat to low, cover and keep it warm.
7 To serve, arrange two parcels on each plate and garnish with the watercress leaves and the chives. Pour the sauce into four small bowls and serve one alongside each plate.

Serving suggestion: a medley of mixed seasonal baby vegetables.

Nutrients per serving

- Calories 269
- Carbohydrate 34 g
- Protein 17 g
- Fat 8 g (including saturated fat 2 g)

Vietnamese fish salad

Toasted rice and peanuts add crunch to these whiting fillets, 'cooked' in a powerful rice vinegar marinade.

PREPARATION TIME: 20 minutes, plus 1 hour marinating
COOKING TIME: 5-7 minutes
SERVES 4

500 g (1 lb 2 oz) whiting fillets, skinned
450 ml (16 fl oz) rice vinegar
250 g (9 oz) onions, finely sliced
1 tablespoon white sugar
1 teaspoon salt
2 tablespoons raw peanuts, shelled
2 tablespoons white rice
1½ tablespoons finely shredded fresh mint
1 fresh red chilli, deseeded and finely chopped
To garnish: shredded fresh mint and thin slivers of red chilli, optional

1. Remove any small bones from the fish, then cut the fillets in half crossways and slice them into long thin strips. Place them in a large bowl and pour over 300 ml (10 fl oz) of the rice vinegar, making sure the fish is covered. Set aside to marinate for 1 hour.
2. Place the onions in a bowl, add the sugar and salt and pour over the remaining vinegar. Stir until the sugar and salt have dissolved, then leave to soak for 30 minutes.
3. Meanwhile, crush the peanuts finely using a pestle and mortar, then dry-fry them in a heavy-based nonstick frying pan over a low heat for 2-3 minutes until they are evenly browned. Remove them from the pan and set aside.
4. Add the rice to the pan and toast it for 3-4 minutes until it is golden brown all over, then place it in the mortar and crush it finely.
5. After the fish and onion have marinated, remove them from the vinegar and pat them both dry with kitchen paper. Place in a large bowl and add the mint and chilli. Toss gently to combine, then sprinkle the toasted crushed peanuts and rice on top and toss again. Garnish with extra mint and chilli if you like, and serve.

Serving suggestion: make this dish part of a Far Eastern banquet by adding bowls of Ratatouille Chinese-style (page 84), Green Vegetable Salad with Garlic and Ginger (page 85) and Rice Vermicelli with Mustard and Chillies (page 212).

Nutrients per serving

- Calories 240
- Carbohydrate 19 g
- Protein 27 g
- Fat 4 g (including saturated fat 1 g)

RED CHILLI

Monkfish and **prawn kebabs** with **tomato salsa**

These grilled kebabs served with a fresh Mexican-style sauce are a tasty example of Pacific Rim cooking.

PREPARATION TIME: 40 minutes, plus 1 hour marinating
COOKING TIME: 6-8 minutes
SERVES 4

1 medium-size monkfish tail, about 700 g (1 lb 9 oz)
4 raw tiger prawns or 8-12 smaller ones, about 100 g (3½ oz) altogether
1 clove garlic, crushed
1 teaspoon ginger purée, or grated ginger
1 green chilli, deseeded and finely chopped
1 tablespoon sunflower or groundnut oil
Salt and black pepper
For the salsa:
500 g (1 lb 2 oz) plum tomatoes
2 teaspoons coriander seeds
1 green chilli, deseeded and finely chopped
1 clove garlic, crushed
1 stalk lemongrass, outer leaves removed, very finely sliced
Juice of 1 lime
To serve: wedges of lime

1 Rinse the fish with cold water, pat it dry with kitchen paper, and remove any grey membrane. Cut the flesh from the cartilage backbone in two long pieces. Cut each piece into 8-12 equal-size chunks.
2 Peel the prawns, removing the legs and heads but leaving the tails on if possible. Run a sharp knife along the back of each prawn and pull away the dark digestive thread. Rinse and pat dry with kitchen paper.
3 Mix the garlic, ginger and chilli with the oil in a large bowl. Add the monkfish and the prawns and mix well. Cover with cling film and chill for 1 hour. If you are using wooden

skewers, soak them in cold water for at least 30 minutes before using.

4 Meanwhile, make the salsa. Put a kettle on to boil. Cover the tomatoes with boiling water and leave for 1 minute. Then skin and deseed them and chop the flesh into a chunky purée. This must be done by hand, not in a food processor.

5 Dry-fry the coriander seeds in a heavy-based frying pan over a high heat for a few seconds until they release their aroma. Then crush them in a spice mill or with a pestle and mortar and add them to the tomato. Mix in the chilli, garlic, lemongrass and lime juice and season well. Cover and chill for 30 minutes or more.

6 When you are ready to cook, heat the grill to medium-high. Thread the monkfish and prawns onto four skewers and grill for 3-4 minutes on each side until the prawns are firm and pink but not overcooked. Season the kebabs to taste, garnish with the lime wedges and serve with the salsa on the side.

Variation: cook the kebabs on a barbecue rather than under the grill for a smokier flavour. Or cook them in a ridged, iron grill pan over a medium-high heat.

Serving suggestion: for a hearty meal, serve with Cellophane Noodles with Chilli Greens (page 213) or Cardamom Rice (page 225).

Nutrients per serving

- Calories 167
- Carbohydrate 4 g
- Protein 29 g
- Fat 4 g (including saturated fat 1 g)

Stuffed squid, Italian-style

Slow cooking guarantees that the squid remains tender in this delicious baked dish.

PREPARATION TIME: 25-45 minutes
COOKING TIME: 30-45 minutes
SERVES 4

8 sun-dried tomatoes, not in oil
1 large prepared tube squid, or 8 small tubes, about 300 g (10½ oz) altogether, tentacles reserved
2 tablespoons capers, finely chopped
75 g (2¾ oz) fresh white breadcrumbs
2 tablespoons chopped mixed fresh herbs, such as basil, oregano, parsley or sage
Salt and black pepper
1 egg white
½ tablespoon olive oil
To garnish: a few drops of balsamic vinegar, lemon juice and olive oil
To serve: mixed salad with cherry tomatoes

1 Put a kettle on to boil. Place the sun-dried tomatoes in a small bowl and cover generously with boiling water. Leave them to soak for 20 minutes to rehydrate them and to remove any excess salt.

2 Heat the oven to 180°C (350°F, gas mark 4). Rinse the squid inside and out and pat it dry with kitchen paper.

3 To make the stuffing, cut off and discard any hard bits on the tentacles then finely dice about a third of them and place in a mixing bowl. (Reserve the rest for another dish, such as a stir-fry.) Add the capers to the bowl.

4 Drain and dry the tomatoes, dice them finely and add them to the tentacles, with the breadcrumbs and herbs. Blend well, season to taste, then stir in the egg white to bind.

5 Spoon the stuffing into the squid, pushing it right down to the tip, and secure the opening with a small skewer or wooden cocktail stick. Lightly brush a baking tray with oil and place the stuffed squid on top. Bake for 45 minutes if using one large tube, 30 minutes if using small tubes, or until lightly golden.

6 To serve, carve the squid crossways into 1 cm (½ in) slices, lay on a plate, and dot with balsamic vinegar, lemon juice and olive oil. Serve with mixed salad and cherry tomatoes.

Serving suggestion: to serve as a main course, accompany with Lemon-braised Spinach with Mushrooms and Croutons (page 230) and Grilled Vegetable Salad (page 232).

Nutrients per serving

- Calories 159
- Carbohydrate 17 g
- Protein 15 g
- Fat 4 g (including saturated fat 1 g)

Blackened swordfish with **warm pineapple salsa**

Nutrients per serving

- Calories 276
- Carbohydrate 21 g
- Protein 24 g
- Fat 11 g (including saturated fat 2 g)

The spicy coating used in this full-flavoured fish dish is brilliantly set off by a sweet, fruity sauce.

PREPARATION TIME: 20 minutes
COOKING TIME: 15 minutes
SERVES 4

1 teaspoon cayenne pepper
1 tablespoon dried garlic granules
1 tablespoon dried onion powder or granules
1 teaspoon dried oregano
2 tablespoons paprika
1 teaspoon dried thyme
Salt and black pepper
A pinch of white pepper
1½ tablespoons sunflower oil, plus oil for greasing
4 swordfish steaks, about 125 g (4½ oz) each

For the salsa:
100 ml (3½ fl oz) sake, or dry sherry
1 tablespoon rice vinegar
1 green chilli
1 tablespoon light muscovado sugar
10-12 strands saffron
450 g (1 lb) fresh pineapple

To garnish: a few fresh basil leaves

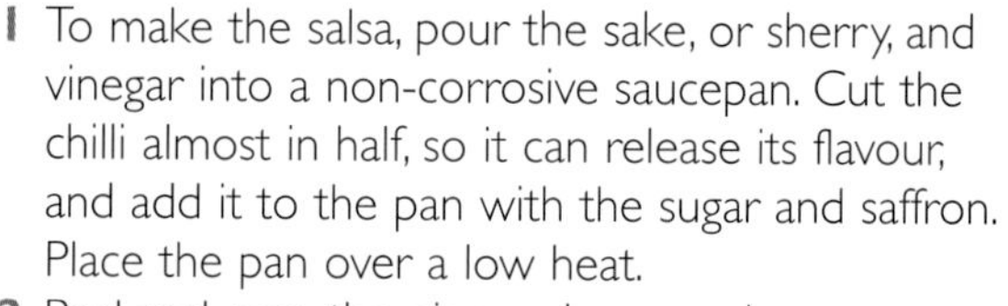

1 To make the salsa, pour the sake, or sherry, and vinegar into a non-corrosive saucepan. Cut the chilli almost in half, so it can release its flavour, and add it to the pan with the sugar and saffron. Place the pan over a low heat.
2 Peel and core the pineapple, removing any eyes, and cut it into 2 cm (¾ in) cubes. As soon as the syrup comes to the boil, add the pineapple and return to the boil, then remove the pan from the heat and leave the pineapple to soften.
3 Mix together the cayenne pepper, garlic granules, onion powder or granules, oregano, paprika and thyme. Season with black and white pepper, and a pinch of salt if you have used onion powder not granules, then stir in 1½ tablespoons of oil to make a paste.
4 Cut any skin off the fish then coat them with the spicy paste. Put the salsa over a low heat to warm through.
5 Lightly grease a ridged, iron grill pan or heavy-based nonstick frying pan and place it over a very high heat. When it is really hot, add the fish and grill for 8-10 minutes, turning them halfway through. The fish will smoke vigorously when they touch the pan – this is part of the 'blackening' process.
6 Serve the blackened fish steaks hot with the warm pineapple salsa, and garnish with basil.

Serving suggestion: saffron rice and a crisp green salad.

Seared tuna with spicy black bean salsa

Nutrients per serving

- Calories 260
- Carbohydrate 12 g
- Protein 30 g
- Fat 11 g (including saturated fat 2 g)

The fresh tomato and lime juice in the salsa balance the richness of the tuna, which can be served hot or chilled.

PREPARATION TIME: 20 minutes, plus overnight soaking and at least 30 minutes marinating

COOKING TIME: 1 hour 15 minutes

SERVES 4

4 tuna fillets, about 100 g (3½ oz) each
For the salsa:
100 g (3½ oz) dried black beans
150 g (5½ oz) tomatoes
½ fresh red chilli, deseeded and finely chopped
2 tablespoons roughly chopped fresh coriander
1 clove garlic, finely chopped
1 tablespoon lime juice
2 tablespoons extra virgin olive oil
Salt and black pepper
To garnish: lime wedges

1 To make the salsa, rinse the beans and soak them overnight in cold water.
2 Next day, drain and rinse the beans, then put them in a saucepan with enough cold water to cover. Bring to the boil and cook vigorously for 10 minutes, skimming off any foam as necessary. Reduce the heat, cover and boil gently for 1 hour, or until the beans are soft but not falling apart. Rinse them under cold water, drain and leave to cool.
3 Put the kettle on to boil. Cover the tomatoes with boiling water and leave for 1 minute. Then skin and deseed them and chop the flesh into bean-size dice.
4 Place the beans and tomatoes in a mixing bowl and stir in the chilli, coriander, garlic, lime juice and 1 tablespoon of the olive oil. Season with salt and pepper, then set aside to marinate for at least 30 minutes.
5 Cut off the skin and any dark-coloured flesh from the tuna, then season. Heat a ridged, iron grill pan or nonstick frying pan over a high heat. Once hot, add the remaining oil. As soon as the oil is hot, add the fish and fry it for 1-2 minutes on each side until it flakes easily. Alternatively, to barbecue the fish, brush the barbecue rack or plate with a little oil and sear the tuna for 2-3 minutes on each side.
6 Serve the fish hot or at room temperature with the black bean salsa spooned over and garnish with lime wedges.

Variation: most supermarkets sell dried black beans, but if you cannot find them, substitute dried chickpeas instead, soaking and cooking them as above. You can also use well-drained and rinsed canned black beans or chickpeas, in which case omit steps 1 and 2.

Serving suggestion: sprouting broccoli.

GARLIC AND TOMATOES

Baked salmon fishcakes with parsley sauce

Nutrients per serving

- Calories 463
- Carbohydrate 54 g
- Protein 28 g
- Fat 16 g (including saturated fat 3 g)

Packed full of flavour, these fishcakes are served with a delicious herb sauce in this tasty and healthy version of an all-time family favourite.

PREPARATION TIME: 15 minutes, plus 1 hour chilling, optional
COOKING TIME: 1 hour
SERVES 4

750 g (1 lb 10 oz) potatoes, peeled and cut into chunks
350 g (12 oz) salmon fillets
300 ml (10 fl oz) skimmed milk
2 tablespoons tomato ketchup
1 tablespoon anchovy essence, optional
1 tablespoon chopped fresh chives or parsley
Salt and black pepper
1 egg
90 g (3¼ oz) dried breadcrumbs
For the sauce:
25 g (1 oz) plain white flour
25 g (1 oz) 70 per cent fat spread
2 tablespoons chopped fresh parsley

Low-fat tip

Baking the fishcakes instead of frying them means that, even with an oily fish like salmon, they contain much less fat than the traditional version.

1 Put the potatoes in a large saucepan, cover with salted water, bring to the boil and cook for 15 minutes, or until they are tender. Drain, mash and set aside.
2 Meanwhile, place the salmon in a frying pan, cover with the skimmed milk and poach for 8-10 minutes until the flesh turns opaque. Lift the fish out and save the milk for the sauce.
3 Heat the oven to 190°C (375°F, gas mark 5). Skin, bone and flake the salmon into a bowl and combine with the mashed potato, tomato ketchup, anchovy essence if using, and fresh herbs. Season to taste and shape into eight fishcakes. If you can chill them for 1 hour in the refrigerator to firm up, it will make them easier to handle while you coat them, but it is not essential.
4 Beat the egg in a shallow bowl and stir in 2 tablespoons of cold water. Place the breadcrumbs in another shallow bowl. One at a time, dip the fishcakes in the beaten egg, then lightly coat them with the breadcrumbs. Place them on a nonstick baking sheet and bake for 20-30 minutes.
5 Meanwhile, heat the grill to medium. To make the parsley sauce, strain the reserved milk into a small pan, add the flour and spread, and slowly bring to the boil, stirring all the time, until the sauce thickens and becomes smooth. Reduce the heat and simmer for 20 minutes. Season to taste, then stir in the parsley.
6 To brown the fishcakes, place them under the grill for about 5 minutes, or until golden brown. Serve the baked fishcakes on a bed of sauce.

Serving suggestion: savoy cabbage, sautéed in stock, or Sweet Roasted Squash with Shallots (page 231).

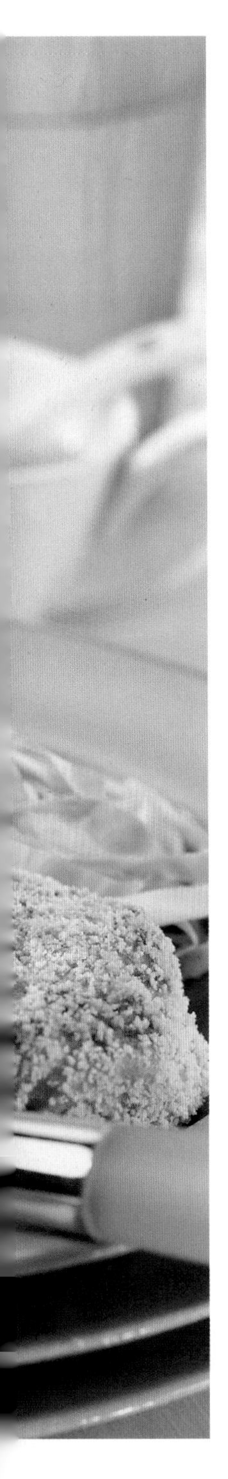

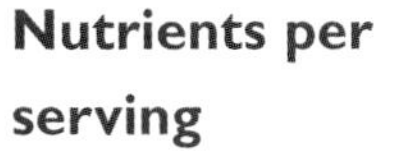

Fabulous fish and chips

From now on you can enjoy this delicious treat without worrying about the high fat content – the secret to golden chips is to coat them with egg white, not fat.

PREPARATION TIME: 20 minutes
COOKING TIME: 40 minutes
SERVES 4

For the chips:
650 g (1 lb 7 oz) baking potatoes, peeled
1 teaspoon oil
1 egg white
For the fish:
4 tail fillets of cod or haddock, about 125 g (4½ oz) each
4 teaspoons reduced-fat mayonnaise
50 g (1¾ oz) fresh white breadcrumbs
1 tablespoon 70 per cent spread, melted
1 tablespoon grated Parmesan cheese
1 tablespoon chopped fresh chives
1 tablespoon chopped fresh parsley
Salt and black pepper
To garnish: sprigs of fresh flat-leaved parsley and 1 lemon cut into wedges

1. Heat the oven to 200°C (400°F, gas mark 6). Put a kettle on to boil.
2. Put the potatoes in a saucepan, cover with boiling water and cook gently for 5 minutes. Drain, then dry on kitchen paper. Cut each potato lengthways into slices about 2 cm (¾ in) thick, then cut each slice into two or three thick wedges.
3. Brush a nonstick baking tray with some of the oil. Beat the egg white until it is frothy. Toss the chips in the egg white, gently shake off any excess, then spread them out on the tray. Bake for 35 minutes, turning them over halfway through cooking.
4. Meanwhile, prepare the fish. Lightly oil another nonstick baking tray. Lay the fillets, skin side down, on the tray. Spread a teaspoon of the mayonnaise over each fillet.
5. Mix together the breadcrumbs, spread, cheese, herbs and season to taste. Spread the mixture evenly over the fish, pressing it in gently.
6. Bake the fish on the top shelf of the oven for the final 10-15 minutes of the chips' cooking time. To serve, divide between four plates and garnish with sprigs of fresh parsley and lemon wedges.

Nutrients per serving

- Calories 302
- Carbohydrate 33 g
- Protein 29 g
- Fat 7 g (including saturated fat 1 g)

Fish biriyani

Spiced cod and basmati rice are baked together to make this traditional Indian one-pot dish.

PREPARATION TIME: 20 minutes, plus 2 hours or overnight marinating
COOKING TIME: 40-45 minutes
SERVES 4

500 g (1 lb 2 oz) skinned cod fillets
½ tablespoon oil
For the marinade:
3 tablespoons sunflower oil
2 tablespoons lemon juice
75 g (2¾ oz) spring onions, chopped
1 teaspoon ground anise
A pinch of cayenne pepper
1 teaspoon ground cumin
1½ teaspoons garlic paste, or 1 clove garlic, crushed
½ teaspoon ginger paste, or very finely chopped ginger
½ teaspoon ground turmeric
Salt and pepper
For the rice:
350 g (12 oz) basmati rice
2 bay leaves, torn in half
10 cm (4 in) cinnamon stick
15 g (½ oz) butter
2 tablespoons chopped fresh coriander
To garnish: sprigs of fresh coriander

1 Mix all the marinade ingredients together and season with salt and pepper to taste.
2 Cut the fillets into 5 cm (2 in) cubes and put them in a shallow dish. Add the marinade and mix them gently together, coating the fish completely. Cover with cling film and leave in a cool place for 2 hours, or overnight in the refrigerator. Bring the fish back to room temperature before you start cooking it.
3 Heat the oven to 150°C (300°F, gas mark 2) and heat the grill to high. Line the grill pan with foil and brush with the oil. Arrange the fish in the grill pan in a single layer. Strain the marinade, reserving the spring onions, and spoon it over the fish. Grill for 6-7 minutes until the edges of the fish begin to brown. Then turn off the grill and gather the corners of the foil, covering the fish loosely to keep it warm.
4 Meanwhile, rinse and drain the rice. Bring 600 ml (1 pint) of water to the boil in a saucepan and add the bay leaves, cinnamon, butter and salt to taste. Add the rice and return to the boil for 3 minutes. Reduce the heat, cover and simmer for 8 minutes until all the water has been absorbed: it will not be completely cooked. Take the pan off the heat and leave it, uncovered, for 4 minutes.
5 Unwrap the fish, pour the cooking juices into the rice and stir them through. Place a few pieces of fish and the reserved spring onions in a single layer in the base of a casserole, leaving small gaps between the fish. Sprinkle with chopped coriander and cover with a layer of rice. Continue alternating layers of fish, coriander and rice, finishing with rice.
6 Soak a clean tea towel in water and wring it out. Place it over the rice, then cover the casserole with a tight-fitting lid. If it is not tight, cover the dish with a piece of foil first, then with the lid. Bake for 20-25 minutes so the rice finishes cooking in the steam and all the flavours develop. Garnish with coriander and serve.

Serving suggestion: grilled poppadoms and Brussels Sprouts with Mustard and Cumin (page 234).

Nutrients per serving

- Calories 541
- Carbohydrate 71 g
- Protein 30 g
- Fat 15 g (including saturated fat 3 g)

Tandoori monkfish with mint relish

Nutrients per serving

- Calories 131
- Carbohydrate 3 g
- Protein 22 g
- Fat 4 g (including saturated fat 1 g)

Pep up your tastebuds with marinated fish and a sweet and sour relish.

PREPARATION TIME: 25 minutes, plus 1 hour 30 minutes marinating
COOKING TIME: 10 minutes
SERVES 4

500 g (1 lb 2 oz) monkfish
2 teaspoons sunflower oil
For the marinade:
2 tablespoons Greek yoghurt
2 tablespoons lemon juice
A pinch of cayenne pepper
A pinch of garam masala
1 clove garlic, crushed
1 teaspoon finely chopped ginger
1 tablespoon paprika
Salt and black pepper
For the relish:
½ teaspoon deseeded and finely chopped green chilli
½ teaspoon garam masala
1-2 tablespoons lemon juice
6 tablespoons finely chopped fresh mint
1 teaspoon caster sugar

1. Remove any membrane from the monkfish, then divide the fish into four equal portions.
2. Mix together the yoghurt, lemon juice, cayenne pepper, garam masala, garlic, ginger and paprika, then season to taste. Rub the spicy yoghurt into the fish, cover and chill for 1 hour 30 minutes.
3. To make the relish, mix the chilli, garam masala, lemon juice and mint together and add salt to taste. Cover and chill until required.
4. Lightly oil a ridged, iron grill pan or heavy-based frying pan and set it over a medium-high heat. Remove the fish from the spicy yoghurt and, using your fingers, gently wipe off the excess marinade. Cook for about 10 minutes, turning the fish regularly so that it cooks evenly. Serve hot with the mint relish.

Variation: halve the quantities and serve as a starter with cucumber, onion and tomato.

Serving suggestion: mixed long-grain and wild rice grains with finely chopped fresh parsley stirred in, or curried vegetables and a starchy accompaniment such as Chilli or Spinach Chapattis (page 291).

GARAM MASALA

Red mullet with Provençale sauce

Nutrients per serving
- Calories 227
- Carbohydrate 5 g
- Protein 25 g
- Fat 11 g (including saturated fat 1 g)

This rosy-skinned Mediterranean fish is traditionally cooked with tomatoes and herbs. Black olives, peppers and vermouth add extra southern flavour.

PREPARATION TIME: 20 minutes
COOKING TIME: 20 minutes
SERVES 4

4 red mullet fillets, skin on, about 125 g (4½ oz) each
Salt and black pepper
2 tablespoons olive oil
For the sauce:
2 cloves garlic, crushed
1 small yellow pepper, chopped
1 shallot, finely chopped
2 tablespoons dry vermouth
1 tablespoon dried herbes de Provence or oregano
350 g (12 oz) plum tomatoes, skinned and roughly chopped
8 large stoned black olives, roughly chopped
2 tablespoons roughly chopped fresh flat-leaved parsley

1 Lightly season the fish fillets and brush the flesh with a little of the oil.
2 To make the sauce, heat 1 tablespoon of the oil in a shallow pan and gently fry the garlic, pepper and shallot for about 8 minutes until they are softened.
3 Stir in the vermouth and cook until it is reduced by half. Add the dried herbs, tomatoes and salt and pepper to taste. Bring to the boil, then reduce the heat, cover and simmer for 10 minutes. Near the end of the cooking, stir in the olives and parsley and adjust the seasoning.
4 Meanwhile, heat the remaining oil in a ridged, iron grill pan or a heavy-based nonstick frying pan and cook the fish fillets, skin side down, for 4 minutes. Turn them carefully and cook for a further 2-4 minutes until they are opaque and flake easily. Or you can grill the fillets in a lightly oiled grill pan under a high heat for about 4 minutes on each side.
5 Spoon the sauce onto four dinner plates, place a fillet on top of each, skin side up, and serve.
Serving suggestion: a ribbon pasta such as linguine, or boiled new potatoes or rice.

Salmon with almond stuffing

Salmon braised in wine with a rich, nutty filling makes a wonderful dinner party dish that can be served hot or cold.

PREPARATION TIME: 20 minutes
COOKING TIME: 30-35 minutes
SERVES 6

Olive oil for greasing
750 g (1 lb 10 oz) piece of middle cut, boned salmon, skin on
250 ml (9 fl oz) white wine or water
For the stuffing:
¼ teaspoon fennel seeds
1 tablespoon finely chopped ginger
150 g (5½ oz) shallots, chopped

50 g (1¾ oz) canned anchovies, drained, dried and chopped
3 tablespoons ground almonds
2 drops almond extract
1 tablespoon capers, drained
1 tablespoon chopped fresh dill
1 tablespoon chopped fresh parsley
Grated zest and juice of ½ lemon
2-3 tablespoons matzo meal, or dried breadcrumbs
1 egg white
To garnish: wedges of lemon and sprigs of fresh dill and parsley

1 Heat the oven to 200°C (400°F, gas mark 6). To make the stuffing, dry-fry the fennel seeds, ginger and shallots in a nonstick frying pan for 2 minutes over a high heat. Keep scraping the pan to prevent them burning.
2 Add the anchovies and 4 tablespoons of water to the pan and bring it to the boil, then reduce the heat and simmer for 4-5 minutes until most of the liquid has evaporated and the shallots are translucent.
3 Place the mixture in a food processor with the ground almonds, almond extract, capers, dill, parsley, lemon zest and juice, matzo meal or breadcrumbs, and egg white, and blend to a smooth paste. If it is too liquid, add more matzo meal or dried breadcrumbs.
4 Lightly grease a deep ovenproof dish with the oil. Cut the salmon across into two equal pieces. Place one piece, skin side down, in the dish and spread the stuffing over it. Cover it with the other piece, skin side up, and pour in enough wine or water to come nearly to the top of the lower piece of salmon, but do not let it moisten the filling.
5 Cover the dish loosely with foil and cook for 25-30 minutes basting with the liquid occasionally, until the salmon is opaque and flakes easily.
6 Lay the salmon on a serving platter and peel off the top skin and any bits of brown flesh. Serve it garnished with lemon, dill and parsley.

Variation: the salmon tastes equally good chilled. Allow it to cool to room temperature, then peel off the skin. Cover tightly with foil and refrigerate. Serve garnished with very finely sliced cucumber.

Serving suggestion: broccoli and potatoes.

Nutrients per serving

- Calories 357
- Carbohydrate 6 g
- Protein 31 g
- Fat 21 g (including saturated fat 3 g)

Light haddock pie with pesto mash

With its firm texture, haddock makes an excellent pie filling, especially when teamed with cider, potatoes and prawns.

PREPARATION TIME: 20 minutes
COOKING TIME: 30-35 minutes
SERVES 4-6

300 g (10½ oz) white haddock fillet
300 g (10½ oz) undyed smoked haddock fillet
1 large bay leaf
500 ml (18 fl oz) skimmed milk
Salt and black pepper
800 g (1 lb 12 oz) floury potatoes, such as King Edwards
40 g (1½ oz) 70 per cent fat spread
1-2 tablespoons pesto
200 g (7 oz) leeks, thinly sliced, or 1 small onion, thinly sliced
150 ml (5 fl oz) dry cider
25 g (1 oz) plain white flour
125 g (4½ oz) cooked, peeled prawns, defrosted if frozen
2 tablespoons half-fat crème fraîche
2 tablespoons dried breadcrumbs
3-4 tomatoes, thinly sliced

1. Place all the haddock in a single layer in a roasting tin or a large frying pan, add the bay leaf, milk and pepper to taste and poach over a medium heat for 6-8 minutes until the flesh turns opaque and flakes easily when tested with a knife.
2. Meanwhile, peel the potatoes and cut them into chunks.
3. Put a large saucepan of lightly salted water on to boil. Remove the fish from the tin, and skin and flake the flesh, checking for any bones. Strain the milk into a measuring jug, discard the bay leaf and set the milk aside.
4. Add the potatoes to the saucepan, bring the water back to the boil and cook the potatoes for 10-15 minutes until they are tender.
5. Drain the potatoes well, reserving a little of the water, and return them to the pan over a medium heat to dry. Mash well, then beat in 1 tablespoon of the spread, check the seasoning and stir in the pesto to taste. (If the potatoes are a little dry, beat in 1-2 tablespoons of the reserved cooking water.) Set the mash aside. Heat the grill to high.
6. Melt the remaining spread in a saucepan, add the leeks or onion and cook for 7 minutes, or until softened. Pour in the cider, increase the heat to high and boil until the cider is reduced by half.
7. Stir in the flour and continue boiling for about 1 minute, then gradually stir in the reserved poaching milk, stirring briskly until the sauce thickens and becomes smooth. Reduce the heat, season to taste and simmer for 3 minutes, stirring occasionally.
8. Stir in the prawns, crème fraîche and flaked fish and reheat for 2 minutes. Be careful not to let the mixture boil or to break up the fish.
9. Spoon the fish mixture into a shallow 20 x 30 cm (8 x 12 in) flameproof serving dish. Spread the pesto mash over the top and smooth the surface. Sprinkle on the breadcrumbs and arrange the tomato slices on top.
10. Reduce the grill heat to medium and grill the pie until it is crisp, but not burnt, then serve.

Serving suggestion: steamed savoy cabbage and chunky carrots.

Nutrients per serving, when serving 4

- Calories 526
- Carbohydrate 52 g
- Protein 49 g
- Fat 14 g (including saturated fat 3 g)

PESTO

Baked fish with **lemon tahini**

Nutrients per serving

- Calories 263
- Carbohydrate 2 g
- Protein 29 g
- Fat 16 g (including saturated fat 1 g)

Low-fat tip

Mixing the tahini paste with virtually fat-free Greek yoghurt reduces the fat content of the traditional sauce by half.

This is a classic from the Middle East where tahini, a nutty-flavoured sesame seed paste, is used like cream to add substance and moisture to simple dishes.

PREPARATION TIME: 5 minutes, plus 30 minutes standing

COOKING TIME: 17 minutes

SERVES 4

4 fish fillets, such as cod, haddock or halibut, about 125 g (4½ oz) each, or 4 small sea fish such as red mullet, cleaned
Salt and black pepper
½ tablespoon olive oil
For the sauce:
3 tablespoons tahini paste
3 tablespoons lemon juice
Grated zest of ½ lemon
3 tablespoons virtually fat-free Greek yoghurt
1 clove garlic, finely crushed
4 tablespoons finely chopped fresh parsley
To garnish: lemon slices and a few sprigs of fresh parsley

1 Sprinkle the fillets on both sides, or whole fish inside and out, with a little salt and leave to stand for about 30 minutes.
2 Heat the oven to 230°C (450°F, gas mark 8) and heat the grill. Pat the fish dry, brush with oil and grill for 6-7 minutes on each side until they are almost cooked through.
3 Meanwhile, whisk or process all the sauce ingredients, except the parsley, with 2-3 tablespoons of water to make a smooth sauce. Add the parsley and mix well.
4 Place the fish in an ovenproof dish, spoon the sauce over them and bake for 10 minutes, or until the sauce bubbles and starts to brown. Serve garnished with slices of lemon and a few sprigs of fresh parsley.

Variation: in the Middle East, during the pomegranate season, the dish is traditionally decorated with the fruit's jewel-like red seeds.

Serving suggestion: a salad of black olives, tomatoes and red onions with sprigs of basil.

Baked halibut with steamed pak choi

Nutrients per serving

- Calories 250
- Carbohydrate 7 g
- Protein 32 g
- Fat 11 g (including saturated fat 4 g)

Soy sauce and ginger bring a taste of the Orient to a simple fish dish, accompanied by sesame-flavoured Chinese cabbage.

PREPARATION TIME: 15 minutes, plus 30 minutes marinating
COOKING TIME: 12-15 minutes
SERVES 4

4 halibut steaks, about 125 g (4½ oz) each
Grated zest and juice of 1 orange
1 fresh red chilli, deseeded and chopped
2 teaspoons clear honey
1 tablespoon soy sauce
1 tablespoon rice vinegar
1 star anise
6 small pak choi, cut in half lengthways
1 teaspoon sesame oil
1 teaspoon lemon juice
Salt and black pepper
For the marinade:
2 cloves garlic, chopped
1 tablespoon grated ginger
1 tablespoon olive oil

1. Heat the oven to 200°C (400°F, gas mark 6). To make the marinade, combine the garlic, ginger, oil and orange zest in a small bowl, then rub the mixture over the halibut steaks. Allow them to marinate for 30 minutes.
2. Lay the halibut in a roasting tin. Mix together the orange juice, chilli, honey, soy sauce and vinegar, pour the liquid around the fish and add the star anise. Cover the tin tightly with foil and bake for 12 minutes. Remove the tin from the oven and leave the fish to rest for 5 minutes.
3. Meanwhile, bring 5 cm (2 in) of water to the boil in a steamer, or a saucepan large enough to hold a basket that all the pak choi will fit into. Steam the pak choi for 3-5 minutes until just tender but retaining a slight crunch.
4. Drain the pak choi halves, drizzle them with sesame oil and lemon juice and season to taste. Transfer them to four plates, top with the halibut and pour the pan juices over.

Tip: pak choi is a Chinese cabbage with long, green or white stems. If it is not available, shredded green cabbage can be used instead.
Serving suggestion: fragrant Thai rice.

STAR ANISE

Lemon sole in a parcel

A chilli flavour contrasts with cool, creamy coconut in the marinade for this Parsee fish dish. It is traditionally baked wrapped in a banana leaf, but you can use greaseproof paper and foil instead.

PREPARATION TIME: 20 minutes, plus 1-2 hours, or overnight, marinating
COOKING TIME: 30 minutes
SERVES 2

2 whole lemon soles, or pomfrets, about 250 g (9 oz) each, cleaned

For the marinade:

25 g (1 oz) unsweetened desiccated coconut
1-2 green chillies, deseeded and roughly chopped
1 tablespoon roughly chopped fresh coriander
2 cloves garlic, roughly chopped
1 tablespoon roughly chopped ginger
Juice of 1 lemon
Salt

To garnish: lemon wedges and fresh coriander leaves

1 Put a kettle of water on to boil. To make the marinade, place the coconut in a small heatproof bowl, pour 150 ml (5 fl oz) of boiling water over it and leave it to soak for 10-15 minutes.
2 Meanwhile, make three slits, 5 cm (2 in) apart, on both sides of each fish to allow the marinade to penetrate, then set the fish aside in a deep glass or china dish.
3 Put the reconstituted coconut into a blender with the chillies, coriander, garlic, ginger and lemon juice and add salt to taste. Process until fairly smooth, or blend with a hand-held mixer.
4 Pour half the marinade over the fish, making sure it covers them, then turn the fish over and repeat with the remaining marinade. Cover the dish and leave the fish to marinate for 1-2 hours in a cool place, or overnight in the refrigerator.
5 Bring the fish to room temperature before cooking, if necessary. Heat the oven to 180°C (350°F, gas mark 4).
6 Line a piece of foil large enough to enclose one fish with greaseproof paper. Lift a fish from the marinade and lay it in the middle of the wrapping, then bring up the sides of the paper and foil and twist them together securely. Do the same with the remaining fish.
7 Lay the parcels side by side in an ovenproof dish and cook them in the centre of the oven for 20 minutes. Undo the foil and bake for a further 10 minutes, or until the flesh flakes easily when tested with a knife.
8 Lift the fish carefully from the foil parcels and transfer them to serving plates. Garnish with lemon wedges and coriander leaves.

Serving suggestion: boiled new potatoes and a green vegetable salad.

Nutrients per serving

- Calories 290
- Carbohydrate 2 g
- Protein 45 g
- Fat 12 g (including saturated fat 7 g)

Poached fish in **Oriental broth**

A spiced broth makes a sophisticated main-course soup of lightly cooked fish fillets and crisp vegetables.

PREPARATION TIME: 15 minutes
COOKING TIME: 20 minutes
SERVES 4

500 g (1 lb 2 oz) cod, haddock or plaice fillets
100 g (3½ oz) broccoli, broken into tiny florets
4 spring onions, thinly sliced
50 g (1¾ oz) Chinese leaves, shredded
100 g (3½ oz) carrots, coarsely grated
½ teaspoon sesame oil

For the broth:
300 ml (10 fl oz) chicken stock
2 tablespoons rice wine, or dry sherry
2 tablespoons soy sauce
5 mm (¼ in) cube ginger, thinly sliced
2 cloves garlic, crushed
2 slices of lemon

1 To make the broth, put the stock, rice wine or sherry, soy sauce, ginger, garlic and lemon into a wok or wide non-corrosive saucepan and bring to the boil.
2 Measure the thickness of the fish at its thickest point. Reduce the heat under the broth and slip the fish in, making sure it is completely submerged. If necessary, add a little more stock or water. Poach the fish for 10 minutes for every 2.5 cm (1 in) of thickness, or until it turns opaque and the flesh flakes easily.
3 Carefully lift the fish from the broth, remove the skins and divide the flesh between four shallow bowls. Cover and keep them warm.
4 Return the broth to the boil and add the broccoli, spring onions, Chinese leaves and carrots in this order at 30 second intervals and cook for a total of 2-3 minutes, or until the vegetables are tender but still crisp. Remove with a slotted spoon and divide them between the bowls with the fish.
5 Boil the broth for 30 seconds. Remove the ginger and lemon slices and stir in the sesame oil. Pour the broth over the fish and vegetables and serve.

Nutrients per serving

- Calories 141
- Carbohydrate 3 g
- Protein 26 g
- Fat 2 g (no saturated fat)

Prawn fajitas with tomato salsa

This Tex-Mex-style dish is an informal affair, with everyone assembling their own fajitas.

PREPARATION TIME: 40 minutes
COOKING TIME: 10-12 minutes
SERVES 4

PRAWN FAJITAS WITH TOMATO SALSA

1 tablespoon sunflower oil
1-2 fresh red chillies, deseeded and very finely chopped
2 teaspoons cumin seeds
2 cloves garlic, crushed
125 g (4½ oz) red onions, finely chopped
2 orange or yellow peppers, finely chopped
2 red peppers, finely chopped
300 g (10½ oz) courgettes, diced
200 g (7 oz) baby sweetcorn, cut into 1 cm (½ in) chunks
8 large soft flour tortillas
450 g (1 lb) large, cooked, peeled prawns, defrosted if frozen
2 tablespoons chopped fresh coriander
Salt and black pepper
300 g (10½ oz) low-fat Greek yoghurt

For the salsa:
500 g (1 lb 2 oz) beef tomatoes, peeled, deseeded and finely chopped
75 g (2¾ oz) onions, very finely diced
1-2 fresh red chillies, deseeded and very finely chopped
1 tablespoon chopped fresh coriander
1 clove garlic, crushed
1 tablespoon freshly squeezed lemon or lime juice

To garnish: sprigs of fresh coriander and lime

1. Heat the oven to 190°F (375°C, gas mark 5). Mix together all the salsa ingredients. Place in a serving bowl and set aside.
2. Heat the oil in a wok and stir-fry the chilli, cumin seeds, garlic, onions and peppers over a high heat for 5-6 minutes until softened. Add the courgettes and baby sweetcorn and continue to stir-fry for 4-5 minutes until they are just tender.
3. Wrap the tortillas in foil and heat them in the oven for 5 minutes.
4. Add the prawns to the vegetables and stir-fry until they are heated through. Stir in the coriander and season to taste. Pile onto a large serving platter.
5. To serve, each diner spreads a spoonful of yoghurt over a warm tortilla and tops it with some of the prawn mixture and a spoonful of the salsa. The tortillas are then rolled up and eaten with the fingers, or you can use a knife and fork. Serve with any remaining salsa, garnished with coriander and lime.

Nutrients per serving

- Calories 549
- Carbohydrate 83 g
- Protein 37 g
- Fat 10 g (including saturated fat 3 g)

SEAFOOD IN CHIVE PANCAKES
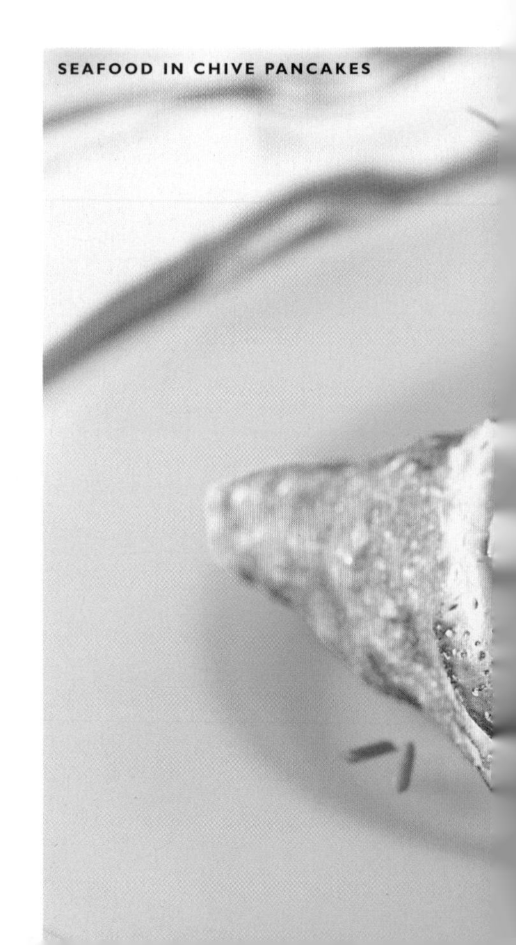

Seafood in chive pancakes

These fluffy pancakes, speckled with herbs, have a delicious monkfish and shellfish filling.

PREPARATION TIME: 20 minutes plus 20 minutes resting
COOKING TIME: 20 minutes
SERVES 4

For the batter:
125 g (4½ oz) plain white flour
1 egg white
300 ml (10 fl oz) skimmed milk
2 tablespoons chopped fresh chives
Salt and black pepper
1 tablespoon oil for greasing

For the filling:
50 g (1¾ oz) onions, thinly sliced
100 ml (3½ fl oz) fish stock
350 g (12 oz) monkfish
150 g (5½ oz) queen scallops
2 teaspoons cornflour
125 g (4½ oz) low-fat fromage frais
125 g (4½ oz) large, cooked, peeled prawns, defrosted if frozen
2 teaspoons wholegrain mustard
A pinch of freshly grated nutmeg

To garnish: fresh chives

1. To make the batter, place the flour, egg white, milk, chives and salt and pepper in a food processor and blend until smooth, or whisk in a bowl with a hand-held mixer until smooth and bubbly. Leave the batter to rest for 20 minutes.
2. Heat a small nonstick frying pan over a medium heat and brush with a little oil. Pour in just enough batter to cover the base, swirling it around to form an even layer. Cook the pancake until it is golden, then turn it over and cook the other side in the same way. Transfer to a plate and cover with kitchen paper to keep it warm. Make seven more pancakes, lightly greasing the pan as necessary.
3. To make the filling, place the onions and stock in a saucepan over a high heat, stir and boil until the liquid is reduced by half.
4. Remove any grey membrane from the monkfish and cut the flesh into bite-size pieces. Remove any corals from the scallops. Put the cornflour in a bowl and toss the monkfish and scallops in it, coating them evenly. Stir in the fromage frais.
5. Add the monkfish to the stock mixture, stirring gently so that the fish does not break up, and simmer, uncovered, for 3 minutes, or until the flesh turns opaque and flakes easily.
6. Add the scallops and simmer for 2-3 minutes. Stir in the prawns and cook for 1 minute, or until they are heated through. Add the mustard, nutmeg and salt and pepper to taste.
7. Divide the seafood mixture between the pancakes, then fold them into cones. Lay two on each plate and spoon over any extra sauce. Garnish with chives and serve.

Serving suggestion: Sauté of Spring Vegetables with Herbs (page 232).

Nutrients per serving

- Calories 335
- Carbohydrate 35 g
- Protein 38 g
- Fat 6 g (including saturated fat 1 g)

Grilled salmon with anchovy dressing

Salty anchovies enhance the subtle flavour of salmon. Lemon and fresh parsley add zest.

PREPARATION TIME: 10 minutes
COOKING TIME: 10 minutes
SERVES 4

4 salmon fillets, about 100 g (3½ oz) each
Olive oil for greasing
For the dressing:
2 canned anchovy fillets, drained
1 clove garlic, crushed
Finely grated zest of 1 lemon
1 tablespoon lemon juice
2 tablespoons chopped fresh parsley
Salt and black pepper
2 tablespoons extra virgin olive oil
To garnish: sprigs of fresh flat-leaved parsley

1. To make the dressing, pat the anchovy fillets dry, then chop them finely. Place them in a bowl with the garlic, lemon zest and juice and parsley. Season to taste and whisk in the oil. As anchovies are salty, you may not need any salt.
2. Place a ridged, iron grill pan or a large nonstick frying pan over a medium-high heat. Brush the pan with oil and season the salmon with salt and pepper on both sides.
3. When the pan is very hot, place the fillets on it, flesh side down, and cook for 6 minutes, then turn them over and continue cooking for a further 4 minutes, or until the flesh is opaque.
4. Arrange on four warm plates, drizzle the dressing over them and garnish with a sprig of parsley. Serve the salmon hot or at room temperature.
Serving suggestion: new potatoes and a green salad lightly dressed with lemon juice.

Nutrients per serving

- Calories 261
- Carbohydrate 1 g
- Protein 15 g
- Fat 22 g (including saturated fat 9 g)

Tuna kebabs with lime marinade

Sharp lime juice and sweet demerara sugar combine to make a flavour-packed marinade.

PREPARATION TIME: 10 minutes, plus 30 minutes or up to 12 hours marinating
COOKING TIME: 5-6 minutes
SERVES 4

500 g (1 lb 2 oz) tuna steak
For the marinade:
1 teaspoon finely chopped fresh coriander
Grated zest and juice of 2 limes
4 teaspoons demerara sugar
1 tablespoon olive oil
Salt and black pepper
To garnish: lime wedges and fresh coriander leaves

1. Cut the tuna into 2.5 cm (1 in) cubes.
2. In a large china or glass bowl, mix together all the marinade ingredients. Carefully stir in the tuna, cover and marinate the fish in the refrigerator for at least 30 minutes, or up to 12 hours.
3. When ready to cook, heat the grill to its highest setting. Remove the tuna from the marinade and divide it between eight skewers.
4. Grill the kebabs for 5-6 minutes, basting frequently with the remaining marinade and turning them over a few times so that the fish is evenly cooked and flakes easily. Garnish with lime wedges and coriander.
Tip: if using bamboo or wooden skewers, soak them in cold water for 30 minutes beforehand.
Serving suggestion: saffron rice.

Nutrients per serving

- Calories 219
- Carbohydrate 6 g
- Protein 30 g
- Fat 9 g (including saturated fat 2 g)

Baked cod with a horseradish crust

These robustly flavoured fillets are baked on a bed of lemon.

PREPARATION TIME: 10 minutes
COOKING TIME: 15-20 minutes
SERVES 4

2 lemons
75 g (2¾ oz) fresh wholemeal breadcrumbs
2 tablespoons grated fresh horseradish, drained if bottled
3 tablespoons chopped fresh parsley
2 spring onions, finely chopped
Salt and black pepper
4 cod fillets, skin on, about 125 g (4½ oz) each
To garnish: paprika

Low-fat tip

Do not use creamed horseradish or horseradish sauce with the cod as it can be high in fat. If you cannot find fresh horseradish, use fresh ginger instead.

TUNA KEBABS WITH LIME MARINADE

1 Heat the oven to 220°C (425°F, gas mark 7). Finely grate the zest from one lemon into a bowl. Stir in the breadcrumbs, horseradish, parsley and spring onions, then season well. Squeeze the juice from the grated lemon and stir it in.
2 Cut the remaining lemon into slices and arrange them on the base of a shallow ovenproof dish. Place the cod on top, skin side down, and spoon the crumb mixture over each fillet, pressing it down lightly.
3 Bake the fish for 15-20 minutes until the flesh turns opaque and flakes easily. Serve sprinkled with paprika.

Serving suggestion: asparagus.

Nutrients per serving

- Calories 177
- Carbohydrate 16g
- Protein 26g
- Fat 1g (no saturated fat)

GRILLED SALMON WITH ANCHOVY DRESSING

BAKED COD WITH A HORSERADISH CRUST

Mediterranean fish casserole

Nutrients per serving

- Calories 232
- Carbohydrate 9 g
- Protein 31 g
- Fat 8 g (including saturated fat 2 g)

Hearty fish steaks baked with garlic, tomatoes and herbs make a dish redolent of the Mediterranean coast.

PREPARATION TIME: 20 minutes
COOKING TIME: 20-25 minutes
SERVES 4

2 teaspoons olive oil
1 tablespoon dry white wine or stock
2 sticks celery, thinly sliced
1 clove garlic, thinly sliced
150 g (5½ oz) red onions, thinly sliced
600 g (1 lb 5 oz) plum tomatoes
1 lemon, thinly sliced
1 tablespoon tomato purée
1 teaspoon sugar, optional
4 fish steaks, such as swordfish or tuna, about 125 g (4½ oz) each
3 sprigs fresh rosemary
3 tablespoons chopped fresh oregano, or 1 tablespoon dried
Salt and black pepper
To garnish: sprigs of fresh rosemary and chopped fresh oregano

1. Heat the oil and wine or stock in a flameproof casserole then add the celery, garlic and onions and fry for 5-6 minutes, stirring frequently, until they have softened.
2. Roughly chop the tomatoes (they can be peeled if you like) and add them to the casserole with the lemon, tomato purée and the sugar, if needed (it depends how acid the tomatoes are). Bring to the boil and simmer, stirring, for 2-3 minutes until the tomatoes begin to soften.
3. Arrange the fish in a single layer on top of the vegetable mixture. Tuck in the sprigs of rosemary, sprinkle with oregano and season to taste.
4. Cover the casserole and leave it to simmer for 10-15 minutes until the flesh is just firm, spooning the juices over the fish occasionally. Serve garnished with chopped oregano and a sprig of rosemary.

Tip: the olive oil can be omitted, if you prefer, but even a little helps to capture the Mediterranean flavour.

Serving suggestion: rice or crusty bread and a green salad, or a side dish of green vegetables such as Roasted Asparagus with Caramelised Shallot Dressing (page 76) or Braised Fennel (page 234).

Sea bass baked with **wine** and **fennel**

Nutrients per serving

- Calories 162
- Carbohydrate 1 g
- Protein 25 g
- Fat 4 g (including saturated fat 1 g)

Flavoured with capers, olives and white wine, this exotic but satisfying dish is surprisingly simple to make.

PREPARATION TIME: 15 minutes
COOKING TIME: 20 minutes
SERVES 4

125 g (4½ oz) fennel
2 shallots, finely sliced
4 skinned sea bass fillets, about 125 g (4½ oz) each
Salt and black pepper
1 lime
1-2 tablespoons capers
1 clove garlic, finely chopped
6 stoned black olives, finely diced
A pinch of paprika
150 ml (5 fl oz) dry white wine

1. Heat the oven to 220°C (425°F, gas mark 7). Trim the fennel, reserve the feathery fronds to use as a garnish and finely slice the rest. Arrange the sliced fennel in a shallow ovenproof dish large enough to take the fish fillets in a single layer. Add the shallots and lay the fish on top. Season with salt and pepper to taste.
2. Pare a few strips of lime zest to use as a garnish and grate the rest. Scatter the capers, garlic, olives, paprika and grated zest over the fish, then pour the wine over the top.
3. Cover the dish with a lid or foil and bake for 20 minutes, or until the fish turns opaque and flakes easily. Serve it hot, garnished with fronds of fennel, lime zest and paprika.

Variation: grey mullet can be substituted for the sea bass.

Serving suggestion: new potatoes and a medley of steamed vegetables such as carrots, cauliflower, mangetout and baby sweetcorn.

Trout baked with **apples** and **cider**

Nutrients per serving

- Calories 397
- Carbohydrate 9 g
- Protein 50 g
- Fat 16 g (including saturated fat 4 g)

The delicate flavours of the fruit and vegetables in cider turn rainbow trout into an impressive dish for entertaining.

PREPARATION TIME: 10 minutes
COOKING TIME: 30 minutes
SERVES 4

150 g (5½ oz) fennel, finely sliced
125 g (4½ oz) leeks, finely sliced
2 tart dessert apples, peeled, cored and diced
4 rainbow trout, about 250 g (9 oz) each
Salt and black pepper
300 ml (10 fl oz) dry cider
4 tablespoons half-fat crème fraîche
To garnish: chopped fresh parsley and chives, sprigs of fresh chervil and lemon wedges, optional

1. Heat the oven to 190°C (375°F, gas mark 5).
2. Cover the base of a shallow ovenproof dish or roasting tin, wide enough to take the fish in a single layer, with the fennel, leeks and apples. Place the trout on top, season generously and pour the cider over. Cover the dish tightly with a lid or foil and bake for 15-20 minutes until the trout is just tender and flakes easily.
3. Transfer the fish to a hot serving plate, cover with foil and keep it warm.
4. Pour the contents of the baking dish into a small saucepan and bring to the boil, then reduce the heat and simmer for 5 minutes until the liquid has reduced a little: it remains quite a thin liquor. Season to taste and stir in the crème fraîche.
5. Serve the trout sprinkled with herbs, with the sauce spooned alongside and garnished with lemon, if liked.

   Serving suggestion: carrots and mashed potatoes.

Seafood casserole with **saffron** and **vegetables**

A cross between a chowder and a casserole, this dish with the wonderful fragrance of saffron is elegant enough to serve on special occasions.

PREPARATION TIME: 15 minutes
COOKING TIME: 30-35 minutes
SERVES 4

1 tablespoon olive oil
150 g (5½ oz) carrots, thickly sliced
2 sticks celery, chopped
150 g (5½ oz) onions, sliced
1 clove garlic, crushed
350 g (12 oz) new potatoes, halved if large
300 ml (10 fl oz) vegetable or fish stock
10-12 strands saffron
500 g (1 lb 2 oz) cod, haddock or salmon
150 g (5½ oz) green beans, halved
125 ml (4 fl oz) dry white wine
1 tablespoon cornflour
1 tablespoon skimmed milk
125 g (4½ oz) cooked, peeled prawns, defrosted if frozen
Salt and black pepper
2 tablespoons chopped fresh herbs, such as chives, parsley, tarragon or thyme

1. Heat the oil in a large, heavy-based flameproof casserole. Add the carrots, celery and onions, cover the casserole and cook over a low heat for 5 minutes.
2. Add the garlic and potatoes and continue to cook, uncovered, for a further 5 minutes, stirring occasionally.
3. Pour in the stock and stir in the saffron. Cover and simmer for 10 minutes, or until the vegetables are just beginning to soften.
4. Meanwhile, skin the fish, remove any bones and cut it into 4 cm (1½ in) chunks. Add the fish, beans and wine to the casserole, cover and simmer for a further 7 minutes.
5. Dissolve the cornflour in the milk, then gently stir it into the casserole, along with the prawns. Allow the sauce to bubble gently and thicken slightly, taking care the fish does not break up and the prawns are warmed right through. Season to taste, stir in the herbs and serve.

Serving suggestion: some rice or fresh crusty bread to mop up the stew's tasty juices.

Nutrients per serving

- Calories 281
- Carbohydrate 23 g
- Protein 33 g
- Fat 5 g (including saturated fat 1 g)

poultry and game

Chicken with **asparagus** in a **white wine sauce**

Nutrients per serving

- Calories 224
- Carbohydrate 15 g
- Protein 33 g
- Fat 2 g (no saturated fat)

Poached chicken served with a light asparagus sauce proves that fine ingredients need only the simplest cooking to make a delicious meal.

PREPARATION TIME: 5 minutes
COOKING TIME: 25 minutes
SERVES 4

4 skinned, boned chicken breasts, about 125 g (4½ oz) each
1 bay leaf
2 shallots, finely chopped
150 ml (5 fl oz) chicken stock
125 ml (4 fl oz) dry white wine
225 g (8 oz) asparagus, cut into 7.5 cm (3 in) lengths
2 tablespoons cornflour
150 ml (5 fl oz) skimmed milk
Salt and black pepper
To garnish: sprigs of fresh flat-leaved parsley

1. Place the chicken breasts in a single layer in a large frying pan with the bay leaf and shallots. Pour in the stock and wine and bring to the boil, then reduce the heat, cover and simmer for 20 minutes, turning the chicken over after 10 minutes.
2. Meanwhile, put a kettle on to boil. Cook the asparagus in a pan of lightly salted boiling water for 4-5 minutes until it is just tender when tested with a knife. Drain and refresh under cold running water, then drain again thoroughly and set aside.
3. Remove the chicken breasts from the frying pan and keep them warm. Blend the cornflour and milk together in a large jug. Strain the hot cooking liquid then whisk it into the jug. Return the sauce to the frying pan and boil, stirring continuously, until thickened and smooth. Season with salt and pepper to taste.
4. Stir the cooked asparagus into the sauce and heat it through for 1 minute. Serve the chicken breasts, spoon the sauce and asparagus over them, sprinkle them with pepper and garnish with sprigs of parsley.

Serving suggestion: boiled new potatoes and puréed carrots.

Chargrilled chicken with fresh mango salsa

Nutrients per serving

- Calories 185
- Carbohydrate 11 g
- Protein 31 g
- Fat 2 g (including saturated fat 1 g)

Sweet mangoes sharpened with chilli make a luscious dressing for lean chicken breasts, cooked in minutes.

PREPARATION TIME: 10 minutes, plus 1 hour chilling
COOKING TIME: 8 minutes
SERVES 4

4 skinned, boned chicken breasts, about 125 g (4½ oz) each
A little vegetable oil for brushing
For the salsa:
2 large juicy mangoes
Juice of 1 lime
1 green chilli, deseeded and finely chopped
2 tablespoons finely chopped fresh coriander
½ tablespoon grated ginger
Salt and black pepper
To garnish: sprigs of fresh coriander and fresh chives

1 First make the salsa to give it time to chill: peel the mangoes over a bowl to catch any juice. Cut the flesh away from the stone and dice it into 5 mm (¼ in) cubes. Place the pieces in the bowl with any mango juice and the lime juice.
2 Stir the chilli into the diced mango along with the coriander and ginger. Add salt and pepper to taste, then cover the bowl and leave the salsa to chill for at least 1 hour to allow all the flavours to develop.
3 When you are ready to start cooking, place the chicken breasts one at a time between two sheets of cling film and flatten them lightly with a mallet or rolling pin.
4 Put a ridged, iron grill pan or a heavy-based nonstick frying pan over a high heat. Brush a little oil onto both sides of the chicken breasts, then chargrill or fry them for 4 minutes on each side. The juices must run clear when the breasts are pierced with a knife. Serve them hot with the chilled mango salsa.

Serving suggestion: mixed salad leaves or Roasted Asparagus with Caramelised Shallot Dressing (page 76).

Roasted lemon and **paprika poussins**

These young chickens, stuffed with lemon and flavoured with paprika, are equally enjoyable served hot, or cool with a salad.

PREPARATION TIME: 5 minutes
COOKING TIME: 45-50 minutes
SERVES 4

4 oven-ready poussins, about 400 g (14 oz) each
2 lemons, cut in half
1 clove garlic, crushed
2 tablespoons olive oil
2 teaspoons paprika
Salt and black pepper
To garnish: bay leaves and sprigs of fresh thyme

1. Heat the oven to 220°C (425°F, gas mark 7). Arrange the poussins breast side up in a non-corrosive roasting tin. Squeeze some of the juice from half a lemon over one poussin, then rub the bird all over with the lemon before stuffing the squeezed half inside its cavity. Repeat with the remaining birds and lemon halves.
2. Rub each bird with a little of the garlic, then coat them with olive oil and sprinkle them all over with paprika and salt and pepper to taste.
3. Roast the birds in the centre of the oven for 15 minutes. Turn them breast side down and roast for a further 15 minutes. Finally, stand the birds upright, baste them liberally with the pan juices and roast for a further 15-20 minutes until the juices run clear when each is pierced with a knife in the thickest part of a thigh.
4. Remove the poussins from the oven, discard the lemons and leave the birds in a warm place for 5 minutes.
5. Meanwhile, skim off any excess fat from the pan juices and transfer the dark lemony gravy to a jug to serve separately. Garnish the poussins with bay leaves and thyme, then serve.

Serving suggestion: serve hot with a selection of cooked vegetables, or chilled with crusty bread, cos lettuce, cucumber, spring onions and finely chopped fresh mint.

Nutrients per serving

- Calories 285
- Carbohydrate 1 g
- Protein 47 g
- Fat 10 g (including saturated fat 2 g)

Chicken braised in yoghurt and coconut

This superbly flavoured dish uses toasted spices to give pungency to a yoghurt sauce enriched with coconut.

PREPARATION TIME: 20 minutes
COOKING TIME: 45 minutes
SERVES 4

8 skinned chicken thighs on the bone, about 700 g (1 lb 9 oz) altogether
175 g (6 oz) onions, finely chopped
2 teaspoons garlic purée, or crushed garlic
2 teaspoons ginger purée, or grated ginger
½ teaspoon ground turmeric
50 g (1¾ oz) low-fat natural set yoghurt
2 teaspoons coriander seeds
1 teaspoon cumin seeds
1 dried red chilli, chopped, or ¼ red pepper, deseeded and cut into strips
2.5 cm (1 in) cinnamon stick, broken in half
Salt
40 g (1½ oz) coconut milk powder
1 tablespoon sunflower oil
5-6 large cloves garlic, finely sliced
1 fresh red chilli, deseeded and sliced
2 tablespoons chopped fresh coriander
1 tablespoon lemon juice
To garnish: sprigs of fresh coriander

1. Trim any excess fat from the thighs and put them into a heavy-based saucepan with the onions, garlic, ginger, turmeric and yoghurt, stirring until well blended. Place the pan over a medium heat and bring to the boil. Reduce the heat, cover and simmer for 20 minutes, stirring occasionally.
2. To toast the spices, heat a small, heavy-based frying pan over a medium heat. Add the coriander and cumin seeds, dried chilli or red pepper and cinnamon and dry-fry them, stirring continuously, for up to 1 minute, or until they release their aromas. Turn off the heat and continue to stir the spices for a few seconds, then transfer them to a plate and allow to cool. When they are cool, grind them finely in a spice mill or with a pestle and mortar.
3. After the chicken has simmered for 20 minutes, increase the heat slightly, uncover and cook for 5 minutes, stirring frequently, or until the sauce in the pan reduces to a thick paste. Meanwhile, put a kettle on to boil.
4. Stir in the toasted spices and a pinch of salt, then reduce the heat and simmer, stirring, for 3-4 minutes.
5. Blend the coconut milk powder with 300 ml (10 fl oz) of boiling water, then stir it into the chicken mixture and continue simmering, uncovered, for 6-8 minutes, stirring occasionally, until the juices run clear when the chicken is pierced with a knife.
6. Meanwhile, in a small pan, heat the oil over a low heat and fry the garlic until it has browned slightly. Add the fresh chilli and cook for 30 seconds, then add them to the chicken.
7. Reserve a little of the chopped coriander and stir the remainder into the chicken mixture with the lemon juice. Remove the pan from the heat, sprinkle the chicken with the reserved chopped coriander, garnish with sprigs of coriander and serve.

Variation: boned chicken can be used instead of chicken thighs with bones, though it has less flavour. If using boned meat, reduce the initial cooking time by 15 minutes.

Serving suggestion: naans, chapattis or boiled long-grain rice, and Brussels Sprouts with Mustard (page 234).

Nutrients per serving

- Calories 373
- Carbohydrate 10 g
- Protein 36 g
- Fat 22 g (including saturated fat 9 g)

Poussins with a **spicy fruit** and **vegetable stuffing**

Nutrients per serving

- Calories 302
- Carbohydrate 20 g
- Protein 28 g
- Fat 14 g (including saturated fat 6 g)

Indian royal cooks devised this dish of marinated baby chickens stuffed with spiced vegetables and dried fruits.

PREPARATION TIME: 1 hour, plus overnight marinating
COOKING TIME: 55 minutes
SERVES 4

2 oven-ready poussins, about 400 g (14 oz) each
1 tablespoon unsalted butter
For the marinade:
1½ tablespoons korma curry powder
2 teaspoons garlic purée, or crushed garlic
2 teaspoons ginger purée, or grated ginger
75 g (2¾ oz) natural set yoghurt
Salt and black pepper
2 teaspoons white poppy seeds
2 teaspoons sesame seeds

For the stuffing:
1 tablespoon unsalted butter
1 green chilli, deseeded and chopped
1 teaspoon ginger purée, or grated ginger
50 g (1¾ oz) onions, finely chopped
25 g (1 oz) flaked rice, or fresh breadcrumbs
50 g (1¾ oz) ready-to-eat dried apricots, chopped
25 g (1 oz) seedless raisins
50 g (1¾ oz) sweetcorn kernels, drained if canned or defrosted if frozen
1 tablespoon chopped fresh coriander
1 tablespoon fromage frais
50 g (1¾ oz) button mushrooms, finely chopped
To garnish: a few sprigs of fresh coriander

1 Take all the skin off the poussins, using a cloth to pull back the skin, which is slippery to hold.
2 To make the marinade, stir the curry powder, garlic, ginger and yoghurt together in a large bowl and season with salt to taste. Finely grind

the poppy and sesame seeds in a spice mill, or with a pestle and mortar, then stir them into the yoghurt marinade.

3 Add the poussins to the bowl, rubbing the marinade all over them, inside and out. Cover and marinate in the refrigerator overnight.
4 Next day, bring the birds to room temperature. Heat the oven to 190°C (375°F, gas mark 5).
5 To make the stuffing, melt half the butter over a medium-low heat and sauté the chilli, ginger and onions for 3-4 minutes until the onions are soft.
6 Rinse the flaked rice, if using, with cold water to moisten it. Add the rice or breadcrumbs to the onion mixture with the apricots, raisins and sweetcorn. Cook for 5 minutes, stirring, then stir in the coriander, fromage frais, mushrooms and salt and pepper to taste. Remove from the heat and set aside to cool completely.
7 Stuff the poussins, packing the filling in tightly. Tie the birds' legs together with string.
8 In a flameproof casserole large enough to hold the poussins in one layer, melt the rest of the butter over a medium-high heat and fry the birds all over until browned. Cover with the lid or foil, making sure that the foil does not touch the birds, transfer to the oven and roast for 20 minutes.
9 Uncover the poussins and pour 100 ml (3½ fl oz) of warm water into the casserole, but not over the birds. Continue cooking for 20 minutes, basting frequently.
10 Put the poussins on a board and cut them in half lengthways with poultry shears or a carving knife. Put half a bird on each plate and strain the cooking juices over them (the liquid will be absorbed if the birds are really hot). Garnish with sprigs of coriander and serve.

Serving suggestion: complete the meal with Pilau or Cardamom Rice (page 224) and a salad.

Chilled chicken with a **herb** and **tomato sauce**

The smooth, creamy sauce sets off the juicy texture of poached chicken. It is an ideal dish for easy entertaining.

PREPARATION TIME: 5-10 minutes, plus 15-20 minutes cooling

COOKING TIME: 20-25 minutes

SERVES 4

4 skinned, boned chicken breasts, about 125 g (4½ oz) each
1 lemon
1 bay leaf, crumbled, or 1 bouquet garni
1 teaspoon black peppercorns
100 ml (3½ fl oz) dry white wine, or 75 ml (2½ fl oz) dry sherry

For the sauce:
3-4 tablespoons chopped mixed fresh herbs, such as basil, chervil, dill, oregano and parsley
4 teaspoons sun-dried tomato paste
225 g (8 oz) Greek yoghurt
Salt and black pepper

To garnish: a few sprigs of fresh chervil
To serve: mixed salad leaves and radishes

1 Place the chicken breasts in a single layer in a saucepan or flameproof casserole. Cut two slices from the lemon and add them to the chicken with the bay leaf or bouquet garni, peppercorns and wine or sherry.
2 Add enough cold water to cover the chicken, cover the pan, and bring the liquid to the boil. Reduce the heat and poach the chicken for 20-25 minutes until tender and the juices run clear when the breasts are pierced with a knife at their thickest point.
3 Meanwhile, to make the sauce, stir together the herbs, tomato paste and yoghurt in a bowl. Squeeze the juice from the remainder of the lemon and add it, a little at a time, until the sauce has the desired sharpness and texture. Add seasoning to taste, then chill until required.
4 Remove the chicken from the cooking liquid, pat dry with kitchen paper and leave to cool for 15-20 minutes, then chill if not serving at once.
5 To serve, cut the cooled chicken breasts into strips and arrange them on a mixed salad. Spoon the sauce over, garnish with sprigs of chervil and serve.

Tip: save the strained poaching liquid to use as chicken stock in other recipes. Allow it to cool, then chill and lift off any fat. Refrigerate for up to two days or freeze for up to three months.

Nutrients per serving

- Calories 240
- Carbohydrate 3 g
- Protein 32 g
- Fat 9 g (including saturated fat 4 g)

Low-fat tip

Poaching is an effective way to reduce fat, and produces tender, moist meats especially suitable for serving cold.

Poached chicken with spring vegetables

Make the most of new season's vegetables with this simple all-in-one supper dish.

PREPARATION TIME: 10 minutes
COOKING TIME: 25 minutes
SERVES 4

4 skinned, boned chicken breasts, about 125 g (4½ oz) each
900 ml (1 pint 12 fl oz) chicken stock
3 tablespoons dry sherry, or dry white wine
1 bouquet garni
650 g (1 lb 7 oz) mixed vegetables, such as asparagus, baby sweetcorn, broccoli, carrots, cauliflower, leeks and savoy cabbage
To garnish: chopped fresh parsley

1 Place the chicken breasts, stock, sherry or wine and the bouquet garni in a large flameproof casserole or a deep frying pan over a high heat. Bring the liquid to the boil, then lower the heat, cover and poach the chicken for 20 minutes, skimming off any foam as necessary.
2 Meanwhile, cut the vegetables into bite-size pieces.
3 After the chicken has been poaching for 20 minutes, add the vegetables to the pan, cover and continue cooking for 5 minutes, or until the vegetables are tender and the chicken juices run clear when the breasts are pierced.
4 Remove the bouquet garni. Spoon the broth and vegetables into large, shallow bowls and top with the chicken, whole or sliced as you prefer. Sprinkle with parsley and serve.

Nutrients per serving

- Calories 227
- Carbohydrate 6 g
- Protein 37 g
- Fat 5 g (including saturated fat 1 g)

Balsamic grilled chicken

Fast-grilled chicken breasts with a sweet sauce make a great dish for cooks in a hurry.

PREPARATION TIME: 5 minutes
COOKING TIME: 10-12 minutes
SERVES 4

4 skinned, boned chicken breasts, about 125 g (4½ oz) each
1 tablespoon butter, melted
1 clove garlic, crushed
Salt and black pepper
2 teaspoons clear honey
1 tablespoon lemon juice
1 tablespoon balsamic vinegar
To garnish: fresh flat-leaved parsley

1 Heat the grill to medium. Place the chicken breasts between two sheets of cling film and beat them with a rolling pin to an even thickness. Brush them with the butter and place in a wide flameproof dish or pan.
2 Sprinkle the chicken with the garlic, season lightly, then drizzle with the honey and lemon juice.
3 Place the chicken under the grill and cook for 5-6 minutes until golden, then spoon the balsamic vinegar over. Turn the breasts over, baste with the pan juices and continue grilling for 5-6 minutes until the chicken juices run clear when the breasts are pierced with a knife.
4 Serve the chicken breasts, spoon the pan juices over them and garnish with parsley.
Serving suggestion: roasted tomatoes and crusty bread.

Nutrients per serving

- Calories 226
- Carbohydrate 3 g
- Protein 40 g
- Fat 6 g (including saturated fat 3 g)

Chicken breasts with grape sauce

Good enough for a dinner party, this easy dish makes the most of the sharp, fresh flavour of white grapes.

Nutrients per serving
- Calories 368
- Carbohydrate 43 g
- Protein 29 g
- Fat 10 g (including saturated fat 2 g)

PREPARATION TIME: 35 minutes
COOKING TIME: 50 minutes
SERVES 4

1 kg (2 lb 4 oz) large white grapes
Finely grated zest and juice of 1 lemon
4 skinned, boned chicken breasts, about 125 g (4½ oz) each
Salt and black pepper
2 tablespoons olive oil
1 clove garlic, crushed
4 shallots, finely sliced
1 tablespoon plain white flour
4 tablespoons finely chopped fresh parsley
To garnish: a few sprigs of fresh parsley

1. Pull the grapes off the stalks and reserve 200 g (7 oz). Put the remainder in a saucepan with 3 tablespoons of water. Cover and simmer over a low heat for 20 minutes, or until they soften and burst. Crush them thoroughly to release their juice, then cover and simmer for a further 10 minutes. Strain and reserve 350 ml (12 fl oz) of the liquid, then set it aside.
2. Meanwhile, cover the reserved grapes with boiling water and leave for 15 seconds. Drain, peel and halve them and remove their pips. Toss them in half the lemon juice.
3. Cut the chicken breasts into 2.5 cm (1 in) pieces and season. Heat the oil in a saucepan over a medium heat. Add half the chicken and fry briskly until coloured. Remove, repeat with the remaining chicken and set both batches aside.
4. Reduce the heat, add the garlic and shallots to the pan and sauté for 3 minutes, or until soft. Sprinkle the flour in and cook, stirring, for a further 1 minute. Stir in the lemon zest, the remaining lemon juice and the grape liquid, then bring to the boil and cook for 2 minutes.
5. Reduce the heat and return the chicken, with its juices, to the pan. Season to taste and simmer for 7 minutes, or until the chicken is tender and the juices run clear when the breasts are pierced with a knife at their thickest point.
6. Add the halved grapes, their juice and the chopped parsley and adjust the seasoning. Serve hot, garnished with sprigs of parsley.

Serving suggestion: mashed potato, steamed broccoli and carrots.

CHICKEN BREASTS WITH GRAPE SAUCE

GRILLED CHICKEN, BROCCOLI AND PASTA GRATIN

Grilled chicken, broccoli and pasta gratin

Use leftover chicken for this simple family supper dish, made in less than 30 minutes.

PREPARATION TIME: 5 minutes
COOKING TIME: 20 minutes
SERVES 4

175 g (6 oz) dried pasta shapes, such as spirals (fusilli)
Salt and black pepper
225 g (8 oz) broccoli florets
2 sticks celery, thinly sliced
300 g (10½ oz) canned condensed half-fat tomato soup
200 ml (7 fl oz) skimmed milk
350 g (12 oz) skinned, boned cooked chicken
25 g (1 oz) fresh white breadcrumbs
¼ teaspoon dried herbes de Provence, or dried mixed herbs

1. Bring a large saucepan of water to the boil over a high heat, add the pasta and a pinch of salt and cook according to the instructions on the packet. Drain well and set aside.
2. Meanwhile, bring another pan of water to the boil, then add the broccoli, celery and a pinch of salt and boil for 5 minutes, or until the broccoli is just beginning to soften. Drain well, rinse under cold water, drain again and set aside.
3. Heat the grill to medium-high. Put the soup and milk into a large pan over a medium heat and bring to a simmer, stirring occasionally.
4. Trim any fat off the chicken and cut it into bite-size pieces. Add them to the tomato soup mixture along with the broccoli, celery and pasta, and reheat at a simmer for 5 minutes. Season to taste.
5. Pour the chicken mixture into four individual gratin dishes, or a single shallow 1.75 litre (3 pint) flameproof serving dish. Scatter the breadcrumbs and herbs evenly over the top, then grill until the sauce is bubbling and the crumbs are crisp and golden. Serve hot.

Variation: ring the changes by replacing the broccoli with slices of courgettes or cauliflower florets.

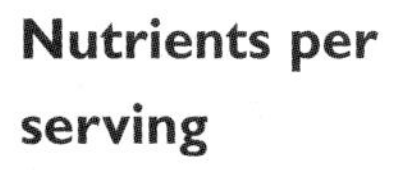

Nutrients per serving

- Calories 419
- Carbohydrate 57 g
- Protein 38 g
- Fat 4 g (including saturated fat 1 g)

Chicken chermoula with fruity couscous

Nutrients per serving

- Calories 361
- Carbohydrate 32 g
- Protein 31 g
- Fat 13 g (including saturated fat 2 g)

Chermoula, a North African mix of spices, gives a warming flavour to this chicken served on a mild and fruity salad.

PREPARATION TIME: 15 minutes, plus 2 hours marinating

COOKING TIME: 6-8 minutes

SERVES 4

4 skinned, boned chicken breasts, about 125 g (4½ oz) each

For the marinade:

2 tablespoons extra virgin olive oil
Pinch of cayenne pepper
1 tablespoon chopped fresh coriander
½ teaspoon ground coriander
½ teaspoon ground cumin
1 clove garlic, crushed
Juice of 1 lemon
1 teaspoon paprika
2 tablespoons chopped fresh parsley
Salt and black pepper

For the couscous:

175 g (6 oz) couscous
25 g (1 oz) ready-to-eat dried peaches, finely chopped
25 g (1 oz) raisins
175 g (6 oz) tomatoes, chopped
1 tablespoon chopped fresh coriander
1 tablespoon olive oil

To garnish: a few sprigs of fresh coriander

1. To make the marinade, put the olive oil, cayenne pepper, fresh and ground coriander, cumin, garlic, lemon juice, paprika and parsley in a shallow dish and stir until smooth. Season with salt and pepper to taste.
2. Cut several slashes in each chicken breast. Add the chicken to the marinade and turn it until it is coated all over, rubbing the marinade into the slashes. Cover and chill for 2 hours.
3. Put a kettle on to boil. Put the couscous into a pan and pour 300 ml (10 fl oz) of boiling water over it. Cover and leave for 5 minutes to fluff up.
4. Meanwhile, stir the peaches, raisins, tomatoes, coriander and olive oil into the couscous. Adjust the seasoning to taste, cover and set aside.
5. Heat the grill to medium. Grill the chicken breasts for 3-4 minutes on each side, until the juices run clear when they are pierced with a knife. Carve them into slices and serve on top of the fruity couscous, garnished with a few sprigs of coriander.

Braised chicken with **mushroom** and **lemon sauce**

Nutrients per serving

- Calories 180
- Carbohydrate 1 g
- Protein 28 g
- Fat 7 g (including saturated fat 2 g)

This simple casserole shows how just a few flavours can become a feast.

PREPARATION TIME: 15 minutes
COOKING TIME: 30-35 minutes
SERVES 4

1 tablespoon sunflower oil
4 skinned, boned chicken breasts, about 125 g (4½ oz) each
Salt and black pepper
Juice of 2 lemons
150 g (5½ oz) mushrooms, quartered
125 ml (4 fl oz) chicken stock
1 tablespoon chopped fresh thyme or marjoram
6 spring onions, finely chopped
To garnish: a few sprigs of fresh thyme

1 Heat the oil in a flameproof casserole large enough to hold the chicken breasts in a single layer. Add the chicken and brown them all over.
2 Season the chicken with salt and pepper, then add the lemon juice, mushrooms and stock. Cover and bring to the boil, then lower the heat and simmer, stirring occasionally, for 20 minutes, or until the chicken juices run clear when the breasts are pierced with a knife. Add a little more stock or water if the liquid is evaporating too quickly; there should be some liquid left when the chicken is cooked.
3 Remove the chicken breasts from the casserole and keep them warm. Boil the remaining cooking liquid until it thickens slightly. Stir in the chopped thyme or marjoram and spring onions and adjust the seasoning. Serve the chicken, spoon the mushroom sauce over it and garnish with sprigs of thyme.
Serving suggestion: steamed new potatoes and runner beans or fresh peas.

Spicy chicken with **tomatoes** and **spinach**

Chicken thighs are tastier than breast meat, and here their flavour is boosted with mild spices and vegetables.

PREPARATION TIME: 15 minutes
COOKING TIME: 30-35 minutes
SERVES 4

500 g (1 lb 2 oz) skinned, boned chicken thighs
150 g (5½ oz) onions, finely chopped
4 green cardamom pods, split open at the top
½ teaspoon cayenne pepper
5 cm (2 in) cinnamon stick, broken in half
2 teaspoons garlic purée, or crushed garlic
2 teaspoons ginger purée, or grated ginger
½ teaspoon turmeric
50 g (1¾ oz) low-fat natural yoghurt
Salt
250 g (9 oz) spinach, defrosted if frozen
225 g (8 oz) canned chopped tomatoes
50 g (1¾ oz) low-fat fromage frais
A pinch of garam masala

1 Trim any fat off the chicken thighs, then cut each in half. Put them into a large saucepan with the onions, cardamom, cayenne pepper, cinnamon, garlic, ginger, turmeric, yoghurt and salt to taste.
2 Place the pan over a medium-high heat and stir until the chicken starts sizzling. Continue to cook, stirring frequently, until the chicken begins to release its juices, then reduce the heat to low, cover the pan and simmer for 12 minutes, stirring occasionally.
3 Meanwhile, chop the spinach, discarding any thick stems. If using defrosted leaf spinach, place it between two plates and squeeze out the excess liquid before chopping.
4 Uncover the saucepan and increase the heat to medium-high. Continue cooking for 5-6 minutes until most of the liquid has evaporated and the sauce has thickened, stirring frequently to prevent it sticking to the bottom of the pan.
5 Stir the tomatoes into the chicken mixture and continue to cook, uncovered, for 1-2 minutes until they are well blended into the sauce.
6 Add the spinach in batches, stirring well. As soon as the first batch begins to wilt, add the next and keep stirring. Reduce the heat to low and cook, uncovered, for 5 minutes, or until the chicken juices run clear when the pieces are pierced.
7 Add the fromage frais and garam masala, stirring until well blended. Remove the cinnamon stick and serve.

Serving suggestion: spicy poppadoms, Pilau Rice (page 224) or boiled rice and naan breads.

Nutrients per serving

- Calories 220
- Carbohydrate 8 g
- Protein 28 g
- Fat 9 g (including saturated fat 3 g)

POPPADOMS

Chicken and cheese envelopes

Nutrients per serving

- Calories 310
- Carbohydrate 17 g
- Protein 50 g
- Fat 5 g (including saturated fat 2 g)

Crunchy-coated chicken breasts are filled with a luscious, but low-fat, cream cheese and marjoram stuffing.

PREPARATION TIME: 30-40 minutes
COOKING TIME: 20-25 minutes
SERVES 4

4 skinned, boned chicken breasts, about 175 g (6 oz) each
For the filling:
100 g (3½ oz) low-fat cream cheese
15 g (½ oz) fresh white breadcrumbs
1 egg yolk
2 tablespoons chopped fresh marjoram
Black pepper
For the coating:
1 tablespoon plain white flour
1 egg white
50 g (1¾ oz) fine fresh white breadcrumbs
1 teaspoon paprika
To garnish: 1 tablespoon chopped fresh flat-leaved parsley, plus a few whole sprigs

1. Heat the oven to 220°C (425°F, gas mark 7). Place each chicken breast between two sheets of cling film and flatten lightly with a rolling pin. Cut a deep pocket lengthways in each breast.
2. To make the filling, mix together the cream cheese, breadcrumbs, egg yolk, marjoram and pepper to taste. Spoon the mixture into the pockets in the chicken. Reshape each breast and secure the pockets with wooden cocktail sticks.
3. To make the coating, put the flour onto a large plate. Lightly beat the egg white in a shallow bowl. Spread the breadcrumbs out on a plate.
4. Dip each chicken breast in the flour, shaking off the excess. Brush with egg white, then coat well with breadcrumbs, gently pressing them on.
5. Place the breasts on a nonstick baking tray and sift the paprika lightly over them. Bake for 20-25 minutes until the chicken juices run clear when the breasts are pierced with a knife.
6. Remove the cocktail sticks from the chicken breasts, garnish them with the parsley and serve.

Serving suggestion: new potatoes with asparagus or mangetout. For a dinner party, try Roasted Asparagus with Caramelised Shallot Dressing (page 76).

Minted turkey and **mushroom kebabs**

These light, fresh-tasting kebabs flavoured with honey, lime juice and masses of fresh mint are perfect for a summer barbecue.

Nutrients per serving
- Calories 199
- Carbohydrate 13 g
- Protein 34 g
- Fat 2 g (including saturated fat 1 g)

PREPARATION TIME: 20 minutes, plus 1-2 hours, or overnight, marinating
COOKING TIME: 8-10 minutes
SERVES 4

500 g (1 lb 2 oz) lean turkey breast fillet
1 clove garlic, crushed
2 tablespoons clear honey
Finely grated zest and juice of 1 lime
3 tablespoons chopped fresh mint
150 g (5½ oz) low-fat natural yoghurt
300 g (10½ oz) button mushrooms
Salt and black pepper
To serve: lime wedges

1. Cut the turkey into bite-size pieces and place them in a bowl. Add the garlic, honey, lime zest and juice, mint and yoghurt. Toss well to coat evenly. Place the turkey in the refrigerator to marinate for 1-2 hours, or preferably overnight, to allow the flavours to develop.
2. Heat a barbecue or grill to a medium heat. Toss the mushrooms in the turkey mixture to coat them with the marinade. Thread the turkey pieces and mushrooms alternately onto skewers, then sprinkle with salt and pepper to taste.
3. Grill for 8-10 minutes, turning the skewers occasionally, until the turkey is golden brown and the juices run clear when the pieces are pierced with a knife. Serve with wedges of lime.

Serving suggestion: grilled pitta bread and a crisp salad.

ZESTING LIME

Braised turkey crown with apples and plums

Nutrients per serving

- Calories 410
- Carbohydrate 30 g
- Protein 47 g
- Fat 10 g (including saturated fat 2 g)

Turkey breast, gently braised to keep it moist and tender, is served with apples and plums for a special Sunday lunch, or a small Christmas dinner.

PREPARATION TIME: 25 minutes
COOKING TIME: 1 hour 50 minutes
SERVES 6

1½ tablespoons olive oil
1.8 kg (4 lb) turkey breast crown joint
400 g (14 oz) onions, cut into quarters
4 dessert apples such as Cox's or Russets, cut into quarters and cored
1 tablespoon caster sugar
400 g (14 oz) plums, halved and stoned
Salt and black pepper
225 ml (8 fl oz) dry white wine
225 ml (8 fl oz) concentrated turkey or chicken stock

For the garnish:
1 tablespoon caster sugar
3 plums, halved, stoned and thickly sliced
2 dessert apples, cored, quartered and thickly sliced

1. Heat the oven to 220°C (425°F, gas mark 7). Warm the oil in a large, lidded flameproof casserole over a medium heat. Add the turkey crown and lightly brown it all over, taking care not to let the oil burn. Transfer the turkey crown to a plate and set aside.
2. Add the onions and the apples to the oil remaining in the casserole, sprinkle them with the sugar and cook for 3-4 minutes until lightly browned, stirring occasionally. Then mix in the plums and season with salt and a generous grinding of pepper.
3. Place the turkey, flesh side up, on top of the fruit and onion mixture and pour in the wine. Bring to the boil, then remove the casserole from the heat, cover with a tight-fitting lid and transfer it to the oven.
4. After 15 minutes, baste the turkey well with the wine, then replace the lid and return the casserole to the oven. Reduce the temperature to 190°C (375°F, gas mark 5) and cook for a further 15 minutes. Baste the turkey again, then cook it for 45 minutes - 1 hour, basting every 15 minutes, until the turkey juices run clear when the breast is pierced at its thickest point with a knife.
5. Meanwhile, to prepare the garnish, pour 225 ml (8 fl oz) of water into a frying pan, add the sugar, stir to dissolve and bring to the boil. Then add the plum and apple slices. Reduce the heat to low and simmer for 2-3 minutes, until the fruit is just tender. Lift the fruit onto a plate. Boil the cooking juices until they become slightly syrupy, then return the fruit to the pan. Remove the pan from the heat and set aside.
6. When the turkey is cooked through, lift it onto a serving dish, cover and set aside in a warm place while you complete the sauce.
7. Purée the onion, fruit and cooking juices from the casserole dish in a food processor, or with a hand-held mixer, then pass the purée through a fine sieve into a saucepan. Stir in the stock and bring to the boil. Taste and adjust the seasoning, then pour the sauce into a serving jug.
8. Reheat the fruit garnish, spoon it around the turkey crown, and serve with the sauce.

Serving suggestion: new potatoes and green beans.

Turkey with smoked chilli sauce

Nutrients per serving
- Calories 156
- Carbohydrate 4 g
- Protein 33 g
- Fat 1 g (no saturated fat)

Dried chipotle chillies have an aromatic flavour quite unlike regular dried chillies. They make a hot, subtly smoky sauce, which enhances this turkey casserole.

PREPARATION TIME: 10 minutes, plus 30 minutes soaking
COOKING TIME: 50 minutes
SERVES 4

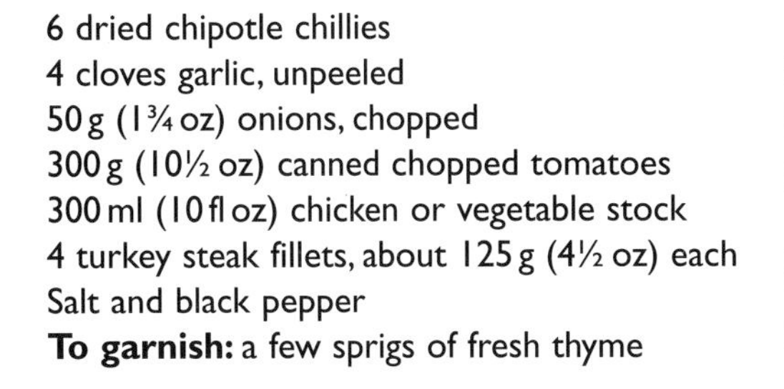

6 dried chipotle chillies
4 cloves garlic, unpeeled
50 g (1¾ oz) onions, chopped
300 g (10½ oz) canned chopped tomatoes
300 ml (10 fl oz) chicken or vegetable stock
4 turkey steak fillets, about 125 g (4½ oz) each
Salt and black pepper
To garnish: a few sprigs of fresh thyme

1. Heat the oven to 200°C (400°F, gas mark 6) and put a kettle on to boil. Put the dried chillies into a small heatproof bowl, cover them with 125 ml (4 fl oz) of boiling water and leave them to soak for 30 minutes.
2. Meanwhile, put the cloves of garlic on a baking tray and roast them for 10-15 minutes until tender. Remove the garlic and set aside to cool, but do not turn off the oven. When the soft garlic cloves are cool enough to handle, peel and chop them.
3. Line a sieve with clean muslin or kitchen paper and strain the soaking water from the chillies into a jug. Halve and deseed the chillies, then chop the flesh roughly and add it to the jug. Purée the chillies and water in a food processor or with a hand-held mixer.
4. Place the chilli purée, garlic, onions, tomatoes and stock in a large, lidded flameproof casserole and mix well. Add the turkey steaks and submerge them in the liquid. Cover with a tight-fitting lid and cook the casserole in the oven for 20-25 minutes.
5. Transfer the casserole to the hob. Remove the turkey steaks and keep them warm. Bring the sauce to the boil, then reduce the heat and simmer for 10 minutes, or until it has reduced to a thick coating consistency. Season with salt and pepper to taste. Pour the sauce liberally over the turkey steaks and serve them garnished with sprigs of thyme.

Tip: dried chipotle chillies from Mexico are available from large supermarkets and some delicatessens. If you cannot find them, you can get a similar smoky flavour by roasting a large fresh red chilli over a gas flame or in a 200°C (400°F, gas mark 6) oven until the skin is charred. Place it in a bowl and cover until cool enough to handle, then peel and deseed and proceed from Step 3.

Serving suggestion: plain or wholemeal pasta spirals or other shapes.

Turkey and red wine casserole

Nutrients per serving

- Calories 394
- Carbohydrate 12 g
- Protein 37 g
- Fat 8 g (including saturated fat 2 g)

Lean meat and chunky vegetables make this dish both healthy and satisfying.

PREPARATION TIME: 20 minutes
COOKING TIME: 1 hour
SERVES 4

2 tablespoons plain white flour
Salt and black pepper
500 g (1 lb 2 oz) turkey steaks
2 rashers back bacon, rind cut off
2 tablespoons olive oil
250 g (9 oz) baby carrots
1 stick celery, chopped
250 g (9 oz) button mushrooms
250 g (9 oz) shallots, left whole
750 ml (1 pint 7 fl oz) light red wine
600-700 ml (1 pint-1 pint 5 fl oz) chicken stock
4 large cloves garlic, chopped
1 large bouquet garni, or 4 sprigs of fresh parsley or thyme and 1 bay leaf tied together
To garnish: sprigs of fresh chervil or parsley

1 Put the flour, salt and pepper into a large plastic bag. Cut the turkey into 2.5 cm (1 in) cubes, add them to the bag and shake to coat them evenly.
2 Cut the bacon into strips and put them into a flameproof casserole over a very low heat. Fry the bacon until the fat melts in the pan, stirring frequently, then remove it and set it aside.
3 Add 1 tablespoon of the oil to the bacon fat and fry the turkey over a medium heat for 2-3 minutes until lightly browned all over: if it starts to burn, add 1 tablespoon of water to the pan and stir. Remove the turkey and set it aside.
4 Add the remaining oil to the casserole and cook the carrots, celery, mushrooms and shallots for about 5 minutes, or until softened and lightly browned. Remove them and set aside.
5 Increase the heat, add the wine and scrape up the sticky meat juices. Boil the mixture until it has reduced by half, then add the stock, return to the boil and cook until it has reduced by a third.
6 Return the bacon, turkey and vegetables to the casserole with the garlic and bouquet garni or the bunch of herbs. Reduce the heat and simmer, uncovered, for 20-30 minutes until the turkey is tender and the sauce is quite dark and syrupy. Remove the bouquet garni, or herbs, and serve garnished with fresh herbs.

Serving suggestion: Potatoes Boulangère (page 241) or French bread.

Creamy turkey and **mushroom** with **horseradish**

Nutrients per serving

- Calories 251
- Carbohydrate 19 g
- Protein 35 g
- Fat 4 g (including saturated fat 1 g)

The unexpected heat of horseradish sharpens the appetite for this lean yet filling turkey dish, quickly prepared and cooked.

PREPARATION TIME: 10 minutes
COOKING TIME: 20 minutes
SERVES 4

450 g (1 lb) skinned turkey fillets
1 tablespoon sunflower oil
75 g (2¾ oz) onions, chopped
225 g (8 oz) button mushrooms, sliced
50 g (1¾ oz) plain white flour
600 ml (1 pint) skimmed milk
1-2 tablespoons grated horseradish or horseradish relish (not creamed horseradish)
2 tablespoons chopped fresh parsley or chives
Salt and black pepper
To garnish: sprigs of fresh flat-leaved parsley

1. Cut the turkey into 1 cm (½ in) strips.
2. Heat 1 teaspoon of the oil in a large nonstick frying pan or wok and sauté the onions for 5 minutes, or until softened.
3. Lightly coat the turkey strips with another teaspoon of the oil, using your hands. Add them to the onions and stir-fry for 5 minutes.
4. Add the mushrooms and the remaining oil and stir-fry 2-3 minutes more.
5. Sprinkle in the flour. Cook for 1 minute, then gradually stir in the milk, scraping any bits from the pan. Bring it to the boil and cook for a further 1 minute, then reduce the heat to a simmer.
6. Stir in the horseradish to taste, add the herbs and season. Simmer for a further 5 minutes, then garnish with parsley and serve.

Variation: you can replace the horseradish with wholegrain mustard.

Serving suggestion: mashed sweet potatoes.

Simply delicious soft drinks

There are often times when you and your guests will prefer alcohol-free drinks. And there is no reason to feel that you are missing out on anything when you can have one of these sophisticated and unusual soft drinks.

Ginger and Lemongrass Cordial and Mint Lassi are natural partners for spicy Indian and other Oriental dishes. They are also good thirst-quenchers on hot summer days. Rhubarb Refresher, another hot-weather favourite, makes a pretty addition to any drinks tray.

Serve Cardamom-spiced Grape Juice over ice in the summer, or hot in winter to stave off the cold. And if you need a real 'comfort drink', the fragrance of hot cinnamon, cloves and raisins in Apple and Cinnamon Warmer will remind you of homely apple pie.

Good enough to eat

The Cardamom-spiced Grape Juice can also be used to make a lovely jelly. Simply add three sachets of powdered gelatine to the hot, strained juice, stir gently until it has dissolved then pour it into a jelly mould. Leave the mixture to cool, then chill until set.

Ginger and lemongrass cordial

This aromatic cordial is a great partner to Thai food.

PREPARATION TIME: 8 minutes
SERVES 10

175 g (6 oz) preserved stem ginger
4 tablespoons ginger syrup from the jar
1 tablespoon lemongrass purée
2 litres (3 pints 10 fl oz) sparkling mineral water
Ice cubes

1. Put the stem ginger, syrup, lemongrass purée and 150 ml (5 fl oz) of the sparkling mineral water into a blender and process to a smooth purée.
2. Pour into glasses, add mineral water to taste and ice cubes, and serve.

Tip: lemongrass purée is available in small jars from supermarkets.

Nutrients per serving

- Calories 75
- Carbohydrate 17 g
- No protein
- Fat 1 g (no saturated fat)

CARDAMOM-SPICED GRAPE JUICE (LEFT) AND GINGER AND LEMONGRASS CORDIAL

RHUBARB REFRESHER AND MINT LASSI

Cardamom-spiced grape juice

Spicy grape juice, served chilled or hot, is a drink for all seasons.

PREPARATION TIME: 5 minutes, plus 2 hours cooling and chilling, if serving cold
COOKING TIME: 15 minutes
SERVES 4

1 litre (1 pint 15 fl oz) red grape juice
Pared zest and juice of 1 large orange
A pinch of ground allspice
12 green cardamom pods, lightly crushed
10 cm (4 in) cinnamon stick
6 cloves
25 g (1 oz) caster sugar
Crushed ice, optional

1. Combine all the ingredients in a large saucepan and simmer over a medium heat for 5 minutes, then reduce the heat to low and continue simmering for 10 minutes. Remove from the heat and leave to cool for 1 hour.
2. Strain the juice into a jug. Chill for 1 hour, or serve over crushed ice.

Variation: to serve the drink hot, strain the juice as in Step 2, then reheat gently and serve it with a cinnamon stick in each glass to stir.

Nutrients per serving

- Calories 145
- Carbohydrate 37 g
- Protein 1 g
- No fat

Apple and cinnamon warmer

Raisins, cinnamon and cloves give this drink a festive aroma – perfect for a chilly evening.

PREPARATION TIME: 5 minutes, plus 1 hour soaking

COOKING TIME: 25 minutes

SERVES 4

10 cm (4 in) cinnamon stick
6 cloves
1 litre (1 pint 15 fl oz) unsweetened apple juice
2 tablespoons clear honey
25 g (1 oz) raisins
1 small dessert apple
2 tablespoons lemon juice

1 Tie the cinnamon stick and cloves in a small piece of muslin to make a spice bag.
2 Mix the apple juice, honey and raisins together in a large saucepan, add the spice bag and leave for 1 hour to allow the raisins to soften.
3 Peel, core and cut the apple into four rings. Put the pan of juice over a low heat, add the apple rings and simmer, without letting the mixture boil, for 20 minutes, or until the apples are just tender.
4 Remove from the heat, discard the spice bag and stir in the lemon juice. Place an apple ring in each tumbler and pour in the hot drink, making sure you place a teaspoon into each tumbler first to absorb the heat and prevent the glass from cracking. Serve piping hot.

Variation: Calvados or brandy can be added to give a spirited kick.

Nutrients per serving

- Calories 154
- Carbohydrate 40 g
- Protein 1 g
- No fat

Rhubarb refresher

Tart rhubarb makes a surprisingly delicate rosy drink for sophisticated entertaining.

PREPARATION TIME: 5 minutes, plus 1 hour cooling and 45 minutes chilling

COOKING TIME: 10 minutes

SERVES 4

450 g (1 lb) rhubarb, cut into 5 cm (2 in) lengths
7-8 tablespoons caster sugar
2 tablespoons lemon juice
600 ml (1 pint) sparkling mineral water

1 Put the rhubarb, sugar, lemon juice and 350 ml (12 fl oz) of water in a non-corrosive saucepan over a medium heat. Bring to the boil, then reduce the heat and simmer, uncovered, for 5 minutes, or until the rhubarb begins to collapse. Remove from the heat and leave to cool for about an hour.

APPLE AND CINNAMON WARMER

2 Strain the rhubarb, reserving the liquid and discarding the pulp. Chill the rhubarb liquid for about 45 minutes.
3 Combine equal amounts of rhubarb liquid and sparkling mineral water in each glass, and serve.

Variation: for an alcoholic cocktail, add a dash or two of Pernod, which will impart a subtle aniseed taste.

Nutrients per serving

- Calories 146
- Carbohydrate 38 g
- Protein 1 g
- No fat

Mint lassi

Cooling lassis are traditionally served with fiery Indian curries.

PREPARATION TIME: 5 minutes

SERVES 2

150 ml (5 fl oz) skimmed milk
75 g (2¾ oz) low-fat natural yoghurt
4 tablespoons chopped fresh mint leaves
Salt
Crushed ice

1 Put the milk, yoghurt, mint and a pinch of salt into a blender and process for 45 seconds.
2 Fill two tumblers with crushed ice and pour the lassi over. (You can crush the ice in a food processor if necessary.)

Variation: for sweet fruit lassis, use half of the milk and make up the difference with equal quantities of fruit and yoghurt. Use sugar instead of salt.

Nutrients per serving

- Calories 48
- Carbohydrate 7 g
- Protein 5 g
- No fat

Seared duck breasts with **wild rice** and **grapes**

Dark wild rice fragrant with orange zest and balsamic vinegar makes a great partner for chargrilled duck.

PREPARATION TIME: 10 minutes
COOKING TIME: 45 minutes
SERVES 4

Nutrients per serving
- Calories 430
- Carbohydrate 46 g
- Protein 32 g
- Fat 14 g (including saturated fat 3 g)

200 g (7 oz) wild rice
Salt and black pepper
25 g (1 oz) pecan nuts, chopped
4 duck breasts, about 175 g (6 oz) each
Oil for greasing
Grated zest and juice of 1 orange
2 teaspoons balsamic vinegar
150 g (5½ oz) seedless red grapes, halved
3 spring onions, thinly sliced

1 Bring a saucepan of water to the boil. Add the rice and a pinch of salt and cook for 45 minutes, or according to the instructions on the packet.
2 Meanwhile, heat a heavy-based nonstick frying pan and toast the pecan nuts for 2 minutes until they are lightly browned, then set them aside.
3 Remove the skin and fat from the duck breasts. Lightly grease a ridged, iron grill pan or the frying pan with oil and place over a medium heat. When it is hot, add the duck breasts and cook them for 1-2 minutes on each side until they are golden brown. Reduce the heat and cook for a further 8-10 minutes until the juices run clear when the thickest part of the breasts is pierced with a knife, turning them occasionally.
4 Mix the orange juice with the balsamic vinegar and drizzle it over the duck breasts, then take them off the heat.
5 Drain the rice, stir in the grapes and spring onions and season with black pepper.
6 Divide the rice mixture between four plates. Slice the duck breasts and arrange them over the rice. Scatter them with orange zest and pecans and spoon the pan juices over them.
Serving suggestion: Lemon-braised Spinach with Mushrooms and Croutons (page 230) or Sauté of Spring Vegetables with Herbs (page 232).

Low-fat tip
Although duck has a reputation for being fat, most of it lies just under the skin; remove them both and you can still enjoy duck in your low-fat diet.

SEARED DUCK BREASTS WITH WILD RICE AND GRAPES

DUCK DO-PIAZA

Duck do-piaza

One of the courtly dishes of the Mughals, do-piaza combines onions and tomatoes with Eastern spices as a foil for rich duck.

PREPARATION TIME: 30 minutes
COOKING TIME: 1 hour 30 minutes
SERVES 4

500 g (1 lb 2 oz) onions
700 g (1 lb 9 oz) duck breasts
2 tablespoons sunflower oil
2 bay leaves, crumbled
4 green cardamom pods, split open at the top
5 cm (2 in) cinnamon stick, broken in half
4 cloves
½-1 teaspoon cayenne pepper
2 teaspoons ground coriander
1 teaspoon ground cumin
2 teaspoons garlic purée, or crushed garlic
2 teaspoons ginger purée, or grated ginger
1 teaspoon paprika
½ teaspoon turmeric
125 g (4½ oz) canned chopped tomatoes
Salt
½ teaspoon garam masala
2 tablespoons chopped fresh coriander
To garnish: chopped fresh coriander, sliced cucumber and red onion

1. Peel and roughly chop half the onions and put them in a saucepan with 250 ml (9 fl oz) of water. Bring to the boil, then reduce the heat to low and cook, covered, for 10 minutes. Purée them in a food processor or with a hand-held mixer and set them aside.
2. Meanwhile, finely chop the remaining onions. Remove the skin and fat from the duck breasts, then cut the flesh into 2.5 cm (1 in) cubes.
3. Heat the oil in a heavy-based saucepan over a medium-high heat and fry the duck cubes for 4 minutes, or until they just start to turn brown. Remove with a slotted spoon and set aside.
4. Take the pan off the heat so that the oil cools a little. Add the bay leaves, cardamom pods, cinnamon and cloves and let them sizzle gently for 15-20 seconds. Return the pan to the heat, add the chopped onions and fry them, stirring frequently, for 8 minutes, or until they have softened and browned.
5. Stir in the cayenne pepper, coriander, cumin, garlic, ginger, paprika and turmeric and cook for 1 minute. Then stir in the puréed onions, increase the heat slightly and cook for 5 minutes, stirring frequently.
6. Add the tomatoes, with their juice, and continue to cook over a low heat for a further 5 minutes. Then return the browned duck to the pan and add 175 ml (6 fl oz) of water. Cover, bring to the boil then reduce the heat and simmer for 30 minutes, checking occasionally and adding more water if necessary.
7. Add salt to taste, cover and continue to cook for a further 20-25 minutes, stirring occasionally, until the duck is tender and has absorbed the flavours of the sauce. Then increase the heat slightly and cook, uncovered, for 3 minutes, stirring frequently, to thicken the sauce.
8. Add the garam masala and chopped coriander, simmer for 1 minute then serve garnished with coriander and slices of cucumber and onion.

Serving suggestion: plain boiled long-grain rice or Chilli Chapattis (page 291).

Nutrients per serving

- Calories 283
- Carbohydrate 11 g
- Protein 27 g
- Fat 15 g (including saturated fat 3 g)

Chargrilled duck with **plum** and **chilli salsa**

A spicy sauce made with sweet and sour plums is a wonderful companion for tender duck breasts.

PREPARATION TIME: 25 minutes, plus 30 minutes, or overnight, marinating

COOKING TIME: 10-15 minutes

SERVES 4

2 Barbary duck breasts, about 350 g (12 oz) each, or 4 ordinary duck breasts about 175 g (6 oz) each
Oil for greasing
A pinch of Chinese 5-spice powder

For the salsa:
1 tablespoon olive or sunflower oil
150 g (5½ oz) onions, finely chopped
2 large cloves garlic, crushed
2 green chillies, deseeded and finely chopped
8 red plums, stoned and diced
1 small yellow or red pepper, finely chopped
2 tablespoons coarsely chopped fresh coriander leaves
Juice of 2 limes
Salt and black pepper, or Chinese Sichuan peppercorns, ground

To garnish: a few sprigs of fresh coriander

PLUMS

1. First make the salsa: heat the oil in a small frying pan, add the onions and garlic and cook over a high heat for 1-2 minutes until lightly browned. Remove and leave to cool.
2. Mix together the chillies, plums, pepper and coriander with the lime juice, add salt and pepper to taste, then stir in the onions and garlic. Set aside for at least 30 minutes, or overnight, to allow the flavours to develop.
3. Cut the skin and fat from the duck breasts and slash them several times.
4. Lightly brush a ridged, iron grill pan or heavy nonstick frying pan with oil and heat it until you feel a steady heat rising. Fry the breasts for at least 3 minutes on each side, or until they feel springy when pressed with the back of a fork. Larger breasts will need longer cooking, and the length of time depends on how pink you like to serve your meat.
5. Sprinkle the breasts lightly with salt, pepper and 5-spice powder, then leave them to stand for 5 minutes.
6. Spoon the salsa in mounds onto four dinner plates. Slice the duck breasts diagonally and arrange them on top of the salsa. Garnish with sprigs of coriander.

Serving suggestion: new potatoes or flat rice noodles and some steamed mangetout.

Nutrients per serving

- Calories 269
- Carbohydrate 15 g
- Protein 26 g
- Fat 12 g (including saturated fat 3 g)

Duck stir-fry with orange and honey

A piquant marinade brings out the succulence of duck meat, stir-fried to seal in its juices.

PREPARATION TIME: 15 minutes, plus 30 minutes marinating
COOKING TIME: 6-8 minutes
SERVES 2

2 duck breasts, about 175 g (6 oz) each
1 teaspoon olive oil
2 spring onions, cut into 2.5 cm (1 in) lengths
50 g (1¾ oz) watercress, stalks removed
1 orange, peeled and segmented

For the marinade:
1 small red chilli, deseeded and finely chopped
1 teaspoon cornflour
1 clove garlic, crushed
1 teaspoon grated ginger
Grated zest and juice of 1 orange
1 teaspoon clear honey
1 teaspoon sesame oil
1 tablespoon dry sherry or rice wine
1 tablespoon dark soy sauce

1 To make the marinade, mix all the ingredients together in a bowl.
2 Cut the skin and fat off the duck breasts and discard. Slice the flesh into thin strips and add them to the marinade. Stir to mix well then cover and leave to marinate for 30 minutes, or refrigerate until required.
3 Remove the duck strips, reserving the marinade, and pat them dry. Heat the oil in a wok or large nonstick frying pan over a high heat, then stir-fry the duck for 4-5 minutes until browned.
4 Pour the marinade onto the duck and allow it to bubble until it reduces and becomes dark and syrupy.
5 Add the spring onions and watercress, stir-fry for 1 minute, then toss in the orange segments and heat them through.

Variation: replace the watercress with shredded Chinese leaf, ribbons of courgettes and carrots, or baby spinach.

Serving suggestion: plain wheat or rice noodles, or rice.

Nutrients per serving

- Calories 281
- Carbohydrate 17 g
- Protein 27 g
- Fat 11 g (including saturated fat 3 g)

Pheasant breasts with port

Lean pheasant is cooked in a glistening ruby sauce packed with healthy fresh fruit.

PREPARATION TIME: 15 minutes
COOKING TIME: 25-30 minutes
SERVES 4

4 boned pheasant breasts, about 150 g (5½ oz) each
1 teaspoon olive oil
3 shallots, chopped
200 ml (7 fl oz) ruby port
2 tablespoons red wine vinegar
150 ml (5 fl oz) meat stock
1 sprig of fresh thyme
2 purple figs
100 g (3½ oz) redcurrants
1 teaspoon Dijon mustard
Salt and black pepper
To garnish: redcurrants and sprigs of fresh thyme

1 Remove and discard the skin and any excess fat from the pheasant breasts. Brush a heavy-based nonstick frying pan with the oil and place it over a medium heat. When the oil is hot, add the pheasant breasts and shallots and brown the meat for 1 minute on each side.
2 Remove the pheasant breasts and set them aside. Add the port and vinegar to the shallots, then boil to reduce it by about half. Stir in the stock and thyme and return to the boil, then reduce the heat to low.
3 Return the pheasant to the pan, cover and simmer for 8-10 minutes until the breasts are tender: be careful not to overcook them or they will become tough.
4 Meanwhile, cut each fig into eight wedges and strip the redcurrants from their stalks with a fork.
5 When the pheasant juices run clear after a breast is pierced with a knife at its thickest point, remove the meat from the pan and keep it warm.
6 Boil the sauce to reduce it by one-third then stir in the mustard. Add the figs and redcurrants, let them heat through, then adjust the seasoning. Serve the sauce alongside the pheasant, garnished with redcurrants and sprigs of thyme.

Variation: if redcurrants are not in season, use frozen ones, defrosted, or 2 tablespoons of redcurrant jelly for the sauce instead.

Serving suggestion: jacket potatoes and a green vegetable.

Nutrients per serving

- Calories 304
- Carbohydrate 11 g
- Protein 41 g
- Fat 5 g (including saturated fat 1 g)

Pheasant and turkey terrine

This make-ahead game terrine uses puréed chestnuts instead of fat to keep it moist.

PREPARATION TIME: 1-2 hours, plus 2-3 days maturing
COOKING TIME: 1 hour 15 minutes
SERVES 6 as a main course, 12 as a starter

400 g (14 oz) whole peeled chestnuts, frozen, vacuum packed or canned and drained
425 ml (15 fl oz) turkey or chicken stock
350 g (12 oz) skinned and boned turkey thighs
500 g (1 lb 2 oz) skinned and boned pheasant breasts
12 large ready-to-eat stoned prunes
5 tablespoons brandy
1 teaspoon allspice berries, ground, or 1½ teaspoons ground allspice
Salt and black pepper
150 g (5½ oz) turkey or chicken livers
2 leeks, at least 35 cm (14 in) long
1 egg, beaten
1 tablespoon olive oil
25 g (1 oz) shelled, unsalted pistachio nuts

1 Put the chestnuts into a saucepan with the stock and bring to the boil, then reduce the heat, partially cover and simmer for 20-25 minutes until the chestnuts are just tender. Drain them, reserving the stock, and leave them to cool.
2 Remove any sinews from the turkey and pheasant. Check the pheasant for lead shot then cut it into long strips about 5 mm (¼ in) wide. Put 200 g (7 oz) of the neatest strips into a bowl, then add the prunes, 3 tablespoons of the brandy and half the allspice and season to taste. Stir then set aside.
3 Trim any membrane and white tissue from the livers. In a food processor or with a hand-held mixer, finely mince the remaining pheasant, the turkey and the livers. Mix well together, then mince once more and put the mixture into a large bowl.
4 Roughly chop a quarter of the chestnuts and set them aside. Mince the remaining chestnuts and stir them into the minced meats with the remaining brandy and allspice, a little salt and plenty of pepper.
5 Put a kettle on to boil. Trim the leeks to 30 cm (12 in) long, then cut them in half lengthways, discard the fine centre leaves and rinse well under cold running water. Lay them in a roasting tin or frying pan big enough to hold them in a single layer, cover with boiling water and leave for 1-2 minutes until just pliable. Refresh in cold water, separate the leaves and drain on kitchen paper.
6 Heat the oven to 180°C (350°F, gas mark 4). Lightly oil a nonstick loaf tin, measuring about 22 x 11 x 6 cm (8½ x 4¼ x 2½ in). Working widthways, line the tin with overlapping leeks, allowing the excess to hang over the sides.
7 Strain the brandy from the pheasant and prunes into the bowl of minced meat and stir it in. Add the egg, olive oil, pistachio nuts and 2 tablespoons of the reserved stock from the chestnuts and mix well. Gently stir in the chopped chestnuts – do not overmix or they will break up.
8 Spoon one-third of the mixture into the loaf tin and spread it out evenly. Arrange half the drained prunes, end to end, in a line along the centre, then lay half the pheasant strips on either side of the prunes.
9 Cover the pheasant and prunes with another third of the terrine mixture, then arrange the remaining prunes and pheasant strips on top as before. Spread the rest of the mixture evenly over the top.
10 Put a kettle of water on to boil. Cover the terrine lengthways with a layer of overlapping leek strips, trimming them to fit exactly, then bring the overhanging leek strips over the top.
11 Cover the tin tightly with foil and stand it in a small roasting tin. Pour in boiling water to halfway up the side of the loaf tin, then bake for 1 hour-1 hour 15 minutes until a skewer inserted into the centre feels hot on the back of your hand.
12 Stand the loaf tin on a large plate, place a small board on top of the foil, then place some heavy weights, or cans of beans, on top. Allow it to cool, then refrigerate for 2-3 days to allow the flavours to mature.
13 Take the terrine out of the refrigerator 1 hour before serving. Remove the foil and drain off any juices. Loosen it by gently running a palette knife between the leeks and the tin, then turn the terrine out, cut into slices and serve.

Variation: the terrine can be made with duck and pheasant, goose and duck, all pheasant or all duck.

Serving suggestion: as a main course, serve with a green salad and some crusty bread; as a starter, serve with baby gherkins and toast.

Nutrients per serving, when serving 6

- Calories 435
- Carbohydrate 33 g
- Protein 46 g
- Fat 11 g (including saturated fat 2 g)

Quails baked on a bed of rosemary

Celebrate a special occasion with quails marinated in wine, and fruit-stuffed apples.

PREPARATION TIME: 30 minutes, plus 1 hour marinating

COOKING TIME: 25-30 minutes

SERVES 2 as a main course, 4 as a starter

4 oven-ready quails
1 lemon, cut into quarters
4-5 bushy sprigs of fresh rosemary

For the marinade:

300 ml (10 fl oz) fruity dry white wine
1 tablespoon olive oil
1 clove garlic, crushed
Salt and black pepper

For the stuffed apples:

3 tablespoons brandy, warmed
75 g (2¾ oz) currants
50 g (1¾ oz) preserved stem ginger, drained and chopped
2 rashers of rindless smoked streaky bacon, chopped
1 teaspoon chopped fresh thyme
4 small dessert apples

1 To make the marinade, combine the wine, olive oil and garlic in a bowl and add salt to taste. Add the quails and coat well, rubbing the marinade inside and out. Cover and leave them to marinate for 1 hour, turning the birds over a few times.
2 Meanwhile, to make the stuffing for the apples, stir together the brandy, currants and ginger in a small bowl and leave to stand for 30 minutes.
3 Heat the oven to 200°C (400°F, gas mark 6). Arrange sprigs of rosemary over the base of a roasting tin, saving a few for a garnish.
4 Stir the bacon and thyme into the brandy and add salt and pepper. Core the apples, then cut a ring around each circumference, so that they can expand as they bake. Using a teaspoon, stuff the apples with the fruit mixture.
5 Remove the quails from the marinade and place a lemon quarter inside each. Place the quails and apples on the rosemary, pour the marinade over them and loosely cover the roasting tin with foil.
6 Bake for 15 minutes, then uncover and baste. Increase the heat to 230°C (450°F, gas mark 8) and bake for a further 10-15 minutes until the quails are tender and the juices run clear when pierced in the thighs.
7 Transfer the quails and apples to a plate and keep them warm. (If the apples are not completely tender, leave them in the oven while you make the sauce.)
8 Strain the pan juices into a small pan and boil hard until slightly thickened. Pour the sauce over the quails and serve.

Serving suggestion: serve alone as a starter. For a main course add carrots and spinach, with potato and pumpkin mash to soak up the sauce.

Nutrients per serving, when serving 4

- Calories 414
- Carbohydrate 32 g
- Protein 31 g
- Fat 11 g (including saturated fat 3 g)

Guinea fowl fricassée

Tender poached guinea fowl is served in a tangy sauce enriched with lemon and yoghurt.

PREPARATION TIME: 30 minutes, plus 20 minutes cooling
COOKING TIME: 1 hour 20 minutes
SERVES 4

1 oven-ready guinea fowl, about 1.25 kg (2 lb 12 oz)
35 g (1¼ oz) carrots, sliced
60 g (2¼ oz) onions, cut into quarters
1 large sprig of fresh parsley
8 black peppercorns
300 ml (10 fl oz) chicken stock
1 teaspoon olive oil
250 g (9 oz) small chestnut mushrooms, cut into quarters
25 g (1 oz) 70 per cent fat spread
25 g (1 oz) plain white flour
Finely grated zest of 1 lemon
2 tablespoons lemon juice
150 g (5½ oz) low-fat Greek yoghurt
Salt and black pepper
2 tablespoons chopped fresh parsley
To garnish: sprigs of fresh parsley and toast triangles, optional

1 Put the guinea fowl into a saucepan with the carrots, onions, parsley, peppercorns and stock. Bring to the boil, then reduce the heat, cover and simmer for 45-55 minutes until the guinea fowl is tender and the juices run clear when the thigh is pierced with a knife.
2 Transfer the guinea fowl to a plate and leave to cool for 20 minutes. Meanwhile, strain the stock into a measuring jug. There should be 300 ml (10 fl oz); if not, make it up to this amount with water.
3 Heat the oven to 180°C (350°F, gas mark 4). When the guinea fowl is cool enough to handle, remove and discard the skin, then cut the meat from the bones and chop or roughly tear it into large chunks.
4 Heat the oil in a large frying pan, add the mushrooms and stir-fry them over a high heat for 2-3 minutes until lightly browned. Remove them from the heat and set aside.
5 Melt the fat spread in a saucepan over a medium heat, stir in the flour then gradually stir in the cooking liquid from the guinea fowl. Bring to the boil and stir continuously until the sauce thickens. Reduce the heat and simmer for 3 minutes, stirring occasionally.
6 Remove the sauce from the heat and stir in half the lemon zest, the lemon juice and the yoghurt. Season with salt and pepper, then stir in the guinea fowl and mushrooms.
7 Pour the fricassée into an ovenproof serving dish, cover and bake for 25-30 minutes until heated through.
8 Stir the fricassée to blend in any mushroom juices, then sprinkle it with the rest of the lemon zest and the chopped parsley. Serve garnished with sprigs of parsley, and toast triangles if you like.

Variation: you can substitute a small chicken for the guinea fowl.

Serving suggestion: steamed savoy cabbage, and plain or mixed rice or baked potatoes.

Nutrients per serving

- Calories 117
- Carbohydrate 8 g
- Protein 5 g
- Fat 8 g (including saturated fat 2 g)

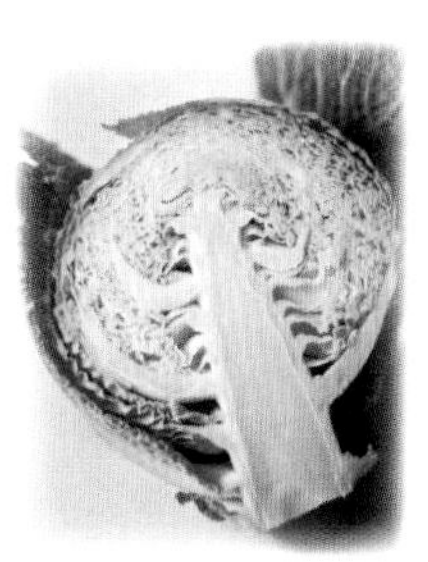

SAVOY CABBAGE

SUPER ROAST PARTRIDGE

Super roast partridge

Lean gamy partridge tastes especially good served with an autumn-fruit preserve.

PREPARATION TIME: 10 minutes
COOKING TIME: 40 minutes
SERVES 4

4 oven-ready partridges, about 350 g (12 oz) each
2 tablespoons olive oil
Salt and black pepper
A pinch of ground mace
300 ml (10 fl oz) chicken stock
100 ml (3½ fl oz) dry white wine
To serve: blackberry or crab apple jelly

1 Heat the oven to 220°C (425°F, gas mark 7). Rub the partridges with olive oil and season to taste with salt, black pepper and mace.
2 Put the birds in a roasting tin and cook in the centre of the oven for 30 minutes, basting regularly, until the juices run clear when the thigh is pierced with a knife. Transfer the birds to a plate and leave them to rest in a warm place while you make the gravy.
3 Place the roasting tin over a medium-high heat and pour in the chicken stock and wine. Let the gravy bubble vigorously, scraping any sediment off the bottom of the roasting tin with a wooden spoon, until it is reduced to 4-6 tablespoons.
4 Spoon a little of the hot gravy onto each serving plate, lay a partridge on top and accompany it with some blackberry or crab apple jelly.

Serving suggestion: a peppery salad such as red mustard and red chard leaves.

Nutrients per serving

- Calories 438
- Carbohydrate 8 g
- Protein 59 g
- Fat 17 g (including saturated fat 4 g)

Rabbit with garlic

Garlic, aromatic herbs and spices transform humble rabbit into a tasty stew.

PREPARATION TIME: 30 minutes
COOKING TIME: 1 hour
SERVES 4

2 tablespoons olive oil
150 g (5½ oz) whole baby carrots, or large carrots cut into batons
1 whole head of garlic, outer skin removed but left whole
12 pickling onions, or small shallots
1 bay leaf
1 sprig of fresh rosemary
2 sprigs of fresh sage
3 sprigs of fresh thyme
2 strips of lemon zest, about 5 cm (2 in) long
3-4 cloves
150 ml (5 fl oz) dry white wine
300 ml (10 fl oz) chicken stock
4 rabbit legs, about 225 g (8 oz) each
Salt and black pepper
2 tablespoons lemon juice
To garnish: sprigs of fresh thyme

1 Heat the oil in a large, heavy-based frying pan and add the carrots, the head of garlic and pickling onions or shallots. Fry the vegetables over a high heat for about 5 minutes, or until they start to brown.
2 Meanwhile, tie the bay leaf, rosemary, sage, thyme and lemon zest together.

RABBIT WITH GARLIC

3 Add the cloves to the carrots and fry for a few seconds so that they release their aroma. Then add the wine, stock and herbs. Bring to the boil, then reduce the heat and let it simmer for a few minutes.
4 Add the rabbit legs and bring to a rapid boil, turning them in the liquid. Season to taste then reduce the heat, skim well, cover and simmer for about 45 minutes, or until the legs are tender. Remove the rabbit and keep it warm.
5 Discard the herbs and the garlic. Raise the heat and boil the sauce hard until it is reduced by half.
6 Return the rabbit to the pan, add the lemon juice and heat the meat through. Serve it with the vegetables, sprinkled with thyme.
Tip: wild rabbit has more flavour and less fat than farmed, but it is tougher and will need cooking for at least 1 hour 15 minutes. The legs are smaller, so you may need two each.
Serving suggestion: a bed of pasta or some chunky bread.

Nutrients per serving

- Calories 260
- Carbohydrate 6 g
- Protein 30 g
- Fat 11 g (including saturated fat 3 g)

VENISON WITH A RUBY SAUCE

Venison with a **ruby sauce**

A glowing sauce of red wine and sweet-sour cranberries turns lean venison into a dinner party dish.

PREPARATION TIME: 10 minutes, plus several hours, or overnight, marinating
COOKING TIME: 15-20 minutes
SERVES 4

4 venison fillet steaks, about 125 g (4½ oz) each
1 bay leaf
50 g (1¾ oz) red onions, thinly sliced
250 ml (9 fl oz) red wine
125 g (4½ oz) cranberries, defrosted if frozen
2 tablespoons tomato purée
4 tablespoons cranberry sauce
Salt and black pepper

1 Place the venison, bay leaf and onions in a bowl and pour the wine over them. Cover and leave to marinate in the refrigerator for several hours, or overnight.
2 Heat a grill to medium heat. Drain the venison thoroughly, reserving the marinade, and grill for 10-15 minutes, turning once, until the steaks are tender and cooked to your liking.
3 Meanwhile, pour the marinade with the onions into a small pan, bring to the boil and simmer rapidly for 1 minute. Add the cranberries and simmer for 4-5 minutes until the fruit bursts.
4 Stir in the tomato purée and cranberry sauce and adjust the seasoning with salt and pepper. Remove the bay leaf, then serve the venison and spoon the cranberry wine sauce over it.
Serving suggestion: polenta or mashed potatoes, or Sweet Roasted Squash with Shallots (page 231).

Nutrients per serving

- Calories 209
- Carbohydrate 9 g
- Protein 28 g
- Fat 2 g (including saturated fat 1 g)

Venison cottage pie

Venison stays juicy when it is cooked slowly and gently. Here it is combined with lots of vegetables to make a healthy, hearty family meal.

PREPARATION TIME: 25 minutes, plus 10 minutes resting
COOKING TIME: 1 hour
SERVES 4-6

1 kg (2 lb 4 oz) potatoes, peeled and cubed
100 ml (3½ fl oz) semi-skimmed milk
Freshly ground nutmeg, to taste
Salt and black pepper
3 rashers of rindless streaky bacon, chopped
500 g (1 lb 2 oz) minced venison
150 g (5½ oz) carrots, coarsely grated
1 stick of celery, chopped
400 g (14 oz) leeks, sliced
125 g (4½ oz) mushrooms, sliced
150 g (5½ oz) canned sweetcorn, drained
1 teaspoon dried mixed herbs
2 tablespoons plain wholemeal flour
300 ml (10 fl oz) stock, or half water and half ale
2 tablespoons soy sauce
1 tablespoon Worcestershire sauce
2 tablespoons dried white or brown breadcrumbs

1. Bring a large saucepan of water to the boil. Add the potatoes and a pinch of salt and boil until tender. Drain well and mash them until smooth. Beat in the milk, nutmeg and salt and pepper to taste then set aside.
2. Heat a large nonstick frying pan and dry-fry the bacon until it is lightly browned and some fat starts to run. Add the venison, raise the heat and stir-fry until the meat is crumbly and browned.
3. Stir in the carrots, celery, leeks and mushrooms, cover the pan and let the vegetables sweat for 5 minutes, or until softened. Meanwhile, heat the oven to 190°C (357°F, gas mark 5).
4. Add the sweetcorn and herbs to the pan and stir in the flour. Continue cooking for 1 minute, then stir in the stock or water and ale mixture, soy sauce and Worcestershire sauce and season to taste. Bring to the boil, stirring, then simmer, uncovered, for 10 minutes.
5. Put the mixture into a shallow, 1.5 litre (2¾ pint) pie dish. Spoon the mashed potato over the meat, roughing up the top slightly. Sprinkle with the breadcrumbs and place the dish on a baking sheet. Cook for 25-30 minutes until the top is golden brown. Remove the pie from the oven and let it rest for 10 minutes, then serve.

Nutrients per serving, when serving 4

- Calories 476
- Carbohydrate 63 g
- Protein 41 g
- Fat 9 g (including saturated fat 3 g)

Low-fat tip

Venison is a lean, low-cholesterol meat and so it is a good substitute for beef and lamb.

beef, lamb and pork

Beef stew with parsley dumplings

Nutrients per serving

- Calories 385
- Carbohydrate 36 g
- Protein 34 g
- Fat 13 g (including saturated fat 3 g)

Warm up on a winter evening with a nourishing beef stew, made extra-satisfying with low-fat, herb dumplings.

PREPARATION TIME: 40 minutes
COOKING TIME: 2 hours 50 minutes
SERVES 6

1 kg (2 lb 4 oz) lean beef stewing steak
1 tablespoon olive oil
400 g (14 oz) onions, cut into wedges
250 g (9 oz) carrots, sliced
250 g (9 oz) swede, diced
1 tablespoon plain white flour
2 teaspoons dried mixed herbs
400 g (14 oz) canned chopped tomatoes
600 ml (1 pint) meat stock
Salt and black pepper

For the dumplings:
175 g (6 oz) self-raising white flour
50 g (1¾ oz) 70 per cent fat spread
3 tablespoons chopped fresh parsley

1 Remove the fat, membrane and gristle from the stewing steak, then cut the meat into 2.5 cm (1 in) cubes.
2 Heat the oil in a large, flameproof casserole, add the onions and cook them over a medium heat for 5 minutes, or until they are lightly browned, stirring occasionally.
3 Transfer the onions to a large bowl, then put half the meat in the casserole and cook it for 2-3 minutes until browned, stirring occasionally. Do not worry if there is very little oil in the casserole, but take care not to let the meat burn. Remove the browned meat and add it to the onions, then brown the remaining meat and add that to the onions.
4 Stir the carrots and swede into the meat juices remaining in the casserole and cook them over a medium heat for 1-2 minutes. Return the meat and onions with their juices to the pan and stir in the flour so that the meat and vegetables are evenly coated.
5 Stir in the herbs, tomatoes and stock and bring to the boil. Reduce the heat to very low, cover the pan with a tight-fitting lid and simmer for 2 hours-2 hours 15 minutes until the meat is tender, stirring occasionally. Do not allow the stew to boil or the meat will become tough.
6 Meanwhile, make the dumplings: sift the flour and a pinch of salt into a mixing bowl and rub in the spread. Add the parsley and season to taste. Make a well in the centre of the mixture, pour in 6 tablespoons of cold water and mix with a round-bladed knife to form a soft, slightly sticky dough.
7 When the meat is tender, adjust the seasoning of the stew to taste and increase the heat a little, but do not allow it to boil. Take a rounded dessertspoon of the dumpling mixture and drop it on top of the stew. Add 11 more spoonfuls, spacing them well apart, then cover the pan and continue cooking for 20 minutes, or until the dumplings are well risen and cooked through. Serve two dumplings with each helping.

Serving suggestion: steamed broccoli, or a leafy vegetable such as spring greens or cabbage.

Cottage pie, American-style

Nutrients per serving

- Calories 424
- Carbohydrate 42 g
- Protein 36 g
- Fat 14 g (including saturated fat 6 g)

Low-fat tip

Extra-lean minced beef still contains enough fat to be dry-fried. If you cannot find extra-lean mince, soak up any fat from the browned meat with kitchen paper.

Two firm favourites – baked beans and traditional cottage pie – are combined here to provide a hearty and nutritious dish for all the family.

PREPARATION TIME: 10 minutes
COOKING TIME: 35-40 minutes
SERVES 4

500 g (1 lb 2 oz) extra-lean minced beef
175 g (6 oz) onions, diced
1 meat stock cube, crumbled
400 g (14 oz) canned baked beans in tomato sauce
2 teaspoons Worcestershire sauce
1 tablespoon maple syrup
Salt and black pepper
600 g (1 lb 5 oz) potatoes, peeled and cubed
60-75 ml (2¼-2½ fl oz) low-fat fromage frais
To garnish: a few sprigs of fresh thyme

1. In a large frying pan, dry-fry the mince and onion for 6-7 minutes, stirring frequently, until the meat is browned and the liquid has evaporated.
2. Put a large saucepan of water on to boil. Add the stock cube, baked beans, Worcestershire sauce and maple syrup to the frying pan, cover and simmer for 10 minutes, stirring occasionally. Moisten the mixture with a little water, if necessary, and season with black pepper.
3. Meanwhile, prepare the topping: put the potatoes in the boiling water, add a pinch of salt, return to the boil and cook for 15-20 minutes until tender. Drain and mash them with the fromage frais then season to taste.
4. Heat the grill to high. Spoon the meat mixture into a 1.5 litre (2¾ pint) flameproof serving dish and spread the mashed potato evenly over the top. Grill for 4-5 minutes until the potato topping is golden brown. Serve garnished with sprigs of thyme.

Serving suggestion: green beans or carrots.

Roast beef with **broad beans** and **mushrooms**

Juicy fresh vegetables replace Yorkshire pudding as an accompaniment to the Sunday joint, giving a lighter touch.

PREPARATION TIME: 40 minutes
COOKING TIME: 1 hour 5 minutes-1 hour 40 minutes
SERVES 4

1 beef topside joint, about 750 g (1 lb 10 oz)
250 g (9 oz) shelled broad beans, defrosted if frozen
250 g (9 oz) mixed mushrooms, such as chanterelles (girolles), oysters and shiitake
2 tablespoons Madeira, sherry or red wine
150-200 ml (5-7 fl oz) meat stock
Salt and black pepper

1. Heat the oven to 180°C (350°F, gas mark 4). Weigh the beef and calculate the cooking time: for rare meat, 35 minutes per kg (15 minutes per lb) plus 15 minutes; for medium, 45 minutes per kg (20 minutes per lb) plus 20 minutes; for well done, 55 minutes per kg (25 minutes per lb) plus 25 minutes. Place the beef in a roasting tin and cook.
2. Meanwhile, bring a large saucepan of water to the boil and cook the broad beans for 5-10 minutes until tender, then drain and refresh them under cold running water. When they are cool enough to handle, peel off their skins to reveal the bright green inner bean. Set aside.
3. Finely slice or tear the mushrooms and set aside.
4. When the joint is done, remove it from the roasting tin and put it to rest in a warm place while you cook the mushrooms and make the sauce.
5. Remove any excess fat from the roasting tin and place the tin over a low heat. Add the mushrooms and fry them for about 10 minutes until they have softened.
6. Raise the heat and add the Madeira, sherry or wine, stirring to take in the cooking juices. When the alcohol has almost evaporated, add the stock and bring it to the boil, stirring frequently. Then lower the heat and simmer for 5-10 minutes to make a syrupy sauce. Season to taste, then stir in the broad beans and heat them through.
7. Spoon the bean and mushroom mixture onto a platter and lay the joint on top. Carve the meat at the table, and serve it with the beans and mushrooms spooned over it.

Serving suggestion: Sweet Roasted Squash with Shallots (page 231) or Roasted Vegetables with Horseradish Sauce (page 233).

Nutrients per serving

- Calories 270
- Carbohydrate 5 g
- Protein 48 g
- Fat 6 g (including saturated fat 2 g)

Daube of beef and vegetables Provençale

A rich stew of beef and vegetables is slow-cooked to melting tenderness and infused with Mediterranean flavours.

PREPARATION TIME: 20 minutes

COOKING TIME: 3 hours

SERVES 4-6

600 g (1 lb 5 oz) braising beef
125 g (4½ oz) piece of lean smoked bacon
175 g (6 oz) carrots, chopped
150 g (5½ oz) onions, chopped
2 red peppers, diced
400 g (14 oz) canned chopped tomatoes
2 sticks celery, sliced
2 cloves garlic, crushed
2 bay leaves
4 strips of orange zest
2 small sprigs of fresh rosemary
4 sprigs of fresh thyme
2 tablespoons tomato purée
300 ml (10 fl oz) meat stock
150 ml (5 fl oz) red wine
4 canned anchovy fillets, drained, dried and chopped
225 g (8 oz) button mushrooms
75 g (2¾ oz) stoned black olives
4 tablespoons chopped fresh parsley
Black pepper

1 Heat the oven to 150°C (300°F, gas mark 2). Remove any excess fat and gristle from the beef and cut it into 4 cm (1½ in) cubes. Trim the bacon of fat and cut it into 1 cm (½ in) dice.
2 Put the beef and bacon into a large flameproof casserole and add the carrots, onions, red peppers, canned tomatoes, celery, garlic, bay leaves, orange zest, rosemary, thyme, tomato purée, stock, and wine. Bring to the boil, cover the casserole, transfer it to the oven and cook for 2 hours.
3 Stir in the anchovies, mushrooms, olives and parsley, reserving a little for garnish, then season with black pepper to taste (the anchovies will provide enough salt). Cover and cook for a further 1 hour. Check the seasoning, sprinkle with the reserved parsley and serve.

Serving suggestion: mashed potatoes.

Nutrients per serving, when serving 4

- Calories 351
- Carbohydrate 14 g
- Protein 39 g
- Fat 13 g (including saturated fat 4 g)

VEAL ESCALOPES WITH SHIITAKE MUSHROOMS

Veal escalopes with shiitake mushrooms

Ginger and rice wine spice up an Oriental-style mushroom sauce to accompany tender pan-fried veal.

PREPARATION TIME: 10 minutes
COOKING TIME: 6-15 minutes
SERVES 4

8 lean veal escalopes, about 400 g (14 oz) altogether
2 tablespoons plain white flour, seasoned with salt and pepper
2 tablespoons vegetable oil
2 cloves garlic, crushed
1 teaspoon finely chopped ginger
250 g (9 oz) shiitake mushrooms, destalked and thickly sliced
4 tablespoons soy sauce
4 tablespoons sake, dry sherry or vermouth

1. Place a veal escalope between two sheets of greaseproof paper or cling film and beat it with a rolling pin until it has flattened slightly. Lightly toss it in the seasoned flour, then shake off any excess flour and set aside. Repeat with the remaining seven escalopes.
2. Heat 1 tablespoon of the oil in a large nonstick frying pan. Add the escalopes and sear for 2-3 minutes until browned, then flip them over and cook for a further 2-3 minutes – you may need to cook them in two batches. Divide them between four plates and keep them warm.
3. Add the remaining oil to the pan and heat it, then add the garlic and ginger and stir-fry for 30 seconds. Add the mushrooms, soy sauce, sake, sherry or vermouth and 100 ml (3½ fl oz) of water and boil for 2-3 minutes to cook the mushrooms and reduce the sauce slightly. Spoon the mushrooms and sauce over the escalopes and serve.

Serving suggestion: lightly cooked spinach and plain boiled rice.

Nutrients per serving

- Calories 204
- Carbohydrate 10 g
- Protein 25 g
- Fat 8 g (including saturated fat 1 g)

Beef stroganoff

Quick and easy to cook, this version has half the fat of the much-loved traditional recipe.

PREPARATION TIME: 15 minutes
COOKING TIME: 20 minutes
SERVES 2

300 g (10½ oz) rump steak
Salt and black pepper
150 g (5½ oz) onions, thinly sliced
125 g (4½ oz) button mushrooms, thinly sliced
100 ml (3½ fl oz) meat stock, or medium sherry
1 tablespoon Worcestershire sauce
1 tablespoon brandy, optional
1 clove garlic, crushed, optional
4 tablespoons sour cream
2 teaspoons chopped fresh parsley
To garnish: a few sprigs of fresh flat-leaved parsley

1. Trim any fat off the steak then cut the meat into strips and season with pepper.
2. Heat a large, lidded nonstick frying pan and dry-fry the onions and mushrooms for 2-3 minutes over a medium heat.
3. Pour in the stock or sherry and Worcestershire sauce, cover and simmer for 5 minutes, shaking the pan occasionally. Remove the lid and boil for 2 minutes, until there are only 4-5 tablespoons of liquid left. Lift out the vegetables and keep them warm.

BEEF STROGANOFF

4 Add the beef to the pan and simmer for 3-4 minutes until browned.
5 If using the brandy, turn up the heat slightly to warm the base of the pan, pour in the brandy and ignite it. When the flames have died down, stir in the garlic, if using.
6 Return the onions and mushrooms to the pan and cook for 2 minutes. Stir in the sour cream and parsley and adjust the seasoning to taste. Serve garnished with sprigs of parsley.

Serving suggestion: mixed wild and plain rice.

Nutrients per serving

- Calories 304
- Carbohydrate 9 g
- Protein 29 g
- Fat 17 g (including saturated fat 9 g)

FILLET STEAK WITH ROASTED SHALLOTS AND GARLIC

Fillet steak with roasted shallots and garlic

Slowly roasted in their skins, shallots and garlic have a mellow sweetness that marries beautifully with juicy chargrilled fillet steak.

PREPARATION TIME: 10 minutes
COOKING TIME: 45-55 minutes
SERVES 4

- 500 g (1 lb 2 oz) shallots
- 2 whole heads garlic, roots and tops trimmed off
- 3 tablespoons olive oil
- 1 teaspoon balsamic vinegar
- 2 tablespoons chopped fresh flat-leaved parsley
- Salt and black pepper
- 4 lean fillet steaks, about 125 g (4½ oz) each
- 1 teaspoon Worcestershire sauce

1 Heat the oven to 200°C (400°F, gas mark 6). Cut off the roots of the shallots, leaving them in their skins, and place them in a small roasting tin. Add the garlic to the shallots. Drizzle with 1 tablespoon of oil, cover with foil and roast for 40-50 minutes until they are very soft.
2 When the shallots and garlic are cool enough to handle, slip them out of their skins and place them in a small mixing bowl. Dress with 1 tablespoon of olive oil and the balsamic vinegar, stir in the parsley and season to taste.
3 Heat a ridged, iron grill pan over a high heat. Cut any fat off the steaks and rub them with the remaining olive oil and the Worcestershire sauce. Season to taste, then grill them for 2 minutes on each side for medium-rare steaks, or longer to taste. Serve with the garlic and shallot dressing.

Serving suggestion: new potatoes roasted in their skins and sprinkled with chopped fresh thyme, and a green vegetable or salad.

Nutrients per serving

- Calories 291
- Carbohydrate 7 g
- Protein 30 g
- Fat 16 g (including saturated fat 5 g)

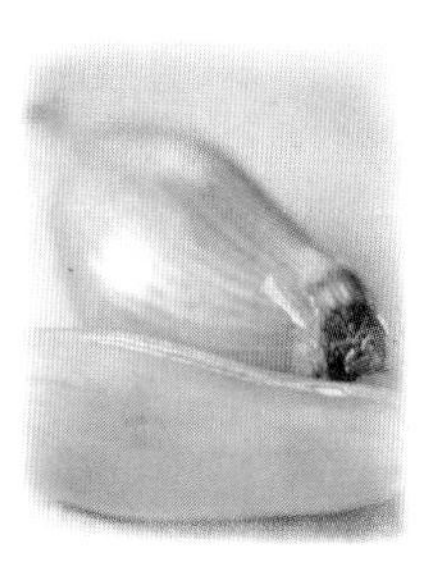
SHALLOTS

Luxury beefburgers

Extra-lean burgers, with capers, anchovies and sun-dried tomatoes added for extra flavour, become a gourmet treat when served with sizzling tender artichoke hearts.

PREPARATION TIME: 40 minutes
COOKING TIME: 10 minutes
SERVES 4

600 g (1 lb 5 oz) rump or sirloin steak
1 tablespoon capers, drained and roughly chopped
35 g (1¼ oz) sun-dried tomatoes, finely chopped; if packed in oil, pat them dry first
50 g (1¾ oz) canned anchovy fillets, drained, dried and roughly chopped
2 tablespoons olive oil
2 teaspoons black peppercorns
400 g (14 oz) canned artichoke hearts in water, well drained
1 clove garlic, sliced
2 tablespoons finely chopped fresh parsley
1 tablespoon lemon juice
25 g (1 oz) stoned black olives, chopped
To garnish: a few sprigs of fresh flat-leaved parsley

1 Remove any fat, membrane and gristle from the steak. Cut the meat into thin strips lengthways, then crossways into small dice.
2 To retain all the succulence of the steak and avoid it turning into a pulp in a food processor, mince the meat by hand. Take a large, sharp knife in each hand, and, holding them loosely, lift each up and down in turn to chop the steak, using a rhythmic action. Lift and turn the meat with the flats of the knives and continue chopping it to a fine mince.
3 Put the chopped steak, capers, sun-dried tomatoes, anchovy fillets and 2 teaspoons of the olive oil into a large bowl and mix well. (The anchovies will provide enough salt.)
4 Divide the mixture into four equal portions, shaping each one into a neat burger 9-10 cm (3½-4 in) in diameter. Crush the peppercorns with a rolling pin or with a pestle and mortar and use them to coat both sides of each burger, pressing them gently into the meat.
5 Cut each artichoke heart into four slices lengthways. Put 1 tablespoon of the remaining olive oil in a frying pan and add the garlic. When the oil starts to sizzle, remove the garlic.
6 Add the artichokes to the pan and sauté them for 2-3 minutes until heated through, then stir in the parsley, lemon juice, black olives and garlic. Remove from the heat and cover to keep warm.
7 Heat a ridged, iron grill pan or heavy-based frying pan. Lightly brush it with the remaining oil and grill the burgers for 1-2 minutes on each side, turning them over carefully. If you prefer, cook them for 2-3 minutes each side under a hot grill. The steak is lean and tender, so take care not to overcook the burgers.
8 Serve the burgers on individual plates, spoon the hot artichoke hearts with their dressing over them and garnish with sprigs of parsley.

Serving suggestion: lightly toasted rolls or new potatoes, and a green salad.

Low-fat tip

Buying steak to mince yourself means that you can cut off every trace of fat before you make the burgers.

Nutrients per serving

- Calories 294
- Carbohydrate 3 g
- Protein 31 g
- Fat 17 g (including saturated fat 4 g)

CAPER BERRIES

Beef and **pork meatballs** in a **caper sauce**

Nutrients per serving

- Calories 314
- Carbohydrate 15 g
- Protein 37 g
- Fat 9 g (including saturated fat 3 g)

Anchovies, lemon and parsley turn choice cuts of meat into delicious meatballs, given extra piquancy with a caper sauce.

PREPARATION TIME: 30 minutes, plus 1 hour chilling

COOKING TIME: 30 minutes

SERVES 4

300 g (10½ oz) sirloin or rump steak
300 g (10½ oz) pork fillet
50 g (1¾ oz) canned anchovy fillets, drained, dried and finely chopped, optional
30 g (1¼ oz) fresh white or brown breadcrumbs
1 egg, beaten
Finely grated zest of 1 lemon
6 tablespoons chopped fresh parsley
Black pepper

For the sauce:
425 ml (15 fl oz) chicken or meat stock
150 ml (5 fl oz) dry white wine
150 g (5½ oz) low-fat Greek yoghurt
2 tablespoons plain white flour
2 tablespoons caper berries or capers, drained

1. Remove any fat, membrane and gristle from the steak and pork. Cut the meat into thin strips lengthways, then crossways into small dice.
2. To retain all the succulence of the meat, mince it by hand. Take a large, sharp knife in each hand, and, holding them loosely, lift each up and down in turn to chop, using a rhythmic action. Lift and turn the meat with the flats of the knives and continue chopping it to a fine mince.
3. In a large bowl, mix the minced meat, anchovy, if using, breadcrumbs, egg, lemon zest and 5 tablespoons of the parsley. Season with pepper only (the anchovies will provide enough salt).
4. Use your hands to roll the meat mixture into 20 meatballs the size of large walnuts. Then place them in a dish, cover with cling film and chill for 1 hour to allow their flavour to develop.
5. To make the sauce, pour the stock and wine into a large frying pan or wok and bring to the boil, then reduce the heat to low. Add the meatballs and poach them, uncovered, for 20 minutes, turning them once or twice as they cook. Do not allow the stock to boil or the meatballs will break up. Lift out the meatballs with a slotted spoon, dry them on kitchen paper and keep them warm.
6. Put the yoghurt and flour into a small bowl, whisk until smooth, then gradually whisk the mixture into the simmering stock. Raise the heat and continue whisking until the sauce comes to the boil, then reduce the heat to low, add the capers and simmer for 3 minutes.
7. Season the sauce with pepper, pour it over the meatballs, sprinkle with the remaining parsley and serve.

Serving suggestion: some rice and a mixed-leaf salad.

Country lamb and vegetable cobbler

Nutrients per serving

- Calories 514
- Carbohydrate 64 g
- Protein 36 g
- Fat 12 g (including saturated fat 1 g)

If you enjoy hearty stews topped with dumplings or crumbly pastry, you'll love this low-fat version.

PREPARATION TIME: 20 minutes
COOKING TIME: 1 hour-1 hour 10 minutes
SERVES 4

500 g (1 lb 2 oz) lean lamb steak
400 g (14 oz) carrots, thickly sliced
225 g (8 oz) celery, thickly sliced
450 g (1 lb) leeks, thickly sliced
350 ml (12 fl oz) strong dry cider
350 ml (12 fl oz) lamb or chicken stock
Salt and black pepper
200 g (7 oz) peas, defrosted if frozen
A few sprigs of fresh rosemary, sage and thyme, tied together to make a bouquet garni

For the topping:
250 g (9 oz) self-raising white flour
4 tablespoons chopped fresh parsley and sage
150 g (5½ oz) low-fat fromage frais
1-2 teaspoons skimmed milk, optional

1. Heat the oven to 200°C (400°F, gas mark 6). Trim any fat off the lamb and cut the meat into 2.5 cm (1 in) cubes. In a large flameproof casserole, dry-fry the lamb over a medium-high heat for 6-8 minutes until it is lightly browned, stirring frequently.
2. Add the carrots, celery and leeks and cook for a further 3-4 minutes, stirring occasionally.
3. Pour in the cider and stock, add salt and pepper to taste and bring to the boil. Cover and simmer over a low heat for 20-25 minutes until the vegetables are tender.
4. Meanwhile, make the topping. Sift the flour into a bowl and stir in the parsley and sage and a good sprinkling of salt and pepper. Stir in the fromage frais and bring the mixture together with your fingertips to make a fairly firm dough. If it is too dry, add 1-2 teaspoons of skimmed milk. Roll out the dough to about 1.5 cm (½ in) thick and cut it into 18-20 triangles.
5. Add the peas and bouquet garni to the casserole and arrange the triangles on top, covering the surface. Transfer the casserole to the oven and cook for 25-30 minutes until the topping is well risen and golden brown.

Roasted Mediterranean lamb and potatoes

Nutrients per serving
- Calories 346
- Carbohydrate 27 g
- Protein 29 g
- Fat 14 g (including saturated fat 5 g)

This one-dish meal is an easy Greek-style roast bursting with the fresh flavours of lemon and herbs.

PREPARATION TIME: 15-20 minutes
COOKING TIME: 1 hour-1 hour 5 minutes
SERVES 4

550 g (1 lb 4 oz) lean lamb leg steak
300 g (10½ oz) onions, cut into quarters, or shallots, peeled but left whole
500 g (1 lb 2 oz) small new potatoes, scrubbed
1 large lemon, cut into 8 wedges
1 tablespoon olive oil
12 cloves garlic, peeled
6 sprigs each of fresh rosemary and thyme
Salt and black pepper
180 g (6½ oz) cherry or baby plum tomatoes, cut in half
1 tablespoon mint sauce, or 2 tablespoons mint jelly, melted

1. Heat the oven to 200°C (400°F, gas mark 6). Trim any fat off the lamb, cut the meat into 2.5 cm (1 in) cubes and arrange them in a large roasting tin with the onions or shallots and potatoes, cut in half if large.
2. Squeeze the juice from four of the lemon wedges, whisk it into the oil and drizzle it over the meat and vegetables. Tuck all eight lemon wedges, the garlic and half of the herbs into the dish and season to taste. Cover the tin tightly with foil and cook for 45 minutes.
3. Remove the foil and the herbs and discard them, then increase the oven heat to 220°C (425°F, gas mark 7). Add the tomatoes and remaining herbs and baste the meat and vegetables with the mint sauce or melted jelly. Roast for a further 15-20 minutes, uncovered, until the meat and vegetables are browned and tender.
4. Divide the lamb and vegetables between four plates, spoon on any roasting juices and serve.

THYME

GLAZED LAMB FILLET WITH A HERB AND YOGHURT SAUCE

Stir-fried lamb with black bean sauce

Black beans impart an intense flavour to this dish, inspired by a classic Chinese recipe.

PREPARATION TIME: 10 minutes, plus 20 minutes soaking if using fermented black beans
COOKING TIME: 25 minutes
SERVES 4

3 tablespoons salted, fermented black beans, or 2 tablespoons ready-made black bean sauce
400 g (14 oz) lean lamb neck fillet or leg steak
2 tablespoons nut or olive oil
100 g (3½ oz) carrots, cut into matchsticks
100 g (3½ oz) shallots, sliced
1 fresh red chilli, deseeded and sliced
4 cloves garlic, sliced
1 tablespoon finely sliced ginger
100 g (3½ oz) shiitake mushrooms, large ones roughly sliced, small ones left whole
2 tablespoons dark soy sauce
1 tablespoon tomato purée
300 ml (10 fl oz) lamb or chicken stock, or dry white wine
To garnish: chopped fresh coriander

1 If using fermented black beans, put them in a bowl, pour boiling water over them and leave them to soak for 20 minutes, then drain.
2 Trim any fat off the lamb and slice the meat across the grain into 5 mm (¼ in) slices and then with the grain into 5 mm (¼ in) strips.
3 Heat 1 tablespoon of the oil in a wok or heavy-based frying pan and when it is very hot, add the meat and stir-fry for 1-2 minutes until lightly browned. Lift the lamb out and keep it hot. If your wok or pan is small, cook the lamb in two batches to prevent it stewing.
4 Wipe the wok or pan clean with kitchen paper, add the rest of the oil and, when it is very hot, add the carrots, shallots, chilli, garlic and ginger and stir-fry for 3-4 minutes until they start to brown. Add the mushrooms and continue frying for 2-3 minutes.
5 Add the soy sauce, tomato purée, stock or wine and fermented black beans or black bean sauce. Bring the mixture to the boil then simmer for 10 minutes.
6 Increase the heat and boil the sauce hard until it is slightly reduced, then add the meat and warm it through for 1 minute. Sprinkle with the coriander and serve.

Variation: you could use chicken, lean duck or seafood instead of lamb.
Serving suggestion: plain rice noodles or rice, and Soy-Dressed Green Beans (page 235).

Nutrients per serving

- Calories 266
- Carbohydrate 5 g
- Protein 20 g
- Fat 18 g (including saturated fat 6 g)

Glazed lamb fillet with a herb and yoghurt sauce

A herby sauce makes a mouth-watering meal of sliced lean lamb and vegetables.

PREPARATION TIME: 20 minutes
COOKING TIME: 20 minutes
SERVES 4

650 g (1 lb 7 oz) small new potatoes, cut in half lengthways
250 g (9 oz) green beans, trimmed and cut in half
400 g (14 oz) lean lamb neck fillet
1 tablespoon mustard powder
1 tablespoon soft brown sugar
175 g (6 oz) tomatoes

For the sauce:

1 tablespoon clear honey
1 tablespoon Dijon or English mustard
150 g (5½ oz) low-fat natural yoghurt
2 cloves garlic, chopped
2 tablespoons capers, drained and chopped
12 fresh basil leaves, torn
2 tablespoons finely chopped fresh mint
2 tablespoons finely chopped fresh parsley
1 tablespoon red wine or sherry vinegar
Salt and black pepper

1. First make the sauce: mix together the honey, mustard and yoghurt. Stir in the garlic, capers, basil, mint and parsley, add the wine or vinegar and season to taste. Cover and chill.
2. Bring a saucepan of water to the boil, add the potatoes and a pinch of salt and cook for 10-15 minutes, adding the beans for the last 2 minutes.
3. Meanwhile, heat the grill to high and put a kettle on to boil. Trim the lamb of any fat. Combine the mustard powder and sugar and rub it all over the meat, then grill it for 5 minutes on each side, or until tender.
4. Cover the tomatoes with the boiling water, leave them for 1 minute, then skin, deseed and chop them.
5. When the vegetables are just tender, drain them thoroughly and mix them with the tomatoes.
6. Divide the potatoes and beans between four plates. Cut the lamb into thin slices and arrange them on top of the vegetables. Spoon a little sauce onto the lamb and serve the remainder on the side.

Nutrients per serving

- Calories 402
- Carbohydrate 39 g
- Protein 27 g
- Fat 16 g (including saturated fat 7 g)

STIR-FRIED LAMB WITH BLACK BEAN SAUCE

Poached lamb with herb and caper sauce

Try this tender young lamb with its piquant sauce as a light alternative to a more traditional Sunday roast.

PREPARATION TIME: 15 minutes
COOKING TIME: about 1 hour, according to weight of lamb
SERVES 4-6

1 small leg of lamb, about 1 kg (2 lb 4 oz)
2 bay leaves
2 cloves
1 small carrot, peeled but left whole
1 small onion, peeled but left whole
1 teaspoon black peppercorns
For the sauce:
15 g (½ oz) fresh mint
15 g (½ oz) fresh parsley
Grated zest and juice of 1 lemon
1 tablespoon olive oil
1 tablespoon capers, drained
1 teaspoon Dijon mustard
1 small clove garlic, crushed, optional
Salt and black pepper
To garnish: bay leaves

1. Trim any fat and skin off the lamb and weigh the meat to calculate the cooking time: it will take 35 minutes per kg (15 minutes per lb).
2. Place the lamb in a stockpot and add 750 ml (1 pint 7 fl oz) of water and the bay leaves, cloves, carrot, onion and peppercorns. Cover and slowly bring to the boil, then lower the heat so the liquid just simmers. Poach the meat, beginning the timing from this point. Skim off any foam as necessary during poaching.
3. Remove the lamb from the stock and leave it in a warm place to stand. Boil the stock hard until it has reduced by half.
4. Meanwhile, make the sauce. Strip the mint leaves from the stems. Place the parsley (tender stalks and leaves) into the bowl of a food processor with the mint leaves, lemon zest and juice, oil, capers, mustard and garlic, if using. Process for just long enough to chop the leaves.
5. Add 6 tablespoons of the reduced stock to the processed mixture and blend until it forms a reasonably smooth sauce. Season to taste then gently reheat it. (The remainder of the stock can be frozen for another use.)
6. Slice the lamb, garnish with a bay leaf and serve with the sauce.

Serving suggestion: Sweet Roasted Squash with Shallots (page 231) or Grilled Vegetable Salad (page 232).

Nutrients per serving, when serving 4
- Calories 333
- Carbohydrate 2 g
- Protein 39 g
- Fat 19 g (including saturated fat 8 g)

Roast lamb with sweetcorn and apricot stuffing

Sumptuously thick slices of roasted lamb and a sweet and savoury filling make a robust main course.

PREPARATION TIME: 20 minutes
COOKING TIME: 1 hour
SERVES 4

700 g (1 lb 9 oz) best end of neck of lamb, boned
Salt and black pepper
75 g (2¾ oz) ready-to-eat dried apricots
125 g (4½ oz) wholemeal breadcrumbs
175 g (6 oz) sweetcorn, drained if canned, defrosted if frozen
2 tablespoons chopped fresh chives
1 egg white
1 tablespoon Dijon mustard
To garnish: fresh chives

1 Heat the oven to 200°C (400°F, gas mark 6). If the boned lamb has been rolled, remove any string and unroll it. Cut off the meatless flap at the thin end of the joint and trim away any excess fat. Lay the meat flat, skin side down, on a board and sprinkle it with salt and pepper to taste.
2 Roughly chop the apricots and mix them with the breadcrumbs, sweetcorn, chives, egg white and mustard. Season well and spread the mixture over the surface of the lamb, pressing it down evenly.
3 Starting at the fleshy end of the lamb, roll it up into a tight cylinder. Tie it firmly but not too tightly with fine cotton string at 2.5 cm (1 in) intervals, then place it seam downwards on a rack in a roasting tin. Roast it for 1 hour, or until golden brown. Cut the roast into thick slices and serve hot, garnished with chives.

Serving suggestion: steamed runner beans and new potatoes.

Nutrients per serving

- Calories 449
- Carbohydrate 37 g
- Protein 41 g
- Fat 16 g (including saturated fat 7 g)

Lamb noisettes with fig and kumquat sauce

Tender pieces of lamb spread with garlic and herbs are served with a fruity sauce.

PREPARATION TIME: 45 minutes
COOKING TIME: 25 minutes
SERVES 4

2 cloves garlic
2 tablespoons finely chopped fresh basil
2 tablespoons finely chopped fresh parsley
Salt and black pepper
1 kg (2 lb 4 oz) best end of neck of lamb, boned
Whole nutmeg, for grating
8 large sprigs fresh rosemary
2 teaspoons olive oil

For the sauce:
100 g (3½ oz) ready-to-eat dried figs
100 g (3½ oz) kumquats, thinly sliced and seeds removed
125 ml (4 fl oz) dry white wine
300 ml (10 fl oz) chicken stock

1 Crush the garlic, basil, parsley and a little salt almost to a paste.
2 If the boned lamb has been rolled, remove any string and unroll it. Cut off the meatless flap at the thin end of the joint and trim any excess fat.
3 Lay the lamb skin side down, season with black pepper and grated nutmeg to taste, and spread the herb paste over it. Starting at the fleshy end of the lamb, roll it up into a cylinder and tie it at 2.5 cm (1 in) intervals with fine string, starting 1 cm (½ in) in from the end. Then cut it into eight noisettes halfway between each tie.
4 Push a sprig of rosemary through each noisette, then brush both sides of each noisette with oil. Cover and set aside while you make the sauce.
5 Remove any stalks from the figs, cut the stalks in half and put them into a saucepan with the kumquats, wine and stock. Bring to the boil then reduce the heat, cover and cook gently for 10 minutes. Uncover the pan, raise the heat slightly and allow the sauce to bubble for 3-4 minutes until reduced to a slightly syrupy consistency. Put the lid back on and keep the sauce warm over a low heat.
6 Heat a ridged, iron grill pan or heavy-based nonstick frying pan until very hot, add the noisettes and cook them for 3-4 minutes each side. Or cook them under a hot grill or on a barbecue: they will take a minute or so longer to cook.
7 Remove the string from the noisettes before serving them, accompanied with some sauce.

Serving suggestion: potatoes and a green vegetable such as broccoli.

Nutrients per serving

- Calories 337
- Carbohydrate 15 g
- Protein 32 g
- Fat 15 g (including saturated fat 6 g)

Indian baked lamb

Nutrients per serving, including 1 chapatti

- Calories 368
- Carbohydrate 33 g
- Protein 36 g
- Fat 13 g (including saturated fat: trace)

Make an Indian version of stuffed pancakes with minced lamb marinated in a tantalising mix of herbs and spices.

PREPARATION TIME: 5-10 minutes, plus 1-2 hours, or overnight, marinating

COOKING TIME: 30 minutes

SERVES 4

500 g (1 lb 2 oz) extra-lean minced lamb
4 chapattis
1 tablespoon each chopped cucumber, red onion and tomatoes
4 tablespoons low-fat fromage frais
2 teaspoons paprika
A few fresh mint leaves

For the marinade:

125 g (4½ oz) low-fat natural yoghurt
175 g (6 oz) onions, chopped
2 tablespoons chopped ginger
8 cloves garlic, chopped
2 green chillies, deseeded and chopped
6 sprigs fresh coriander, including tender stems
6-8 fresh mint leaves, or ½ teaspoon dried mint
½ teaspoon ground turmeric
Salt
1½ tablespoons ground cumin
1½ tablespoons ground coriander
1 teaspoon garam masala

1. Put all the marinade ingredients into a food processor and blend them to a smooth purée.
2. Place the minced lamb in a mixing bowl, add the marinade and blend thoroughly. Cover and leave to marinate for 1-2 hours, or refrigerate overnight, to allow the flavours to develop. Bring the meat to room temperature before cooking.
3. Heat the oven to 200°C (400°F, gas mark 6). Spread the meat out evenly in a 25 x 20 cm (10 x 8 in) ovenproof dish and bake it in the top half of the oven for 10 minutes.
4. Remove the dish from the oven and break the mince down with a fork to chunky pieces, then stir it thoroughly so that it absorbs any cooking juices. Return it to the oven and cook for a further 15-20 minutes, stirring halfway through, until the mince is lightly browned and most of the cooking juices have evaporated. Then give it a final stir so that any remaining juices are absorbed.
5. Spoon equal portions of lamb on top of each chapatti, then top each with some chopped salad vegetables and a little fromage frais. Serve garnished with a sprinkle of paprika and a few mint leaves.

Lamb Rogan Josh

Nutrients per serving

- Calories 292
- Carbohydrate 9 g
- Protein 28 g
- Fat 17 g (including saturated fat 4 g)

Lean lamb releases its juices during slow, gentle cooking in this mild curry flavoured with dry-roasted spices.

PREPARATION TIME: 35 minutes
COOKING TIME: 1 hour 10 minutes
SERVES 4

75 g (2¾ oz) natural yoghurt
½-1 teaspoon cayenne pepper
2 teaspoons ground coriander
1½ teaspoons ground cumin
2 teaspoons garlic purée, or crushed fresh garlic
2 teaspoons ginger purée, or grated fresh ginger
1 teaspoon paprika
½ teaspoon ground turmeric
550 g (1 lb 4 oz) lamb neck fillet or leg steak
300 g (10½ oz) onions, finely chopped
1½ tablespoons tomato purée
Salt
25 g (1 oz) unsalted butter
2 bay leaves, crumbled
2 green cardamom pods, split open at the top
5 cm (2 in) cinnamon stick, broken in half
4 whole cloves
½ teaspoon freshly grated nutmeg
1 tablespoon chopped fresh mint
2 tablespoons chopped fresh coriander

1. Mix the yoghurt with the cayenne pepper, coriander, cumin, garlic, ginger, paprika and turmeric.
2. Trim the lamb of any fat and cut it into 5 cm (2 in) cubes. Put them into a nonstick saucepan with the onions, place the pan over a medium heat and stir until the contents begin to sizzle.
3. Add the yoghurt mixture, reduce the heat to low, cover and cook for about 30 minutes, stirring occasionally, until the lamb has released all its natural juices.
4. Remove the lid, increase the heat to medium and cook for 5-6 minutes, stirring frequently, until the sauce has reduced to a paste-like consistency.
5. Put a kettle on to boil. Add the tomato purée, some salt and 15 g (½ oz) of the butter to the lamb. Reduce the heat to low again and cook, uncovered, for 3-4 minutes, stirring frequently. Then add 350 ml (12 fl oz) of boiling water from the kettle, cover and simmer for 15 minutes.
6. In a small pan, melt the remaining butter over a low heat, add the bay leaves, cardamom, cinnamon and cloves and allow them to sizzle for 35-40 seconds. Add the nutmeg, stir once and pour the contents over the meat. Mix well, cover and cook for a further 10-12 minutes. Stir in the chopped mint and coriander and serve.

Serving suggestion: Cardamom Rice (page 224).

Aubergine stuffed with **lamb** and **rice**

Middle Eastern flavours infuse these aubergines filled with a mixture of lamb and rice.

PREPARATION TIME: 15 minutes
COOKING TIME: 45 minutes
SERVES 4

2 medium aubergines, about 325 g (11½ oz) each
250 g (9 oz) lean minced lamb
1 tablespoon olive oil
2 cloves garlic, crushed
150 g (5½ oz) onions, chopped
1 teaspoon ground coriander
½ teaspoon ground cumin
100 g (3½ oz) long-grain rice
300 ml (10 fl oz) stock or water
Salt and black pepper
1 tablespoon chopped fresh mint or dill
2 tablespoons chopped fresh parsley
To garnish: chopped fresh mint and flat-leaved parsley
To serve: natural yoghurt, or half-fat crème fraîche, optional

1. Bring a large pan of lightly salted water to the boil. Meanwhile, cut the aubergines in half lengthways, cut out the flesh, taking care not to puncture the skins, and chop it into 1 cm (½ in) chunks.
2. Put the aubergine shells in the boiling water, reduce the heat and simmer for 2-3 minutes until they have softened. Remove the shells, then place them cut side down on kitchen paper to drain and pat them dry.
3. Heat a large nonstick frying pan and dry-fry the minced lamb until it has browned, stirring frequently to break up any lumps. Remove the meat, drain off any fatty juices and wipe the pan clean with kitchen paper.
4. Heat the oven to 180°C (350°F, gas mark 4). Add the oil and 2 tablespoons of water to the frying pan and sauté the chopped aubergine flesh, garlic and onions for 5 minutes, or until they have softened. Return the meat to the pan, stir in the coriander, cumin and rice and cook for 1 minute, stirring.
5. Stir in the stock or water, add seasoning to taste and bring to the boil, then reduce the heat, cover and simmer for 10-15 minutes until the rice has absorbed the liquid. Stir in the mint or dill and parsley, and remove from the heat.
6. Put the aubergine shells into a shallow ovenproof dish and spoon in the filling, piling it up. Bake for 15-20 minutes until the filling is lightly browned. Serve the aubergines hot, garnished with parsley and mint, and topped with spoonfuls of yoghurt or half-fat crème fraîche, if you like.

Serving suggestion: Moroccan Carrot Dip (page 72) and Marinated Leeks (page 90).

Nutrients per serving

- Calories 249
- Carbohydrate 27 g
- Protein 17 g
- Fat 8 g (including saturated fat 1 g)

Spicy lamb tagine with couscous

Capture the atmosphere of Morocco with this filling stew of lamb, fruit and vegetables, served with fluffy couscous.

PREPARATION TIME: 35 minutes
COOKING TIME: 2 hours
SERVES 6

800 g (1 lb 12 oz) lean lamb leg steak
125 g (4½ oz) onions, chopped
2 cloves garlic, chopped
½ teaspoon cayenne pepper
5 cm (2 in) cinnamon stick, broken in half
1 teaspoon ground ginger
1 teaspoon paprika
10-12 saffron strands
Salt and black pepper
125 g (4½ oz) ready-to-eat dried apricots, quartered
175 g (6 oz) carrots, diced
100 g (3½ oz) courgettes, diced
350 g (12 oz) tomatoes, chopped
2 tablespoons chopped fresh coriander
2 tablespoons chopped fresh parsley
300 g (10½ oz) couscous
To garnish: 1 tablespoon each of chopped fresh coriander and parsley

1. Trim any fat off the lamb and cut it into 2.5 cm (1 in) cubes. Put the meat, onions, garlic, cayenne pepper, cinnamon, ginger, paprika and saffron into the bottom of a double boiler or a large saucepan, season to taste and add enough water to cover. Bring the contents to the boil, then cover the pan, reduce the heat to low and simmer for 1 hour 30 minutes.
2. Add the apricots, carrots, courgettes, tomatoes, coriander and parsley to the pan and cook, covered, for a further 15 minutes.
3. Meanwhile, put the couscous into a bowl, add just enough cold water to cover it and leave it for 5 minutes to absorb the liquid.
4. Transfer the couscous to the top of the double boiler, or, if using a saucepan, put it into a sieve, and steam the couscous over the stew for 15 minutes until warm, fluffed up and tender. Add salt to taste.
5. To serve, spoon the couscous onto a serving dish; lift the lamb and vegetables from the pan with a slotted spoon and lay them on top of the couscous and sprinkle them with chopped coriander and parsley. Pour the broth into a jug or bowl to serve separately and let people help themselves at the table.

Nutrients per serving

- Calories 381
- Carbohydrate 41 g
- Protein 32 g
- Fat 11 g (saturated fat: trace)

SAFFRON STRANDS

HAM SIMMERED IN CIDER

Chargrilled pork with **little baked apples**

Seared pork fillet is made deliciously sweet with the contrasting flavours of apples, lemon and rosemary.

PREPARATION TIME: 30 minutes, plus 1 hour or overnight marinating
COOKING TIME: 25 minutes
SERVES 4

500g (1 lb 2oz) pork fillet
4 dessert apples, such as Cox's Orange Pippin
4 sprigs fresh rosemary
4 teaspoons golden caster sugar, optional

For the marinade:
1 sprig fresh rosemary
1 clove garlic, crushed
Grated zest of 1 lemon
2 tablespoons olive oil
Salt and black pepper

To garnish: a few sprigs of fresh rosemary

1. Trim any fat from the pork, cut the meat into 1 cm (½ in) thick medallions and place them in a mixing bowl.
2. To make the marinade, remove the leaves from the sprig of rosemary, chop them roughly and add them to the pork with the garlic, lemon zest, olive oil and pepper. Cover and chill for at least 1 hour – overnight is best as it allows the flavours to permeate the meat.
3. Heat the oven to 180°C (350°F, gas mark 4). Thirty minutes before you want to serve, core the apples and cut a ring through the skin around their circumference, so they can expand as they cook. Tuck a sprig of rosemary into the centre of each apple, with a teaspoon of caster sugar if using, and bake the apples for 25 minutes, or until just soft.
4. Meanwhile, heat a ridged, iron grill pan or nonstick frying pan over a medium-high heat. Remove the medallions from their marinade, season with salt and sear them for 2-4 minutes on each side until browned. Serve with the baked apples and garnish with sprigs of rosemary.

Variation: make a simple gravy by reducing some chicken or pork stock. You could also deglaze the grill pan or frying pan with a little dry cider.
Serving suggestion: steamed courgettes and plain boiled rice.

Nutrients per serving

- Calories 247
- Carbohydrate 15g
- Protein 25g
- Fat 10g (including saturated fat 2g)

Ham simmered in cider

Poaching ham keeps it moist without adding any fat. For a succulent dish, serve it with a selection of vegetables.

PREPARATION TIME: 10 minutes, plus 15 minutes standing

COOKING TIME: 1 hour 20 minutes

SERVES 6

1 kg (2 lb 4 oz) gammon joint
1 litre (1 pint 15 fl oz) dry or medium cider
4 cloves
1 medium onion, cut in half
1 bouquet garni
75 g (2¾ oz) carrots, sliced
1 stick celery, sliced
6 juniper berries
6 black peppercorns

1. Place the gammon in a large saucepan, cover it with water and bring to the boil, then drain and rinse any foam from the joint. Clean the pan.
2. Return the gammon to the pan and add the cider. Push two cloves into each onion half, then add them to the pan with the bouquet garni, carrots, celery, juniper berries and peppercorns. Pour in enough water to cover the joint and bring to the boil, then lower the heat and simmer the gammon for 1 hour 15 minutes. Take care not to cook it any longer or it will become tough and dry.
3. Remove the gammon from the pan, discard the cooking liquid and the flavourings, and leave the joint to stand for 15 minutes.
4. Trim away any fat from the joint, then carve the meat into slices and serve.

Variation: to serve the joint cold, leave it to cool in the cooking liquid before slicing it. This keeps the meat succulent.

Serving suggestion: mashed potatoes and a selection of steamed vegetables.

Nutrients per serving

- Calories 276
- Carbohydrate 7 g
- Protein 24 g
- Fat 12 g (including saturated fat 4 g)

CHARGRILLED PORK WITH LITTLE BAKED APPLES

Baked pork with **coconut** and **lemongrass**

Succulent chunks of pork, coated in a spicy yoghurt marinade, are baked then simmered in a light, lemony coconut broth.

PREPARATION TIME: 20 minutes, plus 3-4 hours, or overnight, marinating

COOKING TIME: 45 minutes

SERVES 4

600 g (1 lb 5 oz) boneless pork steak
40 g (1½ oz) coconut milk powder or 250 ml (9 fl oz) canned coconut milk
2 stalks lemongrass, bruised with a rolling pin
Salt
1-2 green chillies, deseeded and cut into matchsticks
2 tablespoons chopped fresh coriander

For the marinade:
50 g (1¾ oz) natural yoghurt
125 g (4½ oz) onions, finely sliced
½ teaspoon cayenne pepper
1½ teaspoons ground coriander
½ teaspoon garam masala
2 teaspoons garlic purée, or crushed garlic
2 teaspoons ginger purée, or grated ginger
½ teaspoon ground turmeric

LEMONGRASS

1 Trim the rind and fat from the pork, then cut the meat into 5 cm (2 in) cubes and place them in a large mixing bowl.
2 Mix together all the marinade ingredients, then spoon the mixture over the cubed pork, coating it well, and set aside for 3-4 hours, or overnight, in the refrigerator. Bring to room temperature before cooking.
3 Heat the oven to 200°C (400°F, gas mark 6). Spread out the marinated meat evenly in an ovenproof dish and bake it in the centre of the oven for 30 minutes, or until the onions and the edges of the meat have browned.
4 Blend the coconut milk powder, if using, with 250 ml (9 fl oz) of hot water. Transfer the pork mixture to a saucepan, pour the coconut milk over it and add the lemongrass, and salt to taste. Slowly bring the pan to a simmer, cover it and cook for a further 10-12 minutes.
5 Stir in most of the chopped chilli and the coriander, reserving a little of both for garnish. Discard the lemongrass and serve.

Serving suggestion: plain boiled rice.

Nutrients per serving

- Calories 198
- Carbohydrate 7 g
- Protein 30 g
- Fat 6 g (including saturated fat 2 g)

Chinese roasted pork

A hoisin and soy marinade adds rich colour and an Oriental flavour to roasted pork.

PREPARATION TIME: 10 minutes, plus 2 hours marinating
COOKING TIME: 25 minutes
SERVES 4-6

2 pork fillets, about 350 g (12 oz) each
1 teaspoon Chinese 5-spice powder
2 cloves garlic, crushed
75 g (2¾ oz) caster sugar
125 ml (4 fl oz) hoisin sauce
3 tablespoons soy sauce
2 tablespoons Chinese rice wine, sake, or dry sherry

1 Trim any fat from the pork. Rub the meat all over with the 5-spice powder and then the crushed garlic. Place the spiced pork in a china or glass dish.
2 Mix together the caster sugar, hoisin sauce, soy sauce and rice wine, sake or sherry and pour the mixture over the pork, making sure it is evenly coated. Cover and leave the meat to marinate in the refrigerator for 2 hours.
3 Heat the oven to 200°C (400°F, gas mark 6). Put about 2.5 cm (1 in) of water in the bottom of a roasting tin, place the marinated pork on a rack in the tin, and roast it for 25 minutes. Baste the meat frequently with the marinade, and turn the meat over halfway through roasting.
4 Take the pork out of the oven and leave it to stand for 15 minutes, then carve it into slices.

Variation: while the meat is resting, make a sauce from the marinade left in the roasting tin by simmering the juices in a saucepan for 10 minutes.

Serving suggestion: ribbons of carrots, courgettes and spring onions stir-fried in chicken stock with a little oyster sauce, tossed with egg thread noodles.

Nutrients per serving, when serving 4

- Calories 347
- Carbohydrate 33 g
- Protein 37 g
- Fat 7 g (including saturated fat 2 g)

Chilli pork tortillas

Eat this dish the Mexican way, with a delicious combination of spicy pork and fried beans neatly rolled up in soft tortillas.

PREPARATION TIME: 15 minutes, plus 30 minutes marinating
COOKING TIME: 20 minutes
SERVES 4

450 g (1 lb) pork fillet or boned loin
1 teaspoon ground coriander
1 small fresh red chilli, deseeded and chopped
1 clove garlic, crushed
4 tablespoons lime juice
2 teaspoons sunflower oil
75 g (2¾ oz) onions, thinly sliced
400 g (14 oz) canned red kidney beans, rinsed and drained
150 g (5½ oz) beef tomatoes, skinned, deseeded and diced
Salt and black pepper
8 flour tortillas
To serve: 4 tablespoons low-fat natural yoghurt; 2 tablespoons chopped fresh mint; 2 limes cut into wedges

1. Trim any fat from the pork, cut the meat into thin strips and place them in a bowl with the coriander. Add the chilli, garlic and lime juice, toss well to coat the meat evenly, then cover and leave it to marinate for 30 minutes.
2. Heat the oil in a heavy-based frying pan or wok and fry the onions over a medium-high heat for 3-4 minutes until they just begin to brown, stirring frequently. Add the marinated pork and continue cooking for a further 10 minutes, or until the meat is browned, stirring frequently.
3. Add the kidney beans and tomatoes to the pan, season well and simmer for 3-4 minutes until the tomatoes have softened.
4. Heat the grill to high, then warm the tortillas through for about 1 minute, turning once.
5. Divide the pork mixture between the tortillas. Top each one with yoghurt and mint and fold the tortillas over. Serve them with lime wedges.

Nutrients per serving

- Calories 528
- Carbohydrate 79 g
- Protein 41 g
- Fat 8 g (including saturated fat 1 g)

Chilli-stuffed pork rolls with raita

Nutrients per serving

- Calories 154
- Carbohydrate 7 g
- Protein 23 g
- Fat 4 g (including saturated fat: trace)

Cucumber and yoghurt provide a cooling contrast to pork escalopes rolled around a hot, ginger-spiced stuffing.

PREPARATION TIME: 15 minutes, plus 10 minutes standing

COOKING TIME: 10 minutes

SERVES 4

4 pork escalopes, about 100 g (3½ oz) each
1 green chilli, deseeded and roughly chopped
1 shallot, or 35 g (1¼ oz) onions, roughly chopped
2 tablespoons chopped fresh coriander
1 tablespoon roughly chopped ginger
50 ml (2 fl oz) apple juice, or any natural fruit juice
50 ml (2 fl oz) light soy sauce

For the raita:

10 cm (4 in) piece cucumber, peeled, deseeded and diced
Salt
150 g (5½ oz) low-fat natural yoghurt
2 tablespoons finely chopped red pepper
2 spring onions, chopped

1 To make the raita, place the diced cucumber in a sieve, sprinkle it liberally with salt and leave to stand for 10 minutes to draw out the moisture. Rinse it under cold running water and pat dry. Mix it with the remaining raita ingredients and chill while you cook the pork, but for no longer than 30 minutes or it will separate.
2 Lay each escalope between two sheets of cling film and beat it out with a rolling pin until 5 mm (¼ in) thick. Cut each escalope in half.
3 Process the chilli, shallot or onion, coriander and ginger in a food processor or with a hand-held mixer until they form a coarse paste. Spread this evenly over one side of each escalope half.
4 Roll up each piece of meat, enclosing the filling, and secure it with wooden cocktail sticks. Heat a nonstick frying pan or wok to very hot then dry-fry the rolls for about 4 minutes, turning them frequently, until browned all over.
5 Add the fruit juice and soy sauce to the pan and boil hard for 5 minutes or until almost evaporated, turning the rolls once or twice to glaze them. Serve them hot, with the chilled raita on the side.

Serving suggestion: boiled rice, steamed green beans and Ratatouille Chinese-Style (page 84).

Pork and mushroom crespelli

Nutrients per serving
- Calories 373
- Carbohydrate 42 g
- Protein 32 g
- Fat 10 g (including saturated fat 2 g)

Pancakes are too good for Shrove Tuesday alone. These baked Italian-style pancakes, with a piquant pork filling, are enjoyable any time of the year.

PREPARATION TIME: 30 minutes
COOKING TIME: 1 hour
SERVES 4

350 g (12 oz) extra-lean minced pork
125 g (4½ oz) leeks, thinly sliced
125 g (4½ oz) mushrooms, chopped
A pinch of cayenne pepper
½ teaspoon dried sage
A little vegetable oil for greasing
1 tablespoon cornflour
A pinch of mustard powder
300 ml (10 fl oz) skimmed milk
Salt and black pepper

For the batter:
125 g (4½ oz) plain white flour
1 egg
300 ml (10 fl oz) skimmed milk
2 teaspoons vegetable oil for frying
For the topping:
3-4 tomatoes, thickly sliced
15 g (½ oz) Parmesan cheese, finely grated
To garnish: chopped fresh flat-leaved parsley and a little freshly grated Parmesan cheese, optional

1. Prepare the batter: place the flour, egg, milk and a pinch of salt into a food processor and blend until smooth, or put them in a bowl and blend with a hand-held mixer or a whisk. Allow the batter to stand while you fry the meat. Heat the oven to 190°C (375°F, gas mark 5).
2. To make the filling, dry-fry the minced pork in a nonstick saucepan or lidded frying pan over a medium heat until browned and crumbly. Add the leeks, mushrooms, cayenne pepper and sage. Cover, reduce the heat and let the mixture simmer, stirring occasionally, for 15 minutes, adding a little water if it becomes too dry.
3. Heat a small nonstick frying pan over a medium heat and brush with a little vegetable oil. Swirl 2 tablespoons of the batter into the hot pan and quickly tilt it to coat the base with a thin layer. Cook the pancake until lightly set, flip it over with a palette knife and cook it for a further 30 seconds. Remove it from the pan and keep it warm under a clean tea towel. Make seven more pancakes the same way, greasing the pan as necessary.
4. To complete the filling, blend the cornflour and mustard with 2 tablespoons of the milk. Bring the remaining milk to the boil in a large saucepan, briskly stir in the cornflour mixture and continue to boil until it is thickened. Season to taste.
5. Drain off any cooking juices from the pork, stir in the sauce and adjust the seasoning if necessary.
6. Spoon a strip of filling down one side of each pancake. Then roll them up and fit them snugly, seam side down, in a lightly oiled, shallow ovenproof dish. Arrange the tomato slices over the top and sprinkle with the cheese.
7. Bake the pancakes for 15-20 minutes until the tomatoes have softened and the pancake edges are just crisp. Serve garnished with a little chopped parsley, and Parmesan, if wished.

Serving suggestion: Sauté of Spring Vegetables with Herbs (page 232) or Brussels Sprouts with Mustard and Cumin (page 234).

Glazed pork kebabs

Nutrients per serving
- Calories 277
- Carbohydrate 20 g
- Protein 36 g
- Fat 7 g (including saturated fat: trace)

An orange marmalade marinade gives the classic combination of pork and apricots a very special lift.

PREPARATION TIME: 15 minutes, plus 30 minutes, or overnight, marinating
COOKING TIME: 20 minutes
SERVES 4

600 g (1 lb 5 oz) extra-lean boneless pork
12 ready-to-eat dried apricots
2 small courgettes, about 125 g (4½ oz) altogether, thickly sliced
2 small red or white onions, about 125 g (4¼ oz) altogether, cut into quarters

For the marinade:
4 tablespoons fine-shred orange marmalade
30 ml (1 fl oz) orange juice or sherry
2 tablespoons coarse-grained mustard
½ teaspoon ground ginger
½ teaspoon dried thyme or oregano

1 To make the marinade, melt the marmalade in a small saucepan over a gentle heat for 1-2 minutes. Stir in the remaining marinade ingredients and set aside to cool.
2 Trim any fat off the pork and cut the meat into 4 cm (1½ in) cubes. Place them in a large bowl, pour the marinade over and stir. Cover and leave at room temperature for 30 minutes, or refrigerate overnight, to allow the meat to soak up the flavours, then bring back to room temperature.
3 When you are ready to cook, heat the grill to a medium heat. Thread the meat cubes, apricots, courgettes and onions alternately onto four metal skewers. Grill the kebabs for 12-15 minutes, turning and brushing them with the reserved marinade, until the pork is tender and the juices run clear when the cubes are pierced with a knife.

Variation: boil up the remaining marinade and the pan juices from grilling the meat to make a hot sauce. Or stir ½ tablespoon each of chopped fresh coriander leaves and spring onion into 150 g (5½ oz) of low-fat natural yoghurt as a cool accompaniment.

Serving suggestion: plain rice and Fruity Brussels Sprouts (page 84).

DRIED APRICOTS

Pork koftas with **cider** and **cinnamon**

Gingery meatballs in an aromatic sauce of cider and roasted spices make an irresistible supper dish.

PREPARATION TIME: 25 minutes
COOKING TIME: 1 hour - 1 hour 10 minutes
SERVES 4

1 large thick slice white bread, crusts removed
100 ml (3½ fl oz) skimmed milk
500 g (1 lb 2 oz) lean minced pork
1-2 green chillies, deseeded and finely chopped
2 tablespoons chopped fresh coriander
1 tablespoon grated ginger
Salt
2 tablespoons sunflower oil
For the sauce:
2 cinnamon sticks, about 5 cm (2 in) long, broken in half
2 cloves garlic, crushed
1 teaspoon grated ginger
275 g (9½ oz) onions, finely chopped
1 teaspoon paprika
½ teaspoon ground turmeric
250 ml (9 fl oz) dry cider
2 teaspoons coriander seeds
½ teaspoon cumin seeds
½ teaspoon black peppercorns
30 g (1¼ oz) half-fat crème fraîche
To garnish: sprigs of fresh coriander

1 Lay the slice of bread in a shallow dish and pour the milk over it. Let it soak for 1-2 minutes, then squeeze out most of the milk.
2 Put the pork in a mixing bowl with the chilli, half the chopped coriander, all the ginger and a pinch of salt. Add the bread and mix thoroughly, then knead the mixture for 1-2 minutes. Divide it into 16 equal balls, each slightly larger than a walnut.
3 In a nonstick saucepan, heat the oil over a medium heat, add half the meatballs and fry for 2-3 minutes, stirring, until browned. Remove the meatballs and keep them warm, then brown the remaining meatballs. Add them to the first batch of meatballs and keep them warm.
4 Remove the pan from the heat and add the cinnamon sticks to the oil remaining in the pan. Allow them to sizzle for 20-25 seconds, then return the pan to the heat and add the garlic, ginger and onions. Fry over a medium-low heat for 8-9 minutes, stirring frequently, until the onions have softened and start to colour.
5 Stir in the paprika and turmeric and continue to fry for 1-2 minutes, then add the cider, some salt and the browned meatballs. Bring the liquid to a simmer, cover the pan and reduce the heat to low, then cook for 15 minutes.
6 Meanwhile, heat a small heavy-based pan over a medium heat. Add the coriander and cumin seeds and the peppercorns and dry-fry them for 30 seconds, stirring, until they release their aromas. Remove them from the pan and leave them to cool, then grind them in a spice mill or with a pestle and mortar.
7 Add the spice mixture to the meat, cover and continue simmering for a further 25-30 minutes.
8 Remove the cinnamon sticks and stir in the crème fraîche and the remaining chopped coriander. Serve garnished with sprigs of coriander.
Serving suggestion: Turmeric Rice (page 224) and a mixed salad.

Nutrients per serving

- Calories 315
- Carbohydrate 14 g
- Protein 31 g
- Fat 14 g (including saturated fat 5 g)

pasta and grains

Low-fat tip

Lamb fillet is so tender it can be seared briefly over a high heat, using hardly any fat.

Spicy noodles with seared lamb

Nutrients per serving

- Calories 559
- Carbohydrate 69 g
- Protein 34 g
- Fat 17 g (including saturated fat 5 g)

Thin noodles are laced with Thai-style flavourings to make a great partner for quickly cooked slices of tender lamb.

PREPARATION TIME: 10 minutes
COOKING TIME: 10-15 minutes
SERVES 2

½ tablespoon olive oil
200 g (7 oz) lamb fillet, thinly sliced
2-3 teaspoons sesame oil
250 g (9 oz) fresh mixed egg, spinach and tomato tagliolini, or other long, thin pasta
4 tablespoons chopped fresh coriander
2 tablespoons chopped fresh parsley
2 mild fresh red chillies, deseeded and finely chopped
2 mild green chillies, deseeded and finely chopped
1 clove garlic, crushed
Juice of ½ lime
Salt and black pepper
Tabasco sauce, optional

1 Put a large saucepan of salted water on to boil. Heat a large nonstick frying pan to a high heat and brush it with the olive oil. Sear the lamb for 1-2 minutes until browned all over. Transfer it to a plate, sprinkle the sesame oil over it and keep it warm.
2 Put the pasta in the boiling water and cook according to the instructions on the packet.
3 Drain the pasta and toss it with the coriander and parsley, chillies, garlic, lime juice, a pinch of salt and plenty of freshly ground black pepper. Add a dash of Tabasco sauce, if using, and a few extra drops of sesame oil if liked.
4 Arrange a mound of the spiced pasta on each plate and top with the slices of lamb.

GREEN CHILLIES

Tagliatelle carbonara

Nutrients per serving
- Calories 588
- Carbohydrate 84 g
- Protein 24 g
- Fat 16 g (including saturated fat 6 g)

Ribbons of pasta coated in bacon, eggs and cream make a warming supper dish, with less than half the fat of other versions of this popular Italian dish.

PREPARATION TIME: 10 minutes
COOKING TIME: 15-20 minutes
SERVES 2

1 clove garlic, crushed
1 shallot, finely chopped
2 tablespoons dry white wine
200 g (7 oz) dried tagliatelle or fettuccine
Salt and black pepper
50 g (1¾ oz) rindless streaky smoked bacon
2 tablespoons single cream
2 eggs
1 tablespoon freshly grated Parmesan cheese
1 tablespoon chopped fresh parsley

Low-fat tip

The white wine in this recipe adds flavour to make up for reducing the large amount of double cream traditionally used in this dish.

1. Cook the garlic, shallot and wine in a nonstick saucepan over a high heat for 2-3 minutes until the wine has evaporated.
2. Bring a large saucepan of water to the boil, add the pasta and a pinch of salt and cook according to the instructions on the packet.
3. Meanwhile, cut the bacon into thin strips and add it to the shallot mixture. Sauté over a high heat for 2-3 minutes until the bacon has cooked through and is crisp.
4. In a small bowl, whisk together the cream, eggs, Parmesan and parsley and season to taste.
5. Drain the pasta, then return it to the pan, stir in the bacon and shallot mixture and heat through for 1 minute.
6. Take the pan off the heat and stir in the cream and egg mixture. The eggs should thicken and lightly scramble in the heat of the pasta, but if they do not, place the pan over a low heat and cook for 1-2 minutes, stirring continuously, until the mixture is thick and creamy. Spoon into bowls and serve.

Variation: replace the bacon with wafer-thin smoked ham, which has less fat. Vegetarians could replace it with sliced button mushrooms.

Aubergine lasagne

Aubergine slices are the ideal filling for this superb vegetarian lasagne, which can be made a day in advance.

Nutrients per serving

- Calories 313
- Carbohydrate 33 g
- Protein 14 g
- Fat 15 g (including saturated fat 4 g)

PREPARATION TIME: 30 minutes, plus 30-40 minutes infusing
COOKING TIME: 1 hour 30 minutes - 1 hour 45 minutes
SERVES 4

600 g (1 lb 5 oz) aubergines, cut into 5 mm (¼ in) slices
Salt and black pepper
9-12 sheets dried spinach lasagne
Olive oil for greasing
25 g (1 oz) Parmesan cheese, grated
For the béchamel sauce:
600 ml (1 pint) skimmed milk
35 g (1¼ oz) carrots, sliced
1 shallot, thinly sliced
1 bay leaf
1 clove
1 large sprig of fresh flat-leaved parsley
12 black peppercorns
35 g (1¼ oz) 70 per cent fat spread
35 g (1¼ oz) plain white flour
Whole nutmeg for grating
For the tomato sauce:
1 tablespoon olive oil
250 g (9 oz) onions, finely chopped
1 clove garlic, crushed
800 g (1 lb 12 oz) canned chopped tomatoes
1 teaspoon dried oregano
4-6 tablespoons finely shredded fresh basil

1 First make the béchamel sauce. Pour the milk into a saucepan, add the carrots, shallot, bay leaf, clove, parsley and peppercorns, and bring to the boil. Remove the pan from the heat, cover and leave the mixture to infuse for 30-40 minutes.
2 Meanwhile, make the tomato sauce. Heat the olive oil in a large saucepan over a medium heat, add the onions and fry for 6-8 minutes until they are softened but not browned.
3 Add the garlic to the pan and cook for a further 1-2 minutes. Add the tomatoes and oregano and bring to the boil then simmer, uncovered, for 45 minutes, stirring frequently, or until it has reduced by about one-third. Season to taste.
4 Meanwhile, steam the aubergines in single-layer batches, for 4-5 minutes each batch, until they have softened. Then set them aside.
5 While the aubergines are steaming, bring a large saucepan of water to the boil. Cook the lasagne, a few sheets at a time, for 8 minutes, or until softened. Rinse them under cold water, drain well and set aside.
6 To complete the béchamel sauce, strain the infused milk and discard the flavourings. Melt the fat spread in a saucepan, stir in the flour and cook for 1 minute. Then slowly whisk in the milk and bring to the boil, whisking continuously until the sauce is thick enough to thinly coat the back of a spoon. Let it simmer for 3 minutes then add salt, pepper and freshly grated nutmeg to taste.
7 Meanwhile, heat the oven to 180°C (350°F, gas mark 4). Lightly grease a 25 x 20 x 5 cm (10 x 8 x 2 in) ovenproof dish with oil.
8 Place three sheets of pasta in the bottom of the dish, pour half the tomato sauce over them and sprinkle it with half the basil. Arrange half the aubergines in a single layer on top and spoon a third of the béchamel sauce over them. Repeat the layers and top with a layer of lasagne. Pour the remaining béchamel over the top and sprinkle with the Parmesan cheese.
9 Bake the lasagne for 35-40 minutes until it is golden brown and bubbling hot. Serve straight from the dish.

Variation: to prepare the lasagne in advance, assemble it in the dish, then cover it loosely with foil and refrigerate until ready to cook it.

Low-fat tip

Steaming the aubergines for this dish avoids having to cook them in a large amount of oil, which they soak up like a sponge.

Pasta e fagioli

This Italian stew marries small pasta shapes and beans to make a filling supper dish.

PREPARATION TIME: 25 minutes
COOKING TIME: 50-55 minutes
SERVES 6

2 tablespoons olive oil
75 g (2¾ oz) carrots, diced
1 stick celery, chopped
3 cloves garlic, crushed
50 g (1¾ oz) onions, chopped
1 tablespoon chopped fresh rosemary
400 g (14 oz) canned borlotti or pinto beans, drained and rinsed
600 ml (1 pint) tomato passata
300 ml (10 fl oz) vegetable stock
1 teaspoon caster sugar
125 g (4½ oz) dried small pasta shapes, such as shells
2 tablespoons chopped fresh parsley
Salt and black pepper
To garnish: a few fresh sprigs of rosemary
To serve: 25 g (1 oz) Parmesan cheese, grated

1 Heat the oil in a flameproof casserole and gently fry the carrots, celery, garlic, onions and rosemary for 10 minutes, or until softened but not coloured.
2 Stir in the beans, passata, stock and sugar and bring to the boil. Then cover, reduce the heat and simmer for 25 minutes, or until the vegetables are tender.
3 Add the pasta and parsley and season to taste then simmer, covered, for a further 10-15 minutes until the pasta is al dente. Serve sprinkled with rosemary and Parmesan cheese.

Nutrients per serving

- Calories 228
- Carbohydrate 35 g
- Protein 9 g
- Fat 6 g (including saturated fat 1 g)

Tagliatelle with summer vegetables

Nutrients per serving
- Calories 211
- Carbohydrate 34 g
- Protein 9 g
- Fat 5 g (including saturated fat 1 g)

Choose vegetables at their peak of freshness for this light pasta dish, which uses lemon, tarragon and garlic to bring out their delicate flavours.

PREPARATION TIME: 15 minutes
COOKING TIME: 15-20 minutes
SERVES 4

250 g (9 oz) thin asparagus
150 g (5½ oz) green beans
200 g (7 oz) small courgettes
150 g (5½ oz) young leeks
Salt and black pepper
500 g (1 lb 2 oz) fresh egg tagliatelle, or other thin pasta
1 tablespoon olive oil
1 clove garlic, finely chopped
4 tablespoons lemon juice, or to taste
2 teaspoons chopped fresh tarragon
2-3 tablespoons finely chopped fresh flat-leaved parsley

1. Put two saucepans of water on to boil. Trim off the woody stems of the asparagus and cut the spears into 2.5 cm (1 in) lengths. Trim the green beans and cut them in half. Slice the courgettes thinly. Trim and cut the leeks into quarters lengthways, then into 1 cm (½ in) slices.
2. Put the asparagus and beans into one pan of boiling water and cook them for 4 minutes, or until just tender. Drain, refresh them with cold water and set aside.
3. Add the pasta to the remaining pan of boiling water and cook according to the instructions on the packet.
4. Meanwhile, heat the olive oil in a wok or heavy-based nonstick frying pan over a medium-high heat. Add the garlic and stir-fry for 30 seconds, then add the courgettes and leeks and stir-fry for 3 minutes, or until the courgettes are tender but not too soft.
5. Add the asparagus and beans to the wok or pan and stir-fry for 1 minute, then mix in the lemon juice and tarragon. Remove from the heat and season with salt and pepper to taste.
6. Drain the pasta, reserving the cooking water. Stir the pasta into the vegetables, using a few teaspoons of the cooking water to moisten, if necessary. Sprinkle with the parsley and extra black pepper and serve.

Catalan-style pasta in tomato broth

This Spanish way of cooking pasta in a thick fresh sauce makes a rich side dish to accompany meat or fish.

PREPARATION TIME: 20 minutes
COOKING TIME: 30 minutes
SERVES 4

Nutrients per serving

- Calories 280
- Carbohydrate 55g
- Protein 7g
- Fat 4g (including saturated fat 1 g)

500g (1 lb 2oz) tomatoes, chopped
1 whole head garlic, separated into individual cloves and peeled
150g (5½ oz) onions, chopped
A strip of orange zest, about 5cm (2in) long
2 bay leaves and 2 sprigs of fresh thyme, tied together
10-12 strands saffron
600ml (1 pint) vegetable stock
A pinch of caster sugar
1 tablespoon olive oil
225g (8oz) vermicelli, broken into pieces
Salt and black pepper
To garnish: sprigs of fresh basil

1. Put the tomatoes, garlic, onions, orange zest, herbs, saffron, stock and sugar into a saucepan and bring to the boil. Cover, reduce the heat and simmer for 20 minutes.
2. Discard the herbs and zest, then purée the broth in a food processor or with a hand-held mixer.
3. Return the purée to the pan and stir in the oil, vermicelli, and some salt and pepper to taste. Bring to the boil then simmer, uncovered, for 8-10 minutes, stirring occasionally, until the pasta is cooked and the broth has thickened. Season to taste and serve, garnished with basil.

Pappardelle with **aubergine sauce**

East and West combine in this appetising supper dish of pasta and an unusual aubergine sauce flavoured with soy.

PREPARATION TIME: 10 minutes
COOKING TIME: 30 minutes
SERVES 4

- 1 tablespoon olive or groundnut oil
- 1-2 fresh red chillies, deseeded and roughly chopped
- 4 cloves garlic, roughly chopped
- 100 g (3½ oz) onions, chopped
- 1 red pepper, roughly chopped
- 600 g (1 lb 5 oz) baby aubergines, cut in half lengthways and sliced
- 2 tablespoons lemon juice
- 3 tablespoons dark soy sauce
- 300 ml (10 fl oz) vegetable or chicken stock
- 2 teaspoons tomato purée
- Salt
- 400 g (14 oz) dried pappardelle, or other ribbon pasta
- 3 tablespoons chopped fresh coriander or parsley
- **To garnish:** chopped fresh flat-leaved parsley

1. Heat the oil in a large frying pan over a high heat, add the chillies, garlic, onions and red pepper and stir-fry for 3-4 minutes until the onions begin to brown.
2. Add the aubergines to the pan and continue frying for 3-4 minutes, stirring frequently.
3. Stir the lemon juice, soy sauce, stock, tomato purée and salt to taste into the vegetables. Bring to the boil, then reduce the heat and simmer for 20 minutes. Raise the heat and boil for 3-4 minutes until most of the liquid has evaporated.
4. Meanwhile, put some water on to boil and cook the pappardelle according to the packet instructions.
5. Drain the pasta and divide it between four plates or bowls. Stir the coriander or parsley into the aubergine mixture, then spoon the vegetables over the pasta and garnish with chopped parsley.

Nutrients per serving

- Calories 425
- Carbohydrate 84 g
- Protein 16 g
- Fat 5 g (including saturated fat 1 g)

PAPPARDELLE

Soba noodles with **lentils, spinach** and **carrots**

Buckwheat soba noodles have a strong, nutty flavour which goes well with this combination of earthy lentils and vegetables.

PREPARATION TIME: 15 minutes
COOKING TIME: 20-30 minutes
SERVES 4

125 g (4½ oz) Puy lentils
1 bay leaf
2 teaspoons olive oil
3 cloves garlic, chopped
100 g (3½ oz) red onions, chopped
75 g (2¾ oz) carrots, finely diced
1 stick celery, finely chopped
2 teaspoons Dijon mustard
2 tablespoons dry sherry
Salt and black pepper
150 g (5½ oz) fresh spinach leaves, coarsely shredded
250 g (9 oz) dried soba noodles
2 tablespoons chopped fresh parsley

1. Put the lentils into a saucepan with the bay leaf, cover them with cold water and bring to the boil. Then reduce the heat and simmer for 10-15 minutes until the lentils are tender. Drain and set them aside.
2. Meanwhile, heat the olive oil in a nonstick saucepan over a very low heat. Add the garlic and onions, cover the pan and cook them for 7-10 minutes until they have softened. Meanwhile, put a kettle on to boil for the pasta.
3. Add the drained lentils, carrots, celery, mustard and sherry to the onions in the pan, season with salt and pepper to taste and mix well. Raise the heat to medium, cover the pan and cook for 2-3 minutes.
4. Add the spinach and 75 ml (2½ fl oz) of hot water, cover the pan again and continue cooking for a further 1 minute, or until the vegetables are tender, adding more hot water if the pan is very dry. Adjust the seasoning to taste.
5. Cook the pasta in the boiling water in a large pan, according to the instructions on the packet.
6. Drain the pasta, reserving a little of the cooking water. Toss the lentil mixture and parsley with the pasta, adding a little of the cooking water to moisten if necessary. Adjust the seasoning to taste and serve.

Tip: French Puy lentils are used in this dish because they keep their shape and texture better than other varieties of lentil.

Nutrients per serving

- Calories 347
- Carbohydrate 61 g
- Protein 18 g
- Fat 4 g (including saturated fat 1 g)

Black spaghetti with yellow pepper sauce

Nutrients per serving
- Calories 403
- Carbohydrate 81 g
- Protein 14 g
- Fat 5 g (including saturated fat 1 g)

Roasted peppers and balsamic vinegar make a wonderful balance of flavours and provide a dramatic visual contrast to coloured pasta.

PREPARATION TIME: 15 minutes, plus 5 minutes standing
COOKING TIME: 20 minutes
SERVES 4

4 yellow peppers, about 650 g (1 lb 7 oz) altogether
400 g (14 oz) black spaghetti, or other long, thin dried pasta
2 teaspoons balsamic or sherry vinegar
1 tablespoon extra virgin olive oil
1 tablespoon chopped fresh herbs, such as basil, chives or flat-leaved parsley
Salt and black pepper

1. Heat the grill to high and line the grill pan with foil. Cut the peppers in half and remove the cores and seeds, then place them on the grill pan, cut side down, and flatten them with the palm of your hand. Grill them for 20 minutes, or until the skins are blistered and charred but the interior flesh is still moist.
2. Remove the grill pan from the heat, fold the foil up around the peppers and seal it to make a pouch. Leave them to stand for 5 minutes.
3. Meanwhile, put some water on to boil and cook the pasta according to the packet instructions.
4. To make the sauce, peel the peppers, discarding the charred skins. Place the flesh in a food processor with the vinegar, olive oil and most of the chopped herbs, reserving some to use as a garnish. Process the mixture until it is smooth. Alternatively, place the ingredients in a bowl and purée with a hand-held mixer. Season to taste and reheat gently if necessary.
5. When the pasta is cooked, drain it and divide it between four bowls. Top with the sauce and serve, garnished with the reserved herbs.

Crab, basil and ginger ravioli

Nutrients per serving

- Calories 433
- Carbohydrate 59 g
- Protein 46 g
- Fat 3 g (no saturated fat)

Canned crabmeat is given a twist with fresh herbs and hot spices in this delectable filling for home-made pasta.

PREPARATION TIME: 1 hour, plus at least 30 minutes resting
COOKING TIME: 25 minutes
SERVES 4

For the pasta:
180 g (6½ oz) semolina flour or Italian type '00' pasta flour
125 g (4½ oz) plain white flour, plus extra for dusting
Salt and black pepper
For the filling:
850 g (1 lb 14 oz) canned crabmeat
2 egg whites
4 tablespoons chopped fresh basil
4 tablespoons chopped fresh coriander
1 large fresh red chilli, deseeded and finely chopped
2 teaspoons finely chopped garlic
2 teaspoons finely grated ginger
To garnish: sesame oil and sprigs of fresh basil
To serve: steamed vegetables

1. To make the pasta, sift the flours and a pinch of salt into a mixing bowl. Make a well in the centre, pour in 175 ml (6 fl oz) of water and stir to make a firm but not sticky dough. Add another tablespoon of water if the mixture is too dry, or of flour if it is too wet.
2. Knead the dough for 3-4 minutes until it becomes elastic, then cover loosely with cling film and set aside for at least 30 minutes to rest.
3. Meanwhile, to make the filling, put the crabmeat in a sieve and leave it to drain. Then place it in a bowl with the egg whites, basil, coriander, chilli, garlic and ginger and mix well. Season with black pepper to taste and set aside.
4. Cut the pasta dough into eight equal pieces, then roll each piece into a long strip. Set the pasta machine to its widest setting and roll one strip of dough through it. Fold the dough in half, lightly dust it with flour to prevent sticking and roll it through the machine again. Fold, dust and roll the dough through the machine once more, then set it aside. Repeat the process with the remaining strips.
5. Set the machine to the next setting and roll each strip of dough through once, then lower the setting and roll each piece of dough through again. Continue lowering the settings and rolling the dough through until you get to the fifth or sixth setting – the dough should be very thin but not transparent.
6. Put a large pan of water on to boil.
7. Use a serrated 4-5 cm (1½-2 in) biscuit cutter to stamp out rounds of dough. Place 1-2 heaped teaspoons of filling in the centre of half the rounds, dampen the edges with water and lay the remaining rounds on top. Press the edges firmly together to enclose the filling and to thin the double layer of dough slightly. Alternatively, cut and fill the ravioli with ravioli trays, following the manufacturer's instructions.
8. Working in batches, lower the ravioli into the boiling water and cook for 3 minutes, then drain them in a colander and keep them warm. Arrange the ravioli on plates and sprinkle them lightly with a few drops of sesame oil and fresh basil. Serve with steamed vegetables such as ribbons of carrot and leek.

Variation: if you do not have a pasta machine, use won ton wrappers to enclose the filling, and steam them for 5 minutes. If you cannot find semolina flour or Italian pasta flour, use strong plain white flour.

Tagliatelle with mussels in a rich dill sauce

Nutrients per serving

- Calories 652
- Carbohydrate 95 g
- Protein 38 g
- Fat 8 g (including saturated fat 3 g)

Fresh mussels, fragrant with dill and saffron, make a luxurious dish.

PREPARATION TIME: 50 minutes
COOKING TIME: 20-25 minutes
SERVES 4

2 kg (4 lb 8 oz) live mussels
300 ml (10 fl oz) dry white wine
2 bay leaves
2 sprigs fresh flat-leaved parsley
2 slices of lemon
Salt and black pepper
400 g (14 oz) dried tagliatelle
1 tablespoon cornflour
10-12 strands saffron, optional
3 tablespoons chopped fresh dill
250 g (9 oz) fromage frais

1 Scrub the mussels thoroughly, debeard them and rinse them well. Discard any that are damaged or remain open.
2 Divide the mussels between two large saucepans, then add half the wine, 1 bay leaf, 1 sprig of parsley and 1 slice of lemon to each pan. Cover and cook for 6-8 minutes over a high heat, shaking the pans frequently, until all the mussels have opened. Do not overcook them or they will be tough. Discard any that do not open.
3 Meanwhile, place a large colander over a large bowl and line it with muslin or kitchen paper. As soon as the mussels have opened, pour them into the colander to drain and cool, reserving the liquid. When the mussels are cool enough to handle, remove them from their shells and put them into a bowl.
4 Bring a large pan of salted water to the boil and cook the tagliatelle according to the instructions on the packet.
5 Meanwhile, pour the strained mussel liquid into a saucepan, bring it to the boil, then let it boil until reduced to 300 ml (10 fl oz), pouring it into a measuring jug from time to time to check.
6 Blend the cornflour with 1 tablespoon of cold water and stir it into the reduced mussel liquid. Add the saffron, if using, and return to the boil, stirring continuously. Then reduce the heat, add 2 tablespoons of the dill and let the sauce simmer for 5 minutes for the flavours to infuse.
7 Gradually whisk the fromage frais into the sauce, then add the mussels and heat them through over a medium heat. Do not let the sauce boil or it will curdle and the mussels will be tough. There is no need to add salt as the mussel liquid has a salty flavour.
8 Drain the pasta and stir it into the sauce. Divide the pasta between four bowls, garnish with pepper and the remaining dill and serve.

Spaghetti with **scallops** and **roasted peppers**

Nutrients per serving

- Calories 618
- Carbohydrate 86 g
- Protein 40 g
- Fat 15 g (including saturated fat 2 g)

Luscious roasted peppers and seared scallops make a perfect pairing in this delightfully simple affair.

PREPARATION TIME: 25 minutes
COOKING TIME: 20 minutes
SERVES 4

2 red peppers
2 yellow peppers
½ teaspoon flaked or crushed dried red chillies, or to taste
Grated zest and juice of 1 large lemon
4 tablespoons olive oil
6 tablespoons finely chopped fresh parsley
Salt and black pepper
400 g (14 oz) dried spaghetti
450 g (1 lb) fresh scallops
3 large cloves garlic, crushed
To garnish: 1 lemon, cut into 8 wedges, and grated Parmesan cheese, optional

1. Heat the grill. Cut the peppers into quarters, deseed them and arrange them, cut side down, on the grill pan. Grill for 8 minutes, or until their skins blister and blacken. Transfer them to a bowl and cover with cling film.
2. When the peppers are cool enough to handle, peel them and dice finely. Place them in a bowl with the chilli, lemon zest and 2 tablespoons of oil. Stir in the parsley, reserving a little for a garnish, and set aside.
3. Bring a large pan of salted water to the boil and cook the spaghetti according to the instructions on the packet. Drain and keep the pasta warm.
4. Meanwhile, gently remove the tough white muscle and the coral, if attached, from the scallops and pull away any dark digestive thread. Then rinse and pat each scallop dry. If they are very large, cut them into bite-size pieces. Toss them in 1 tablespoon of oil and season with salt and pepper to taste.
5. Heat a ridged, iron grill pan or large nonstick frying pan. When the spaghetti is nearly cooked, sear the scallops for 2-3 minutes on the grill pan, turning them over once. They should be very lightly browned but opaque and cooked through if cut open. Do not overcook them or they will be tough.
6. Heat 1 tablespoon of oil in a nonstick frying pan. Fry the garlic for 1 minute then stir in the roasted pepper mixture. When it is warm, add the scallops, lemon juice and spaghetti. Mix thoroughly and garnish with the reserved parsley and a sprinkling of black pepper. Serve the pasta with lemon wedges, and freshly grated Parmesan, if you like.

GRATING PARMESAN CHEESE

Tuna and seafood spaghetti

Spaghetti marinara, served without grated cheese, makes a quick and easy low-fat dish.

PREPARATION TIME: 5 minutes
COOKING TIME: about 20 minutes
SERVES 4

2 teaspoons olive oil
2 cloves garlic, chopped
100 g (3½ oz) onions, chopped
A pinch of cayenne pepper
400 g (14 oz) canned chopped tomatoes with herbs, or plain chopped tomatoes mixed with 1 teaspoon dried mixed herbs
1 tablespoon tomato purée
2 tablespoons chopped fresh parsley
250 g (9 oz) dried spaghetti
225 g (8 oz) ready-cooked mixed seafood, defrosted if frozen
200 g (7 oz) canned tuna in brine or water, drained
Salt and black pepper
To garnish: sprigs of fresh flat-leaved parsley

1 Heat the oil in a nonstick saucepan and fry the garlic and onions for 4-5 minutes until softened.
2 Add the cayenne pepper and cook for a further 1 minute, then stir in the tomatoes, tomato purée and parsley and simmer for 5 minutes, stirring occasionally.
3 Meanwhile, bring a large saucepan of water to the boil and cook the spaghetti according to the packet instructions.
4 Add the mixed seafood and tuna to the tomato sauce, heat them gently for 3-4 minutes, then season to taste.
5 Drain the spaghetti and divide between four bowls. Spoon the sauce over the pasta and serve, garnished with sprigs of parsley.

Nutrients per serving

- Calories 355
- Carbohydrate 54 g
- Protein 30 g
- Fat 4 g (including saturated fat 1 g)

Tiger prawn, tomato and basil tagliatelle

Mouth-watering large prawns are quickly fried, then tossed into fresh pasta with a juicy tomato and basil dressing.

PREPARATION TIME: 40 minutes
COOKING TIME: 10 minutes
SERVES 4

750 g (1 lb 10 oz) tomatoes
1 tablespoon finely chopped fresh basil
1½ tablespoons champagne vinegar or other white wine vinegar
2 tablespoons olive oil
Salt and black pepper
500 g (1 lb 2 oz) headless raw tiger prawns, defrosted if frozen
250 g (9 oz) fresh tagliatelle
3 cloves garlic, crushed
To garnish: fresh basil leaves

1 Put a kettle on to boil. Cut a cross in the base of the tomatoes, cover them with boiling water, leave them for 1-2 minutes then peel off the skins. Cut them into quarters and scrape the seeds into a nylon sieve set over a large mixing bowl. Strain as much of the juice as possible into the bowl and discard the seeds.
2 Dice the tomato flesh and add it to the juice in the bowl, then stir in the basil, vinegar and 1 tablespoon of oil. Season to taste and set aside. Put a pan of water on to boil for the pasta.
3 Peel the prawns then run a small sharp knife along the length of each back and pull away the dark digestive thread. Rinse the prawns and pat them dry with kitchen paper.
4 Put the pasta in the boiling water and cook it according to the instructions on the packet.
5 Meanwhile, heat 1 tablespoon of oil in a large nonstick frying pan over a high heat. When it is really hot, season the prawns and stir-fry them for 2 minutes. Add the garlic and continue stir-frying for a further 2-3 minutes until the prawns turn completely pink.
6 Drain the pasta and toss it into the tomato vinaigrette. Stir in the cooked prawns and the garlic-flavoured oil, garnish with basil and serve.

Nutrients per serving

- Calories 352
- Carbohydrate 40 g
- Protein 30 g
- Fat 8 g (including saturated fat 1 g)

Rice vermicelli with mustard and chillies

Rice vermicelli is partnered with seeds and coconut to make a savoury meat-free dish.

PREPARATION TIME: 10 minutes
COOKING TIME: 15 minutes
SERVES 4

225 g (8 oz) dried rice vermicelli
25 g (1 oz) unsweetened desiccated coconut
Salt
2 tablespoons sunflower oil
½ teaspoon black mustard seeds
1 green chilli, deseeded and chopped
1 dried red chilli, deseeded and chopped
½ teaspoon cumin seeds
12 curry leaves, optional
5 spring onions, chopped
To garnish: 4 grilled or microwaved poppadoms, lightly crushed

1. Put a kettle on to boil. Break up the vermicelli and set aside. Put the coconut in a small bowl with a pinch of salt, cover with 150 ml (5 fl oz) of boiling water and set aside.
2. Heat the oil in a large nonstick saucepan over a medium heat, then add the mustard seeds. As soon as they start popping, add the chillies, cumin seeds and curry leaves, if using, and stir-fry for 20-25 seconds. Add the spring onions and stir-fry for a further 2 minutes.
3. Stir in the noodles, 450 ml (16 fl oz) of boiling water, the coconut and its soaking water, then increase the heat to high. As soon as the water returns to the boil, reduce the heat to very low, cover the pan and cook for 10-12 minutes, stirring occasionally, until all the water has been absorbed.
4. Spoon the noodles into bowls and top with crushed poppadom.

Low-fat tip

In India, rice vermicelli is topped with deep-fried Bombay mix, but here grilled poppadoms are used instead.

RICE VERMICELLI

Nutrients per serving

- Calories 317
- Carbohydrate 49 g
- Protein 8 g
- Fat 10 g (including saturated fat 4 g)

Vietnamese chicken noodles

This chicken noodle soup is given an unusual twist with raw vegetables and exotic flavours.

PREPARATION TIME: 20 minutes
COOKING TIME: 15 minutes
SERVES 4

500 g (1 lb 2 oz) skinned and boned chicken, diced
1 litre (1 pint 15 fl oz) chicken stock
4 tablespoons Thai fish sauce
1 tablespoon grated ginger
350 g (12 oz) dried rice noodles
50 g (1¾ oz) beansprouts
60 g (2¼ oz) onions, finely sliced
2 tablespoons each chopped fresh Thai or ordinary basil leaves, coriander and mint
2-4 fresh bird's-eye red chillies or any small, hot red chillies, deseeded and finely sliced
2 spring onions, finely sliced
To serve: 1 lime, cut into quarters

1 Place the chicken, stock, fish sauce and grated ginger in a large saucepan and bring to the boil, then cover and simmer for 10-15 minutes until the chicken is cooked through.
2 Meanwhile, put a kettle on to boil, and soak the noodles in boiling water according to the packet instructions.
3 Drain the noodles and divide them between four serving bowls. Spoon the chicken, beansprouts and onions over the top, then sprinkle with the basil, coriander and mint. Drench the mixture with the chicken broth, then scatter the chillies and spring onions over the top.
4 Serve with the lime wedges.

Nutrients per serving

- Calories 522
- Carbohydrate 76 g
- Protein 40 g
- Fat 5 g (including saturated fat 1 g)

Cellophane noodles with chilli greens

Oriental vegetables with chilli is a deliciously different dish.

PREPARATION TIME: 30 minutes
COOKING TIME: 10 minutes
SERVES 4

100 g (3½ oz) cellophane noodles
2 tablespoons vegetable oil
2 spring onions, finely sliced
2 eggs, beaten
1 fresh red chilli, deseeded and finely chopped
2 cloves garlic, finely sliced
1 teaspoon finely chopped ginger
50 g (1¾ oz) water chestnuts, drained and roughly chopped
300 g (10½ oz) Chinese leaves, such as choi sum or pak choi, separated
4 tablespoons soy sauce
3 tablespoons mirin, or sweet sherry
Salt
50 g (1¾ oz) unsalted peanuts

1 Put the noodles in a bowl, cover them with plenty of cold water and leave to soak for 30 minutes while you prepare the vegetables.
2 Bring a large pan of water to the boil, drain the noodles and cook them according to the instructions on the packet. Drain and set aside.
3 Heat 1 tablespoon of the oil in a nonstick omelette pan, add the spring onions and allow them to sizzle for 5 seconds, then pour in the beaten egg and let it spread across the pan to form a thin omelette. Remove the omelette from the heat, roll it up and shred it finely.
4 Put the remaining 1 tablespoon of oil in a large wok or frying pan. When it is sizzling hot, add the chilli, garlic, ginger and water chestnuts and stir-fry for 20 seconds.
5 Add the greens to the pan, continue to stir-fry for 1 minute, or until they begin to wilt. Then add the shredded omelette, soy sauce and mirin or sherry and season to taste. Allow the liquid to bubble up, then stir in the noodles. Chop the peanuts, and sprinkle over the top to serve, with some extra soy sauce on the side.

Tip: cellophane noodles are made from mung beans and become transparent when cooked. If you cannot find them, you can use fine rice noodles instead, but they will be opaque.

Nutrients per serving

- Calories 290
- Carbohydrate 26 g
- Protein 10 g
- Fat 15 g (including saturated fat 3 g)

Pea orzotto

Parmesan cheese and white wine or sherry add body to this versatile barley dish.

PREPARATION TIME: 10 minutes
COOKING TIME: 1 hour
SERVES 4

850 ml (1 pint 10 fl oz) vegetable stock
2 teaspoons olive oil
50 g (1¾ oz) onions, finely chopped
125 g (4½ oz) pearl barley
50 ml (2 fl oz) white wine or sherry
150 g (5½ oz) frozen peas, defrosted
2 tablespoons freshly grated Parmesan cheese
Salt and black pepper

1. Put a kettle on to boil. Heat the stock to simmering point in a small saucepan. Meanwhile, in a larger saucepan, heat the olive oil then add the onions and fry them over a medium heat for 5 minutes, stirring frequently, until tender.
2. Add the pearl barley to the pan and stir continuously for 1-2 minutes until the grains are evenly coated with the oil and onion mixture. Increase the heat, add the wine or sherry to the pan and simmer for 1-2 minutes until the barley has absorbed the liquid.
3. Add a ladle of the hot stock to the barley, stirring continuously until it has been absorbed. Continue to add the stock a ladle at a time, stirring, and add half the peas before the last few ladles of stock. Continue stirring frequently until all the stock has been absorbed and the barley is al dente. This takes 35-45 minutes.
4. Meanwhile, place the remaining peas in a bowl and pour 100 ml (3½ fl oz) of boiling water over them, or just enough to cover them. Leave them to stand for 1-2 minutes, then purée them with their liquid using a food processor or a hand-held mixer.
5. Just before serving, stir the puréed peas and Parmesan into the orzotto and quickly heat them through. Season with salt and pepper to taste.

Tip: using barley gives this mixture a slightly firmer, more granular texture than a risotto made with rice, as barley grains do not release much starch during cooking.

Serving suggestion: serve as a side dish to accompany plainly cooked fish or meat, or as the main course of a vegetarian meal.

Nutrients per serving

- Calories 193
- Carbohydrate 32 g
- Protein 7 g
- Fat 5 g (including saturated fat 1 g)

Polenta with a **rich mushroom sauce**

Italian cornmeal is topped with a dark sauce combining dried and fresh mushrooms in this luxurious dinner dish.

PREPARATION TIME: 10 minutes, plus 30 minutes soaking
COOKING TIME: 30 minutes
SERVES 4

300 g (10½ oz) instant polenta
2 teaspoons salt
For the mushroom sauce:
20 g (¾ oz) dried wild mushrooms
2 tablespoons olive oil
4 cloves garlic, roughly chopped
1 kg (2 lb 4 oz) button or chestnut mushrooms, or a mixture of the two, thickly sliced
1 tablespoon tomato purée
2 teaspoons dried thyme
50 ml (2 fl oz) red wine
5 teaspoons brandy
Salt and black pepper
To garnish: chopped fresh parsley and sprigs of thyme

1. Put a kettle on to boil. Put the dried mushrooms into a heatproof bowl, cover with boiling water and leave them to soak for 30 minutes.
2. Meanwhile, heat the olive oil in a large saucepan over a medium-high heat. Add the garlic and stir-fry for 15 seconds, then add the fresh mushrooms and continue stir-frying for 10 minutes, or until they have wilted.
3. Strain the soaking liquid off the wild mushrooms through a fine sieve lined with muslin or kitchen paper, and add 50 ml (2 fl oz) of it to the cooked mushrooms.
4. Roughly chop the rehydrated wild mushrooms and add them to the pan with the tomato purée, thyme, wine and brandy. Season to taste and simmer, covered, for 20 minutes, or until you have a thin, richly flavoured sauce.
5. Meanwhile, put the polenta and salt into a large saucepan and pour in 1.4 litres (2 pints 10 fl oz) of water, whisking continuously to prevent any lumps. Bring the mixture to the boil, then simmer for 10 minutes, stirring frequently until it becomes firm but not stiff.
6. Arrange spoonfuls of the polenta on individual plates, spoon the mushroom sauce alongside and garnish with the parsley and thyme.

Nutrients per serving

- Calories 377
- Carbohydrate 58 g
- Protein 12 g
- Fat 8 g (including saturated fat 1 g)

Grilled vegetable couscous with chilled tomato sauce

Nutrients per serving
- Calories 234
- Carbohydrates 40 g
- Protein 7 g
- Fat 6 g (including saturated fat 2 g)

Lightly charred vegetables and herbs lend a wonderful flavour to this easy couscous.

PREPARATION TIME: 30 minutes
COOKING TIME: 20 minutes
SERVES 6

250 g (9 oz) couscous
3 red peppers
200 g (7 oz) leeks
200 g (7 oz) courgettes
150 g (5½ oz) fennel
1 tablespoon olive oil
Juice of 2 lemons
8 fresh mint leaves, shredded
2 tablespoons chopped fresh parsley
Salt and black pepper
For the sauce:
2 tablespoons sherry vinegar or white wine vinegar
4 teaspoons caster sugar
700 ml (1 pint 5 fl oz) tomato passata
450 g (1 lb) plum tomatoes
2 tablespoons chopped fresh basil
To garnish: 200 g (7 oz) Greek yoghurt; fresh basil leaves

1 Heat the grill to its highest setting. Put the couscous into a large heatproof bowl and pour over 400 ml (14 fl oz) of boiling water. Stir and leave to stand for 20 minutes.
2 Meanwhile, make the sauce. Heat the vinegar and sugar in a small saucepan, stirring until the sugar has dissolved, then allow this syrup to cool a little.
3 Place the passata in a large bowl. Dice the tomatoes and add them to the bowl with the basil and the vinegar syrup. Season with salt and plenty of black pepper, then chill until required.
4 Cut the peppers in half lengthways and grill them, cut side down, until the skin is well blackened. Transfer them to a bowl, cover with cling film and leave to cool for 2-3 minutes.
5 Thickly slice the leeks and courgettes and cut the fennel into thin wedges, chopping and reserving any leaves. Spread out the leeks, courgettes and fennel wedges on the grill pan, brush them all over with oil and grill for 5-10 minutes until lightly browned, turning them over halfway through cooking and removing each piece as soon as it is done.
6 When the peppers are cool enough to handle, skin and deseed them, then dice the flesh and add it to the couscous, with the other grilled vegetables. Stir in the lemon juice, mint, parsley and fennel leaves, and season to taste.
7 Serve the couscous at room temperature. Pile it in mounds on individual dishes, surround with a moat of chilled tomato sauce, spoon a little yoghurt onto the sauce and garnish with basil leaves.

Grilled grainburgers

Made with rice and rolled oats instead of mashed beans, these vegetarian burgers have an unexpectedly light texture.

PREPARATION TIME: 10 minutes, plus 30 minutes soaking

COOKING TIME: 20-25 minutes

SERVES 4

300 ml (10 fl oz) vegetable stock
50 g (1¾ oz) couscous
50 g (1¾ oz) rolled oats
50 g (1¾ oz) long-grain rice
Salt and black pepper
100 g (3½ oz) low-fat natural cottage cheese

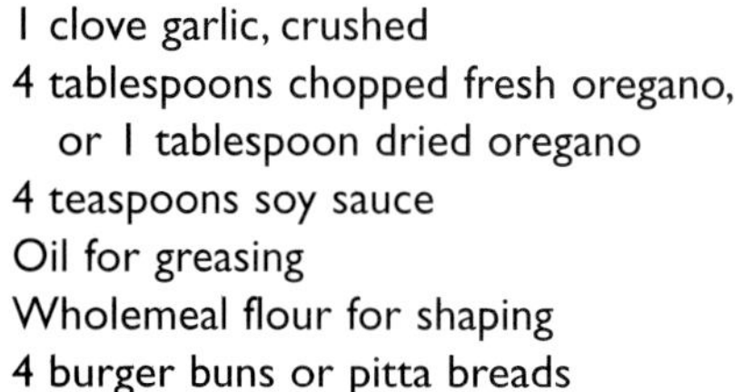

1 clove garlic, crushed
4 tablespoons chopped fresh oregano, or 1 tablespoon dried oregano
4 teaspoons soy sauce
Oil for greasing
Wholemeal flour for shaping
4 burger buns or pitta breads
To serve: mixed salad

1. Bring the stock to the boil. Place the couscous and oats in a large heatproof bowl and pour the stock over them. Stir well and leave them to stand for 30 minutes to absorb the liquid.
2. Meanwhile, bring a large saucepan of water to the boil and cook the rice according to the instructions on the packet. Drain thoroughly and set aside to cool.
3. Add the cooked rice, cottage cheese, garlic, oregano and soy sauce to the couscous and oats and mix well. Season with salt and pepper to taste.
4. Heat the grill to medium. Line the grill pan with foil and lightly brush with oil. Divide the grain mixture into eight balls and use lightly floured hands to shape them into round, flat burgers.
5. Grill the burgers for 3-5 minutes each side until they are golden brown. Serve them hot in burger buns, with a mixed salad.

Variation: substitute wholemeal pitta bread for the burger buns, and serve with chutney on the side.

Tip: use ordinary long-grain rice rather than the easy-cook variety, as it helps to bind the mixture and gives the burgers a better texture.

Nutrients per serving

- Calories 309
- Carbohydrate 55 g
- Protein 12 g
- Fat 6 g (including saturated fat 1 g)

Kashtouri

This popular Egyptian dish of rice, macaroni and lentils in a spicy tomato sauce makes a quick light meal.

PREPARATION TIME: 5 minutes
COOKING TIME: 20 minutes
SERVES 4

150 g (5½ oz) risotto rice, such as arborio
Salt and black pepper
150 g (5½ oz) short-cut macaroni
2 teaspoons olive oil
150 g (5½ oz) onions, chopped
2 large cloves garlic, crushed
1 teaspoon cayenne pepper or paprika
1 teaspoon ground coriander
400 g (14 oz) canned chopped tomatoes
400 g (14 oz) canned green lentils, including liquid
2 tablespoons chopped fresh parsley

1. Bring a large saucepan of water to the boil, add the rice and a pinch of salt, return the water to the boil, then reduce the heat and simmer for 5 minutes. Add the macaroni and stir, increase the heat to medium and cook for a further 10 minutes, or until both rice and macaroni are tender. Drain and set aside in a colander.
2. Meanwhile, put the oil and 2 tablespoons of water in a saucepan, add the onions and garlic and sauté for 5 minutes or until they have softened. Stir in the spices and cook for a further 1 minute.
3. Add the tomatoes and lentils and their canned liquid to the onions, season to taste and bring the mixture to the boil. Reduce the heat and simmer for 10 minutes, stirring occasionally.
4. Mix in the rice and macaroni then add the parsley, reserving a small amount for garnish, and heat through. Serve hot, garnished with parsley.

Nutrients per serving

- Calories 623
- Carbohydrate 117 g
- Protein 32 g
- Fat 4 g (no saturated fat)

Bulgur wheat pilaf with nuts and seeds

Nutrients per serving

- Calories 390
- Carbohydrate 67 g
- Protein 12 g
- Fat 10 g (including saturated fat 1 g)

Although high in fat, nuts and seeds are extremely nutritious, and just a handful gives a satisfying crunch to this pilaf.

PREPARATION TIME: 10 minutes
COOKING TIME: 20 minutes
SERVES 4

150 g (5½ oz) onions, thinly sliced
800 ml (1 pint 9 fl oz) vegetable stock
300 g (10½ oz) bulgur wheat
25 g (1 oz) unsalted, raw cashew nuts
25 g (1 oz) pumpkin seeds
1 tablespoon sesame seeds
1 pomegranate, or 1 dessert apple, or 6 apricots
2 tablespoons chopped fresh mint
Salt and black pepper
To garnish: sprigs of fresh mint

PUMPKIN SEEDS

1. Sauté the onions in 2 tablespoons of the stock over a medium-high heat for 2-3 minutes, stirring occasionally, until the onions have softened and the liquid evaporated. Heat the grill to high.
2. Stir the bulgur wheat and the remaining stock into the pan and bring to the boil. Then cover and simmer gently over a low heat, stirring occasionally, for 12-15 minutes until the bulgur is tender and the liquid has been absorbed.
3. Meanwhile, toast the cashew nuts under the grill for 30 seconds, or until they are golden. Place the pumpkin and sesame seeds in a small frying pan and dry-fry them for 3-5 seconds over a high heat shaking the pan until the seeds begin to pop. Stir all the nuts and seeds into the bulgur wheat.
4. Cut the pomegranate into quarters and scoop the seeds and juice into the bulgur wheat. If pomegranates are not available, add chopped apple or apricots instead. Stir in the mint and adjust the seasoning to taste. Serve hot or at room temperature, garnished with sprigs of mint.

Variation: for a fresh, raw salad, place 200 g (7 oz) of bulgur wheat in a large bowl and cover it with boiling water. Leave it to soften and swell for 30 minutes, then drain and squeeze out the excess water. Stir in 4-6 diced tomatoes, ½ diced cucumber, 1 crushed garlic clove and 6-8 tablespoons of chopped, fresh mint and parsley. Dress with 3 tablespoons of lemon juice and 2 tablespoons of olive oil. This has only 7 g of fat (1 g saturated) per serving.

Paella

This version of a traditional Spanish dish combines tender chicken and mixed seafood in saffron-scented rice.

PREPARATION TIME: 45 minutes
COOKING TIME: 1 hour 5 minutes-1 hour 15 minutes
SERVES 6

600 ml (1 pint) chicken stock
10-12 strands saffron
3 rashers dry-cured, smoked back bacon
350 g (12 oz) skinned and boned chicken breasts
2 tablespoons olive oil
200 g (7 oz) onions, thinly sliced
1 green and 1 red pepper, thinly sliced
2 cloves garlic, crushed
400 g (14 oz) canned chopped tomatoes
250 g (9 oz) long-grain rice
Salt and black pepper
250 g (9 oz) baby squid tubes
400 g (14 oz) live mussels
200 g (7 oz) frozen peas
2 tablespoons white wine, optional
200 g (7 oz) large peeled prawns, defrosted if frozen
12 whole unpeeled prawns, optional
3 tablespoons chopped fresh parsley
To serve: wedges of lemon, optional

1. Bring the stock to the boil, stir in the saffron and set aside until needed. Trim the rind and fat off the bacon and cut it into 1 cm (½ in) strips. Cut the chicken into 2.5 cm (1 in) cubes.
2. Heat 1 tablespoon of olive oil in a large paella pan, lidded frying pan, or flameproof casserole. Add the bacon and chicken and cook over a medium heat for 5 minutes, or until they are lightly browned, turning the pieces frequently. Then remove them and set aside.
3. Add the remaining oil to the pan, then add the onions, peppers and garlic, and cook over a low heat for 10-15 minutes until they are softened but not coloured.
4. Stir in the tomatoes and bring the mixture to the boil. Then reduce the heat to medium and continue to cook for a further 9-10 minutes, stirring frequently, until some of the liquid from the tomatoes has evaporated and the mixture has thickened slightly.
5. Stir the rice into the pan, add the chicken and bacon, the stock and a pinch of salt and bring to the boil. Then reduce the heat to low, cover the pan with a tight-fitting lid or foil and simmer for 25 minutes without looking.
6. Meanwhile, clean the squid tubes and cut them into quarters lengthways. Scrub and debeard the mussels, discarding any that are open or damaged.
7. Stir the squid, mussels and peas into the rice and cook the paella for a further 10 minutes, or until the rice has absorbed all the stock and the mussels have all opened (discard any that do not open). If the mixture sticks to the pan, add the white wine, if using, or a little water.
8. Season with plenty of black pepper, then add the peeled prawns and mix them in gently with a fork. Scatter the whole prawns on top, if using, and cook for 3-4 minutes more until all the prawns are heated through.
9. Sprinkle the parsley over the paella and serve it with lemon wedges on the side, if you like.

Nutrients per serving

- Calories 441
- Carbohydrate 45 g
- Protein 42 g
- Fat 10 g (including saturated fat 2 g)

Peppers stuffed with minted rice

Sweet roasted peppers are filled with savoury rice and topped with sharp feta cheese.

PREPARATION TIME: 20-30 minutes
COOKING TIME: 50-55 minutes
SERVES 4

4 red peppers, cut in half lengthways, seeds removed but stalks left on
3 sun-dried tomatoes in oil, chopped, plus 2 teaspoons of the oil
150 g (5½ oz) onions, finely chopped
1-2 cloves garlic, crushed
200 g (7 oz) long-grain white rice
450 ml (16 fl oz) vegetable stock or water
4 tablespoons dry white wine
450 g (1 lb) plum tomatoes
25 g (1 oz) green olives, stoned and chopped
2 spring onions, finely chopped
25 g (1 oz) pine nuts, toasted
2-3 tablespoons chopped fresh mint
Salt and black pepper
100 g (3½ oz) feta cheese, drained and crumbled

1 Heat the oven to 200°C (400°F, gas mark 6). Place the peppers closely together, cut side up, in an ovenproof dish and bake for 20 minutes, or until softened. Remove from the oven and set aside.
2 Meanwhile, heat 2 teaspoons of oil from the jar of sun-dried tomatoes in a large nonstick saucepan and sauté the onions for 5 minutes, or until softened. Add the garlic and sun-dried tomatoes and continue cooking for a further 2 minutes, then stir in the rice.
3 Pour the stock or water and wine into the rice mixture, stir well and bring to the boil. Cover and simmer for 15-20 minutes until the liquid has been absorbed and the rice is tender. Add a little more water if the rice dries out during cooking.
4 Meanwhile, cover the tomatoes with boiling water, leave for 1 minute, then skin, deseed and chop them. Add them to the cooked rice mixture with the olives, spring onions, pine nuts and mint, season well and stir to combine. Spoon the rice into the peppers and sprinkle the feta cheese over the top.
5 Return the peppers to the top shelf of the oven and cook for a further 15 minutes, then serve.

Nutrients per serving

- Calories 414
- Carbohydrate 57 g
- Protein 12 g
- Fat 15 g (including saturated fat 5 g)

Tomato risotto

A simple risotto of fresh and sun-dried tomatoes is an easy dish for a light lunch.

PREPARATION TIME: 10 minutes
COOKING TIME: 30 minutes
SERVES 4

1 tablespoon olive oil
60 g (2¼ oz) onions or shallots, finely chopped
1 clove garlic, crushed
500 ml (18 fl oz) tomato juice
200 g (7 oz) risotto rice, such as arborio
1 tablespoon tomato purée
100 g (3½ oz) plum tomatoes, peeled, deseeded and diced
50 g (1¾ oz) sun-dried tomatoes, drained, dried and cut into strips
2 tablespoons fresh torn basil leaves
Salt and black pepper
To garnish: a few fresh basil leaves
To serve: 50 g (1¾ oz) Parmesan cheese, grated

1 Heat the oil in a large nonstick saucepan. Add the onions or shallots and garlic and sauté gently for 10 minutes, or until they are softened but not coloured.
2 Put the tomato juice in another pan and bring it to simmering point.
3 Add the rice to the onions and cook for a further 1-2 minutes, stirring

frequently, until the rice becomes transparent.

4 Add a small ladle of tomato juice to the rice mixture and stir continuously until all the juice has been absorbed. Repeat, stirring after each ladle of juice has been added, and cook for 10-15 minutes until the rice is tender and has a creamy consistency, adding more water if necessary.
5 Stir the tomato purée, fresh and sun-dried tomatoes and basil leaves into the rice and season to taste.
6 Serve garnished with basil and pass the Parmesan cheese separately.

Variations: add 50 g (1¾ oz) of diced mushrooms at the end of Step 2 or, for a creamier risotto, stir in 4 tablespoons of fromage frais.

Nutrients per serving

- Calories 288
- Carbohydrate 46 g
- Protein 10 g
- Fat 8 g (including saturated fat 3 g)

Chicken mayonnaise rice salad

Tarragon, chives and lemon liven up this simple salad.

PREPARATION TIME: 30 minutes, plus 30 minutes marinating
COOKING TIME: 30-35 minutes
SERVES 4

4 skinned and boned chicken breasts, about 125 g (4½ oz) each
250 g (9 oz) long-grain white rice
Salt and black pepper
½ cucumber, peeled and diced
150 g (5½ oz) button mushrooms, cut into quarters
300 g (10½ oz) radishes, cut into quarters
2 tablespoons chopped fresh chives
1 teaspoon chopped fresh tarragon
5 tablespoons low-fat mayonnaise
Juice of 1 lemon
A few drops of Tabasco sauce
A few drops of Worcestershire sauce

For the marinade:
Grated zest of 1 lemon
2 cloves garlic, crushed
2 tablespoons olive oil
Juice of ½ lemon

1 Mix the marinade ingredients together in a large bowl. Add the chicken, mix well, then set it aside to marinate for 30 minutes.
2 Meanwhile, place the rice in a saucepan with 500 ml (18 fl oz) of water and a pinch of salt. Cover, bring to the boil then reduce the heat and simmer, covered, for 20 minutes, or until tender. Transfer the rice to a large plate and leave it to cool until tepid, stirring occasionally with a fork.
3 Heat a ridged, iron grill pan or a nonstick frying pan over a medium heat. Remove the chicken from the marinade, season and cook for 10-12 minutes, turning regularly, until it is browned and the juices run clear when pierced with a knife. Transfer the chicken to a plate to rest for 5 minutes, then dice it.
4 In a large bowl, mix together the cooled rice, chicken, cucumber, mushrooms, radishes and herbs. Stir in the mayonnaise, lemon juice and Tabasco and Worcestershire sauce. Season to taste and serve.

Nutrients per serving

- Calories 496
- Carbohydrate 54 g
- Protein 34 g
- Fat 16 g (including saturated fat 2 g)

Pilau rice

A lower-fat form of traditional pilau rice is the ideal partner for a range of spicy dishes.

PREPARATION TIME: 10 minutes, plus 30 minutes soaking and 8-10 minutes standing
COOKING TIME: 20 minutes
SERVES 4

225 g (8 oz) basmati rice
1 tablespoon natural yoghurt
Salt
10-12 strands saffron
15 g (½ oz) unsalted butter
1½ tablespoons sunflower oil
2 bay leaves, crumbled
4 green cardamom pods, split open
7.5 cm (3 in) cinnamon stick, broken in half
2 cloves
1 teaspoon royal cumin
125 g (4½ oz) red onions, cut in half and finely sliced

1. Rinse the rice in cold water until the water runs clear, then drain it well and put it into a bowl. Stir in the yoghurt, add salt to taste and set aside for 30 minutes.
2. Put a kettle on to boil. Pound the saffron once or twice in a pestle and mortar until it crumbles.
3. Melt the butter with 1 tablespoon of oil in a large saucepan over a low heat. Add the bay leaves, cardamom, cinnamon, cloves and royal cumin and stir-fry for 1 minute. Stir in the rice, increase the heat to medium and stir-fry for 2-3 minutes.
4. Pour in 350 ml (12 fl oz) of boiling water and add the saffron.
5. Return to the boil, then reduce the heat to very low, cover the pan with a tight-fitting lid and simmer for 10 minutes without lifting the lid. Remove the pan from the heat and leave it for 8-10 minutes. Freshly cooked basmati is quite fragile. Letting it rest ensures fluffy, dry grains.
6. Meanwhile, heat ½ tablesooon of oil in a nonstick frying pan over a medium heat. Add the onions and stir-fry for 2-3 minutes. Reduce the heat, add a pinch of salt and continue stir-frying for 4-5 minutes until the onion is soft and lightly browned. If necessary, sprinkle a little water on the onions to prevent them burning.
7. Fluff up the rice with a fork and serve, garnished with the fried onion.

Tip: royal cumin (*shahi jeera*) is a rare variety of cumin seed grown only in Kashmir and is available in Indian shops. Stored in an airtight jar, it will retain its aroma for two years. If you cannot find it, you can use caraway seeds instead.

Nutrients per serving

- Calories 287
- Carbohydrate 48 g
- Protein 5 g
- Fat 8 g (including saturated fat 3 g)

PILAU RICE

Turmeric rice

A colourful mixture of rice and flavourings makes a perfect background to any curry.

PREPARATION TIME: as Pilau Rice
COOKING TIME: 15 minutes
SERVES 4

225g (8oz) basmati rice
2 tablespoons sunflower oil
½ teaspoon black mustard seeds
1 dried red chilli, deseeded and finely chopped
½ teaspoon turmeric
Finely grated zest of 1 lime
1 tablespoon finely chopped fresh coriander
Salt

1. Rinse the rice well, put it in a bowl, cover with cold water and leave it to soak for 30 minutes. Then drain and leave it in a sieve until required.
2. Put a kettle on to boil. Heat the oil in a large saucepan over a medium heat. When it is hot, add the mustard seeds and as soon as they begin to pop, add the chilli and let it blacken.
3. Add the rice and turmeric, reduce the heat and stir-fry for 2-3 minutes.
4. Add the lime zest, coriander and salt to taste, then add 475 ml (17 fl oz) of boiling water. Cook and let the rice stand as in Step 5 of the Pilau Rice recipe.
5. Fluff up the rice lightly with a fork and serve.

Nutrients per serving

- as for Cardamom Rice, below

Cardamom rice

Aromatic cardamom lends its rich flavour to this simple but luxurious side dish.

PREPARATION TIME: as Pilau Rice
COOKING TIME: 15 minutes
SERVES 4

225 g (8 oz) basmati rice
2 tablespoons sunflower oil
6 green cardamom pods, split open
1 teaspoon royal cumin
Salt

1. Rinse the rice well, put it in a bowl, cover with cold water and leave it to soak for 30 minutes. Then drain and leave it in a sieve until required.
2. Put a kettle on to boil. Heat the oil in a large saucepan over a medium heat. When it is hot but not smoking, reduce the heat to low, add the cardamom and royal cumin (see Pilau Rice tip) and stir-fry for 1 minute.
3. Add the drained rice to the spices, increase the heat to medium and continue stir-frying for 2-3 minutes. Add salt to taste.
4. Pour in 475 ml (17 fl oz) of hot water from the kettle. Cook and let the rice stand as in Step 5 of the Pilau Rice recipe.
5. Fluff up the rice lightly with a fork and serve.

Nutrients per serving

- Calories 251
- Carbohydrate 45 g
- Protein 4 g
- Fat 6 g (including saturated fat 1 g)

Risotto primavera

This wholesome risotto is packed with fresh vegetables.

PREPARATION TIME: 20 minutes, plus 5 minutes standing
COOKING TIME: 40-45 minutes
SERVES 4

1.2 litres (2 pints) vegetable stock
10-12 strands saffron
2 tablespoons olive oil
175 g (6 oz) carrots, diced
2 cloves garlic, crushed
200 g (7 oz) leeks, halved lengthways then sliced into half-moons
225 g (8 oz) risotto rice, such as arborio
125 g (4½ oz) asparagus spears, chopped into 2 cm (¾ in) lengths
125 g (4½ oz) green beans, chopped into 2 cm (¾ in) lengths
125 g (4½ oz) peas, defrosted if frozen
4 tablespoons chopped fresh herbs, such as chives, dill, flat-leaved parsley and tarragon
50 g (1¾ oz) Parmesan cheese, grated
Salt and black pepper

1. Warm the stock, then add the saffron and leave it to infuse for 10 minutes. Meanwhile, heat the oil in a large frying pan and fry the carrots, garlic and leeks over a low heat for 10 minutes, until they are softened but not coloured.
2. Bring the stock to simmering point. Meanwhile, add the rice to the vegetables and stir for 1 minute or until the grains are glossy.
3. Keep the stock simmering and add a ladleful to the rice. Stir continuously until it has been absorbed. Continue adding the stock a ladleful at a time, and stirring, for 15 minutes.
4. Add the asparagus, beans and peas to the rice and continue stirring and adding stock for a further 15-20 minutes until the rice and vegetables are tender.
5. Remove the pan from the heat and stir in the herbs and Parmesan, then cover and leave to rest for 5 minutes. Season to taste and serve.

Nutrients per serving

- Calories 364
- Carbohydrate 54 g
- Protein 13 g
- Fat 12 g (including saturated fat 4 g)

Marinated turkey pilaf

Fragrant seeds and spices infuse a captivating all-in-one dish with Eastern flavours.

PREPARATION TIME: 25 minutes, plus 2-3 hours marinating and 10 minutes standing
COOKING TIME: 30 minutes
SERVES 4

- 500 g (1 lb 2 oz) skinned and boned turkey thighs
- 2 teaspoons crushed garlic
- 2 teaspoons crushed ginger
- ½ teaspoon ground turmeric
- 75 g (2¾ oz) low-fat natural yoghurt
- 225 g (8 oz) basmati rice
- 1-2 dried red chillies, deseeded and finely chopped
- 1 tablespoon coriander seeds
- 1 teaspoon cumin seeds
- 2 teaspoons white poppy seeds
- 2 teaspoons sesame seeds
- 1 tablespoon sunflower oil
- 6 green cardamom pods, split open
- 7.5 cm (3 in) cinnamon stick, broken in half
- 4 cloves
- 250 g (9 oz) onions, thinly sliced
- 1-2 green chillies, deseeded and finely chopped
- Salt

To garnish: 1 egg, a pinch of paprika and sprigs of fresh parsley

1. Trim any fat from the turkey thighs and cut them into 5 cm (2 in) cubes. Put them into a mixing bowl, add the garlic, ginger, turmeric and yoghurt and mix thoroughly. Cover and leave to marinate for 2-3 hours.
2. Meanwhile, rinse the rice then cover it with cold water and leave it to soak for 30 minutes. Hard-boil the egg for the garnish. Drain the rice.
3. Coarsely grind the red chilli and coriander and cumin seeds in a spice mill or with a pestle and mortar. Add the poppy seeds, if using, and sesame seeds and grind to a fine mixture.
4. Heat the oil in a nonstick saucepan over a low heat, add the cardamom, cinnamon and cloves and let them sizzle for 20-25 seconds. Add the onions and green chilli, increase the heat to medium and fry for 7-8 minutes until the onions are lightly browned, stirring frequently.
5. Add the ground spices to the onions, continue to fry for 1-2 minutes, then add the marinated turkey. Increase the heat to high and fry the meat for 7-8 minutes, stirring frequently. Put a kettle on to boil.
6. Add the rice to the pan, add salt to taste and fry for 2-3 minutes. Then pour in 475 ml (17 fl oz) of boiling water, bring it back to the boil and

BROWNED BASMATI RICE WITH KOFTAS

Browned basmati rice with koftas

Flavoured basmati rice, fried with caramelised sugar, is partnered with lamb meatballs.

PREPARATION TIME: 20 minutes, plus 40 minutes chilling, soaking and standing
COOKING TIME: 35 minutes
SERVES 4

For the koftas:

- 1 large slice of white bread, crust removed
- 150 ml (5 fl oz) skimmed milk
- 500 g (1 lb 2 oz) lean minced lamb
- 1-2 green chillies, deseeded and chopped
- 1 tablespoon roughly chopped fresh coriander
- 1 teaspoon garam masala
- 2-3 cloves garlic, roughly chopped
- 1 teaspoon chopped ginger
- ½ tablespoon chopped fresh mint

boil hard for 1 minute. Then reduce the heat to very low, cover the pan with a piece of foil and place the lid on top. Cook for 10 minutes, without uncovering the pan. Remove from the heat and allow the rice to stand, undisturbed, for 10 minutes.

7 Transfer the pilaf to a serving dish, garnish with sliced egg, sprinkle paprika and a few sprigs of parsley over the top and serve.

Variation: you can leave the turkey to marinate overnight in the refrigerator, but bring it to room temperature before cooking.

Nutrients per serving

- Calories 434
- Carbohydrate 52 g
- Protein 34 g
- Fat 11 g (including saturated fat 2 g)

MARINATED TURKEY PILAF

Salt
125 g (4½ oz) onions, roughly chopped
1 tablespoon unsalted butter

For the rice:
225 g (8 oz) basmati rice
1 tablespoon sunflower oil, plus oil for greasing
1 tablespoon sugar
4 green cardamom pods, split open
7.5 cm (3 in) cinnamon stick, broken in half
4 cloves

To garnish: cherry tomatoes and a few sprigs of fresh coriander

1 To make the koftas, soak the bread in the milk for 2 minutes, then squeeze out the milk. Place the bread in a food processor, add the lamb, chilli, coriander, garam masala, garlic, ginger, mint, and salt to taste, then processs to a smooth mixture. Add the onions and pulse for 1 or 2 seconds, so they are mixed in but not puréed.

2 Transfer the mixture to a bowl, cover and chill for 30 minutes, or overnight in an airtight container.

3 Meanwhile, rinse the rice then place it in a bowl, cover with cold water and leave it to soak for 30 minutes.

4 Heat the grill to high, line the grill pan with foil and brush it with oil.

5 Divide the lamb kofta mixture into two portions. Lightly grease your palms and make 12 equal-sized balls out of each portion. Place them on the grill pan 1 cm (½ in) apart and grill for 5 minutes. Meanwhile, melt the butter.

6 Brush the koftas with half the butter and continue grilling for a further 2-3 minutes until they have browned.

7 Turn the koftas and brush with the remaining butter. Grill for 3-4 minutes until browned. Wrap them in a piece of foil and keep them warm.

8 Drain the rice and set it aside. Put a kettle on to boil.

9 Heat the oil in a large heavy saucepan or flameproof casserole over a medium heat. Sprinkle in the sugar and cook for 1-2 minutes until it has caramelised.

10 Add the cardamon, cinnamon and rice and fry them for 2-3 minutes, stirring continuously. Then pour in 475 ml (17 fl oz) of boiling water and add salt to taste.

11 As soon as the water returns to the boil, add the meatballs in a single layer, plus any cooking juices, then reduce the heat to very low. Cover the pan with a piece of foil and then the lid. Cook for 10 minutes without lifting the lid or the foil.

12 Take the pan off the heat and let it stand, undisturbed, for 10 minutes.

13 Transfer the rice and koftas to a serving dish and serve, garnished with cherry tomatoes and coriander.

Serving suggestion: yoghurt raita (page 192) and microwaved or grilled poppadoms.

Nutrients per serving

- Calories 532
- Carbohydrate 62 g
- Protein 32 g
- Fat 19 g (including saturated fat 8 g)

vegetables

Lemon-braised spinach with mushrooms and croutons

This swift and delicious way to serve spinach is enlivened with soy sauce and crunchy croutons.

PREPARATION TIME: 10 minutes
COOKING TIME: 5-10 minutes
SERVES 4

400 g (14 oz) spinach
½ lemon
200 g (7 oz) oyster mushrooms, thinly sliced
2 teaspoons soy sauce
3 spring onions, thinly sliced
Black pepper
For the croutons:
2 thin slices wholemeal bread, crusts removed
½ teaspoon garlic purée, or crushed garlic
Tabasco sauce, to taste

1 Heat the grill to medium. Rinse the spinach, remove any tough stems and drain well.
2 To make the croutons, cut the bread into small dice. Mix the garlic purée or crushed garlic and Tabasco sauce together in a bowl, then stir in the bread. Transfer the spiced bread to a baking sheet or grill pan in a single layer and grill for 1-2 minutes, turning the dice over occasionally, until the croutons are golden brown. Set aside.
3 Remove a few strips of lemon zest and reserve, then squeeze the juice. Put the lemon juice, mushrooms, soy sauce and spring onions in a saucepan over a medium-high heat and cook, shaking the pan occasionally, for 2-3 minutes until the vegetables have softened.
4 Turn the heat to high, add the spinach and stir for 2 minutes, or until the spinach has wilted and most of the juices have evaporated. Season with pepper. Serve the spinach hot, with the croutons and reserved lemon zest scattered over the top.

Nutrients per serving

- Calories 55
- Carbohydrate 7 g
- Protein 4 g
- Fat 1 g (no saturated fat)

Sweet roasted squash with shallots

Roasted vegetables are sweetened with a touch of maple syrup. Serve these instead of roast potatoes to accompany meat.

PREPARATION TIME: 15 minutes
COOKING TIME: 30-35 minutes
SERVES 4

900 g (2 lb) butternut squash
8 shallots
A few sprigs of fresh thyme
1 teaspoon olive oil
2 teaspoons maple syrup, or clear honey
Salt and black pepper

1. Heat the oven to 190°C (375°F, gas mark 5). Cut the squash in half lengthways, remove the seeds and peel then cut the flesh into 3 cm (1¼ in) cubes. Put them into a large mixing bowl.
2. Peel the shallots and add them to the squash with most of the sprigs of thyme, reserving a few to use as a garnish.
3. Mix together the oil and maple syrup or honey and add salt and pepper to taste, then pour it into the vegetables, tossing to coat them evenly.
4. Tip the vegetables into a roasting tin and cook for 30-35 minutes, turning them occasionally, until they are tender and golden brown. Garnish with the reserved sprigs of thyme and serve.

Nutrients per serving

- Calories 93
- Carbohydrate 20 g
- Protein 3 g
- Fat 1 g (no saturated fat)

BUTTERNUT SQUASH

GRILLED VEGETABLE SALAD

Grilled vegetable salad

Succulent vegetable juices and sherry vinegar moisten this salad so that you do not need an oily dressing.

PREPARATION TIME: 15 minutes, plus at least 3 hours standing
COOKING TIME: 20-35 minutes
SERVES 4

350 g (12 oz) aubergines
700 g (1 lb 9 oz) courgettes
Salt and black pepper
1 large red pepper, cut into quarters
2 tablespoons olive oil
For the dressing:
A pinch of cayenne pepper
2 cloves garlic, crushed
1 tablespoon sherry vinegar
To garnish: chopped fresh parsley

1. Line two baking trays with kitchen paper. Cut the aubergine and courgettes lengthways into 2 cm (¾ in) thick slices, put them on the trays in a single layer and sprinkle with salt. Set aside for 15 minutes.
2. Meanwhile, make the dressing. Mix the cayenne, garlic, and vinegar together, season to taste and set aside.
3. Heat a ridged, iron grill pan over a medium-high heat or set the grill to medium-high. Brush the skin side of the pepper with oil and cook the pieces, skin side down on the grill pan or skin side up under the grill, for 5 minutes, or until the pepper has softened and the skin has blackened a little.
4. Place the pepper in a large bowl, sprinkle over one-third of the dressing and stir.
5. Rinse the aubergine and courgette slices and pat them dry, then brush them lightly with oil. Grill for 3-4 minutes on each side for the aubergines and 2-3 minutes on each side for the courgettes. (You will need to cook them in batches if you are using a ridged grill pan.)
6. Cut the grilled aubergine and courgette slices in half crossways and add them to the pepper. Pour on the remaining dressing and mix well.
7. Cover and refrigerate for 3 hours, or overnight, so that the flavours develop. Serve at room temperature.

Nutrients per serving

- Calories 106
- Carbohydrate 8 g
- Protein 4 g
- Fat 7 g (including saturated fat 1 g)

Sauté of spring vegetables with herbs

A fresh-tasting sauté of peas, beans and green salad leaves is served in a light lemon stock.

PREPARATION TIME: 15 minutes
COOKING TIME: 20 minutes
SERVES 4

25 g (1 oz) butter
1 clove garlic, crushed
300 g (10½ oz) leeks, chopped
225 g (8 oz) green beans
125 g (4½ oz) peas, defrosted if frozen
150 ml (5 fl oz) vegetable stock
225 g (8 oz) escarole or frisée
2 tablespoons chopped fresh mixed chervil, chives and mint
Juice of ½ lemon
Salt and black pepper
To garnish: fresh chives and mint

SAUTÉ OF SPRING VEGETABLES WITH HERBS

1 Melt the butter in a deep frying pan or saucepan, add the garlic and leeks and sauté them for 5 minutes, or until they have softened. Add the green beans and peas and continue sautéeing for a further 2 minutes.
2 Pour in the stock, cover and simmer for 5 minutes. Separate the leaves of the escarole or frisée, add them to the pan, cover and continue simmering for a further 5 minutes, or until all the vegetables are tender.
3 Stir in the herbs, lemon juice and salt and pepper to taste. Serve garnished with fresh chives and mint.

Nutrients per serving

- Calories 106
- Carbohydrate 8 g
- Protein 5 g
- Fat 6 g (including saturated fat 4 g)

ROASTED VEGETABLES WITH HORSERADISH SAUCE

Roasted vegetables with horseradish sauce

A sharp purée makes a tasty accompaniment to a choice selection of vegetables roasted with minimum fat.

PREPARATION TIME: 15 minutes
COOKING TIME: 1 hour - 1 hour 15 minutes
SERVES 4

250 g (9 oz) raw beetroot
250 g (9 oz) carrots
250 g (9 oz) parsnips
400 g (14 oz) potatoes
1 whole head garlic
2 sprigs fresh rosemary
2 sprigs fresh thyme
1 tablespoon olive oil
25 g (1 oz) day-old bread, crusts removed
100 ml (3½ fl oz) skimmed milk
2 tablespoons creamed horseradish
Salt and black pepper
To garnish: a few sprigs of fresh thyme

1 Heat the oven to 220°C (425°F, gas mark 7). Cut the beetroot, carrots, parsnips and potatoes into large chunks and place them in a roasting tin, keeping the beetroot in one corner of the tin to prevent it from staining the other vegetables.
2 Slice off the top of the head of garlic and discard, then add the garlic to the vegetables. Scatter the rosemary and thyme over them and pour on the oil and 3 tablespoons of cold water. Roast for 40 minutes, stirring occasionally to prevent the vegetables from burning.
3 Remove the garlic and set it aside to cool a little, and continue roasting the vegetables for a further 20-35 minutes until they are tender.
4 Meanwhile, tear the bread into small pieces and soak it in the milk for 10 minutes. Squeeze the garlic cloves out of their skins, mash them well and beat them into the soaked bread to make a sauce. Stir in the horseradish and season to taste. Serve the roasted vegetables with the sauce, garnished with a sprig of fresh thyme.

Variation: if you cannot find raw beetroot, use cooked vacuum-packed beetroot, adding them to the roasting tin when you remove the garlic.

Nutrients per serving

- Calories 200
- Carbohydrate 35 g
- Protein 6 g
- Fat 5 g (including saturated fat 1 g)

Brussels sprouts with mustard

Spice up your sprouts with this quick-and-easy Indian recipe, ideal to serve with plainly cooked meat and poultry.

PREPARATION TIME: 15 minutes
COOKING TIME: 15-20 minutes
SERVES 4

500 g (1 lb 2 oz) small Brussels sprouts
1 tablespoon sunflower oil
½ teaspoon black mustard seeds
½ teaspoon cumin seeds
2 large cloves garlic, finely chopped
¼-½ teaspoon cayenne pepper
Salt and black pepper
1 tablespoon gram flour, sifted

1. Trim the sprouts and cut a cross into each stem end. Bring a pan of water to the boil, add the sprouts and return it to the boil. Cover and simmer for 2-3 minutes. Reserve 150 ml (5 fl oz) of the cooking liquid and drain off the remainder.
2. Heat the oil in a large nonstick saucepan over a medium heat, then throw in the mustard seeds – they will start jumping around so you may need to cover the pan briefly until they have settled down. Then add the cumin, garlic and cayenne pepper in that order. Reduce the heat to low and stir-fry for 1 minute, or until the garlic begins to brown.
3. Add the sprouts to the pan, season to taste, stir well, cover and cook for 2-3 minutes.
4. Pour in the reserved sprout stock, increase the heat to medium and simmer the mixture, uncovered, until the stock has reduced by half.
5. Sprinkle the gram flour evenly over the top, then stir until all the stock has been absorbed and the sprouts are coated with a thin sauce.

Variation: if fresh sprouts are not available, use frozen. Or substitute green cabbage and vegetable stock. Do not cook the cabbage first: fry the spices, then add the greens and continue from Step 3.

Tip: gram flour, sometimes called besan, is a soft, yellow flour made from ground chickpeas and is used to thicken dishes. Look for it in supermarkets and Indian food shops.

Nutrients per serving

- Calories 86
- Carbohydrate 7 g
- Protein 5 g
- Fat 5 g (including saturated fat 1 g)

Braised fennel

The distinctive aniseed flavour of fennel makes it a pleasing partner to most fish or chicken main courses.

PREPARATION TIME: 15 minutes
COOKING TIME: 30-40 minutes
SERVES 4

900 g (2 lb) fennel
1 tablespoon butter
150 ml (5 fl oz) dry white wine
2 bay leaves, optional
1 clove garlic, crushed
4 sprigs fresh thyme
300 ml (10 fl oz) vegetable stock
Salt and black pepper
To garnish: 2 tablespoons chopped fresh dill and 1 tablespoon chopped fresh thyme

1. Discard the tough outer layer of the fennel, then cut it lengthways into 1 cm (½ in) thick slices. Melt 1 teaspoon of the butter in a deep heavy-based frying pan over a medium-low heat and fry the fennel, in batches if necessary, for 3 minutes on each side, or until it is golden, adding a little butter with each batch.
2. Return all the fennel to the pan, add the wine and boil for 5 minutes, or until only a small amount of the liquid remains.
3. Add the bay leaves, if using, garlic, thyme and stock and bring to the boil. Reduce the heat to low, cover and simmer for 15-20 minutes until the fennel is tender.
4. Season to taste, scatter with the chopped dill and thyme and serve.

Nutrients per serving

- Calories 79
- Carbohydrate 4 g
- Protein 2 g
- Fat 4 g (including saturated fat 2 g)

Soy-dressed green beans

Young, thin beans are tossed in soy sauce with fresh ginger in this stylish side dish. It tastes fabulous with grilled meats such as lamb.

PREPARATION TIME: 10 minutes
COOKING TIME: 5 minutes
SERVES 4

500 g (1 lb 2 oz) green beans
Salt
2 cloves garlic, finely chopped
½ teaspoon finely chopped ginger
2 tablespoons soy sauce
½ teaspoon sugar

1. Line up the green beans in bunches and cut them in half crossways.
2. Bring a saucepan of water to the boil, then add the beans and a pinch of salt and return to the boil. Reduce the heat and simmer for 3 minutes, or until the beans are tender.
3. Place the garlic, ginger, soy sauce and sugar in a serving bowl and stir them together until the sugar has dissolved. Drain the beans, toss them into the dressing, then serve.

Variation: substitute sliced carrots, runner beans or baby corn cobs, adjusting the cooking time in Step 2 until they are tender.

Nutrients per serving

- Calories 32
- Carbohydrate 5 g
- Protein 2 g
- Fat 1 g (no saturated fat)

Creole-style beans

Nutrients per serving

- Calories 146
- Carbohydrate 24 g
- Protein 10 g
- Fat 2 g (no saturated fat)

Robust beans in a spicy sauce, cooked with the traditional Creole trinity of celery, onion and green pepper, make a substantial dish.

PREPARATION TIME: 10 minutes, plus overnight soaking
COOKING TIME: 1 hour 15 minutes
SERVES 4

150 g (5½ oz) dried haricot or cannellini beans
1 teaspoon olive oil
200 ml (7 fl oz) vegetable stock
1 small fresh red chilli, deseeded and finely chopped
1 clove garlic, finely chopped
3 sticks celery, roughly chopped
60 g (2¼ oz) onions, roughly chopped
1 green pepper, roughly chopped
1-2 teaspoons cayenne pepper, or paprika
1 bay leaf
400 g (14 oz) canned chopped tomatoes
Salt and black pepper

1. Place the beans in a bowl, cover them with cold water and leave to soak overnight.
2. Drain the beans thoroughly, rinse them in fresh water and drain again. Put them in a large saucepan with enough water to cover and bring to the boil. Boil rapidly for 15 minutes, skimming the surface as necessary. Drain well, rinse and set aside to drain thoroughly.
3. Place the oil in a saucepan with 1 tablespoon of the stock, then add the chilli, garlic, celery, onions and green pepper. Cover the pan and cook over a medium heat for 10 minutes, or until the vegetables have softened, shaking the pan occasionally to prevent them sticking. Stir in the cayenne pepper or paprika and cook for a further 1 minute.
4. Add the bay leaf, boiled beans, remaining stock and tomatoes and bring the mixture to the boil, then reduce the heat to low. Cover the pan and simmer for 45 minutes, or according to the instructions on the packet, until the beans are tender, removing the lid for the last 10 minutes so that the juices reduce. Season with salt and pepper to taste and serve.

Baked aubergine and apple layers

Serve this versatile bake, with its fresh tomato sauce, as a vegetarian main course or as a vegetable accompaniment.

PREPARATION TIME: 15 minutes, plus 30 minutes standing

COOKING TIME: 40 minutes

SERVES 4

500 g (1 lb 2 oz) aubergines, cut into 1 cm (½ in) slices
Salt and black pepper
300 g (10½ oz) cooking apples or tart dessert apples, cored and cut into 5 mm (¼ in) slices

For the sauce:
2 cloves garlic, crushed
2 tablespoons olive oil
2 tablespoons chopped fresh flat-leaved parsley
1 tablespoon chopped fresh thyme
2 tablespoons tomato purée
500 g (1 lb 2 oz) plum tomatoes, peeled, deseeded and chopped

To garnish: 1 tablespoon chopped fresh herbs, such as parsley and thyme

1. Sprinkle both sides of the aubergine slices with salt, place them in a colander and set aside to drain for 30 minutes.
2. To make the sauce, put all the ingredients in a food processor, or use a hand-held mixer, and blend until smooth. Set aside.
3. Heat the oven to 220°C (425°F, gas mark 7) and heat a ridged, iron griddle or heavy-based frying pan over a medium-high heat. Rinse the aubergine slices and dry them with kitchen paper. Dry-fry them for 2-3 minutes on each side until they have softened and browned.
4. Arrange half the aubergine slices in a single layer in a 25 x 20 cm (10 x 8 in) ovenproof dish and cover them with 2 tablespoons of the sauce, spreading it out evenly. Layer all the apple slices on top and cover with another 2 tablespoons of sauce. Top with the remaining aubergines and smooth the remaining sauce over the top. Bake for 30 minutes.
5. Sprinkle the dish with the herbs. It tastes equally good served hot or at room temperature. Serve as a vegetarian main course with red or brown rice, or as a side dish to grilled pork.

AUBERGINES

Nutrients per serving

- Calories 132
- Carbohydrate 17 g
- Protein 3 g
- Fat 7 g (including saturated fat 1 g)

Roasted vegetable tart

A scattering of fresh herbs and melting cheese add the finishing touches to vegetables baked in a crisp filo crust.

PREPARATION TIME: 15 minutes
COOKING TIME: 50 minutes-1 hour 10 minutes
SERVES 4

400 g (14 oz) aubergines
400 g (14 oz) courgettes
1 red pepper, thickly sliced
1 yellow pepper, thickly sliced
150 g (5½ oz) red onions, thickly sliced
1 clove garlic, chopped
1 teaspoon chopped fresh rosemary or thyme, plus extra fresh sprigs for topping
3 tablespoons olive oil
Salt and black pepper
4 sheets filo pastry, about 125 g (4½ oz) altogether
75 g (2¾ oz) half-fat mozzarella cheese, shredded

1. Heat the oven to 200°C (400°F, gas mark 6). Cut the aubergines and courgettes into 1 cm (½ in) slices. Arrange all the vegetables in a single layer in a roasting tin, scatter the garlic and rosemary or thyme over them, then drizzle with 2 tablespoons of the olive oil. Season to taste.
2. Roast the vegetables for 40-60 minutes until they have softened and browned.
3. Meanwhile, place a baking sheet in the oven to warm. Line a 20-23 cm (8-9 in) loose-based tart tin with the sheets of filo pastry, brushing each layer with oil before adding the next. Crumple up any overhanging edges to form a rim. Place the tin on the baking sheet and bake the pastry case for 5-8 minutes until golden brown.
4. Reduce the oven to 160°C (325°F, gas mark 3). Spoon the roasted vegetables into the pastry case and scatter the cheese and chopped rosemary and thyme evenly over the top. Return the tart to the oven for 10 minutes, or until the cheese has just melted. Cut into quarters and serve it warm.

Variation: replace the mozzarella cheese with 2 teaspoons of grated Parmesan cheese mixed with 1 teaspoon of toasted breadcrumbs and the rosemary and thyme.

Nutrients per serving

- Calories 260
- Carbohydrate 28 g
- Protein 10 g
- Fat 12 g (including saturated fat 3 g)

Hot Cajun potato wedges

These easy-to-make spicy wedges make a tasty side dish or a flavoursome snack.

PREPARATION TIME: 5 minutes
COOKING TIME: 35-40 minutes
SERVES 4-6

1 kg (2 lb 4 oz) large potatoes
1½ teaspoons sunflower oil
2 tablespoons fresh wholemeal breadcrumbs
A pinch of cayenne pepper
½ teaspoon ground cumin
1 teaspoon garlic salt
1 teaspoon paprika
1 teaspoon ground black pepper
1 teaspoon dried thyme

1 Heat the oven to 220°C (425°F, gas mark 7). Scrub the potatoes, leaving the skins on, and cut each one lengthways into eight wedges. Place them in a large mixing bowl, add the oil and toss to coat the wedges thinly and evenly.
2 Mix together the breadcrumbs, cayenne pepper, cumin, garlic salt, paprika, pepper and thyme in a large bowl. Add the potatoes and toss until they are evenly coated.
3 Arrange the wedges in a single layer on a large nonstick baking sheet and bake for 35-40 minutes until they are golden brown and crisp. Serve them hot.
Variation: serve the wedges as a snack with some low-fat Greek yoghurt for a dip.

Nutrients per serving, when serving 4

- Calories 227
- Carbohydrate 49 g
- Protein 6 g
- Fat 2 g (no saturated fat)

Potato and horseradish rösti

Tasty horseradish brings unusual piquancy to these golden brown potato cakes.

PREPARATION TIME: 10 minutes
COOKING TIME: 8-12 minutes
SERVES 4

400 g (14 oz) floury potatoes, such as King Edwards, peeled and grated
1 egg, beaten
1 tablespoon creamed horseradish
6 spring onions, finely chopped
Salt and black pepper
1 tablespoon sunflower oil
To garnish: chopped fresh parsley
To serve: 4 tablespoons half-fat crème fraîche

1 Squeeze out any moisture from the grated potatoes with your hands, then place them in a bowl. Add the egg, horseradish, spring onions and salt and pepper and mix thoroughly.
2 Heat the oil in a large, nonstick frying pan over a medium heat. Drop eight mounds of the mixture into the pan and press down with the back of the spoon to make 5 mm (¼ in) thick potato cakes.
3 Fry the rösti for 2-3 minutes on each side until they are firm and golden. You may need to cook the rösti in two batches to prevent them sticking together.
4 Drain them well on kitchen paper. Serve hot, topped with the crème fraîche and garnished with parsley.
Variation: serve the rösti without the crème fraîche as a potato side dish.

Nutrients per serving

- Calories 144
- Carbohydrate 15 g
- Protein 4 g
- Fat 8 g (including saturated fat 3 g)

Potatoes boulangère

Slowly baked potato dishes are always popular, and this version is made with stock instead of the usual cream and cheese.

PREPARATION TIME: 15 minutes, plus 15 minutes soaking and 5 minutes standing
COOKING TIME: 1 hour 30 minutes
SERVES 4-6

750 g (1 lb 10 oz) floury potatoes, such as King Edwards, peeled
225 g (8 oz) onions, thinly sliced
Salt and black pepper
Freshly grated nutmeg
1-2 cloves garlic, crushed
600 ml (1 pint) vegetable stock
1 tablespoon 70 per cent fat spread

1 Slice the potatoes by putting them through the thin blade of a food processor or using a sharp knife. Put them in a bowl with the onions, cover with cold water and leave to soak for 15 minutes to remove some of the starch and soften the onions.
2 Heat the oven to 180°C (350°F, gas mark 4). Drain the potatoes and onions and pat them dry with kitchen paper. Arrange a layer of onions and potatoes in the base of a shallow ovenproof serving dish. Season with salt, pepper and nutmeg to taste, then repeat to make four or five layers in total, ending with the seasonings.
3 Stir the garlic into the stock, then pour it over the vegetables. Dot the top with the fat spread. Bake for 1 hour 30 minutes, or until the top is browned and the potatoes feel soft when they are pierced with a skewer. Leave the dish to stand for 5 minutes before serving.

Nutrients per serving, when serving 4

- Calories 161
- Carbohydrate 31 g
- Protein 4 g
- Fat 4 g (including saturated fat 1 g)

A Tex-Mex vegetarian buffet

When you have friends who do not eat meat coming to visit, it can be hard to please everyone. But this sumptuous vegetarian buffet, based on bold Mexican flavours, will satisfy all tastes so that no one will miss the meat or realise it is also low in fat.

The main dish of black beans has a rich, smoky flavour and tastes good with lemon-scented rice flecked with spinach, spring onions and dill.

The easy cabbage slaw adds a refreshing element to the buffet, and the stir-fried vegetables are delicious served either warm or at room temperature. Long, slow cooking gives the onions a sweet, intense flavour, and the fresh tomato salsa adds a crunchy contrast.

Each recipe serves eight, but can be doubled, or an extra half added, for larger numbers. A lime or lemon sorbet would be the best choice for a piquant finish.

Nutrients per person, for one helping of every dish

- Calories 492
- Carbohydrates 88 g
- Protein 19 g
- Fat 8 g (no saturated fat)

Too hot to handle
To avoid discomfort when preparing chillies, wear thin rubber gloves, easily obtained from the chemist, and take care not to touch your eyes or mouth until after you have removed the gloves.

GREEN RICE

BLACK BEAN CHILLI

Black bean chilli

PREPARATION TIME: 15 minutes, plus overnight soaking
COOKING TIME: 1 hour 30 minutes-2 hours 30 minutes

500 g (1 lb 2 oz) black beans
1 bay leaf
2 tablespoons cumin seeds
2 tablespoons dried oregano
½ teaspoon cayenne pepper
1-2 tablespoons chilli powder
1 tablespoon paprika
2 tablespoons sunflower oil
350 g (12 oz) onions, chopped
6 cloves garlic, chopped
400 g (14 oz) canned chopped tomatoes
½ teaspoon Liquid Smoke, optional
Salt
2 tablespoons red wine vinegar
To garnish: chopped fresh coriander

1. Soak the beans overnight in water to cover. Next day, drain them, cover with fresh water, bring to the boil and cook for 15 minutes. Drain again, add 1.2 litres (2 pints) of fresh water and the bay leaf and bring to the boil, then simmer for 20 minutes.
2. Meanwhile, heat a small, heavy-based frying pan. Add the cumin seeds; when they begin to darken, add the oregano and stir for 10 seconds. Take the pan off the heat, stir in the cayenne pepper, chilli powder and paprika, then crush to a powder with a pestle and mortar.
3. Heat the oil in a frying pan over a medium heat and cook the onions for 5 minutes. Add the garlic and fry for 1 minute, then add the spices and cook for a further 2 minutes, stirring.
4. Add the tomatoes with their juice and the Liquid Smoke, if using, and cook the sauce over a medium heat for 2 minutes.
5. Pour the spiced tomato sauce into the beans and simmer for 30 minutes-1 hour 30 minutes, depending on the age of the beans (older beans take longer to cook), until they are thoroughly soft, but not breaking apart. Add more water during cooking if necessary and stir occasionally to ensure they do not burn on the base. Add salt and extra cayenne to taste.
6. Just before serving, stir in the vinegar and garnish with chopped coriander.

Tip: Liquid Smoke, available in some supermarkets, adds an unusual, smoky overtone to food, but use it sparingly.

Green rice

PREPARATION TIME: 15 minutes
COOKING TIME: 30 minutes

125 g (4½ oz) frozen spinach, defrosted
7-8 spring onions
1 teaspoon sunflower oil
4 cloves garlic, finely chopped
2-3 tablespoons finely chopped fresh dill, or 1 tablespoon dried dill
400 g (14 oz) long-grain white rice
2 tablespoons lemon juice
Salt and black pepper

1. Squeeze the spinach dry and chop it finely. Chop the spring onions, including most of the green parts.
2. Heat the oil in a heavy-based saucepan. Stir-fry the garlic for 30 seconds, then add the spring onions and stir-fry for 1 minute. Add the spinach and dill and cook for a further 1 minute.
3. Add the rice to the pan and cook for a further 1 minute, then pour in 650 ml (1 pint 2 fl oz) of water, the lemon juice, and salt and pepper to taste. Bring to the boil, then cover and simmer for 20 minutes, or until the water has been absorbed. Serve warm.

Salsa cruda

PREPARATION TIME: 20 minutes

85 g (3 oz) red onions
3 cloves garlic
750 g (1 lb 10 oz) tomatoes
1-2 green chillies, deseeded and finely chopped
3 tablespoons finely chopped fresh coriander
½ teaspoon sugar
Juice of 3 limes
A pinch of salt

1. Very finely chop the onions and garlic. Cut the tomatoes into quarters, scoop out and discard the seeds and dice the flesh. You must chop the ingredients by hand or the sauce will be too liquid.
2. Put all the ingredients into a bowl and mix well. Chill for no more than 1 hour before serving to preserve the fresh flavours.

SALSA CRUDA

Stir-fried vegetables

PREPARATION TIME: 20 minutes
COOKING TIME: 15 minutes

100 g (3½ oz) onion, chopped
2 cloves garlic, finely chopped
750 g (1 lb 10 oz) courgettes, thinly sliced
1 red pepper, diced
125 g (4½ oz) sweetcorn kernels, defrosted if frozen
2 tablespoons oil
Salt and black pepper
2 tablespoons lemon or lime juice

1. Prepare all the vegetables and divide each into two equal piles: you will need to stir-fry in two batches so as not to overcrowd the wok.
2. Heat 1 tablespoon of the oil in a wok until it starts to smoke slightly. Starting with the first half, add the onions and stir-fry for 1 minute. Add the garlic, stir once, then add the courgettes, red pepper and sweetcorn. Season with salt and pepper and continue to stir-fry for about 5 minutes, until the vegetables are cooked but still crisp and bright.
3. Sprinkle with half of the lemon or lime juice and stir. Transfer the stir-fry to a bowl and keep it warm. Cook the remaining vegetables the same way.

Rich roast onions

PREPARATION TIME: 5 minutes
COOKING TIME: 1 hour-1 hour 15 minutes

4 very large white onions, about 300 g (10½ oz) each
100 ml (3½ fl oz) balsamic vinegar
1 tablespoon brown sugar
Salt and black pepper

1. Heat the oven to 200°C (400°F, gas mark 6). Cut the onions in half through the root, leaving the skin on, and place them, cut side down, in a single layer in a roasting tin.
2. Mix the vinegar and sugar with 200 ml (7 fl oz) of water, pour it over the onions and roast for 1 hour-1 hour 15 minutes until they are soft.
3. Arrange the onions, cut side up, on a platter, season and serve warm.

Coriander and cabbage slaw

PREPARATION TIME: 30 minutes, plus 1 hour chilling

200 g (7 oz) cucumber
500 g (1 lb 2 oz) green cabbage, shredded
50 g (1¾ oz) red onion, thinly sliced
2 tablespoons chopped fresh coriander
For the dressing:
2 cloves garlic
Salt and black pepper
3 tablespoons lime juice
100 g (3½ oz) low-fat natural yoghurt

1. Peel the cucumber, halve it lengthways and remove the seeds with a teaspoon. Slice it into matchsticks about 2.5 cm (1 in) long. Put them in a bowl and stir in the cabbage, onion and coriander.
2. To make the dressing, crush the garlic into a paste with ½ teaspoon of salt, then whisk in the lime juice and yoghurt and season with pepper. Pour the dressing over the slaw, mix well and chill for about 1 hour to let the flavours develop.

CORIANDER AND CABBAGE SLAW

RICH ROAST ONIONS

STIR-FRIED VEGETABLES

Marinated tofu and **mango kebabs** with **green mango salsa**

Protein-rich tofu comes with a Thai salsa flavoured with chilli, coconut cream and lime.

PREPARATION TIME: 15 minutes, plus 30 minutes draining and 30 minutes marinating
COOKING TIME: 6-8 minutes
SERVES 4

500 g (1 lb 2 oz) fresh tofu
1 large ripe mango, peeled and cubed
For the marinade:
1-2 fresh red chillies, deseeded and chopped
2 cloves garlic, crushed
1 tablespoon grated ginger
1 tablespoon clear honey
Grated zest and juice of 1 lime
3 tablespoons dry sherry
2 tablespoons dark soy sauce
For the salsa:
3 tablespoons coconut cream
Juice of ½ lime
1 large green unripe mango, peeled and coarsely grated
Salt
To garnish: lemon wedges and sliced spring onions

1. Cover a large plate with several layers of kitchen paper. Arrange the tofu on top and cover with more paper, then put a plate on top and weigh down with a tin. Allow the tofu to drain for 30 minutes, then pour off the liquid and cut the tofu into 2.5 cm (1 in) cubes.
2. To make the marinade, combine all the ingredients in a shallow bowl. Add the tofu to the bowl and marinate for at least 30 minutes, stirring and turning a few times.
3. Meanwhile, make the salsa. Mix all the ingredients together with salt to taste in a small bowl and set aside. Heat the grill or light the barbecue.
4. Lift the tofu out of the marinade and thread it onto skewers alternately with the mango pieces. Add the remaining marinade to the salsa.
5. Grill the kebabs for 6-8 minutes, turning them once or twice, until the tofu is browned and heated through. Serve hot with the salsa, garnished with the strips of spring onions, and lime wedges.

Variation: if you cannot find green unripe mango, substitute diced ripe mango in the salsa.

Nutrients per serving

- Calories 230
- Carbohydrate 17 g
- Protein 16 g
- Fat 10 g (including saturated fat 6 g)

Chinese-style tofu omelettes

Nutrients per serving

- Calories 304
- Carbohydrate 9 g
- Protein 26 g
- Fat 18 g (including saturated fat 5 g)

A sweet sauce blends delicate rice wine with hoisin, garlic and green peas in this traditional Oriental omelette.

PREPARATION TIME: 10 minutes
COOKING TIME: 30-35 minutes
SERVES 4

600 g (1 lb 5 oz) silken tofu, firm or soft
3 eggs
3-4 spring onions, chopped
Salt and black pepper
2 tablespoons oil
For the sauce:
175 ml (6 fl oz) vegetable stock
2 tablespoons hoisin sauce
2 tablespoons Chinese rice wine, or dry sherry
1 clove garlic, crushed
150 g (5½ oz) peas, defrosted if frozen

1 Heat the oven to low to keep the omelettes warm.
2 Mash the tofu with a fork in a large bowl until it is thoroughly broken down, then beat in the eggs and spring onions and season generously with salt and pepper.
3 Heat ½ tablespoon of the oil in a large nonstick frying pan until it is very hot. Add a quarter of the tofu mixture to the pan to make two omelettes at a time, keeping them well apart. Fry them for 3-4 minutes on each side until they have turned golden brown, turning them carefully because the mixture breaks up easily.
4 Transfer the omelettes to a heatproof plate as they are made and put them in the oven to keep warm. Repeat the process three more times, adding oil to the pan as necessary, to make eight omelettes in total.
5 After all the omelettes have been made, add the vegetable stock to the pan and scrape up any caramelised cooking juices on the base, then bring the liquid to the boil. Stir in the hoisin sauce, Chinese rice wine or sherry, garlic and peas and let them simmer for 2-3 minutes until the sauce has thickened slightly and the flavours have combined. Adjust the seasoning to taste.
6 Lay two omelettes on each plate, pour the sauce over them and serve while they are still hot.

Tip: silken tofu contains more liquid than plain tofu, which gives it a smooth texture, almost like an egg custard, and makes it easy to mash. Fresh silken tofu is sold chilled in health food shops and some supermarkets. If unobtainable, substitute plain tofu.

Baby vegetable fricassée

Nutrients per serving

- Calories 279
- Carbohydrate 28 g
- Protein 9 g
- Fat 15 g (including saturated fat 5 g)

Tender poached vegetables are served in a herb-packed béchamel sauce and given a crunchy cheese topping.

PREPARATION TIME: 15 minutes
COOKING TIME: 30-35 minutes
SERVES 4

750 g (1 lb 10 oz) mixture of young and baby vegetables such as broccoli, carrots, cauliflower, fennel, leeks, mushrooms, onions, patty pan squash or courgettes, and red or yellow peppers
2 tablespoons dry vermouth
1 bay leaf
2-3 fresh parsley stalks
1 sprig fresh thyme
Salt and black pepper
25 g (1 oz) Parmesan cheese, grated
2 tablespoons wholemeal breadcrumbs
For the béchamel sauce:
50 g (1¾ oz) 70 per cent fat spread
3 tablespoons plain white flour
150 ml (5 fl oz) semi-skimmed milk
3 tablespoons half-fat crème fraîche
2 tablespoons coarsely chopped fresh parsley or marjoram

1 Prepare your chosen vegetables: trim broccoli or cauliflower into small florets; top and tail carrots; top, tail and chop fennel finely; slice leeks thickly; slice mushrooms; cut onions into quarters; halve patty pan squash or top and tail baby courgettes; and cut peppers into squares.
2 Put 600 ml (1 pint) of water into a large saucepan and add the vermouth, bay leaf, parsley stalks, thyme, salt and pepper, then bring to the boil. Add the vegetables, reduce the heat and simmer for 5 minutes.
3 Using a slotted spoon, transfer the vegetables to a shallow 1.5 litre (2 pint 15 fl oz) flameproof dish. Set aside and keep warm.
4 Discard the herbs and return the vegetable stock to a fast boil. Cook, uncovered, for 10 minutes, or until it is reduced by half. Heat the grill to a medium heat.
5 To make the sauce, melt the fat spread in a large saucepan and whisk in the flour. Cook for 1-2 seconds, then gradually strain in the stock, add the milk and whisk. Bring to the boil, reduce the heat and simmer for 3 minutes. Remove from the heat, stir in the crème fraîche and chopped herb and season to taste.
6 Pour the sauce over the vegetables, sprinkle the cheese and breadcrumbs over the top, and place under the grill for 2-3 minutes until the topping is lightly browned, then serve.
Serving suggestion: tagliatelle or new potatoes.

Buckwheat crêpes stuffed with spinach and ricotta

A creamy but light filling transforms these nutty-flavoured pancakes, popular in Normandy and Brittany, into a great dish for relaxed entertainment.

PREPARATION TIME: 20 minutes, plus 30 minutes standing
COOKING TIME: 25 minutes
MAKES 8 crêpes

150 g (5½ oz) plain white flour
100 g (3½ oz) buckwheat flour
Salt and black pepper
1 whole egg and 1 egg white
Sunflower oil for greasing
For the filling:
200 g (7 oz) quark
100 g (3½ oz) half-fat cottage cheese
100 g (3½ oz) ricotta cheese
300 g (10½ oz) fresh spinach
2-4 tablespoons lemon juice
½ teaspoon grated nutmeg
To garnish: paprika
To serve: tomatoes and fresh basil leaves

Low-fat tip

Substituting quark and cottage cheese for some of the ricotta makes this filling lighter than the traditional one.

1. Bring the quark, cottage cheese and ricotta to room temperature and set aside.
2. To make the crêpes, sift the flours and 1 teaspoon of salt together. Whisk the egg and egg white together in a small bowl with 450 ml (16 fl oz) of water until well blended, then gradually add the mixture to the flour, whisking well. Set aside for 30 minutes.
3. Rinse the spinach and remove any tough stalks, then put it into a saucepan, with the water still clinging to the leaves. Cover and cook for 3-4 minutes over a medium heat until it is wilted, then drain well.
4. When the spinach is cool enough to handle, squeeze out the excess water and chop it finely. Mix the cheeses and spinach together and season with the lemon juice, nutmeg, and salt and pepper to taste.
5. To cook the crêpes, heat a small nonstick frying pan over a medium-high heat. Stir the batter and check that it is thin enough to pour: if not, add water, 1 tablespoon at a time. When the pan is hot, wipe it with kitchen paper dipped in sunflower oil, then pour in 2-3 tablespoons of the batter and tilt the pan until the batter coats the base. Cook the crêpe for 1½ minutes, or until the edges begin to brown and curl up.
6. Loosen the edges gently with a thin spatula, then turn the crêpe over and cook it for a further 20-30 seconds. Do not be tempted to flip the crêpe too soon as the batter will stick to the pan, and take care not to overcook it: if the crêpe dries out it will be difficult to fold over.
7. Cook seven more crêpes the same way, regreasing the pan when necessary. Either fill and serve each crêpe as you go along or, if you want to serve everyone at once, pile the crêpes up between sheets of kitchen paper and loosely cover with foil.
8. To serve, spread 2-3 tablespoons of the filling along the centre of each hot crêpe, then fold one side over the other. Serve the crêpes sprinkled with paprika and accompanied by tomatoes garnished with basil.

Nutrients per crêpe

- Calories 180
- Carbohydrate 27 g
- Protein 11 g
- Fat 3 g (including saturated fat 1 g)

Lentil loaf with pumpkin sauce

Pumpkin sauce, given a spicy last-minute dressing, makes a mouth-watering accompaniment to this wholesome bake.

Nutrients per serving
- Calories 358
- Carbohydrate 43 g
- Protein 20 g
- Fat 13 g (including saturated fat 2 g)

PREPARATION TIME: 20 minutes, plus 4-5 hours, or overnight, soaking
COOKING TIME: 55 minutes
SERVES 4

For the loaf:
125 g (4½ oz) red split lentils
125 g (4½ oz) yellow split lentils
1-2 green chillies, deseeded and roughly chopped
1-2 dried red chillies, deseeded and roughly chopped
1 tablespoon chopped fresh coriander
1 tablespoon curry leaves
1 tablespoon roughly chopped ginger
½ teaspoon baking powder
1 egg
3 tablespoons sunflower oil
Salt
60 g (2¼ oz) onions, finely chopped

For the sauce:
225 g (8 oz) pumpkin or butternut squash, peeled, deseeded and cut into 2.5 cm (1 in) cubes
1-2 green chillies, deseeded and roughly chopped
10-12 curry leaves
1 tablespoon roughly chopped ginger
1 teaspoon sugar
175 g (6 oz) low-fat natural yoghurt
2 teaspoons sunflower oil
½ teaspoon black mustard seeds
1 dried red chilli, deseeded and roughly chopped
To garnish: chopped fresh coriander and curry leaves

1. Rinse the lentils and soak them in water for 4-5 hours, or overnight.
2. When ready to cook, heat the oven to 190°C (375°F, gas mark 5). Line an 18 x 23 cm (7 x 9 in) ovenproof dish with greaseproof paper.
3. Drain the lentils well and place them in a food processor with the chillies, coriander, curry leaves, ginger, baking powder, egg, oil, and salt to taste. Process until they are well blended and smooth, then stir in the onions and pulse for a few seconds so they are well combined but not puréed.
4. Spoon the mixture into the prepared dish and smooth the top. Bake it on the top shelf for 45-50 minutes until the top has browned.
5. Meanwhile, make the sauce. Put the pumpkin or squash into a saucepan with the green chilli, curry leaves, ginger, sugar, and salt to taste. Add 50 ml (2 fl oz) of water, cover the pan and simmer for 8-10 minutes until the pumpkin is tender, stirring occasionally. Remove it from the heat, allow to cool, then purée the mixture in a food processor or with a hand-held mixer.
6. Mix the yoghurt into the pumpkin purée. Transfer the sauce into a serving bowl, cover and chill until required.
7. Remove the lentil loaf from the oven, gently remove the paper then cut it into slices.
8. In a small saucepan, heat the oil for the sauce over a medium heat. When it is hot, throw in the mustard seeds and cover the pan. As soon as they begin to pop, uncover the pan, add the red chilli and cook until it has just blackened. Pour the spiced oil over the pumpkin sauce.
9. Serve the loaf with a spoonful of pumpkin sauce alongside, garnished with chopped coriander and curry leaves.

Courgette cakes with minted yoghurt sauce

Chargrilled courgette cakes, served with a cool sauce, make a refreshing dish.

PREPARATION TIME: 15-30 minutes, plus 50 minutes standing
COOKING TIME: 20 minutes
SERVES 4-6

750 g (1 lb 10 oz) courgettes
Salt and black pepper
1 egg, beaten
60 g (2¼ oz) matzo meal
A pinch of freshly grated nutmeg
For the sauce:
Finely grated zest and juice of ½ lemon
3-4 tablespoons chopped fresh mint
150 g (5½ oz) low-fat set yoghurt
To garnish: fresh sprigs of mint

1 Finely grate the courgettes into a colander, sprinkle with salt, mix well and allow to drain for 30 minutes. Rinse them under running water and squeeze dry with your hands, then place them in a clean tea towel and squeeze again.
2 Transfer the courgettes to a bowl and add the egg, matzo meal, nutmeg and pepper to taste. Mix them together until well combined, then allow to stand for 20 minutes for the flavours to develop.
3 Meanwhile, to make the sauce, combine the lemon zest and juice, mint and yoghurt in a bowl, then cover and chill until ready to serve.
4 Heat a ridged, iron grill pan or nonstick frying pan over a medium heat. Place dessertspoons of the courgette mixture onto the pan, flattening each to form a thick cake. Dry-fry the cakes for 4-5 minutes on each side, until they are firm and browned. (You may need to cook them in two batches.) Garnish with the mint and serve hot, with the chilled sauce on the side.

Variation: if you cannot find matzo meal, use matzo crackers ground to fine crumbs in a food processor or crushed thoroughly with a rolling pin.

Nutrients per serving, when serving 4

- Calories 129
- Carbohydrate 18 g
- Protein 8 g
- Fat 3 g (including saturated fat 1 g)

Mexican vegetable and cornmeal pie

Nutrients per serving
- Calories 378
- Carbohydrate 56 g
- Protein 19 g
- Fat 10 g (including saturated fat 3 g)

This satisfying dish, with its tasty cornmeal topping, makes an exciting vegetarian alternative to shepherd's pie.

PREPARATION TIME: 20 minutes, plus 5 minutes standing
COOKING TIME: 1 hour
SERVES 4

1 tablespoon sunflower oil
1 stick celery, chopped
1 large clove garlic, crushed
150 g (5½ oz) onions, chopped
½ green pepper, chopped
1 teaspoon cayenne pepper
400 g (14 oz) canned red kidney beans, drained and rinsed
12 stoned green olives, sliced
1 tablespoon chopped jalapeño peppers
75 g (2¾ oz) canned sweetcorn, drained
400 g (14 oz) canned chopped tomatoes
1 tablespoon tomato purée
Salt and black pepper
For the topping:
125 g (4½ oz) cornmeal, or polenta
1 tablespoon plain white flour
2 teaspoons baking powder
1 egg, beaten
100 ml (3½ fl oz) skimmed milk
25 g (1 oz) half-fat mature Cheddar cheese, grated

1. Heat the oven to 200°C (400°F, gas mark 6). Heat the oil in a saucepan over a high heat. Stir in the celery, garlic, onions and green pepper, bring them to a sizzle, then cover, reduce the heat to low and cook for 10 minutes, or until they have softened. Stir in the cayenne pepper and cook for a further 1-2 minutes.
2. Stir in the kidney beans, olives, jalapeño peppers, sweetcorn, canned tomatoes, tomato paste, and salt and pepper to taste. Bring the mixture to the boil and simmer for 5 minutes. Then spoon the mixture into a 3 litre (5 pint 5 fl oz) ovenproof serving dish.
3. To make the topping, mix together the cornmeal or polenta, flour, ½ teaspoon of salt and the baking powder, then beat in the egg and milk. The mixture should look like a thick batter; if not, add 1-2 tablespoons of milk.
4. Spoon the topping over the vegetables, sprinkle with the cheese and bake for 40 minutes, or until the topping is risen and golden brown. Leave the pie to stand for 5 minutes before serving.

MEXICAN VEGETABLE AND CORNMEAL PIE

NEW POTATO AND SPINACH FRITTATA

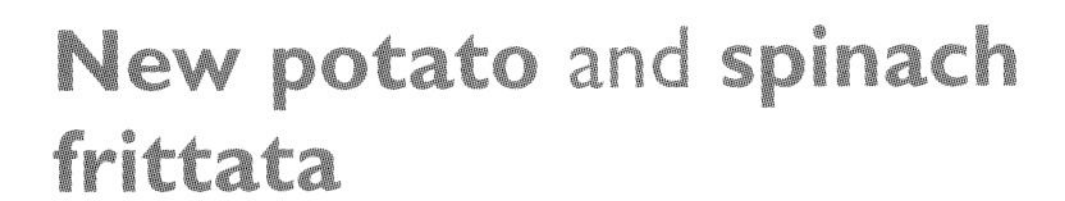

New potato and **spinach frittata**

This chunky omelette makes a perfect light lunch, and is an ideal way of using up leftover new potatoes.

PREPARATION TIME: 20 minutes
COOKING TIME: 20-30 minutes
SERVES 4

1 tablespoon olive oil
150 g (5½ oz) red onions, finely chopped
1 large red pepper, chopped
150 g (5½ oz) baby spinach leaves
1 clove garlic, crushed
6 spring onions, chopped
500 g (1 lb 2 oz) cooked new potatoes, sliced
3 eggs
4 tablespoons skimmed milk
1 tablespoon chopped fresh basil
2 teaspoons finely chopped fresh chives
1 tablespoon chopped fresh flat-leaved parsley
Salt and black pepper
25 g (1 oz) Parmesan cheese, finely grated
25 g (1 oz) half-fat mature Cheddar cheese, finely grated

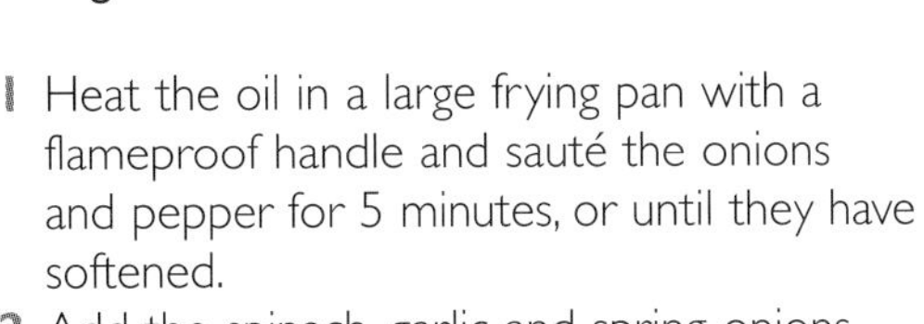

1. Heat the oil in a large frying pan with a flameproof handle and sauté the onions and pepper for 5 minutes, or until they have softened.
2. Add the spinach, garlic and spring onions and continue frying for 2 minutes, or until the spinach has wilted. Then stir in the potatoes.
3. Beat the eggs in a large bowl with the milk, basil, chives and parsley and add salt and pepper to taste. Pour the mixture over the vegetables, reduce the heat and cook for 10-20 minutes until the egg begins to set.
4. Meanwhile, heat the grill to medium. Sprinkle the cheeses over the frittata, then place the pan under the grill for 2 minutes, or until the cheese has melted and turned golden. Cut the frittata into wedges and serve.

Serving suggestion: mixed salad with chives.

Nutrients per serving

- Calories 261
- Carbohydrate 26 g
- Protein 15 g
- Fat 12 g (including saturated fat 4 g)

Onion, feta cheese and marjoram pizzas

In this simple, thin-crust pizza, the sweetness of caramelised onions is balanced by the saltiness of feta cheese.

PREPARATION TIME: 40-50 minutes, plus 1 hour 30 minutes rising

COOKING TIME: 35 minutes

MAKES 2 pizzas, each serving 4

2 teaspoons dried yeast with ¾ teaspoon sugar, or 1 sachet easy-blend yeast
250 g (9 oz) strong plain white flour
Salt and black pepper
2 tablespoons olive oil, plus oil for greasing

For the topping:
1 kg (2 lb 4 oz) onions, peeled and thinly sliced
1 tablespoon sugar
2 tablespoons balsamic vinegar
2 teaspoons dried marjoram
150 g (5½ oz) feta cheese, rinsed, dried and crumbled

Low-fat tip

Cooking the onions in sugar and balsamic vinegar gives them a rich flavour without adding fat.

1 First make the pizza dough. If using dried yeast, dissolve the sugar in 75 ml (2½ fl oz) of lukewarm water, then sprinkle the yeast in and set aside for 10-15 minutes until it is frothy.
2 Meanwhile, sift the flour and a pinch of salt into a large bowl and add the easy-blend yeast, if using. Make a well in the centre and add the olive oil and 125 ml (4 fl oz) of lukewarm water if using easy-blend yeast, or the frothy yeast mixture and 50 ml (2 fl oz) of lukewarm water. Stir with a wooden spoon to form a dough.
3 Turn out the dough onto a lightly floured work surface and knead for 5-10 minutes until it is smooth and elastic, adding extra flour, 1 tablespoon at a time, if necessary to stop it sticking; if it is too dry, add extra water, 1 tablespoon at a time.
4 Shape the dough into a ball and grease the cleaned bowl with a little oil. Put the dough into the bowl, roll it around so that it is lightly coated with oil and loosely cover the bowl with cling film. Leave the dough to rise in a warm place for 1 hour, or until it has doubled in size.
5 Meanwhile, to make the topping, bring a large pan of water to the boil. Add the onions, reduce the heat and let them simmer for 10 minutes, or until they have softened, then drain well.
6 Put the onions into a large nonstick frying pan with the sugar, balsamic vinegar, and salt to taste. Cook them over a medium-high heat, stirring, for 10 minutes, or until the liquid has reduced but not dried out completely. The sugar should have caramelised slightly and the onions should have a rich flavour. Stir in the marjoram and some black pepper and adjust the seasoning if necessary.
7 Turn out the risen dough onto a lightly floured surface, punch it down and knead it for 2-3 minutes. Return it to the bowl, cover it once more and set aside for 30 minutes for the dough to rise again.
8 Meanwhile, heat the oven to 240°C (475°F, gas mark 9). Lightly grease two baking sheets.
9 Turn out the dough, punch it down and divide it into two pieces. Shape each piece into a ball, then roll it out into a 25 cm (10 in) circle and place on a baking sheet. Drain off any liquid from the onions, then spread them evenly over each pizza and sprinkle with the feta cheese.
10 Bake for 12 minutes, or until the cheese has melted and the edges of the pizzas are crisp and golden. Serve them straight from the oven.

Tip: for added flavour, cook the onions ahead of time and use their cooking water as the liquid in the pizza dough.

Nutrients per slice

- Calories 237
- Carbohydrate 37 g
- Protein 8 g
- Fat 8 g (including saturated fat 3 g)

FETA CHEESE

Mushroom and **sweet potato stew**

Orange-fleshed sweet potatoes have a rich, distinctive flavour and combine beautifully with a medley of meaty mushrooms in this warming stew.

PREPARATION TIME: 10-30 minutes, depending on mushrooms used

COOKING TIME: 40-50 minutes

SERVES 4-6

150 g (5½ oz) fresh shiitake mushrooms, or 75 g (2¾ oz) dried Chinese mushrooms
150 g (5½ oz) oyster mushrooms
150 g (5½ oz) field mushrooms
1 tablespoon sesame or groundnut oil
200 g (7 oz) onions, chopped
500 g (1 lb 2 oz) orange sweet potatoes, scrubbed and cut into large chunks
3 tablespoons dark soy sauce
750 ml (1 pint 7 fl oz) vegetable stock or water
Salt and black pepper
3 tablespoons chopped fresh coriander

1. Slice the shiitake mushrooms, or, if using dried mushrooms, cover them in boiling water and leave for 20 minutes to rehydrate. Lift out the mushrooms, strain the liquid through a sieve lined with kitchen paper and set it aside. Slice the mushrooms. Chop the oyster and field mushrooms into large chunks.
2. Heat the oil in a large saucepan, add the onions and fry over a high heat for 5 minutes, or until they start to brown. Add the mushrooms and continue frying for a further 1-2 minutes.
3. Add the sweet potatoes, soy sauce, stock or water, replacing some of the stock with the mushroom liquid if you used dried mushrooms. Bring to the boil, reduce the heat to low and simmer, uncovered, for 30-40 minutes until the sweet potatoes have softened and most of the liquid has evaporated. Stir occasionally during cooking.
4. Season to taste, stir in the coriander and serve.

Variation: this recipe works equally well with yellow or white-fleshed sweet potatoes, although the orange sweet potato is the most widely available variety.

Nutrients per serving, when serving 4

- Calories 215
- Carbohydrate 41 g
- Protein 6 g
- Fat 5 g (including saturated fat 1 g)

Watercress and red pepper quiche

In this savoury tart, peppery watercress, caramelised onions and sweet red pepper combine for a terrific taste.

PREPARATION TIME: 40 minutes, plus at least 30 minutes chilling and 20 minutes cooling

COOKING TIME: 1 hour -1 hour 10 minutes

SERVES 6

For the pastry:
100 g (3½ oz) plain white flour
75 g (2¾ oz) plain wholemeal flour
Salt and black pepper
90 g (3¼ oz) 70 per cent fat spread, diced
1 egg, beaten

For the filling:
1 teaspoon olive oil
400 g (14 oz) onions, cut in half and sliced thinly lengthways
1 tablespoon soft dark brown sugar
2 eggs
225 ml (8 fl oz) skimmed milk
200 g (7 oz) watercress, tough stalks removed, leaves finely chopped
25 g (1 oz) Parmesan cheese, grated
1 large red pepper, diced

1 To make the pastry, sift the flours and a pinch of salt into a mixing bowl, adding any bran remaining in the sieve. Rub in the fat spread until the mixture resembles fine breadcrumbs, then mix in enough of the egg to form a slightly soft, but not sticky, dough.
2 Knead the dough on a lightly floured work surface for a few seconds until it is smooth, then roll it out into a 30 cm (12 in) round. Line a 25 cm (10 in) flan tin with the dough, trim the edge and place in the refrigerator for at least 30 minutes to chill.
3 To make the filling, put the oil, onions, brown sugar and a pinch of salt into a nonstick frying pan, mix them together and fry over a fairly low heat for 25-30 minutes, stirring frequently, until the onions are softened and lightly caramelised. Remove from the heat and set aside.
4 Heat the oven to 220°C (425°F, gas mark 7) and put a baking sheet in to warm.
5 Break the eggs into a mixing bowl, add the milk and pepper to taste and whisk well. Then stir in the watercress and half the Parmesan cheese.
6 Spoon the cooled onions into the pastry case, spreading them out evenly, then pour in the watercress mixture and sprinkle the diced pepper and remaining Parmesan over the top.
7 Place the quiche on the hot baking sheet and cook for 35-40 minutes until the filling is set and the topping is lightly browned. Serve it hot or at room temperature.

Variation: for added flavour, you can sprinkle 15 g (½ oz) of pine nuts over of the quiche before baking it, but they will add 2 g of fat per serving. Cover the quiche loosely with foil if the pine nuts start to brown before the filling is set.

Nutrients per serving

- Calories 331
- Carbohydrate 33 g
- Protein 12 g
- Fat 17 g (including saturated fat 4 g)

desserts

Banana and **summer berry salad**

The flavours of cinnamon and cloves perk up this simple fruit salad, dressed with yoghurt and orange juice.

PREPARATION TIME: 20 minutes, plus 2 hours chilling
SERVES 4

250 g (9 oz) mixed berries, such as blueberries, loganberries, raspberries or strawberries
2 bananas
250 g (9 oz) natural low-fat yoghurt
3 tablespoons clear honey
4 tablespoons freshly squeezed orange juice
1-2 teaspoons ground cinnamon
A pinch of ground cloves
To garnish: fresh mint leaves and ground cinnamon

1 Hull and slice the strawberries, then put them and the rest of the berries into a large bowl. Slice the bananas and add them to the berries.
2 Stir the yoghurt into the fruit, then stir in the honey and orange juice and add ground cinnamon and cloves to taste.
3 Chill for 2 hours to allow the flavours to blend. Garnish with fresh mint leaves, sprinkle cinnamon over the fruit and serve.

Nutrients per serving

- Calories 154
- Carbohydrate 34 g
- Protein 5 g
- Fat 1 g (no saturated fat)

Shrikhand with **exotic fruits**

Shrikhand is a creamy strained yoghurt dessert from western India served here with dates, lychees, papaya and pomegranate.

PREPARATION TIME: 45 minutes-1 hour, plus 4 hours, or overnight, draining and 1 hour chilling
SERVES 4-6

900 g (2 lb) natural set yoghurt
10-12 strands saffron, pounded
2 tablespoons skimmed milk
50 g (1¾ oz) caster sugar, or to taste
½ teaspoon ground cardamom
250 g (9 oz) natural dates
250 g (9 oz) fresh lychees, or 400 g (14 oz) canned lychees, drained
1 small papaya
1 pomegranate

Mango mousse

The sweet flavours of mango and honey balance the citrus tang of this fluffy mousse.

PREPARATION TIME: 10 minutes, plus 2 hours chilling

COOKING TIME: 10 minutes

SERVES 6

1 kg (2 lb 4 oz) fully ripe mangoes
100 ml (3½ fl oz) sweet white wine or water
1 tablespoon clear honey
Grated zest and juice of ½ lemon
Juice of 1 large orange
1 teaspoon orange flower water, optional
2 egg whites
2 tablespoons caster sugar

1 Peel the mangoes, cut the flesh from the stones and purée it in a food processor or with a hand-held mixer.
2 Put the wine or water, honey, lemon zest and juice, orange juice and orange flower water, if using, in a saucepan and bring them to the boil. Boil hard until the liquid has reduced to about 3 tablespoons. Allow the mixture to cool slightly, then stir it into the mango purée.
3 Whisk the egg whites until they form soft peaks, then gradually whisk in the sugar until they are shiny and stiff. Fold the egg whites into the mango mixture. Spoon into individual glasses or one large serving bowl and chill for 2 hours, or until set.

Nutrients per serving

- Calories 137
- Carbohydrate 30 g
- Protein 2 g
- No fat

1 Pour the yoghurt onto a fine muslin cloth, then tie the corners in a knot. Suspend the muslin over the sink for 4 hours, or overnight, until all the water content has drained through. Alternatively, put the muslin bag into a sieve, place it over a bowl and chill until the yoghurt is well drained.
2 When the yoghurt has drained, warm the milk a little, remove it from the heat and infuse the saffron in it for 10 minutes.
3 Untie the muslin cloth and empty the strained yoghurt into a large bowl. Stir in the sugar and cardamom and whisk until the mixture is smooth.
4 Stir in the saffron milk until it is well blended, then cover the shrikhand and chill for 1 hour before serving.
5 Meanwhile, stone and chop the dates.
6 Peel the lychees. Working over a bowl to collect the juice, make two or three slits in the flesh of each and remove the stones. If using canned lychees, halve or quarter each one.
7 Cut the papaya into quarters, scrape out the seeds and the membrane with a teaspoon, then peel each quarter and cut the flesh into bite-size pieces.
8 Cut the pomegranate in half and remove the skin and the white membrane attached to the seeds. Reserve all the seeds.
9 In individual dishes, arrange alternate layers of shrikhand and fruits and seeds (reserving a few pomegranate seeds for a garnish), along with any fresh lychee juice. Garnish with the reserved seeds and serve.

Variation: if you do not like cardamom, use ½ teaspoon of freshly grated nutmeg instead.

Nutrients per serving, when serving 4

- Calories 392
- Carbohydrate 84 g
- Protein 14 g
- Fat 2 g (including saturated fat 1 g)

Summer pudding

This luscious fruit dessert truly captures the flavours of summer.

PREPARATION TIME: 30 minutes, plus 8 hours, or overnight, chilling
COOKING TIME: 7 minutes
SERVES 4-6

250 g (9 oz) blackcurrants
250 g (9 oz) redcurrants
250 g (9 oz) strawberries, cut in half if large
125 g (4½ oz) caster sugar
4 tablespoons kirsch or Cointreau
250 g (9 oz) raspberries
1 small white loaf, thinly sliced lengthways if possible
To garnish: raspberries and redcurrants

1 Strip the currants from their stalks with a fork. Place them in a large, non-aluminium saucepan with the strawberries, sugar and the liqueur.
2 Cover the pan and simmer over a low heat for 5 minutes, or until the sugar has dissolved and the fruit has released plenty of juice. Stir in the raspberries and continue to simmer, covered, for a further 2 minutes, then set aside and leave to cool.
3 Cut the crusts off the bread and, using an 850 ml (1 pint 10 fl oz) pudding basin as a template, cut one round of bread to fit its base and one to fit its top. Cut the remaining slices into wedges. Cover the bottom of the basin with the smaller round, then neatly arrange the bread wedges so that they just overlap one another and flop over the top.
4 Ladle the fruit and some of the juices into the basin, holding the bread lining in place. Set aside any leftover fruit. Fold the bread over the top of the fruit and seal with the remaining bread round.
5 Stand the basin in a dish, then cover with a saucer or small plate that fits snugly into the top of the basin. Put a heavy weight on it and refrigerate for at least 8 hours. Cover and chill any excess fruit and juices.
6 Before serving, gently run a round-bladed knife between the bread and basin. Invert the basin onto a plate, giving it a sharp shake so that the pudding slips out. Pour any reserved juices over the top. Serve garnished with raspberries and redcurrants, with any remaining juices on the side.
Variation: replace the redcurrants with black or red berries instead.

Nutrients per serving, when serving 4
• Calories 373
• Carbohydrate 79 g
• Protein 8 g
• Fat 1 g (no saturated fat)

Cinnamon pineapple with Malibu

In this fat-free dessert, pineapple in syrup is enhanced with a coconut-flavoured liqueur.

PREPARATION TIME: 15-20 minutes, plus 45 minutes cooling and 30 minutes chilling
COOKING TIME: 30-40 minutes
SERVES 4

25 g (1 oz) glacé cherries, halved, rinsed and dried
75 ml (2½ fl oz) Malibu, or other coconut-flavoured liqueur
1.3 kg (3 lb) pineapple
5 cm (2 in) cinnamon stick, halved
2 star anise
75 g (2¾ oz) dark brown sugar
25 g (1 oz) seedless raisins
To garnish: sprigs of fresh mint

1 Put the glacé cherries into a bowl, pour 30 ml (1 fl oz) of liqueur over them, mix well and set aside.
2 Slice off both ends of the pineapple. Peel it with a sharp knife and, using a small knife, remove the 'eyes'. Cut the flesh into quarters lengthways. Remove the fibrous core from each quarter and cut the flesh into bite-size pieces.
3 To make the syrup, put 450 ml (16 fl oz) of water into a saucepan and bring to the boil. Add the pineapple, cinnamon, star anise and sugar and stir until the sugar has dissolved. Return to the boil, reduce the heat, cover and simmer for 8-10 minutes until the pineapple is cooked, but still firm.
4 Remove the pan from the heat and use a slotted spoon to transfer the pineapple to a bowl, squeezing the chunks to remove excess liquid.
5 Add the raisins to the syrup, return it to the heat and simmer for 15-20 minutes until it has reduced by a quarter. Stir in the remaining liqueur and continue simmering for 1 minute. Remove the pan from the heat and discard the cinnamon.
6 Stir the cherries into the syrup, then spoon the mixture over the pineapple. Cool and serve chilled, or at room temperature, garnished with mint.

Nutrients per serving
• Calories 219
• Carbohydrate 46 g
• Protein 1 g
• No fat

Rhubarb, orange and ginger crumble

Nutrients per serving

- Calories 437
- Carbohydrate 70 g
- Protein 15 g
- Fat 13 g (including saturated fat 3 g)

Aromatic ginger and tangy orange liven up this warm, fruity dish with its crisp, oaty topping. And it is just as delicious served chilled.

PREPARATION TIME: 15 minutes
COOKING TIME: 40-45 minutes
SERVES 4

1 large orange
450 g (1 lb) rhubarb, sliced into 2.5 cm (1 in) pieces
2 teaspoons chopped stem ginger
1-2 tablespoons caster sugar
For the crumble:
125 g (4½ oz) plain white flour
75 g (2¾ oz) half-fat butter, chilled and diced
25 g (1 oz) demerara sugar
50 g (1¾ oz) porridge oats
To serve: Low-fat Custard (page 272)

1. Heat the oven to 190°C (375°F, gas mark 5). Finely grate 1 teaspoon of orange zest and set it aside. Then peel the orange, removing all the pith, and divide the flesh into segments, cutting any large ones in half.
2. Place the orange segments in a pie dish and add the rhubarb, stem ginger and caster sugar to taste. Cover the dish with foil and bake for 15 minutes.
3. Meanwhile, prepare the crumble. Place the flour, butter and demerara sugar in a bowl and combine with your fingertips until the mixture resembles breadcrumbs, or whizz them for 10-15 seconds in a food processor. Stir in the oats and the reserved orange zest.
4. Uncover the fruit and sprinkle the crumble topping over them. Return the dish to the oven, uncovered, and bake for 25-30 minutes until the topping is crisp and golden.
5. Allow the crumble to cool slightly, then serve with hot custard.

Variation: you can substitute gooseberries for the rhubarb or strawberries for the oranges.

RHUBARB

Apple and cinnamon filo tartlets

Delectably crisp and golden individual apple pastries are arranged in a whirl and spiced with cinnamon to make a stunning finale to a meal.

PREPARATION TIME: 15 minutes
COOKING TIME: 20 minutes
MAKES 4

6 filo pastry sheets, each measuring at least 24 x 24 cm (9½ x 9½ in)
25 g (1 oz) unsalted butter, melted
2 dessert apples, halved, cored and thinly sliced
2 tablespoons caster sugar
½ teaspoon ground cinnamon
To serve: 4 tablespoons Greek yoghurt, optional

1 Heat the oven to 200°C (400°F, gas mark 6). Lay a sheet of filo pastry on the work surface, brush it with a little of the melted butter, then lay another sheet on top. Continue brushing with butter and layering until all six filo sheets are stacked on top of each other. Using a 12 cm (4½ in) saucer as a guide, cut out four pastry rounds with a sharp knife.
2 Brush each pastry round with the remaining butter and place them on a baking sheet. Arrange the apple slices on the pastry rounds, fanning them out from the centre.
3 Dust with sugar and cinnamon, then bake for 20 minutes, or until the pastry is golden and the apples are tender. Serve the tartlets warm with 1 tablespoon of Greek yoghurt on each, if you like.

Nutrients per tartlet

- Calories 142
- Carbohydrate 22 g
- Protein 2 g
- Fat 6 g (including saturated fat 3 g)

Plum and **apple meringue tart**

Serve this fruity tart, with its soft, gooey topping, soon after it is baked so that the juices do not make the crust soggy.

PREPARATION TIME: 30 minutes, plus at least 30 minutes chilling
COOKING TIME: 1 hour 10 minutes
SERVES 4-6

100 g (3½ oz) plain white flour
1 teaspoon caster sugar
50 g (1¾ oz) 70 per cent fat spread, diced
1 egg white
For the filling:
600 g (1 lb 5 oz) Bramley apples
90 g (3¼ oz) caster sugar
Finely grated zest of 1 lemon
Juice of ½ lemon
500 g (1 lb 2 oz) sweet, purple dessert plums, such as Victoria
For the meringue:
2 egg whites
80 g (3 oz) caster sugar

1 Sift the flour and sugar into a bowl and rub in the fat spread until the mixture resembles breadcrumbs. Stir in the egg white to make a slightly soft, but not sticky, pastry.
2 Put the pastry onto a lightly floured surface and knead for a few seconds until it is smooth. Roll out thinly into a 23 cm (9 in) round. Use the pastry to line a 20 cm (8 in) round tart tin with a removable base, pressing down firmly. Trim the edges, then lightly prick the base with a fork. Put the pastry case into the refrigerator to chill for at least 30 minutes.
3 Meanwhile, make the filling. Peel and cut the apples into quarters, then core and cut them into 1 cm (½ in) slices. Put the apples into a nonstick saucepan, stir in 50 g (1¾ oz) of the sugar, the lemon zest and juice and 1 tablespoon of water. Cover and simmer over a medium-low heat for 10-15 minutes, stirring occasionally, until the apples are just soft and fluffy, but still retain some texture.
4 Halve and stone the plums. Pour 150 ml (5 fl oz) of water into a large frying pan over a high heat, stir in the remaining sugar and bring to the boil, stirring continuously. Reduce the heat to medium, place the plums in a single layer in the syrup and poach for 15 minutes, turning them over halfway through, until they are soft when pricked with a knife.
5 Spoon the apples into a sieve and leave them to drain. Using a slotted spoon, transfer the plums to a plate. Bring the plum liquid to the boil and continue boiling until it has reduced to a thick syrup. Pour the syrup over the plums and set aside to cool.
6 Meanwhile, heat the oven to 220°C (425°F, gas mark 7) and place a baking sheet in the centre to warm.
7 Line the chilled pastry case with foil, weigh down with baking beans, place it on the hot baking sheet and bake for 15 minutes. Remove the foil and bake the pastry for a further 5-10 minutes until it is golden brown and cooked through.
8 Spoon the apples into the pastry case, spreading them out evenly, then arrange the plums on top. Set aside.
9 To make the meringue, put the egg whites into a clean bowl and whisk until they form soft peaks. Add the caster sugar 1 tablespoon at a time, whisking well between each addition, until the meringue is stiff and shiny.
10 Spoon the meringue on top of the pie and spread it evenly over the plums, then make large peaks in it with a palette knife.
11 Bake the tart for 4-5 minutes until the meringue is golden brown. Leave it to set for 1-2 minutes, then remove it from the tin. Serve the tart warm or at room temperature.

Nutrients per serving, when serving 4
- Calories 431
- Carbohydrate 87 g
- Protein 6 g
- Fat 9 g (including saturated fat 2 g)

Hot fruit slump

Fluffy dumplings in a hot fruit sauce served with cooling ice cream make a melt-in-the-mouth dessert.

PREPARATION TIME: 10 minutes
COOKING TIME: 30-35 minutes
SERVES 4

1 kg (2 lb 4 oz) mixed soft fruit, such as blackberries, blueberries, raspberries and strawberries, defrosted if frozen
1 tablespoon caster sugar
For the dumplings:
250 g (9 oz) self-raising white flour
A pinch of salt
1 tablespoon caster sugar
25 g (1 oz) butter, diced
1 egg, lightly beaten
75 ml (2½ fl oz) skimmed milk
To serve: 4 tablespoons low-fat iced dessert or natural yoghurt

1 Pick over the fruit, rinse it if necessary and place it, still damp, in a wide, deep frying pan or large saucepan, then add the sugar and stir. Cover the pan and simmer the fruit over a low heat for 15 minutes, shaking the pan or stirring frequently to prevent the fruit sticking. As the fruit slowly simmers, it should 'slump', or soften, into a textured sauce.
2 Meanwhile, to make the dumplings, place the flour in a mixing bowl and stir in the salt and sugar. Rub in the butter until the mixture resembles breadcrumbs, then quickly stir in the egg and milk to make a dough. Divide the dough in half and shape each half into eight walnut-size dumplings, to make a total of 16.
3 When the fruit has simmered into a sauce, drop the dumplings into it, spacing them as far apart as possible. Cover and continue simmering for 8 minutes, then turn the dumplings over, cover again and simmer for a further 8 minutes.
4 Serve four dumplings per person with a little sauce, accompanied by 1 tablespoon of low-fat iced dessert or natural yoghurt.

Nutrients per serving, when served with iced dessert

- Calories 392
- Carbohydrate 73 g
- Protein 11 g
- Fat 8 g (including saturated fat 4 g)

Fruit and **carrot puddings**

Prunes replace some of the fat in this unusual dessert.

PREPARATION TIME: 15 minutes, plus 20 minutes cooling

COOKING TIME: 30-35 minutes

MAKES 6

50 g (1¾ oz) ready-to-eat stoned prunes
150 g (5½ oz) carrots, grated
100 g (3½ oz) natural dates, chopped
125 g (4½ oz) raisins or sultanas
40 g (1½ oz) butter, diced
75 g (2¾ oz) canned crushed pineapple, well drained
75 g (2¾ oz) brown sugar
½ teaspoon bicarbonate of soda
Vegetable oil for greasing
75 g (2¾ oz) self-raising white flour
75 g (2¾ oz) plain wholemeal flour
½ teaspoon ground mixed spice
1 egg
4 teaspoons brandy or rum
To serve: low-fat Greek yoghurt, optional

1. Purée the prunes to a smooth paste using a food processor or hand-held mixer. Place the prune paste in a large saucepan with the carrots, dates and raisins or sultanas. Stir in the butter, pineapple, sugar and 125 ml (4 fl oz) of water.
2. Place the pan over a high heat and bring the mixture to the boil, stirring frequently, then reduce the heat and simmer, covered, for 5 minutes.
3. Remove the pan from the heat, stir in the bicarbonate of soda and set the mixture aside to cool for about 15 minutes.
4. Meanwhile, heat the oven to 180°C (350°F, gas mark 4) and place a baking sheet in the centre to warm. Using a pastry brush, grease six 150 ml (5 fl oz) ramekins or pudding tins with the vegetable oil.
5. Sift the flours and mixed spice together, then stir them into the fruit mixture with the egg, brandy or rum and any bran left in the sieve. Divide the mixture between the ramekins or tins and place them on the baking sheet. Bake for 25-30 minutes until the puddings have browned, risen slightly and a skewer inserted in the centre of each comes out clean.
6. Leave the puddings to stand for 5 minutes after baking. To remove them from the ramekins or tins, run a round-bladed knife around the edge of each pudding and carefully shake it out onto a plate. Serve with a little low-fat Greek yoghurt on the side, if you like.

Nutrients per serving

- Calories 302
- Carbohydrate 55 g
- Protein 5 g
- Fat 8 g (including saturated fat 4 g)

Cinnamon-flavoured apple and sultana clafoutis

Clafoutis is a French batter pudding traditionally baked with orchard fruits. This scrumptious low-fat version combines apples with juicy sultanas.

PREPARATION TIME: 15 minutes
COOKING TIME: 30-40 minutes
SERVES 4

75 g (2¾ oz) plain white flour, sifted
75 g (2¾ oz) caster sugar
3 eggs
300 ml (10 fl oz) skimmed milk
1 tablespoon Calvados or other fruit brandy, optional
450 g (1 lb) cooking apples, peeled, cut into quarters, cored and thickly sliced
50 g (1¾ oz) sultanas or raisins
1 teaspoon ground cinnamon, allspice or mixed spice

1. Heat the oven to 200°C (400°F, gas mark 6).
2. Place the flour and half the sugar in a bowl, add the eggs and half the milk then blend the ingredients together using a wire whisk or wooden spoon. Alternatively, blend them in a food processor or with a hand-held mixer for 1 minute. Stir in the remaining milk and fruit brandy, if using, and blend to form a smooth batter.
3. Put the apples and sultanas in the base of a shallow, nonstick 1.5 litre (2 pint 15 fl oz) ovenproof pan or dish. Sprinkle with the spice and all but 1 tablespoon of the remaining sugar, then pour the batter over the top.
4. Bake for 30-40 minutes until well risen and golden brown. Sprinkle with the remaining sugar and serve hot.

Variation: replace the apples with 450 g (1 lb) of apricots or dessert plums, halved and stoned.
Tip: if you do not have a nonstick pan or dish, use an ordinary one, lightly greased with ¼ teaspoon vegetable oil.

Nutrients per serving

- Calories 292
- Carbohydrate 54 g
- Protein 11 g
- Fat 5 g (including saturated fat 2 g)

Baked apples glazed with port

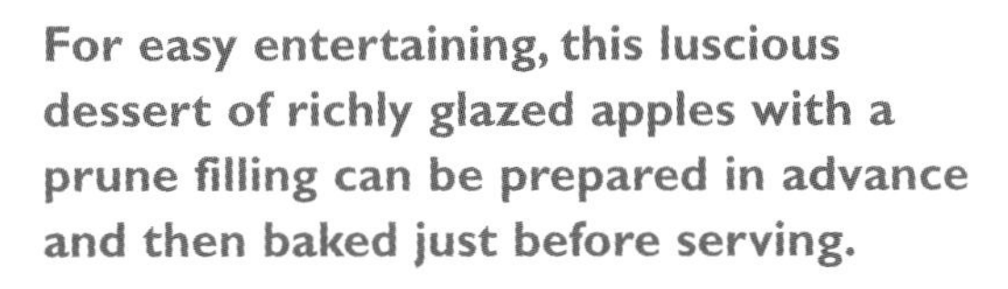

For easy entertaining, this luscious dessert of richly glazed apples with a prune filling can be prepared in advance and then baked just before serving.

PREPARATION TIME: 20 minutes
COOKING TIME: 1 hour-1 hour 15 minutes
SERVES 4

4 large dessert apples, cored
175 g (6 oz) ready-to-eat stoned prunes, chopped
20 g (¾ oz) soft dark brown sugar
450 ml (16 fl oz) port
Finely grated zest of 1 lemon
Finely grated zest of 1 orange
5 cm (2 in) cinnamon stick
2-3 cloves, optional
1 teaspoon icing sugar
To serve: low-fat fromage frais or half-fat Greek yoghurt, optional

1. Heat the oven to 220°C (425°F, gas mark 7).
2. Place one of the apples upright and make deep cuts from the top down through it to within 2 cm (¾ in) of the bottom to divide it into eight equal segments. Do the same with the remaining apples, then place them close together in a shallow ovenproof dish.
3. Gently push a quarter of the prunes into the centre of each apple – they do not have to go all the way down. Sprinkle the apples with the brown sugar and pour the port over them. Add the lemon and orange zests, cinnamon stick and cloves, if using, to the dish.
4. Bake, uncovered, for 15 minutes, then reduce the temperature to 180°C (350°F, gas mark 4) and bake for a further 45 minutes-1 hour, basting the apples with the port every 10-15 minutes until they have softened but not broken up and the port has reduced to a syrupy consistency.
5. Serve the apples on individual plates with the port sauce spooned over them. Sift a little icing sugar over the top and accompany with fromage frais or yoghurt, if you like.

Nutrients per serving

- Calories 363
- Carbohydrate 60 g
- Protein 2 g
- No fat

Spiced seasonal fruit salad

Use any soft fruit in season for this slightly piquant medley of flavours, a perfect follow-on to a spicy main course.

PREPARATION TIME: 20 minutes, plus 1 hour, or overnight, chilling
SERVES 4

1 large mango
125 g (4½ oz) seedless black grapes, cut in half
125 g (4½ oz) seedless green grapes, cut in half
125 g (4½ oz) peaches, skinned, stoned and sliced
125 g (4½ oz) strawberries, hulled and cut in half or into quarters, according to size
25 g (1 oz) unsweetened desiccated coconut
30 g (1¼ oz) caster sugar
A pinch of cayenne pepper
A pinch of mustard powder
Salt

1 Peel the mango, cut away the flesh and thinly slice it.
2 Put the mango into a large mixing bowl and add the black and green grapes, peaches and strawberries.
3 Finely grind the coconut in a spice mill or with a pestle and mortar. Add the sugar, cayenne pepper, mustard and a pinch of salt and mix well.
4 Add the coconut mixture to the fruit, stir well, cover and place in the refrigerator to chill for at least 1 hour, or overnight, to allow the flavours to blend and mature.

Nutrients per serving

- Calories 160
- Carbohydrate 31 g
- Protein 2 g
- Fat 4 g (including saturated fat 3 g)

Honeydew melon with ginger-lemon sauce

A zingy sauce adds a kick to the traditional combination of refreshing melon and ginger in this fat-free dessert.

PREPARATION TIME: 30 minutes, plus overnight chilling
COOKING TIME: 25 minutes
SERVES 8

1 honeydew melon
For the sauce:
50 g (1¾ oz) root ginger
200 g (7 oz) demerara sugar
1-2 tablespoons lemon juice
To garnish: sprigs of fresh mint

1 First make the ginger-lemon sauce. With a small knife, peel off the hard outer skin of the ginger, then grate the flesh finely, discarding any stringy threads.

2. Place the grated ginger, sugar and 1 tablespoon of lemon juice in a saucepan with 250 ml (9 fl oz) of water and bring the mixture to the boil, stirring frequently to dissolve the sugar before it boils. Reduce the heat to low and simmer for 20 minutes, or until the sauce has thickened enough to coat a spoon lightly. Taste it and add extra lemon juice if desired.
3. Transfer the sauce to a bowl to cool for 30 minutes, then place the sauce and the melon in the refrigerator, separately, to chill overnight.
4. When you are ready to serve, cut the melon in half lengthways and scoop out the seeds. Cut each half into four wedges, then trim off the rind. Put a slice of melon on each plate, pour the chilled sauce over it and garnish with a sprig of mint.

Variation: the ginger-lemon sauce can be used to accompany Angel Food Cake (page 296) or ice cream.

Nutrients per serving

- Calories 133
- Carbohydrate 34 g
- Protein 1 g
- No fat

Traditional puddings with a lighter touch

You do not have to give up proper puddings when you are cutting down on fat. Pudding lovers can still tuck into a luscious Sticky Toffee Pudding and other favourites with these lower-fat versions, which do not sacrifice the great flavours of the originals.

You can lower the fat content of a favourite pudding by substituting skimmed milk for whole milk. And instead of cream, offer Low-fat Custard (see box below) or low-fat cream, crème fraîche or fromage frais.

Another delicious alternative accompaniment is a fruit sauce. To make one, purée summer berries in a food processor, pass them through a fine sieve to remove any seeds and sweeten with sugar to taste.

Low-fat custard

To make 600 ml (1 pint), beat 2 eggs with 2 tablespoons of caster sugar and ½ teaspoon of vanilla essence. Bring 600 ml (1 pint) of skimmed milk gently to scalding point, then whisk it slowly onto the beaten eggs. Pour the custard back into the saucepan and cook slowly, stirring, over a low heat until it thickens. Do not let it boil or it will curdle.

Baked bread and marmalade pudding

Marmalade adds a sharp citrus taste to this light version of a popular dessert.

PREPARATION TIME: 10 minutes
COOKING TIME: 35-40 minutes
SERVES 4

Low-fat spread for greasing
90 g (3¼ oz) mixed dried fruit
150 ml (5 fl oz) apple juice
3 tablespoons finely cut Seville orange marmalade
¾ teaspoon ground mixed spice
175 g (6 oz) wholemeal bread, crust removed, cut into cubes
1 egg
300 ml (10 fl oz) skimmed milk
1½ teaspoons demerara sugar
A pinch of freshly grated nutmeg
To serve: 4 tablespoons low-fat cream or fromage frais

1. Heat the oven to 190°C (375°F, gas mark 5), and lightly grease a 1.4 litre (2 pint 10 fl oz) ovenproof serving dish.
2. Place the dried fruit in a saucepan with the apple juice and bring to the boil. Then reduce the heat, cover and simmer for 10 minutes until most of the liquid has been absorbed.
3. Take the pan off the heat, add the marmalade and mixed spice and stir until the marmalade has dissolved.
4. Toss the bread in the pan to coat it evenly, then spoon it into the dish in an even layer.
5. Beat the egg into the milk, then pour it evenly over the bread and sprinkle with the demerara sugar and nutmeg.
6. Bake for 25-30 minutes until just set and golden brown on top. Serve hot, with low-fat cream or fromage frais.

Nutrients per serving

- Calories 287
- Carbohydrate 56 g
- Protein 12 g
- Fat 3 g (including saturated fat 1 g)

Sticky toffee pudding

Dates give this old favourite its delicious toffee texture while keeping the fat content down.

PREPARATION TIME: 10 minutes
COOKING TIME: 45-50 minutes
SERVES 6

175 g (6 oz) stoned natural dates
1 teaspoon bicarbonate of soda
175 g (6 oz) self-raising white flour
175 g (6 oz) dark muscovado sugar
50 g (1¾ oz) 70 per cent fat spread, plus extra for greasing
2 egg whites
1 teaspoon vanilla essence
For the sauce:
1 tablespoon dark muscovado sugar
1 tablespoon golden syrup
3 tablespoons virtually fat-free fromage frais

STICKY TOFFEE PUDDING

BAKED BREAD AND MARMALADE PUDDING

1 Heat the oven to 180°C (350°F, gas mark 4). Lightly grease a 19 cm (7½ in) square cake tin and line the base with baking paper.
2 Roughly chop the dates. Place them in a small pan with 200 ml (7 fl oz) of water and bring to the boil, then reduce the heat and simmer for 5 minutes, or until most of the liquid has been absorbed. Stir in the bicarbonate of soda.
3 Place the flour, sugar, spread, egg whites and vanilla in a bowl and beat until blended and thick. Stir in the dates then spoon the mixture into the cake tin and level the surface. Bake for 35-40 minutes until well risen and firm.
4 To make the sauce, place the sugar, syrup and fromage frais in a pan and heat until melted and smooth, stirring. Cut the pudding into squares and serve with the sauce spooned over.

Nutrients per serving

- Calories 343
- Carbohydrate 65 g
- Protein 6 g
- Fat 8 g (including saturated fat 2 g)

PEAR AND GINGER UPSIDE-DOWN PUDDING

STEAMED ORANGE AND BANANA SPONGE

Steamed orange and banana sponge

If you crave suet puddings, try this rich, fruity version.

PREPARATION TIME: 20 minutes
COOKING TIME: 1 hour 35 minutes
SERVES 4

Vegetable oil for greasing
1 teaspoon golden syrup
2 oranges
75 g (2¾ oz) fresh white breadcrumbs
150 g (5½ oz) self-raising white flour
25 g (1 oz) light vegetable suet
75 g (2¾ oz) golden caster sugar
1 banana
100 ml (3½ fl oz) skimmed milk
To serve: low-fat custard

1 Fill with water the bottom half of a steamer large enough to hold a 1 litre (1 pint 15 fl oz) pudding basin and bring to simmering point. Brush the basin with oil, then spoon in the syrup.
2 Finely grate the zest from 1 orange, then squeeze out the juice and set both aside. Peel the other orange, slice it thinly and arrange the slices inside the basin.
3 Stir together the breadcrumbs, flour, suet, sugar and zest. Mash the banana and add it to the mixture, then beat in the milk and enough orange juice to form a fairly stiff mixture.
4 Spoon the mixture into the basin, without disturbing the orange slices, and level the surface.
5 Cover the pudding with baking paper and a double thickness of foil, pleated in the centre. Tie them to the basin with string and make a string handle to lift the hot pudding. Place the basin in the top of the steamer, cover and cook for 1 hour 30 minutes. Top up the pan with boiling water during steaming if necessary.
6 Remove the basin and take off the paper and foil. Run a round-bladed knife between the pudding and the basin, turn out the pudding onto a plate and serve with the custard.

Nutrients per serving

- Calories 491
- Carbohydrate 92 g
- Protein 16 g
- Fat 9 g (including saturated fat 3 g)

Pear and ginger upside-down pudding

This dessert has all the rich stickiness of a traditional gingerbread pudding.

PREPARATION TIME: 25 minutes
COOKING TIME: 40-45 minutes
SERVES 6

Sunflower oil for greasing
1 tablespoon dark muscovado sugar
450 g (1 lb) firm pears, such as Conference, peeled, cored and sliced
For the batter:
125 g (4½ oz) plain white flour
½ teaspoon bicarbonate of soda
1 teaspoon ground cinnamon
2 teaspoons ground ginger
100 ml (3½ fl oz) skimmed milk
125 g (4½ oz) dark muscovado sugar
3 tablespoons black treacle
1 egg
2 tablespoons sunflower oil
To serve: low-fat custard or natural yoghurt

1 Heat the oven to 180°C (350°F, gas mark 4). Brush a 22 cm (8½ in) round cake tin with oil. Line the base with baking paper and sprinkle it with sugar. Arrange the pears in the base in a wagon wheel pattern.
2 To make the batter, sift together the flour, bicarbonate of soda, cinnamon and ginger. Heat the milk, sugar and treacle together, stirring until the sugar has dissolved. Beat together the egg and oil, then stir them and the milk mixture into the flour, beating well to give a smooth texture.
3 Tip the mixture over the pears and bake for 35-40 minutes until risen and firm to the touch.
4 Run a knife around the edge of the pudding and turn it out onto a plate. Serve hot, with custard or yoghurt.

Nutrients per serving

- Calories 358
- Carbohydrate 65 g
- Protein 10 g
- Fat 8 g (including saturated fat 2 g)

Mango sorbet with tropical fruit salad

A rich sorbet complements this delightful combination of exotic fruits.

PREPARATION TIME: 20 minutes, plus 15 minutes cooling and at least 4 hours 30 minutes freezing
COOKING TIME: 10 minutes
SERVES 4

125 g (4½ oz) caster sugar
Juice of ½ lemon
500 g (1 lb 2 oz) canned mango pieces in syrup, drained
2 tablespoons creamed coconut, crumbled
2 egg whites
For the fruit salad:
1 mango, peeled, stoned and sliced
1 papaya, peeled, deseeded and diced
2 small bananas, sliced
1 star fruit, tough ribs peeled off, then sliced
250 g (9 oz) pineapple, peeled, cored and cut into wedges
Juice of 2 limes or 1 large lemon
To garnish: 4 teaspoons shredded or desiccated coconut

1. Put the sugar and 250 ml (9 fl oz) of water into a small saucepan and bring the mixture to the boil, stirring until the sugar has dissolved. Reduce the heat and simmer for 5 minutes to make a syrup. Strain the lemon juice into the syrup, then set it aside for 15 minutes to cool.
2. Purée the syrup, canned mango and coconut in a food processor, or with a hand-held mixer, to make about 800 ml (1 pint 9 fl oz). Pour the mixture into a freezerproof container, cover and freeze for 2 hours, or until it is just firm. (Use the fast-freeze setting if your freezer has one.)
3. When the mango mixture is frozen, whisk the egg whites until they form soft peaks. Scrape the mango mixture with a fork to form crystals, then use a whisk to beat in the egg whites, making sure they are well mixed. Return the sorbet to the freezer and freeze for 1 hour 30 minutes.
4. Remove the sorbet from the freezer and whisk it again. Press it down with a spatula and return it to the freezer for a further 1 hour, or until it is firm.
5. When the sorbet is almost frozen, prepare the fruit for the salad and put it in a bowl. Add the lime or lemon juice and gently toss it into the fruit, then set the salad aside.
6. Heat a heavy-based nonstick frying pan and dry-fry the coconut for 30 seconds-1 minute, stirring, until it is lightly browned around the edges.
7. Serve the fruit salad with two scoops of sorbet per person, topped with the coconut. Any remaining sorbet will keep, frozen, for three months.

Nutrients per serving

- Calories 262
- Carbohydrate 53 g
- Protein 3 g
- Fat 6 g (including saturated fat 5 g)

GOOSEBERRY GRANITA

Gooseberry granita

This delicately tart water ice, with a crystalline texture, makes an elegant dessert.

PREPARATION TIME: 10 minutes, plus 5 hours freezing
COOKING TIME: 25 minutes
SERVES 4

450 g (1 lb) gooseberries, topped and tailed
150 g (5½ oz) caster sugar
200 ml (7 fl oz) Muscat dessert wine
1 tablespoon lemon juice

1 Place the gooseberries in a saucepan with the sugar and 300 ml (10 fl oz) of water. Bring to the boil, then cover and simmer for 25 minutes, or until the fruit has softened to a pulp.
2 Purée the gooseberry pulp in a food processor or with a hand-held mixer, then strain it through a fine sieve, discarding the pips. Stir in the wine and lemon juice and leave it to cool.
3 Transfer the cooled mixture to a shallow, freezerproof plastic container, cover and freeze for 1 hour.
4 Use a fork to mash into the liquid any ice crystals that have formed around the rim and base, then cover and return to the freezer for a further 4 hours, beating in any ice crystals every hour. Serve the granita in glasses as soon as it is ready.

Variation: if gooseberries are unavailable use seedless green grapes.

Tip: if you want to make the mixture in advance, keep it chilled in the refrigerator until it is time to start the freezing process at Step 3.

Nutrients per serving

- Calories 215
- Carbohydrate 46 g
- Protein 1 g
- No fat

Strawberry yoghurt ice

Creamy Greek yoghurt and fresh strawberries blend well in this honey-sweetened dessert.

PREPARATION TIME: 5-10 minutes, plus 4-6 hours freezing
SERVES 4

450 g (1 lb) strawberries, hulled
4 tablespoons clear honey
1 teaspoon lemon juice
A few drops vanilla essence
500 g (1 lb 2 oz) low-fat Greek yoghurt
To garnish: 4 strawberries

1 Place the strawberries in a liquidiser or food processor with the honey, lemon juice and vanilla essence. Purée until the mixture is smooth, then beat in the yoghurt.
2 Transfer the mixture to a shallow, freezerproof plastic container, cover and freeze for 4-6 hours, beating it with a hand-held whisk after 2 hours and then at hourly intervals until it is frozen. Alternatively, freeze in an ice-cream maker according to the manufacturer's instructions.
3 Spoon into four dessert bowls and garnish each with a fresh strawberry.

Nutrients per serving

- Calories 198
- Carbohydrate 29 g
- Protein 8 g
- Fat 6 g (including saturated fat 4 g)

Sticky black rice pudding

Nutrients per serving
- Calories 398
- Carbohydrate 71 g
- Protein 11 g
- Fat 9 g (including saturated fat 7 g)

Coconut cream and black Oriental rice transform a traditional family pudding into a sophisticated, fragrant delight.

PREPARATION TIME: 5 minutes, plus 20 minutes cooling
COOKING TIME: 1 hour 5 minutes
SERVES 4

250 g (9 oz) glutinous black rice
750 ml (1 pint 7 fl oz) skimmed milk
3-4 tablespoons palm sugar, soft light brown sugar or clear honey
90 ml (3 fl oz) coconut cream
Grated zest of 1 lime
1 tablespoon lime juice
1 tablespoon orange flower water, optional
To serve: slices of ripe mango, optional

1 Place the rice in a sieve and rinse well under cold running water. Put it into a large, heavy-based saucepan, add the milk and bring the mixture to the boil. Reduce the heat to low and simmer, uncovered, for 10 minutes.
2 Add the sugar or honey to the rice, stir until it has dissolved and continue simmering, uncovered, for 55 minutes, or until the rice is almost soft and most of the liquid has been absorbed. From time to time, stir in the skin that forms on the top.
3 Stir in the coconut cream, lime zest and juice and the orange flower water, if using. Remove the pan from the heat and allow the mixture to cool for 20 minutes. Serve warm, or chill it for 1 hour and serve cold, with mango slices, if liked.

Tip: glutinous black rice, which produces dishes with a wonderful dark purple, almost black, colour, is sold in Oriental food shops.

Fluffy banana rice puddings

Nutrients per serving

- Calories 186
- Carbohydrate 38 g
- Protein 6 g
- Fat 2 g (including saturated fat 1 g)

This lovely light milk pudding is sweetened with honey and bananas, which also add nutritional substance.

PREPARATION TIME: 10 minutes
COOKING TIME: 1 hour 15 minutes-1 hour 45 minutes
SERVES 6

60 g (2¼ oz) short-grain pudding rice
600 ml (1 pint) semi-skimmed milk
3 tablespoons clear honey
1 vanilla pod
2 ripe bananas
Finely grated zest of ½ lemon
2 egg whites
A pinch of freshly grated nutmeg

1. Place the rice in a saucepan with the milk, then stir in the honey and add the vanilla pod. Bring gently to the boil, then reduce the heat and cover. Simmer for 1 hour-1 hour 15 minutes, stirring occasionally to prevent it sticking, until the rice is soft and the mixture has thickened but is still sloppy.
2. Meanwhile, heat the oven to 200°C (400°F, gas mark 6). Remove the vanilla pod from the rice. Peel the bananas and slice them thinly, then fold them into the rice with the lemon zest.
3. In a clean, dry bowl, whisk the egg whites until soft peaks form. Fold them into the rice mixture, then spoon it into six 200 ml (7 fl oz) ramekins, or a 1.2 litre (2 pint) soufflé dish, and sprinkle with nutmeg.
4. Place the ramekins or dish on a baking sheet and bake individual puddings for 10-12 minutes, or the large pudding for 25-30 minutes, until golden brown and well risen. Serve warm.

Chocolate roulade with raspberry cream

This version of a classic rolled chocolate sponge can be transformed into an indulgent dessert when it envelops fresh raspberries and fromage frais.

PREPARATION TIME: 30 minutes, plus 30 minutes cooling

COOKING TIME: 7-10 minutes

MAKES 6 slices

3 eggs
75 g (2¾ oz) caster sugar
50 g (1¾ oz) plain white flour
25 g (1 oz) cocoa powder
1 teaspoon icing sugar
For the filling:
125 g (4½ oz) fresh raspberries
200 g (7 oz) low-fat fromage frais
2 teaspoons caster sugar, or to taste

1. Select a saucepan big enough to hold a large heatproof mixing bowl. Fill it with water to a depth that does not reach the bottom of the bowl and bring it to the boil over a high heat. Heat the oven to 220°C (425°F, gas mark 7) and line a 23 x 30 cm (9 x 12 in) swiss roll tin with baking paper.
2. Reduce the heat under the pan to low and place the bowl on top. Put the eggs and sugar in the bowl and, using a hand-held whisk, beat for 12-13 minutes until the mixture is thick and mousse-like and the beaters leave a ribbon-like trail on the surface when lifted out. Remove the bowl from the pan and continue to whisk the mixture for a further 2 minutes.
3. Sift together the flour and cocoa powder and, using a large metal spoon, fold this into the egg mixture with a figure-of-eight motion.
4. Pour the mixture into the prepared swiss roll tin, spreading it gently to cover the whole surface. Bake the sponge for 7-10 minutes until it feels firm yet springy on top.
5. Turn the sponge out immediately onto a sheet of baking paper larger than itself, carefully peel off the lining paper and, using a serrated knife, trim off the crisp edges of the sponge.
6. Roll the sponge up from the short end with the fresh baking paper inside, then leave the roulade on a wire rack for 30 minutes to cool completely.
7. Meanwhile, to make the filling, lightly crush the raspberries in a bowl with a fork. Stir in the fromage frais and add sugar to taste, then cover the mixture and chill until required.
8. Carefully unroll the cooled sponge and remove the paper. Spread the surface with the raspberry filling, leaving it just short of the edges. Roll the sponge up again – do not worry if the surface cracks as you re-roll it: this is part of its attraction.
9. Sift the icing sugar over the roulade and place the cake on a serving plate. To serve, cut into slices with a long, thin serrated knife.

Variation: replace the raspberry filling with a mixture of 1 mashed banana, 2 teaspoons of clear honey and 200 g (7 oz) of fromage frais. Or, if you are in a hurry, use a best-quality, flavoured low-fat yoghurt, such as fruits of the forest, cappuccino, toffee or hazelnut. For an adult dinner party dessert, stir 2 teaspoons of orange-flavoured liqueur, such as Cointreau, into the crushed raspberries in Step 7 before adding the fromage frais.

Nutrients per slice

- Calories 171
- Carbohydrate 24 g
- Protein 8 g
- Fat 5 g (including saturated fat 2 g)

RASPBERRIES

Barbecued fruit

Here is a perfect flavourful, no-fat way to end a barbecue.

PREPARATION TIME: 15 minutes, plus 1 hour, or overnight, marinating
COOKING TIME: 8-10 minutes
SERVES 4

Grated zest of ½ lemon and juice of 1 lemon
4 tablespoons Cointreau or brandy
2-3 tablespoons honey or brown sugar
1 tablespoon bitters, such as Angostura, optional
1 pineapple, peeled and cored
250 g (9 oz) strawberries, hulled
2 tablespoons icing sugar
To decorate: sifted icing sugar

1. In a china or glass bowl, stir together the lemon juice, liqueur and honey or sugar, adding the bitters, if using.
2. Cut the pineapple into 2.5 cm (1 in) cubes and add them to the marinade, then add the strawberries. Stir well, taking care not to break up the fruit, then cover and refrigerate for at least 1 hour, or overnight.
3. Lift the strawberries and pineapple from the marinade, reserving the liquid, and thread them alternately onto eight skewers.
4. Dust the fruit with 1 tablespoon of icing sugar, then place the skewers on the barbecue, sugared side down, and cook for 4-5 minutes. Remove from the barbecue, dust the other side of the fruit with the remaining sugar and barbecue again, sugared side down.
5. Divide the skewers between four plates and drizzle the marinade over. To decorate, sift a little icing sugar over each, then serve.

Variation: try other combinations of fruit, such as pears, strawberries and kiwi fruits, or fresh dates and figs.

Nutrients per serving

- Calories 180
- Carbohydrate 37 g
- Protein 1 g
- No fat

Mulled grape jelly

This refreshing dessert combines sweet, juicy grapes with spiced wine.

PREPARATION TIME: 15 minutes, plus 4 hours setting
COOKING TIME: 15 minutes
SERVES 4

225 g (8 oz) seedless red or black grapes
½ small orange
250 ml (9 fl oz) claret or other rich red wine
2 star anise
40 g (1½ oz) caster sugar
1 sachet powdered gelatine
250 ml (9 fl oz) red grape juice
To garnish: 4 teaspoons Greek yoghurt and a pinch of freshly grated nutmeg

1. Cut the grapes in half and divide them between four large glass tumblers or dishes. Put them in the refrigerator to chill.
2. Meanwhile, make the jelly. Thinly pare a long strip of zest from the half orange, then squeeze the juice and set it aside. Place the zest in a saucepan with the wine and star anise. Heat gently until almost boiling, then reduce the heat, cover and simmer for 10 minutes. Remove the pan from the heat, add the sugar and stir until it has dissolved.
3. Strain the sweetened wine into a bowl. Sprinkle the gelatine over the surface and stir gently until it has dissolved. Add the orange and grape juices and set aside to cool for 5 minutes, or until the liquid is lukewarm.
4. Pour the jelly mixture over the grapes and set aside until completely cool, then put them in the refrigerator for 4 hours, or until set.
5. Serve each glass topped with 1 teaspoon of yoghurt and sprinkle with nutmeg.

Nutrients per serving

- Calories 165
- Carbohydrate 28 g
- Protein 3 g
- Fat 1 g (no saturated fat)

Pan-fried pear and fig pancakes

A rich mixture of fresh and dried fruits fills sweet pancakes drizzled with maple syrup.

PREPARATION TIME: 15-20 minutes, plus 30 minutes resting

COOKING TIME: 35 minutes

SERVES 4

300 ml (10 fl oz) skimmed milk
1 egg
100 g (3½ oz) plain white or plain wholemeal flour, or a mixture
1 tablespoon caster sugar
Salt
2 teaspoons sunflower oil

For the filling:
20 g (¾ oz) butter
700 g (1 lb 9 oz) pears, peeled, cored and chopped
100 g (3½ oz) ready-to-eat dried figs, chopped
½ teaspoon ground cinnamon
A pinch of ground cloves
Grated zest of ½ orange
90 g (3¼ oz) soft brown sugar

To serve: 4 tablespoons half-fat crème fraîche or Greek yoghurt and 4 tablespoons maple syrup, optional

1. To make the pancake batter, place the milk, egg, flour, sugar and a pinch of salt in a food processor and blend for 1 minute to a smooth consistency. Alternatively, place the flour, sugar and a pinch of salt in a bowl, make a well in the centre and pour in the egg and milk. Stir slowly with a wooden spoon to incorporate the flour until a smooth batter forms. Set the batter aside to rest for 30 minutes.
2. Heat the oven to a low setting. Grease an 18 cm (7 in) nonstick frying pan with a little oil and heat the pan until it is very hot. Pour in 1-2 ladles of batter and tilt the pan so that it covers the base. Cook for 30-45 seconds until the underside is golden. Turn the pancake over and cook the other side for 1 minute, or until it is set.
3. Transfer the pancake to a piece of kitchen paper. Repeat the process to make eight pancakes, separating each with a piece of kitchen paper. Wrap the stack of pancakes in foil and place in the oven to keep warm.
4. To make the filling, melt the butter in a small frying pan over a medium heat. Add the pears and figs, reduce the heat and cover, then simmer for about 10 minutes, or until the pears are tender when tested with a knife.
5. Stir the cinnamon, cloves, orange zest and soft brown sugar into the fruit and simmer for a further 5 minutes.
6. Divide the fruit mixture between the warm pancakes. Fold them up and serve two per person, with 1 tablespoon of half-fat crème fraîche or Greek yoghurt, and some maple syrup if desired.

Nutrients per serving

- Calories 420
- Carbohydrate 76 g
- Protein 8 g
- Fat 11 g (including saturated fat 5 g)

Pears in **spiced red wine**

Nutrients per serving

- Calories 204
- Carbohydrate 40 g
- Protein 1 g
- No fat

Peppercorns add a zing to the spicy syrup for this fruit dessert, which can be prepared a day or so in advance.

PREPARATION TIME: 15 minutes, plus 2 hours 30 minutes cooling

COOKING TIME: 55 minutes-1 hour 5 minutes

SERVES 4

4 large firm ripe pears, such as Comice or Packhams, with their stalks

For the syrup:

1 litre (1 pint 15 fl oz) clear apple juice

300 ml (10 fl oz) red wine

1 cinnamon stick, broken in half

2 cloves

2 teaspoons black peppercorns

1 star anise, optional

To serve: Greek yoghurt or half-fat crème fraîche, optional

1 To make the syrup, put the apple juice in a heavy-based saucepan over a high heat with the wine, cinnamon stick, cloves, peppercorns and star anise, if using. Bring to the boil and boil for 10 minutes, or until the mixture has reduced by about half to make a light syrup. Strain it into a bowl and leave to cool, discarding the spices.

2 Meanwhile, push an apple corer through from the base of each pear as far as you can without disturbing the stem; this will make it easier to remove the cores after poaching. Using a vegetable peeler or a small sharp knife, peel the pears, keeping the stalks in place.

3 Pack the pears closely together upright in a saucepan and pour the spiced syrup over them. Wet a large sheet of greaseproof paper and crumple it, then push it down over the top of the pears to keep them submerged.

4 Place the pan over a high heat and bring the syrup to the boil, then reduce the heat, cover and continue simmering for 20-30 minutes until the pears feel tender when pierced with a knife. Remove the pan from the heat and leave the pears to cool in the syrup for 2 hours to enhance their flavour.

5 Remove the pears from the syrup and set them aside. Return the pan to a high heat and boil the syrup for 20 minutes, or until it has reduced by about half. Transfer it to a heatproof bowl and leave for 30 minutes, or until cool. Using a small sharp knife, remove as much core as possible from the base of each pear.

6 To serve, place the pears on individual plates and spoon the syrup over them. Or, for an elegant presentation, slash each pear lengthways four times, almost through to the stalk, and fan them out before pouring the syrup over. Accompany with Greek yoghurt or half-fat crème fraîche, if you like.

Tip: to prepare ahead, store the syrup and pears separately in covered containers in the refrigerator after they have cooled at the end of Step 5 until you are ready to serve them.

Mango cheesecake

Nutrients per slice

- Calories 303
- Carbohydrate 43 g
- Protein 8 g
- Fat 12 g (including saturated fat 7 g)

This mango-topped cheesecake mixes the luscious tropical fruit with saffron and spices on a biscuit base.

PREPARATION TIME: 30 minutes, plus 3-4 hours setting
MAKES 8 slices

Vegetable oil for greasing
125 g (4½ oz) reduced-fat digestive biscuits
60 g (2¼ oz) butter
For the filling:
75 ml (2½ fl oz) semi-skimmed milk
10-12 strands saffron, pounded
500 g (1 lb 2 oz) low-fat Greek yoghurt
50-60 g (1¾-2¼ oz) caster sugar
Finely grated zest of 1 lime
1 sachet powdered gelatine
For the topping:
850 g (1 lb 14 oz) canned mango slices in syrup
Sugar to taste
½ teaspoon freshly grated nutmeg, or 1 teaspoon ground cardamom
1 sachet powdered gelatine

1. To make the filling, heat the milk in a small saucepan, add the saffron strands and set aside to infuse.
2. Brush some vegetable oil on the side and base of a 23 cm (9 in) cake tin with a removable base.
3. Put the biscuits in a plastic bag and crush them into fine crumbs with a rolling pin, or use a food processor. Melt the butter, then stir in the biscuit crumbs. Press the mixture firmly and evenly over the base of the tin. Chill for 10 minutes until firm.
4. Meanwhile, make the filling. Whisk the saffron milk, yoghurt, sugar and lime zest together.
5. Place 3 tablespoons of water in a teacup, sprinkle in the gelatine and leave it to become spongy. Stand the cup in a saucepan of simmering water until the gelatine is runny and clear, then set aside to cool for 5 minutes.
6. Whisk the gelatine into the filling. Pour it over the biscuit base and chill for 1 hour, or until set.
7. To make the topping, drain the cans of mango. Chop a quarter of the slices into 1 cm (½ in) pieces and set them aside. Purée the rest of the mango in a food processor or with a hand-held mixer. Add sugar, if needed, then stir in the nutmeg or cardamom.
8. Dissolve and cool the gelatine as described in Step 5, and stir it into the mango purée. Stir in the reserved pieces of mango, pour the mixture over the filling and chill for 2-3 hours until set.
9. Remove the base of the cake tin, place the cheesecake on a plate and serve.

Raspberry pavlova with red berry sauce

Nutrients per serving, when serving 6

- Calories 313
- Carbohydrate 71 g
- Protein 7 g
- Fat 2 g (including saturated fat 1 g)

A dash of raspberry vinegar makes a slightly tart base for sweet summer fruit.

PREPARATION TIME: 25 minutes, plus 2 hours, or overnight, cooling
COOKING TIME: 1 hour 30 minutes-2 hours
SERVES 6-8

6 egg whites
350 g (12 oz) caster sugar
1 tablespoon raspberry vinegar
A pinch of cream of tartar
300-400 g (10½-14 oz) raspberries and other mixed fruit, such as blueberries, red and white currants or strawberries, halved if necessary
For the sauce:
125 g (4½ oz) fresh raspberries or other red berries such as loganberries or tayberries, defrosted if frozen
300 g (10½ oz) low-fat fromage frais
2 tablespoons icing sugar, or to taste
To garnish: fresh mint leaves, optional

1. Heat the oven to 120°C (250°F, gas mark ½). Line a large baking sheet with greaseproof paper or baking paper.
2. Whisk the egg whites in a very large bowl until soft peaks form, then gradually whisk in the sugar to make a stiff meringue. Whisk in the raspberry vinegar and cream of tartar.
3. Pile the meringue into a round measuring about 30 cm (12 in) across, on the lined baking sheet. Bake for 1 hour 30 minutes-2 hours until it is crisp on the outside and only very slightly coloured.
4. Leave the meringue to cool on the baking sheet for at least 2 hours, or overnight, then transfer it to a serving platter.
5. Meanwhile, make the sauce. Purée the berries and strain them through a fine sieve to remove the seeds. Stir in the fromage frais. Add sugar to taste, cover and chill.
6. Pick over, rinse and dry the mixed soft fruits as necessary. Serve the pavlova cut into wedges, partly covered with chilled sauce and soft fruit, and garnished with mint, if you like.

bread, cakes and biscuits

Pizza bread with **chilli** or **rosemary**

These easy-to-make rustic loaves go perfectly with soup, salads or pasta.

PREPARATION TIME: 15-30 minutes, plus 1 hour 30 minutes rising

COOKING TIME: 15-20 minutes each loaf, or 30-40 minutes altogether

MAKES 3 loaves, each serving 4

2 teaspoons dried yeast with ¾ teaspoon caster sugar, or 1 sachet easy-blend yeast
750 g (1 lb 10 oz) strong plain white flour
1½ teaspoons salt
200 ml (7 fl oz) milk
1 tablespoon olive oil, plus extra for greasing

To top each pizza bread:
1½ teaspoons olive oil
½ teaspoon coarse sea salt, or to taste
A pinch of dried chilli flakes, or finely chopped fresh rosemary

1. If using dried yeast, dissolve the sugar in 225 ml (8 fl oz) of lukewarm water, then sprinkle in the dried yeast and set aside for 15 minutes, or until it is frothy. If using easy-blend yeast, add it directly to the flour.
2. Sift the flour and salt into a large mixing bowl. Pour the yeast mixture, or 225 ml (8 fl oz) of lukewarm water if using easy-blend yeast, into the centre with the milk and olive oil. Stir to form a dough, adding a little extra warm water if it is too dry, then knead until the dough forms a ball and leaves the side of the bowl clean.
3. Turn out the dough onto a lightly floured surface and knead for 5 minutes, or until it is smooth and elastic.
4. Grease a clean bowl with oil. Roll the dough around in the bowl so that it is lightly coated with oil and loosely cover the bowl with cling film. Leave the dough to rise in a warm place for 1 hour 30 minutes, or until it has doubled in size.
5. Put a baking sheet in the oven. Heat the oven to 230°C (450°F, gas mark 8). Turn out the dough onto a lightly floured surface, punch it down and shape it into three equal balls.
6. To make a loaf, roll out one ball to about 1 cm (½ in) thick in whatever shape you wish. For the topping, brush the dough with the oil and sprinkle over the sea salt and either chilli flakes or rosemary, as you wish. Use a sharp knife to score the loaf into quarters so that it will pull apart easily when baked.
7. Put one piece of the dough on the hot baking sheet and cook in the centre of the oven for 15-20 minutes until it is crisp and golden. Do not bake all three loaves together as they will not rise evenly. If you bake two at once, swap their positions in the oven after 8 minutes.
8. Serve the pizza bread warm or at room temperature on the day of baking, broken into four pieces.

Tip: uncooked dough balls will keep in a freezer for up to 3 months, individually wrapped in foil. To use, defrost for about 8 hours in the refrigerator, or for 2-3 hours at room temperature, before proceeding with the recipe from Step 6.

Nutrients per serving

- Calories 240
- Carbohydrate 48 g
- Protein 8 g
- Fat 3 g (including saturated fat 1 g)

Flowerpot rolls

Small flowerpots, bought just for baking, make great moulds for these herb-flavoured rolls.

PREPARATION TIME: 10-25 minutes, plus 1 hour 45 minutes rising
COOKING TIME: 20-25 minutes
MAKES 12 rolls

4 teaspoons dried yeast with 1 teaspoon caster sugar, or 2 sachets easy-blend yeast
1 kg (2 lb 4 oz) strong plain white flour
1 tablespoon salt
6 tablespoons finely chopped mixed fresh herbs, such as coriander, dill, oregano, parsley, rosemary and thyme
Vegetable oil for greasing
2 tablespoons skimmed milk, to glaze

1 If using dried yeast, dissolve the sugar in 750 ml (1 pint 7 fl oz) of lukewarm water, then sprinkle in the dried yeast and set aside for 15 minutes, or until it is frothy. If using easy-blend yeast, add it directly to the flour.

2 Sift the flour and salt into a large bowl and stir in the herbs. Pour the yeast mixture, or 750 ml (1 pint 7 fl oz) of lukewarm water if using easy-blend yeast, into the centre. Stir to form a stiff dough; add a little extra water 1 tablespoon at a time if it is too dry, or a little extra flour, 1 tablespoon at a time, if too wet. Knead until the dough forms a ball and leaves the side of the bowl clean.

3 Shape the dough into a ball and grease a clean bowl with oil. Roll the dough around the bowl so that it is lightly coated with oil and loosely cover the bowl with cling film. Leave the dough to rise in a warm place for 1 hour, or until doubled in size.

4 Meanwhile, soak 12 clean terracotta flowerpots, 9 cm (3½ in) wide and 7.5 cm (3 in) tall, in water for 15 minutes; this helps to prevent the bread sticking to them. Dry the pots then, using a pastry brush, generously brush the insides with oil.

5 Turn out the dough onto a lightly floured surface, punch it down and knead for 1-2 minutes. Divide the dough into 12 equal pieces, then shape them into small balls and place one inside each pot – the dough should come just over halfway up the pots. Place the pots on a baking sheet and loosely cover them with a damp cloth. Leave them to rise in a warm place for 45 minutes, or until the dough has risen to the tops of the pots.

6 Meanwhile, heat the oven to 220°C (425°F, gas mark 7). Bake the rolls for 15 minutes, then lightly brush the tops with milk and continue baking for a further 5-10 minutes until they have risen and are browned on top.

7 Remove the rolls from the oven and allow them to cool in the pots for 15 minutes. Run a round-bladed knife around the inside of the pots and loosen the rolls by pushing a finger through the hole in the bottom. Serve the rolls in the pots.

Variation: shape the dough into two medium-sized loaves and bake for 30 minutes, or into one large loaf and bake for 45 minutes. To check if a loaf is baked through, tap the base – it should sound hollow.

Nutrients per roll

- Calories 292
- Carbohydrate 63 g
- Protein 10 g
- Fat 1 g (no saturated fat)

Crusty olive or sunflower seed rolls

Nutrients per olive roll

- Calories 248
- Carbohydrate 51 g
- Protein 10 g
- Fat 2 g (no saturated fat)

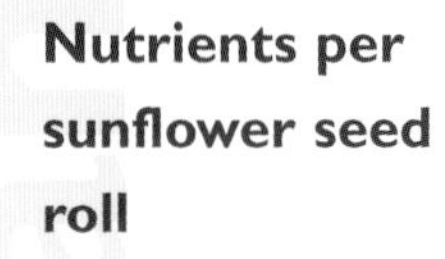

Nutrients per sunflower seed roll

- Calories 257
- Carbohydrate 51 g
- Protein 10 g
- Fat 3 g (no saturated fat)

Buy the very best stoneground flour for these flavoured bread rolls, and enjoy them hot and fragrant from the oven.

PREPARATION TIME: 30-45 minutes, plus 2 hours 30 minutes rising

COOKING TIME: 20-25 minutes

MAKES 10 olive and 10 sunflower seed rolls

2 teaspoons dried yeast with ¾ teaspoon caster sugar, or 1 sachet easy-blend yeast
500 g (1 lb 2 oz) wholemeal flour, plus extra for dusting
250 g (9 oz) strong plain white flour
2 teaspoons salt
1 teaspoon sunflower oil
50 g (1¾ oz) green olives, stoned, patted dry and chopped
20 g (¾ oz) sunflower seeds

1. If using dried yeast, dissolve the sugar in 500 ml (18 fl oz) of lukewarm water, then sprinkle in the dried yeast and set aside for 15 minutes, or until it is frothy. If using easy-blend yeast, add it directly to the flour.
2. Sift both flours and the salt into a large mixing bowl. Pour the yeast mixture, or 500 ml (18 fl oz) of lukewarm water if using easy-blend yeast, into the centre. Stir to form a dough, adding a little extra warm water if it is too dry, then knead until the dough forms a ball and leaves the side of the bowl clean.
3. Turn out the dough onto a lightly floured surface and knead for 5 minutes, or until it is smooth and elastic.
4. Grease a bowl with oil. Roll the dough around in the bowl so that it is lightly coated with oil and loosely cover the bowl with cling film. Leave the dough to rise in a warm place for 2 hours, or until doubled in size.
5. Turn out the dough onto a lightly floured surface, punch it down and knead for 1-2 minutes. Divide the dough in half.
6. Roughly flatten one half. Sprinkle the olives over it, fold the dough over and knead until they are evenly distributed. Cut the dough into ten equal pieces and form them into round or torpedo-shaped rolls. Lightly dust each roll with a little wholemeal flour, then arrange them, at least 2.5 cm (1 in) apart, on a baking sheet and score slashes in the top of each roll.
7. Repeat Step 6 with the remaining dough, using the sunflower seeds instead of the olives.
8. Loosely cover all the rolls with cling film and leave to rise in a warm place for 30 minutes.
9. Meanwhile, heat the oven to 230°C (450°F, gas mark 8). Bake the rolls for 20-25 minutes until they are golden brown and sound hollow when tapped on the bottom. Serve them warm or at room temperature.

Tip: both the baked rolls and the dough freeze well. Freeze the dough after the first rising, before it is shaped into rolls. Defrost for 8 hours in the refrigerator, or for 2-3 hours at room temperature, then proceed from Step 5.

Plain, chilli or spinach chapattis

High in fibre and easy to make, chapatti breads are a classic accompaniment to Indian meals.

PREPARATION TIME: 20 minutes, plus 30 minutes resting
COOKING TIME: 30 minutes
MAKES 16 chapattis

425 g (15 oz) chapatti flour, plus extra for dusting
1 teaspoon salt
2 tablespoons sunflower oil
For chilli chapattis:
1 green chilli, deseeded and finely chopped
1 fresh red chilli, deseeded and finely chopped
A pinch of cayenne pepper
3 cloves garlic, crushed
For spinach chapattis:
1 green chilli, deseeded and finely chopped
2 teaspoons garlic purée, or crushed garlic
1 teaspoon finely grated ginger
250 g (9 oz) spinach leaves, rinsed and finely chopped
½ teaspoon cayenne pepper

1 To make plain chapattis, sift the flour and salt into a large bowl. Add the oil and work it into the flour, then gradually stir in 250 ml (9 fl oz) of lukewarm water, mixing until a soft dough forms.
2 Transfer the dough to a lightly floured surface and knead it for 4-5 minutes until any excess moisture has been absorbed. Add a little more flour if the dough is too sticky to handle. Cover with a damp cloth and leave it to rest for 30 minutes.
3 Meanwhile, line a large piece of foil with kitchen paper to keep the chapattis hot when they are cooked.
4 Cut the dough in half and divide each half into eight equal balls. Cover them with a clean cloth to prevent them from drying out.
5 Heat a nonstick frying pan over a medium heat. Meanwhile, flatten out one ball of dough between your palms, lightly dust it with flour, then roll it out into a 15 cm (6 in) round.
6 Place the dough on the hot pan and cook for 30 seconds, then turn it over and continue cooking until bubbles begin to appear on the surface. Turn it over again, pressing the edges down gently to encourage the chapatti to puff up, and continue cooking until brown patches appear on the underside. Wrap the cooked chapatti in the foil and continue making chapattis in the same way. For a cool contrast, serve them with yoghurt raita (page 192).

To make chilli chapattis: add the chillies, cayenne pepper and garlic to the flour mixture in Step 1 before adding the oil and water.

To make spinach chapattis: heat a large wok or frying pan over a low heat and add the oil. When it is hot, add the chilli, garlic and ginger and stir-fry for 1 minute. Then add the spinach, cayenne pepper and the salt and stir-fry for 5-6 minutes until all the moisture from the spinach has evaporated. Transfer the mixture to a large bowl. Add the flour and 150 ml (5 fl oz) of water (you do not need any more oil) and mix until a soft dough forms. Then continue with the basic recipe from Step 2.

Tip: chapatti flour is available from Indian stores. If you cannot find it, use plain wholemeal flour, adding a little more water to make a stickier dough.

Nutrients per chapatti, for all three types

- Calories 101-108
- Carbohydrate 21 g
- Protein 3 g
- Fat 2 g (no saturated fat)

Oaty scone bread

This country-style bread is delicious served warm, spread with your favourite preserve.

PREPARATION TIME: 10 minutes
COOKING TIME: 15-20 minutes
SERVES 4

225 g (8 oz) self-raising white flour, plus extra for dusting
½ teaspoon baking powder
¼ teaspoon salt
25 g (1 oz) porridge oats, plus 1 tablespoon for topping
30 g (1¼ oz) butter, diced
125 ml (4 fl oz) skimmed milk, plus ½ tablespoon for brushing
To serve: fruit preserve, optional

1 Heat the oven to 220°C (425°F, gas mark 7) and dust a baking tray with flour.
2 Sift the flour, baking powder and salt into a large bowl, and stir in the porridge oats. Using your fingertips, rub the butter into the mixture until it resembles fine breadcrumbs.
3 Using a round-bladed knife, slowly stir in enough of the milk to form a soft, but not sticky, dough.
4 Turn the dough out onto a lightly floured work surface and knead it lightly until smooth. Roll it out into a 14 cm (5½ in) round. With a small sharp knife, score the top into four quarters then place the loaf on the prepared baking tray. Brush the loaf with a little milk and sprinkle the remaining oats over the top.
5 Bake for 15-20 minutes until well risen and golden brown. Transfer to a wire rack to cool slightly. Serve the bread warm, spread with some fruit preserve, if you like.

Nutrients per serving

- Calories 293
- Carbohydrate 51 g
- Protein 7 g
- Fat 8 g (including saturated fat 4 g)

Earl Grey and lemon teabread

The surprise addition of Earl Grey tea with a touch of lemon makes a moist, fruity loaf.

PREPARATION TIME: 10 minutes, plus 6 hours, or overnight, soaking, 2 hours 30 minutes cooling and 24 hours maturing
COOKING TIME: 1 hour 15 minutes
MAKES 10 slices

250 g (9 oz) soft brown sugar
175 g (6 oz) sultanas
50 g (1¾ oz) chopped mixed peel
1 teaspoon finely grated lemon zest
300 ml (10 fl oz) cold, strong Earl Grey tea
1 egg, beaten
300 g (10½ oz) self-raising white flour
To serve: low-fat cream cheese, low-fat spread or half-fat butter, optional

1 Mix together the sugar, sultanas, mixed peel, lemon zest and cold tea in a large bowl, cover it with cling film and leave to soak in a cool place for 6 hours, or overnight.
2 When you are ready to make the teabread, heat the oven to 160°C (325°F, gas mark 3). Line a loaf tin measuring 22 x 11 x 6 cm (8½ x 4¼ x 2½ in) with baking paper.
3 Stir the egg and flour into the fruit mixture, beating thoroughly, then pour it into the tin and smooth the surface. Bake for 1 hour 15 minutes, or until the loaf has risen, is firm and a skewer inserted in the centre comes out clean.
4 Leave the loaf in the tin on a wire rack for 2 hours-2 hours 30 minutes to cool completely.
5 When the loaf is cool, turn it out of the tin, remove the lining paper, then wrap it in greaseproof paper and store in an airtight container for at least one day before slicing. Serve the teabread plain or with your favourite low-fat spread.

Variation: you can use any other distinctive tea for this loaf, including fruit tea.

Nutrients per slice

- Calories 262
- Carbohydrate 62 g
- Protein 4 g
- Fat 1 g (no saturated fat)

Lemon and cornmeal tea time loaf

Fine cornmeal gives this afternoon treat a wonderful golden colour to match its tangy lemon flavour.

Nutrients per slice
- Calories 201
- Carbohydrate 34 g
- Protein 5 g
- Fat 5 g (including saturated fat 1 g)

PREPARATION TIME: 30 minutes
COOKING TIME: 45 minutes
MAKES 12 slices

150 g (5½ oz) fine cornmeal — POLENTA
150 g (5½ oz) plain white flour
1 tablespoon baking powder
60 g (2¼ oz) soft light brown sugar
Finely grated zest and juice of 2 large lemons
225 ml (8 fl oz) buttermilk, or 225 g (8 oz) low-fat natural yoghurt
2 eggs, beaten
4 tablespoons sunflower oil
40 g (1½ oz) caster sugar
60 g (2¼ oz) icing sugar

1. Heat the oven to 190°C (375°F, gas mark 5). Line a loaf tin measuring about 22 x 11 x 6 cm (8½ x 4¼ x 2½ in) with baking paper.
2. Sift the cornmeal, flour and baking powder into a bowl, then stir in the brown sugar and lemon zest.
3. Make a well in the centre and pour in the buttermilk or yoghurt, eggs and oil. Stir with a wooden spoon until the ingredients are just blended and a soft consistency forms. Do not overmix or the loaf will be heavy.
4. Spoon the mixture into the prepared tin and level the surface. Bake for 45 minutes, or until the loaf is well risen, firm to the touch and a skewer inserted into the centre comes out clean.
5. Meanwhile, put the lemon juice into a small bowl and stir in the caster sugar until it dissolves.
6. Remove the loaf from the tin, put it on a wire rack over a plate and leave to cool for 5 minutes.
7. Peel off the baking paper and prick the loaf all over with a fine skewer, inserting it deeply but not quite to the base. Spoon the sweetened lemon juice over the loaf slowly to allow it to soak in.
8. Put 50 ml (2 fl oz) of water into a small saucepan and bring to the boil. Put the icing sugar into a bowl and stir in 1½-2 teaspoons of the boiling water, adding just enough to make an icing that drizzles off the spoon. Using a teaspoon, drizzle the icing from side to side over the warm loaf.
9. Allow the loaf to cool completely on the wire rack, then slice and serve. It will keep fresh for several days stored in an airtight container.

Tip: fine cornmeal, not to be confused with instant polenta, is sold in health food stores.

LEMON AND CORNMEAL TEA TIME LOAF

BANANA BREAD

Banana bread

This moist, wholesome loaf makes a high-energy breakfast or tea time choice.

PREPARATION TIME: 25-40 minutes, plus 2 hours 45 minutes rising and 20 minutes standing
COOKING TIME: 40 minutes
MAKES 8 slices

4 teaspoons dried yeast, or
2 sachets easy-blend yeast
60 g (2¼ oz) caster sugar or soft light brown sugar
150 g (5½ oz) wholemeal flour
150 g (5½ oz) strong white flour
1½ teaspoons ground allspice
1 teaspoon ground cinnamon
4 ripe bananas
1 whole egg plus 1 egg white, beaten together
Vegetable oil for greasing
To serve: fruit preserve or low-fat soft cheese, optional

1. If using dried yeast, dissolve 1 teaspoon of the sugar in 75 ml (2½ fl oz) of lukewarm water, then sprinkle in the dried yeast and set aside for 15 minutes, or until it is frothy. If using easy-blend yeast, add it directly to the flour.
2. Sift the two flours, allspice, cinnamon and remaining sugar into a large bowl, adding any bran left in the sieve. Mash the bananas into a smooth paste, then stir them into the spiced flour with the egg and egg white. Pour the yeast mixture, or 75 ml (2½ fl oz) of lukewarm water if using easy-blend yeast, into the centre. Stir to form a dough, adding a little extra flour if the mixture is too wet.
3. Turn out the dough onto a lightly floured surface and knead for 5 minutes, or until smooth.
4. Grease a bowl with a little oil and roll the dough around so that it is lightly coated with oil. Loosely cover the bowl with cling film and leave the dough to rise in a warm place for 2 hours, or until it has doubled in size. Meanwhile, lightly grease a loaf tin measuring about 19 x 12 x 9 cm (7½ x 4½ x 3½ in) and set aside.
5. Turn out the dough onto a lightly floured surface. Punch it down, knead for 1-2 minutes, then roll it into shape and place it in the tin. Cover it loosely with cling film and leave to rise for 45 minutes, or until it reaches the top of the tin. Heat the oven to 200°C (400°F, gas mark 6).
6. Bake the bread for 40 minutes, or until brown on top and a skewer comes out clean. Stand the tin on a wire rack for 20 minutes before turning the loaf out. Serve it spread with your choice of topping.

Nutrients per slice

- Calories 216
- Carbohydrate 46 g
- Protein 7 g
- Fat 2 g (no saturated fat)

Angel food cake with two preserves

This airy cake is free of fat but tastes heavenly, especially with a fruity accompaniment.

PREPARATION TIME: 25 minutes, plus 1 hour 30 minutes cooling
COOKING TIME: 45 minutes
MAKES 10 slices

10 egg whites
1 teaspoon cream of tartar
1 teaspoon vanilla extract
½ teaspoon almond extract
250 g (9 oz) caster sugar
125 g (4½ oz) plain white flour, sifted

1 Heat the oven to 180°C (350°F, gas mark 4). Whisk the egg whites in a large bowl until foamy. Sprinkle the cream of tartar and the vanilla and almond extracts over them and continue whisking until the mixture is stiff but not dry.
2 Add the sugar, 1 tablespoon at a time, whisking continuously: the mixture should be shiny and form soft peaks.

Apricot oat flapjacks

Soft, chewy bars, packed with sweet fruit and ginger, make an ideal mid-morning or afternoon snack.

PREPARATION TIME: 10 minutes
COOKING TIME: 55 minutes-1 hour 5 minutes
MAKES 8 flapjacks

250 g (9 oz) ready-to-eat dried apricots, cut into quarters
400 ml (14 fl oz) orange juice
Grated zest of ½ orange
50 g (1¾ oz) crystallised ginger, roughly chopped
200 g (7 oz) rolled porridge oats
3 tablespoons light muscovado sugar
25 g (1 oz) sunflower seeds

1 Place the apricots in a pan with the orange juice and zest and bring to the boil. Reduce the heat and simmer, uncovered and stirring occasionally, for 25-30 minutes until the liquid is absorbed. Purée in a food processor or with a hand-held mixer.
2 Meanwhile heat the oven to 180°C (350°F, gas mark 4). Line the base of a 22 cm (8½ in) round cake tin with baking paper.
3 Stir the ginger, oats, sugar and sunflower seeds into the apricot purée and mix well, then tip it into the tin and spread out evenly.
4 Bake for 30-35 minutes until firm and golden brown. Cool slightly, cut into wedges then leave the flapjacks to cool completely in the tin. Peel off the paper before serving.

Variation: for prune and pecan flapjacks, replace the apricot purée with one made from prunes simmered in apple juice, and use chopped pecan nuts in place of the sunflower seeds. For apple and cranberry flapjacks, replace the ginger with dried cranberries, and use a purée made from 3 dessert apples, peeled, cored and roughly chopped; simmer the apples, covered, in 75 ml (2½ fl oz) of cranberry juice for 15 minutes, or until soft.

Nutrients per flapjack

- Calories 235
- Carbohydrate 46 g
- Protein 5 g
- Fat 4 g (including saturated fat 1 g)

3 Fold the flour in with a metal spoon, blending it thoroughly without breaking down the egg whites.
4 Spoon the mixture into an ungreased 23 cm (9 in) ring-shaped cake tin; if you do not have one, use a round cake tin and put an empty can upside-down in the centre to make the hole. Bake on the lowest shelf of the oven for 45 minutes, or until the top is golden brown and feels dry.
5 To cool the cake, leave it in the tin and turn it upside-down, supporting the centre column of the cake tin, or the empty can, on a jar so that the cake is not resting on anything and can 'stretch' downwards. Leave it to cool for at least 1 hour 30 minutes.
6 To take the cake out of the tin, run a knife around its outside and turn it upside-down onto a plate. Serve the cake with one of the following preserves, or with ginger-lemon sauce (see Honeydew Melon with Ginger-Lemon Sauce, page 270).

Tip: leftover yolks can be used to enrich omelettes, scrambled eggs or eggy bread for children, who should not follow a low-fat diet. Or use frozen whites, saved and stored after using the yolks in any other recipe. Allow about 1 hour to defrost before using (do not defrost in a microwave).

Nutrients per slice

- Calories 154
- Carbohydrate 36 g
- Protein 4 g
- No fat

Apple and cranberry preserve

PREPARATION TIME: 5 minutes, plus 30 minutes cooling
COOKING TIME: 20 minutes
MAKES 200 ml (7 fl oz)

125 g (4½ oz) dessert apples
75 g (2¾ oz) fresh or frozen cranberries
100 ml (3½ fl oz) fresh orange juice
100 g (3½ oz) sugar

1 Peel, core and dice the apples and put the pieces into a saucepan with the other ingredients. Bring to the boil then reduce the heat and simmer, stirring frequently, for 20 minutes, or until the preserve has thickened and blended together. Cool to room temperature (about 30 minutes) before serving.

Nutrients per serving

- Calories 50
- Carbohydrate 13 g
- No protein
- No fat

Peach preserve

PREPARATION TIME: 5 minutes, plus 30 minutes cooling
COOKING TIME: 20 minutes
MAKES 200 ml (7 fl oz)

100 g (3½ oz) ready-to-eat dried peaches
100 g (3½ oz) sugar
1 tablespoon kirsch, or other fruit brandy
Fresh lemon juice, optional

1 Finely chop the peaches and put them into a saucepan with the sugar, kirsch or other fruit brandy and 100 ml (3½ fl oz) of water. Bring to the boil then reduce the heat and simmer, stirring frequently, for 15-20 minutes until the preserve has thickened and blended together.
2 Add lemon juice if the preserve is too sweet, and 1-3 tablespoons of water if it is too thick. Cool to room temperature before serving.

Nutrients per serving

- Calories 65
- Carbohydrate 16 g
- No protein
- No fat

Banana and chocolate chip muffins

Chocolate can be part of a healthy diet, as these delicious muffins prove. They use the best-quality chocolate to give more flavour with less fat.

PREPARATION TIME: 15 minutes
COOKING TIME: 25 minutes
MAKES 12 muffins

2 tablespoons vegetable oil
200 g (7 oz) peeled bananas, coarsely chopped
1 whole egg plus 2 egg whites
250 ml (9 fl oz) skimmed milk
400 g (14 oz) self-raising white flour
150 g (5½ oz) caster sugar or soft light brown sugar
½ teaspoon bicarbonate of soda
2 teaspoons finely grated orange zest
50 g (1¾ oz) dark chocolate with 70 per cent cocoa solids, finely chopped

1 Heat the oven to 190°C (375°F, gas mark 5). Using a pastry brush and 1 tablespoon of oil, lightly grease a muffin pan with cups measuring 6 cm (2½ in) across.
2 Using a food processor or hand-held mixer, purée the bananas with 1 tablespoon of oil, the whole egg and egg whites and the milk.
3 Sift the flour, sugar and bicarbonate of soda into a large mixing bowl, and stir in the orange zest and chocolate. Fold in the banana mixture until just blended; if overmixed, the muffins will be heavy. It does not matter if a little flour remains unincorporated.
4 Spoon the mixture into the prepared muffin pan, filling the cups about two-thirds full. Bake for 25 minutes, or until the muffins have risen and are lightly browned.
5 Remove from the oven and take the muffins out of the pan. Serve them hot or at room temperature, preferably on the day of baking.

Nutrients per muffin

- Calories 229
- Carbohydrate 46 g
- Protein 5 g
- Fat 4 g (including saturated fat 1 g)

GRATING ORANGE ZEST

Squidgy chocolate cake

Sweet prunes, not butter, give this luxurious chocolate cake its irresistible fudgy texture.

PREPARATION TIME: 30 minutes, plus 15 minutes standing
COOKING TIME: 1 hour 20 minutes
MAKES 16 squares

125 g (4½ oz) ready-to-eat stoned prunes
100 ml (3½ fl oz) brandy
125 g (4½ oz) butter, diced
150 g (5½ oz) dark chocolate with 70 per cent cocoa solids, roughly chopped
500 g (1 lb 2 oz) caster sugar
375 g (13 oz) plain white flour
60 g (2¼ oz) self-raising white flour
75 g (2¾ oz) cocoa powder
1 whole egg plus 2 egg whites, lightly beaten
To decorate: icing sugar or cocoa powder
To serve: low-fat berry yoghurt, low-fat iced dessert or low-fat cream, optional

1. Put a kettle on to boil. Heat the oven to 160°C (325°F, gas mark 3). Grease a 23 cm (9 in) square cake tin and line it with baking paper.
2. Purée the prunes in a food processor or with a hand-held mixer, adding 1 tablespoon of hot water if necessary to get a smooth consistency. Scrape the purée into a large mixing bowl.
3. Add the brandy, butter, chocolate, sugar and 250 ml (9 fl oz) of boiling water from the kettle. Put the rest of the boiling water into a saucepan over a low heat so that it is simmering and place the bowl on top, making sure the bottom does not touch the water.
4. Stir the mixture frequently until the chocolate melts and forms a smooth sauce. Take the bowl off the pan and leave the mixture to cool for 2-3 minutes until it is lukewarm.
5. Sift both flours and the cocoa powder into a large bowl and make a well in the centre. Pour in the chocolate mixture, then add the whole egg and egg whites and beat to a smooth batter.
6. Pour the mixture into the prepared tin and smooth the surface. Bake for 1 hour 15 minutes, or until a skewer inserted in the centre of the cake comes out clean.
7. Leave the cake to stand in the tin on a wire rack for 15 minutes, then turn it out onto the wire rack to cool completely.
8. Dust the cake with sifted icing sugar or cocoa powder and cut it into 16 squares. Serve plain or with low-fat yoghurt, iced dessert or cream, if you prefer.

Variation: for a sweeter, fruitier flavour, use port instead of brandy.
Tip: this cake will keep well if wrapped in foil.

Nutrients per square

- Calories 368
- Carbohydrate 63 g
- Protein 5 g
- Fat 11 g (including saturated fat 7 g)

Chocolate and coffee éclairs

Mouth-watering chocolate éclairs get a great coffee filling.

PREPARATION TIME: 45 minutes, plus 1 hour infusing, and 3 hours, or overnight, chilling

COOKING TIME: 50 minutes

MAKES 20 éclairs

For the filling:
600 ml (1 pint) semi-skimmed milk
1 vanilla pod, cut in half lengthways
1 tablespoon ground coffee beans
60 g (2¼ oz) cornflour
50 g (1¾ oz) caster sugar
150 g (5½ oz) virtually fat-free Greek yoghurt

For the choux pastry:
75 g (2¾ oz) 70 per cent fat spread
100 g (3½ oz) plain white flour
2 whole eggs plus 1 egg white

For the icing:
100 g (3½ oz) dark chocolate with 70 per cent cocoa solids
2 teaspoons icing sugar, sifted

1 To make the filling, pour the milk into a saucepan and add the vanilla pod and ground coffee. Bring the mixture to the boil then remove from the heat. Cover with a tight-fitting lid and leave to infuse for 1 hour.
2 Meanwhile, make the choux pastry. Line two baking sheets with baking paper and set aside. Pour 200 ml (7 fl oz) of water into a saucepan, add the spread and cover the pan. Heat gently until the spread has melted, then uncover the pan and bring the mixture to the boil.
3 Remove the pan from the heat and stir in the flour. Return to the heat and stir until the mixture forms a ball in the centre of the pan and leaves the sides clean. Remove from the heat and allow the mixture to cool for 2-3 minutes.
4 Whisk the whole eggs and egg white together, then beat them into the cooled pastry mixture a little at a time, preferably with a hand-held mixer, beating well between additions until the mixture is smooth and shiny and will hold a soft peak.
5 Spoon the choux pastry into a large piping bag fitted with a 1 cm (½ in) plain nozzle. Pipe it onto the lined baking sheets in straight lengths about 10 cm (4 in) long, spacing them 2 cm (¾ in) apart. Cut the choux pastry cleanly away from the end of the nozzle with a knife.
6 Freeze the piped choux pastry, uncovered, for 30 minutes, or until firm. Then cover the éclairs with foil and return them to the freezer.
7 Meanwhile, continue making the coffee filling: line a sieve with muslin or kitchen paper and strain the infused milk into a jug, discarding the vanilla pod and ground coffee.
8 Put the cornflour and sugar into a saucepan, gradually stir in the strained milk and bring it to the boil, stirring continuously. The mixture will be lumpy to start with, but continue stirring and it will thicken and become smooth as it reaches the boil. Reduce the heat to low and cook for 2-3 minutes, stirring. Then pour the filling into a bowl, cover with cling film and leave it to cool. Chill for 3 hours, or overnight, for the filling to set.
9 When the filling has set, heat the oven to 220°C (425°F, gas mark 7) and bake the choux pastry from frozen for 25 minutes, or until well risen, golden brown and crisp. Remove the éclairs from the oven and turn it off. Pierce each éclair at one end to allow the steam to escape, then return them to the still-warm oven for 5 minutes to dry out completely. Transfer the éclairs to wire racks to cool.
10 To make the icing, bring a small saucepan half full of water to simmering point. Put 4 tablespoons of cold water, the chocolate and the icing sugar into a small heatproof bowl, place it over the pan of simmering water and stir until the mixture is smooth, then set aside.
11 To fill the cooled éclairs, whisk the chilled coffee filling until smooth, then fold in the yoghurt. Spoon the mixture into a large piping bag fitted with a 1 cm (½ in) star nozzle.
12 Using a serrated knife, carefully slice the top third off each éclair. Pipe the filling generously along the base of each, then replace the tops and return the éclairs to the wire racks.
13 Spoon the chocolate icing along the top of each éclair, allowing it to trickle a little down the sides, and leave in a cool place until set. The éclairs can be kept, covered, in the refrigerator for 3-4 hours before serving.

Variation: if you want to leave the coffee out of the filling, flavour the milk with two vanilla pods instead.

Nutrients per éclair

- Calories 118
- Carbohydrate 15 g
- Protein 3 g
- Fat 5 g (including saturated fat 2 g)

Hazelnut and **coffee meringues**

These nutty treats are good enough to serve on their own, without the usual cream.

PREPARATION TIME: 15 minutes
COOKING TIME: 1 hour 10 minutes-1 hour 25 minutes
MAKES 20 meringues

100 g (3½ oz) roasted hazelnuts, coarsely chopped or ground
2 tablespoons freeze-dried coffee granules
175 g (6 oz) caster sugar
3 egg whites, at room temperature

1. Mix the nuts with the coffee granules. Line a baking tray with baking paper, and heat the oven to 150°C (300°F, gas mark 2).
2. Put the sugar and 50 ml (2 fl oz) of water into a saucepan and bring the mixture slowly to the boil, stirring occasionally until the sugar has dissolved. Increase the heat and boil the syrup for 5-7 minutes to the hard boil stage. To check that it is ready, drop a small amount into a glass of very cold water: it should form a hard, clear ball. (If you have a sugar thermometer, the temperature should be 120°C/250°F.)
3. Meanwhile, whisk the egg whites in a clean bowl until firm and glossy but not dry, and forming soft peaks.
4. With the beaters still running on a slow speed, pour the hot syrup onto the egg whites (try to avoid pouring it onto the metal whisks) and beat until the syrup is well incorporated.
5. Fold in the nut and coffee mixture, creating a speckled effect. For each meringue, drop 2 tablespoons of the mixture onto the baking sheet in cloud shapes, pulled up to form peaks, if you like. You should end up with 20 meringues.
6. Bake for 1 hour-1 hour 15 minutes until the meringues come off the sheet fairly easily but are still a little moist underneath (this will mean that they will be chewy when they are cool). Let them cool completely before serving.

Tip: in this method of making meringue, the hot sugar syrup poured into the egg whites partially cooks them so that they hold their shape better than plain meringues and will keep for up to two days.

Nutrients per meringue

- Calories 73
- Carbohydrate 10 g
- Protein 1 g
- Fat 3 g (no saturated fat)

Blueberry and **cinnamon streusel cake**

Juicy blueberries and a crumble topping combine to make this light, flavourful sponge popular with all the family.

PREPARATION TIME: 20 minutes
COOKING TIME: 50 minutes-1 hour
MAKES 8 squares

50 g (1¾ oz) ready-to-eat stoned prunes
150 g (5½ oz) low-fat natural yoghurt
225 g (8 oz) caster sugar
2 whole eggs plus 2 egg whites
1 teaspoon vanilla essence
350 g (12 oz) plain white flour
1 teaspoon ground cinnamon
A pinch of ground nutmeg
25 g (1 oz) butter
1 tablespoon light muscovado sugar
1½ teaspoons baking powder
250 g (9 oz) blueberries, defrosted if frozen
To garnish: fresh blueberries

1. Heat the oven to 180°C (350°F, gas mark 4). Line the base of a 22 cm (8½ in) square, shallow cake tin with baking paper.
2. Purée the prunes in a food processor or with a hand-held mixer, adding 1 tablespoon of hot water if necessary to get a smooth consistency. Scrape the purée into a large mixing bowl.
3. Add the yoghurt, caster sugar, whole eggs, egg whites and vanilla essence to the bowl and beat until they are evenly mixed.
4. In a separate bowl, sift the flour with the cinnamon and nutmeg. To make the crumble topping, transfer 75 g (2¾ oz) of the spiced flour to another bowl and rub the butter into it, then stir in the muscovado sugar and set aside.
5. Sift the baking powder into the remaining flour mixture. Using a hand-held mixer on low speed or a wooden spoon, beat it into the prune and yoghurt mixture.
6. Tip the mixture into the cake tin, top with the blueberries, then sprinkle the crumble topping evenly over the surface. Bake for 50-60 minutes until the cake is firm and lightly browned.
7. Leave the cake to cool slightly in the tin on a wire rack. Serve just warm or at room temperature, garnished with blueberries.

Variation: instead of blueberries, use other soft fruit such as raspberries.

Nutrients per square

- Calories 345
- Carbohydrate 71 g
- Protein 8 g
- Fat 5 g (including saturated fat 2 g)

Rich dark fruit cake

This moist, fruit-rich cake is so packed with flavour that you will not notice it has none of the fat of traditional recipes.

PREPARATION TIME: 30 minutes
COOKING TIME: 2 hours
MAKES 32 slices

375 g (13 oz) ready-to-eat stoned prunes
6 tablespoons brandy, sherry or orange juice
200 g (7 oz) soft dark brown sugar
4 eggs
Finely grated zest of 1 large lemon
Finely grated zest of 1 large orange
350 g (12 oz) plain white flour
2 teaspoons baking powder
1 teaspoon ground mixed spice
750 g (1 lb 10 oz) luxury mixed dried fruit
4-6 tablespoons skimmed milk

1. Heat the oven to 180°C (350°F, gas mark 4). Line a deep 23 cm (9 in) round cake tin with baking paper.
2. Purée the prunes and brandy, or sherry or orange juice, to a smooth paste in a food processor or with a hand-held mixer. Transfer the purée to a large bowl.
3. Add the sugar, eggs and lemon and orange zest, and whisk until the mixture is pale, thick and fluffy.
4. Sift the flour, baking powder and mixed spice onto the prune mixture, then fold them in with a large metal spoon. Fold in the dried fruit and enough milk to make a soft dropping consistency.
5. Spoon the cake mixture into the prepared tin and smooth over the top. Bake in the centre of the oven for 45 minutes, then reduce the temperature to 160°C (325°F, gas mark 3). Continue baking for a further 1 hour 15 minutes, or until the cake is well risen, firm to the touch and a skewer inserted in the centre comes out clean. If, during baking, the top of the cake appears to be over-browning, cover it loosely with a piece of foil.
6. Leave the cake to cool in the tin on a wire rack for 10-15 minutes. Then remove the cake from the tin, peel off the paper and leave it to cool completely on the rack. Store it wrapped in foil, or in an airtight container.

Tip: the flavour of this cake becomes even fuller if it is left to mature for a day or two before it is cut.

Nutrients per slice

- Calories 157
- Carbohydrate 34 g
- Protein 3 g
- Fat 1 g (no saturated fat)

Mincemeat filo crackers

These cracker-shaped treats make a light, novel alternative to traditional mince pies at Christmas.

PREPARATION TIME: 15 minutes
COOKING TIME: 10-12 minutes
MAKES 12 crackers

12 sheets filo pastry, each at least 15 x 30 cm (6 x 12 in)
1 tablespoon sunflower oil
400 g (14 oz) ready-made luxury mincemeat
2 teaspoons icing sugar, sifted
To serve: low-fat iced dessert, optional

1 Heat the oven to 200°C (400°F, gas mark 6). Fold the sheets of filo pastry in half to make double-layered 15 cm (6 in) squares and brush a little oil around the edges to make a 5 cm (2 in) border.
2 Spoon 1 tablespoon of mincemeat along one half of each pastry square, stopping about 2.5 cm (1 in) short of the ends. Then roll each up loosely to form a cigar shape and place it, seam side down, on a nonstick baking sheet. Pinch in both ends then fan out the edges to form a cracker shape.
3 Brush any remaining oil over the surface of each cracker and bake them for 10-12 minutes until they are golden brown. Leave the crackers to cool slightly before carefully removing them from the baking sheet.
4 Dust the crackers with icing sugar and serve them warm, accompanied by a spoonful of low-fat iced dessert, if you like.

Variation: fold the filo pastry into quarters, spoon the mincemeat into the centre and gather up the edges of the pastry to form a little pouch.

Nutrients per cracker

- Calories 168
- Carbohydrate 34 g
- Protein 2 g
- Fat 3 g (no saturated fat)

Cherry and almond wafers

These crunchy wafers are ideal with all sorts of creamy desserts or after-dinner coffee.

PREPARATION TIME: 20 minutes, plus 1 hour-1 hour 30 minutes cooling
COOKING TIME: 1 hour 10 minutes
MAKES 30 wafers

Oil or butter for greasing
3 egg whites
125 g (4½ oz) caster sugar
225 g (8 oz) plain white flour
100 g (3½ oz) flaked almonds
50 g (1¾ oz) whole unblanched almonds
150 g (5½ oz) glacé cherries, roughly chopped

1 Heat the oven to 180°C (350°F, gas mark 4). Lightly grease a loaf tin measuring about 19 x 12 x 9 cm (7½ x 4½ x 3½ in).
2 In a large, clean bowl, whisk the egg whites until they form soft peaks. Add the sugar 1 tablespoon at a time, whisking well after each addition, to make a meringue mixture. Sift the flour over the top, add the flaked and whole almonds and glacé cherries and fold them in.
3 Spoon the mixture into the tin and level the surface. Bake for 25 minutes, or until the loaf is pale golden on top and just firm to the touch. Turn it out of the tin and leave it to dry out for 1 hour-1 hour 30 minutes, until completely cool.
4 Reduce the heat of the oven to 120°C (250°F, gas mark ½). Using a serrated knife, slice the loaf into 30 thin wafers. Arrange them in a single layer on baking sheets and bake them for 45 minutes, or until dry and crisp. Do not let them go brown.
5 Using a palette knife, transfer the wafers to wire racks to cool. Store them in an airtight container.

Variation: use glacé pineapple instead of cherries, or macadamia nuts for almonds for a tropical taste.

Nutrients per wafer

- Calories 87
- Carbohydrate 14 g
- Protein 2 g
- Fat 3 g (no saturated fat)

the menu planner

Planning meals to provide a mixture of tastes and textures as well as a healthy diet is tricky. To make it easy, the following menus are designed to offer the best of both.

There are carbohydrates to keep hunger at bay, deliciously tempting fruit and vegetables to help you to achieve the five-portions-a-day target without effort and small portions of favourite protein sources to complete the balance.

Whatever the occasion you are catering for – an everyday meal for the family or dinner for guests – just follow our low-fat menu plans and you can be sure that your meals will be well-balanced and bursting with healthy goodness and delicious flavour, too.

GRILLED GRAINBURGERS

RASPBERRY PAVLOVA WITH RED BERRY SAUCE

family meals

Grilled Grainburgers page 217, served with a mixed green salad
Raspberry Pavlova with Red Berry Sauce page 285

Even meat-eaters will enjoy this meal of tasty rice and oat burgers with crisp, fresh salad. A colourful pavlova with a smooth sauce of fresh fruit and soft cheese is easy to make and popular with children and adults alike.

TOTAL NUTRIENTS PER PERSON
- Calories 622
- Carbohydrate 126 g
- Protein 19 g
- Fat 8 g (including saturated fat 2 g)

Country Lamb and Vegetable Cobbler page 175
Pear and Ginger Upside-down Pudding page 273

A hearty meat stew, with generous amounts of carrots, celery, leeks and peas, bubbles beneath a low-fat scone topping. The cold-weather dessert is a spiced-up version of an old-fashioned favourite. Bake the pudding ahead and, to enjoy it piping hot, put it back in the oven when you take out the cobbler.

TOTAL NUTRIENTS PER PERSON
- Calories 872
- Carbohydrate 129 g
- Protein 46 g
- Fat 20 g (including saturated fat 3 g)

Carrot and Butter Bean Soup page 55
Grilled Chicken, Broccoli and Pasta Gratin page 139
Mulled Grape Jelly page 281

Vegetables and fruit make this a colourful feast. The orange soup is given body with creamy beans, and broccoli florets brighten the warming gratin. For a light finish, fresh grapes are set in a crimson jelly.

TOTAL NUTRIENTS PER PERSON
- Calories 769
- Carbohydrate 116 g
- Protein 49 g
- Fat 9 g (including saturated fat 3 g)

Tomato and Bread Soup page 61
Fabulous Fish and Chips page 109
Strawberry Yoghurt Ice page 275

A summery tomato soup is a perfect prelude to crunchy fish and chips, baked in the oven to keep their fat content low without losing the taste. A dessert made with fresh berries, a dash of honey and creamy Greek yoghurt ends the meal on a cool note.

TOTAL NUTRIENTS PER PERSON
- Calories 626
- Carbohydrate 80 g
- Protein 40 g
- Fat 18 g (including saturated fat 6 g)

Chilli Pork Tortillas page 191
Rhubarb, Orange and Ginger Crumble page 262

Children will have great fun assembling the fillings for the floury tortillas and wrapping them up to eat with their fingers. In the oaty-topped crumble, warm pink and orange fruits are flavoured with a little sweet ginger to give the dish just enough bite to complement the spicy main course.

TOTAL NUTRIENTS PER PERSON
- Calories 965
- Carbohydrate 149 g
- Protein 56 g
- Fat 21 g (including saturated fat 4 g)

Cottage Pie, American-style page 167
Banana and Summer Berry Salad page 258

This ever-popular, one-pot main course, packed with extra-lean mince, high-fibre baked beans and masses of vegetables, is easy on the cook and healthy for the family. Colourful summer fruit, tossed with honey, orange juice and yoghurt, provide a luscious, sweet finish.

TOTAL NUTRIENTS PER PERSON
- Calories 578
- Carbohydrate 76 g
- Protein 41 g
- Fat 15 g (including saturated fat 6 g)

Baked Salmon Fishcakes with Parsley Sauce page 108, served with savoy cabbage
Fluffy Banana Rice Puddings page 277

These crispy fishcakes are guaranteed bone-free, which makes them especially appealing to children. Serve them with generous helpings of herb sauce and succulent green cabbage, briskly sautéed in vegetable stock, instead of oil. Individual sweet, creamy puddings, which can be baked while you are eating the fishcakes, have a satisfying, contrasting texture.

TOTAL NUTRIENTS PER PERSON
- Calories 677
- Carbohydrate 96 g
- Protein 36 g
- Fat 19 g (including saturated fat 4 g)

WATERCRESS, KIWI, MUSHROOM AND TOMATO SALAD

SPICY SCRAMBLED EGGS ON TOAST

MINT LASSI

brunches

Whipped Berry Porridge page 31
Sweetcorn Griddlecakes with Yoghurt Sauce page 41
Ratatouille Chinese-style page 84
Apple and Cinnamon Warmer page 151

Soft, fruity porridge is the opener to a warming brunch when followed by fried griddlecakes and an Oriental vegetable stew. Hot, spiced apple juice makes a good accompanying drink.

TOTAL NUTRIENTS PER PERSON
- Calories 489
- Carbohydrate 104 g
- Protein 12 g
- Fat 4 g (including saturated fat 1 g)

Ruby Grapefruit and Grape Refresher page 29
Spicy Scrambled Eggs on Toast page 37
Watercress, Kiwi, Mushroom and Tomato Salad page 93
Mint Lassi page 151

A cool yoghurt drink is the ideal partner for this zingy fruit starter, and the authentic match for the curried egg dish. A salad of vitamin-rich fruit and peppery leaves completes the meal.

TOTAL NUTRIENTS PER PERSON
- Calories 499
- Carbohydrate 57 g
- Protein 26 g
- Fat 20 g (including saturated fat 6 g)

entertaining

CHOCOLATE ROULADE WITH RASPBERRY CREAM

dinners

Roasted Asparagus with Caramelised Shallot Dressing page 76
Chargrilled Duck with Plum and Chilli Salsa page 154, served with new potatoes and steamed mangetout
Chocolate Roulade with Raspberry Cream page 278

Take advantage of the year-round availability of asparagus to make this stylish first course, which sets the tone for the meal. The sophisticated main dish of duck with spiced, diced fruit is served with simple boiled potatoes and colourful mangetout – with no added butter – to counter its richness. You could add an Oriental touch, if you like, by serving flat rice noodles instead of the potatoes. To finish, your guests will not be able to resist the stunning swirled chocolate dessert with fresh raspberries and creamy fromage frais.

TOTAL NUTRIENTS PER PERSON
- Calories 600
- Carbohydrate 63 g
- Protein 42 g
- Fat 21 g (including saturated fat 6 g)

CHARGRILLED DUCK WITH PLUM AND CHILLI SALSA

VEGETARIAN DINNER PARTY
Brandied Chestnut and Mushroom Terrine page 78, served with crusty rolls, salad leaves and red onions
Roasted Vegetable Tart page 239, served with **Braised Fennel** page 234
Cinnamon Pineapple with Malibu page 261

Puréed chestnuts, the only low-fat nuts, make a filling prelude to the filo tart of aubergines, courgettes, peppers and onions, with Braised Fennel as a juicy side dish. Spicy pineapple with coconut rum is a succulent no-fat conclusion.

TOTAL NUTRIENTS PER PERSON
- Calories 951
- Carbohydrate 149 g
- Protein 25 g
- Fat 21 g (including saturated fat 6 g)

MAKE-AHEAD DINNER PARTY
Refreshing Tomato and Watercress Spread page 73
Daube of Beef and Vegetables Provençale page 169, served with mashed potatoes
Angel Food Cake with Two Preserves page 296

Clean, pronounced flavours highlight this menu for carefree catering with style. Everything except the fresh vegetable side dishes can be made a day ahead, and the beef stew is at its best reheated after it has been left overnight.

Serve the starter in its ramekins, or turn each portion onto a plate and accompany them with toast. Anchovies, orange zest and rosemary add the Provençale taste to the main course, which is perfect served with mashed potatoes made with skimmed milk. End the meal with the fat-free, light-as-air cake with fruit preserves.

TOTAL NUTRIENTS PER PERSON
- Calories 872
- Carbohydrate 127 g
- Protein 56 g
- Fat 15 g (including saturated fat 4 g)

NORTH AFRICAN DINNER PARTY
Moroccan Carrot Dip page 72, served with pitta breads
Spicy Lamb Tagine with Couscous page 185
Barbecued Fruit page 280

The warm flavours of North Africa accent this easy-entertaining menu. Start the meal with a spiced dip, which can be prepared in advance. The substantial main course, with chunks of succulent meat, vegetables and apricots in a saffron-flavoured broth, is filling enough not to need any accompaniment other than tender couscous grains to mop up the liquid.

The meal is rounded off with a dessert reminiscent of North African cooking over open fires: strawberries and pineapple, marinated in honey and grilled on skewers.

TOTAL NUTRIENTS PER PERSON
- Calories 839
- Carbohydrate 133 g
- Protein 41 g
- Fat 15 g (including saturated fat 1 g)

lunches

SPECIAL OCCASION LUNCH

Spring Vegetable Soup with Lemon page 57
Balsamic Grilled Chicken page 137, served with **Sauté of Spring Vegetables with Herbs** page 232
Raspberry Pavlova with Red Berry Sauce page 285

Peppery herbs and leaves lace the Oriental-style starter, followed by simple grilled chicken breasts, flavoured with balsamic vinegar and accompanied by a fresh green mix of beans, leeks and peas. The crisp and creamy pavlova is topped with luscious, juicy fresh fruit.

TOTAL NUTRIENTS PER PERSON

- Calories 704
- Carbohydrate 92 g
- Protein 56 g
- Fat 15 g (including saturated fat 8 g)

SUNDAY LUNCH

Roast Beef with Broad Beans and Mushrooms page 168, served with **Potato and Horseradish Rösti** page 240
Baked Bread and Marmalade Pudding page 272

A high-protein roast joint of beef with green beans, earthy mushrooms and meaty sauce is served with a twist on the traditional accompaniment in the crisp side dish of Horseradish Rösti. To finish, the bread pudding with a healthy scattering of plump vine fruits will ensure that everyone is well satisfied.

TOTAL NUTRIENTS PER PERSON

- Calories 701
- Carbohydrate 76 g
- Protein 64 g
- Fat 17 g (including saturated fat 6 g)

SUMMER LUNCH

Chilled Spinach and Yoghurt Soup page 50
Tandoori Monkfish with Mint Relish page 111, served with **Bulgur Wheat Pilaf with Nuts and Seeds** page 219
Summer Pudding page 261

Chilled soups are welcome in hot weather, and this creamy yoghurt one is deliciously cooling. Meaty, white fish is given a tangy, tandoori flavour then accompanied by a fresh mint sauce and a starchy, crunchy pilaf. The classic, fruit pudding rounds the meal off sweetly, but healthily.

TOTAL NUTRIENTS PER PERSON

- Calories 978
- Carbohydrate 159 g
- Protein 50 g
- Fat 16 g (including saturated fat 3 g)

VEGETARIAN LUNCH

Wild Mushrooms and Blueberries on Rice Noodles page 75
Grilled Vegetable Couscous with Chilled Tomato Sauce page 216
Gooseberry Granita page 275

The meaty texture of mushrooms in the starter contrasts well with the chilled main course: smooth, bright tomato sauce, a colourful mixture of vegetables and grainy couscous. A light ice, pale but strongly flavoured with sharp fruit, finishes the meal.

TOTAL NUTRIENTS PER PERSON

- Calories 626
- Carbohydrate 116 g
- Protein 12 g
- Fat 10 g (including saturated fat 3 g)

GRILLED VEGETABLE COUSCOUS WITH CHILLED TOMATO SAUCE

GOOSEBERRY GRANITA

WILD MUSHROOMS AND BLUEBERRIES ON RICE NOODLES

barbecue

Mixed Shellfish and Pasta Salad page 96
Seared Tuna with Spicy Black Bean Salsa page 107 or **Minted Turkey and Mushroom Kebabs** page 144, served with **Roasted Potato Salad with Cumin and Yoghurt Dressing** page 89
Spiced Seasonal Fruit Salad page 270

A make-ahead seafood salad kicks off this summer menu, with barbecued or grilled tuna or turkey to follow. The bean salsa complements both. Crisp potato skins with soft flesh and a creamy dressing make an alternative potato salad, and the mixed fruits with a hint of coconut are a vibrant finish.

TOTAL NUTRIENTS PER PERSON, WHEN SERVING TUNA

- Calories 865
- Carbohydrate 118 g
- Protein 51 g
- Fat 23 g (including saturated fat 7 g)

TOTAL NUTRIENTS PER PERSON, WHEN SERVING TURKEY

- Calories 804
- Carbohydrate 119 g
- Protein 55 g
- Fat 12 g (including saturated fat 6 g)

diet-conscious days

BREAKFAST
Cardamom-spiced Grape Juice page 150
Egg White Omelette with Asparagus page 36
LIGHT MEAL
Black Spaghetti with Yellow Pepper Sauce page 206
Apricot Oat Flapjacks page 296
MAIN MEAL
Black Bean Chilli page 242, served with **Green Rice** page 242 and **Coriander and Cabbage Slaw** page 243
Barbecued Fruit page 280

A nourishing egg white omelette studded with fresh asparagus is a great low-fat option for a cooked breakfast, and a glass of spiced grape juice boosts the day's vitamin intake.

The yellow pepper and herb spaghetti sauce is made without fat, and provides another helping of vegetables. If you are still hungry, the wholesome, fruity flapjacks can be eaten as a dessert, or saved for a low-fat afternoon snack.

The meat-free Tex-Mex-style main meal supplies filling protein and carbohydrate, flavoured with chillies and herbs. Barbecued pineapples and strawberries are a succulent, very low-fat end to the day's eating.

TOTAL NUTRIENTS PER PERSON
- Calories 1399
- Carbohydrate 268 g
- Protein 49 g
- Fat 17 g (including saturated fat 2 g)

LEMON AND CORNMEAL TEA TIME LOAF

BREAKFAST
Whipped Berry Porridge page 31
LIGHT MEAL
Fennel, Pea and Mint Soup page 54
Banana Bread page 295
MAIN MEAL
Tuna and Seafood Spaghetti page 210, served with **Spinach and Apple Salad** page 87
Lemon and Cornmeal Tea Time Loaf page 294

Warm porridge with sweet, colourful berries makes a filling breakfast, and its carbohydrate-packed grains of semolina will give you energy to start the day.

Vegetables form the basis of the light meal, served as an intensely flavoured, slightly chunky soup. Rather than eating it for dessert, the Banana Bread with its slightly sweet flavour, also makes a great mid-morning or afternoon snack.

SPINACH AND APPLE SALAD

TUNA AND SEAFOOD SPAGHETTI

For the main meal, spaghetti is served with a sauce of tomatoes, canned mixed seafood and tuna, accompanied by a fresh salad with crunchy garlic croutons and a herby dressing. The light, yellow dessert cake, moistened with sweetened lemon juice and drizzled with simple, water icing, offers a low-fat way to satisfy a sweet tooth.

TOTAL NUTRIENTS PER PERSON
- Calories 1111
- Carbohydrate 199 g
- Protein 58 g
- Fat 16 g (including saturated fat 2 g)

BREAKFAST
Dried Fruit Compote page 32
LIGHT MEAL
Refreshing Tomato and Watercress Spread page 73, with **Flowerpot Rolls** page 289
MAIN MEAL
Steamed Prawn Won Tons page 80
Poached Chicken with Spring Vegetables page 137
Summer Pudding page 261

This very low-fat day of eating uses vegetables and fruit so cleverly that you will not feel hungry at all.

The colourful mixture of currants, raisins and sultanas with fresh oranges and dried blueberries, cherries or mango is a filling start to the day and is easily made the night before. Sustaining herby rolls, cooked in small terracotta moulds, and a tangy tomato spread make a quick lunch or supper.

The main meal of the day will satisfy your appetite and stimulate your taste buds. Begin with seafood won ton parcels cooked without fat in a steamer and served with strongly flavoured dipping sauces. Follow them with poached chicken and mixed vegetables in a warming broth.

The fruit-packed, sweet and juicy summer pudding is luxurious enough to make sure that you forget any craving for fats.

TOTAL NUTRIENTS PER PERSON
- Calories 1408
- Carbohydrate 248 g
- Protein 79 g
- Fat 12 g (including saturated fat 1 g)

BAKED MIXED MUSHROOMS WITH CIABATTA

supper on a tray

Lemony Lentil Soup page 52
Baked Mixed Mushrooms with Ciabatta page 44

Begin this meat-free meal with a creamy, citrus-flavoured soup whose lentils provide a great source of vegetable protein. Then enjoy the chewy, meaty mushrooms on top of warm, Italian bread, flavoured with olive oil.

TOTAL NUTRIENTS PER PERSON
- Calories 515
- Carbohydrate 74 g
- Protein 27 g
- Fat 14 g (including saturated fat 3 g)

LEMONY LENTIL SOUP

Spiced Pumpkin and Bacon Soup page 58
Irish Grilled Steak Sandwich with Onion Salad page 45

A thick, velvety soup of orange pumpkin lightly flavoured with cumin makes a delicious prelude to the hot sandwich layered with steak and crisp salad ingredients. High-quality protein is perfectly balanced with energy-giving carbohydrates.

TOTAL NUTRIENTS PER PERSON
- Calories 428
- Carbohydrate 67 g
- Protein 41 g
- Fat 17 g (including saturated fat 4 g)

Tagliatelle Carbonara page 199
Baked Apples Glazed with Port page 269

The classic Italian pasta dish of creamy eggs, salty bacon and ribbon noodles is balanced by a piquant no-fat fruit dessert with a richly coloured, spiced red wine sauce.

TOTAL NUTRIENTS PER PERSON
- Calories 951
- Carbohydrate 144 g
- Protein 26 g
- Fat 16 g (including saturated fat 6 g)

Tomato Risotto page 222
Banana and Chocolate Chip Muffins page 298

The fresh flavour of basil is a natural partner for this creamy and filling risotto. Round off this satisfying meal, which would be perfect to follow a vigorous workout, with a sweet fruity muffin.

TOTAL NUTRIENTS PER PERSON
- Calories 517
- Carbohydrate 92 g
- Protein 15 g
- Fat 12 g (including saturated fat 4 g)

index

a

b

c

d

e

f

n,o

p

q,r

s

u,v

acknowledgments

The publishers would like to thank the following for their assistance in the preparation of the **Low fat no fat cookbook.**

Divertimenti, 45-47 Wigmore Street, London W1H 9LE
Lakeland Ltd., Alexandra Buildings, Windermere, Cumbria, LA23 1BQ

Photographs and illustrations in this book are the copyright of Reader's Digest. The photographer for each is listed below.

Cover pictures by **Gus Filgate**

Gus Filgate:
8, 9 T, 10, 11, 10-11, 12 TL, 12 CR, 13 T, 13 B, 14 T, 14 fish, 14 lettuce, 15 T, 15 B, 16 T, 17 T, 18 T, 18 C, 18 BL, 19 L, 19 C, 19 R, 20 TL, 20 BR, 21 T, 21 C, 21 B, 22, 23 T, 23 spoons, 23 steamer, 23 B, 24 TL, 24 B, 25 T, 25 C, 25 B, 26-27, 28, 29, 30, 31, 32, 33, 34, 35, 36, 37, 40, 41, 42, 43, 44, 45 T, 45 B, 46-47, 48-49, 52, 53, 54, 55, 56, 57, 58-59, 60, 61, 62 T, 62 B, 63, 66, 67, 69, 70-71, 72-73, 73, 74, 79 B, 80-81, 82, 83, 86, 87, 88 T, 88 B, 90-91, 94, 95, 97, 98-99, 100, 101, 102-103, 104, 105, 106, 107 T, 107 B, 110, 112, 112-113, 114, 114-115, 116, 117 L, 117 R, 118, 120-121 T, 120-121 B, 122-123, 126, 127, 128-129, 130, 131, 132, 133, 134-135, 136, 137 T, 137 B, 138-139 T, 138-139 B, 140, 142, 143, 146, 147, 148, 156-157, 158-159, 159 L, 159 R, 161, 166, 167, 168, 169, 170 T, 170 B, 171 L, 171 R, 175, 176, 176-177, 180, 180-181, 181, 182, 183, 184, 187, 188-189, 190-191, 192, 193, 194, 199, 200-201, 201, 202-203, 203, 204 L, 206, 208, 209 L, 210, 211, 212 T, 212-213 B, 214, 220-221, 223 T, 228-229, 230, 231 L, 232-233, 235 B, 238-239, 240, 244, 245, 250-251 T, 253, 256-257, 258, 260, 264-265, 268, 270-271, 272 T, 275, 276, 279, 281, 282, 283, 288-289, 289, 290, 291, 292, 294-295 T, 294-295 B, 296, 296-297, 299, 300-301, 302, 305, 306 T, 306 BL, 306 BR, 307 TR, 307 C, 307 CR, 308 L, 308 R, 309 BL

William Lingwood:
9 B, 12 TR, 12 BL, 14 B, 16 B, 18 BR, 20 BL, 23 CR, 24 TR, 46, 58, 64 L, 65 TL, 68 L, 76, 78, 79 T, 85 L, 92, 93 T, 93 BL, 93 BR, 103 L, 125, 151 T, 152, 152-153, 154-155, 157, 172, 174, 179, 189, 195, 207, 215, 216-217 T, 216-217 B, 218, 219 T, 222, 223 B, 224, 224-225, 226, 227, 232, 242 C, 248, 250-251 B, 254, 255, 262 L, 272 C, 272 B, 273 T, 274 T, 285, 303, 311 L, 311

Craig Robertson:
29 R, 68 R, 86 B, 103 R, 185 R, 188, 198 B, 204 R, 212 B, 219 B, 231 R, 262 R, 278 R

Simon Smith:
38 T, 38 C, 38 B, 39, 64 TR, 64 BR, 65 TR, 65 B, 80, 84 T, 84 BL, 84 BR, 85 TR, 96, 108-109, 109, 111 T, 111 B, 119, 124, 144, 144-145, 149, 150 T, 150 B, 151 B, 155, 160, 160-161, 162-163, 178, 185 L, 186-187, 198, 205, 209 B, 212-213, 233, 234, 235, 236, 237 T, 237 B, 241 T, 241 B, 242 T, 242 B, 243 TR, 243 CR, 243 BL, 243 BR, 247, 249, 259 T, 259 B, 261, 263, 266, 267, 269, 271, 273 B, 274 B, 277, 280, 284, 293, 298 L, 298 R, 304, 309 T, 309 BL, 309 BR, 310 TL, 310 TR, 310 B

Philip Webb:
89, 246

Philip Wilkins:
51, 76-77, 90, 141

Indexer **Laura Hicks**

Production credits
Book Production Manager **Chris Reynolds**
Assistant Book Production Manager **Fiona McIntosh**
Pre-press Production Manager **Martin Hendrick**
Pre-press support **Jim Lindsay, Howard Reynolds**

Origination **Rodney Howe Ltd, London, England**
Paper **Perigord-Condat, France**
Printing and binding **Printer Industria Gráfica S.A., Barcelona, Spain**

40-861-01